Childhood
Socialization

Childhood Socialization

Gerald Handel
editor

Second Edition

ALDINETRANSACTION
A Division of Transaction Publishers
New Brunswick (U.S.A.) and London (U.K.)

Library of Congress Catalog Number: 2005041192
ISBN: 0-202-30641-0 (cloth); 0-202-30642-9 (paper)
Printed in the United States of America

Library of Congress Cataloging-in-Publication Data

Childhood socialization / Gerald Handel, editor.—2nd ed.
     p. cm.
  Includes bibliographical references and index.
  ISBN 0-202-30641-0 (cloth : alk. paper)—ISBN 0-202-30642-9 (pbk. : alk. paper)
   1. Socialization. 2. Socialization—Cross-cultural studies. I. Handel, Gerald.

HQ783.C525   2005
303.3'2—dc22   2005041192

To the Memory of My Parents

Pearl Seidman Handel
Louis Handel

Contents

Acknowledgements

I want to thank Richard Koffler, Executive Editor of Aldine de Gruyter, for his interest in this book and for his patience in waiting for this revised edition. My thanks also to Mai Shaikhanuar-Cota and Sara Jackson of Aldine de Gruyter for their contributions to making this book happen. My wife, Ruth D. Handel, has, as always, given moral support and a great deal of practical advice in extricating me from computer blind alleys.

Transaction Publishers acquired Aldine soon after this manuscript was submitted. I thank Mary E. Curtis, President, and Michael Paley, my editor, for carrying the project forward.

Contributors

Patricia A. Adler
University of Colorado

Peter Adler
University of Denver

Jean Anyon
The Graduate Center,
City University of New York

Steven Brint
University of California, Riverside

Scott Coltrane
University of California, Riverside

William Corsaro
Indiana University

William Damon
Stanford University

Gary Alan Fine
Northwestern University

Gerald Handel
The City College and The Graduate
Center, City University of New York

Shirley A. Hill
University of Kansas

Annette Lareau
Temple University

Robin Lynn Leavitt
Illinois Wesleyan University

Catherine C. Lewis
Mills College

David Lisak
University of Massachusetts, Boston

Kristen Myers
North Carolina State University

Barbara J. Risman
North Carolina State University

H. Rudolph Schaffer
University of Strathclyde,
Glasgow, Scotland

Ellen Seiter
University of Southern California

Anthony Synnott
Concordia University, Montreal,
Canada

Judith Van Evra
St. Jerome's College,
University of Waterloo, Canada

Julia Wrigley
The Graduate Center,
City University of New York

Introduction to the Second Edition

The editor of an anthology seeks to bring order to a subject through a judi-cious selection of original writings. The reader has the opportunity to discover first-hand how a variety of scholars approach a subject. This second edition of *Childhood Socialization* has a unity of focus but the reader will see that the sub-ject has many parts, each presented in the words of an original author (or team). The editor's goal is to introduce those writers in their own words. An anthology can both introduce newcomers to a subject and also be of use to readers who are not newcomers to it but have not encountered many of the included selections or the editor's approach to organizing them.

Eleven of the nineteen selections in this second edition are new to it. Those retained from the first edition remain because I consider them to be of contin-uing value and have not discovered any more recent writings that cover the same ground in a comparable amount of space. Knowledge and ideas change over time, and I have dropped those earlier selections that are most evidently obsolete, while keeping those that are not. I also retain the Introduction to the first edition because it remains a valid, concise introduction to the subject.

While the chapters are grouped in Parts, several of them are relevant to other Parts as well. The cross relevancies are noted at the conclusion of the Introductions.

Gerald Handel

Introduction to the First Edition

Socialization is the process by which the newborn human organism is transformed into a social person, a person capable of interacting with others. Interacting with others implies several different kinds of activities—carrying on a conversation; forming affectionate ties; participating as a member of many kinds of organizations, such as a school classroom, a social club, a work group in a shop or office; sharing loyalty with many unknown others who are fellow citizens of a nation or fellow adherents of a church. Being a person means living in a socially organized world and knowing how to move around in some part of that world. It means knowing rules for interacting with others in various contexts and settings and having the various kinds of competence that are required in each. A newborn has the ascribed status of son or daughter but will have to transform it into an achieved status of acceptable son or daughter. Thereafter, in sequence, the child will have to gain the qualifications of an acceptable pupil in nursery school or kindergarten; an acceptable playmate to other children in neighborhood and school, and so on, to a succession of qualifications throughout the life course. Acceptability means knowing the expectations of others and being able to conduct oneself within the limits of those expectations. In all of those settings, expectations change with age, as the child is socialized to increasingly more demanding standards of knowledge, understanding, emotion, and performance.

Socialization is a process that is carried out by persons and organizations that may have official designation as agents of socialization or that may be allowed to function as such an agent. They are agents in a double sense of that term: (1) They act upon the child; and (2) they act on behalf of the larger society (or some particular segment of it that may be acceptable or unacceptable to the larger society). The principal agents in our society, and in many others, are family, school, and peer group. In addition, in the last 35 years, television has come to be considered an important agent in our society. (Churches are probably also significant agents, but, except for a few denominations such as Hutterites and Mennonites, their socialization activity has not been much studied.)

Each of these socialization agents has a somewhat different socialization impact, although there is some overlap in their efforts and impact. In some ways parents and teachers, parents and peer group, teachers and peer group may pull together; in some ways all may pull the child in different directions, offering conflicting goals, standards, expectations. Television may reinforce some aspects of each while also offering its own reality.

The socialization process is not completed in childhood. It continues through adolescence and throughout adulthood. An adult who takes a new job must be socialized into the organization. Social change presents people with opportunities or challenges to alter their beliefs, values, and actions. Major events such as the Vietnam War, the civil rights movement, the women's movement, the Watergate scandal in the Nixon Administration, the rise of AIDS as a threat to public health have led to revised beliefs and values and different actions with regard to patriotism, relationships between blacks and whites, relations between the sexes, trust in government, and standards of openness in the discussion of sexuality. Thus, there is a sense in which the outcomes of socialization are never final because later socialization can have an impact that changes the person. How much change is possible and under what circumstances is still a matter of some uncertainty. Despite this uncertainty, there is widespread agreement that childhood socialization—*primary socialization,* as it is called, to distinguish it from *adult socialization*—is essential in creating the human person and in shaping the identity, outlook, skills, and resources of the evolving person. In the last 20 years or so, sociology has developed a new focus on the life course perspective and psychology on life span development, both of which give a lot of attention to how much people change in adult life. None of this discussion, however, has taken the form that "it does not much matter how children are socialized since they can always change and become whatever kind of person they want to become when they become adults." Studies of gender socialization still deal with the issue of how early socialization prevents girls from developing their full potential in adulthood, and studies of children who grow up both financially and informationally impoverished still find that socialization in such circumstances usually has lifelong consequences, a few dramatic cases to the contrary notwithstanding.

The first agents of socialization, the parents or their surrogates, ordinarily understand that they have some responsibility of preparing their child for adulthood in the society or segment of it into which s/he has been born. Whether they think about it a great deal or not at all, their actions are guided by some notion of what sort of person their child should be upon attaining adulthood. That notion, whether vague or detailed, will be influenced by the community and society in which the family lives. Social class and ethnic group are significant influences that distinguish families within a society, but other kinds of variation also affect how children are socialized.

The purpose of this book is to present a selection of studies that together convey how the agents of socialization operate to induct the human child into society. Although the socialization process largely takes place in face-to-face interaction in small groups, its purpose is to induct the child into his or her particular society. While the book is most fully devoted to socialization in the United States, an effort has been made to communicate something of the variety of socialization by including a few comparative studies and studies from other societies. Space limitation made it necessary to omit some studies of other societies that I had hoped to include.

Gerald Handel

PART I

Socialization, Individuation, and the Self

The newborn baby is a biological organism that will become a grown person functioning in society. This complex transformation is accomplished through numerous processes that can be grouped into several broad categories. One is *maturation* or physical development, which is a passage from small size and uncoordinated body functioning to adult size and body form and coordinated body movement. It includes sexual maturation. A second broad category may be termed *individuation*, the process of becoming a particular person. A third broad category, the one to which this book is devoted, is *socialization*, the process of gaining the capacities for social interaction that enable the person to function in society. Some anthropologists argue for a fourth category—*enculturation*, the process of acquiring a particular culture, which they distinguish from socialization—although others do not find this distinction necessary, considering that socialization necessarily includes acquiring a particular culture. *Cognitive development*, the process of becoming capable of dealing with ever more complex information, concepts, and intellectual relationships, is another broad category.

This classification is useful, but the categories are not independent of each other. Each affects the other to some degree, in complex and subtle ways. This book focuses on social functioning, and the two chapters in Part I introduce the concept of *socialization*. Chapter 1 presents the distinction, and also the connections, between socialization and individuation. Sigmund Freud, the originator of psychoanalysis, viewed society and individual as in opposition. Emile

Durkheim, one of the founding fathers of sociology, believed that autonomy was the freely willed and enlightened acceptance of the social rules to which the child is molded during socialization; the child comes to be but a reflection of the society. Each of these is at best a partial view. Socialization is fundamental in making us human, but the process cannot be understood as simple molding. One reason, as William Damon points out in Chapter 1, is that the child is an active agent in its socialization and does not turn out exactly as socializing adults wish.

Chapter 2 touches briefly on the relationship between socialization and maturation, but it is devoted most fully to explicating the social origin of the self, a key concept in the sociological understanding of socialization. Social participation means being able to regulate one's own conduct in interaction with others; only with the development of a self is self-regulation possible.

When we talk about socialization in terms of the newborn who, as a "raw recruit" into society, is first the object of and then a participant in interaction, we are focusing on socialization as a social–psychological process. This perspective is necessary, but not sufficient, for understanding socialization. Socializing agents have particular positions in society. Parents, for example, are members of a particular social class and usually responsive to and influenced by their class membership. They have a particular position in the economy that is likely to affect their socializing activity. A child whose parents are, say, both assembly-line workers is likely to be socialized somewhat differently from one whose parents are both corporation lawyers because each set of parents participates in a different part of the social structure. There may well be overlap in what the different parental couples know, believe, and value, but there are likely to be significant differences as well. Chapter 2 discusses briefly this structural point of view, as well as the social–psychological. Both perspectives are exemplified in various selections throughout the volume.

References

Durkheim, Emile. *Moral Education: A Study in the Theory and Application of the Sociology of Education* (New York: Free Press of Glencoe, 1961. First published in 1925).

Freud, Sigmund. *Civilization and Its Discontents* James Strachey, transl./ed. (New York: W.W. Norton, 1962. First published in 1930).

1

Socialization and Individuation*

William Damon

Social development is a life process built upon a paradox. The paradox is that at the same time we are *both* social and individual beings, connected with others in a multitude of ways, as well as ultimately alone in the world. This dual condition of connectedness and separateness begins at the moment of birth and remains with us all through life. The phrase *social and personality development* describes a two-fronted life movement within this paradoxical state of affairs. In the course of development, we become better able both to establish connections with others and to realize our own distinctness from others. In short, we become more social while at the same time becoming more individual and unique.

Paradoxes, of course, are only seeming contradictions, not real ones. The strange mix of sociability and individuality that develops in the course of human life can be seen as two complementary developmental functions, rather than as contradictory life directions. These are, respectively, the *social* and the *personality* functions of social development. Although these two functions seem to pull us in opposite ways, in actuality the two functions go hand in hand, each contributing to growth and to the individual's successful social adaptation.

The Two Functions of Social Development

The first of social development's complementary functions usually is called *socialization*. The socialization function includes all of one's tendencies to establish and maintain relations with others, to become an accepted member of society-at-large, to regulate one's behavior according to society's codes

*From *Social and Personality Development, Infancy through Adolescence*, by William Damon. Reprinted by permission of W. W. Norton & Company, Inc. Copyright © 1983 by W. W. Norton & Company, Inc.

and standards, and generally to get along well with other people. We may consider this to be the *integrating* function of social development, since it ensures the integration of the individual into society as a respected participant.

As a child grows, she experiences many different kinds of incentives toward socialization and integration into society. The baby needs close physical and emotional contact with her mother and must respond actively in ways that encourage such contact. The toddler is subject to direct disapproval until she becomes toilet trained. By middle childhood, children must learn to act cooperatively and fairly if they are to enjoy the companionship of friends. By the time of adolescence, the standards of society-at-large must be understood and respected. If an adolescent does not obey the law, there will be legal repercussions; if the adolescent does not do well in school or at work, her future career prospects may suffer. In these and many other ways, children experience the multiple needs and demands of socialization throughout their development.

The second function of social development is the formation of the individual's personal identity. This function, often called *individuation*, includes the development of one's sense of self and the forging of a special place for oneself within the social order. It entails understanding one's idiosyncratic personal characteristics and reconciling these characteristics with the requirements of interpersonal relations, as well as of occupational, sex, and family roles. We may consider this to be the *differentiating* function of social development. The formation of a personal identity requires distinguishing oneself from others, determining one's own unique direction in life, and finding within the social network a position uniquely tailored to one's own particular nature, needs, and aspirations.

As with socialization, the demands of individuation and differentiation begin early and continue throughout life. Babies struggle to recognize themselves as separate persons, distinct from their caregivers. Toddlers learn to say "no" as an assertion of their autonomy (such assertions are so common that during this period children are considered to be in "the terrible twos"). By middle childhood, children in school and at play are busy discovering the particular talents and interests that may set them apart from their peers. The young adolescent's need to establish independence from home and family is well known. Moreover, late adolescence is a primary proving ground for one's personal sense of identity. One's personal identity, once constructed, is continually evaluated and reassessed throughout development.

Both functions of social development are absolutely essential for a person's adaptation to life. Through the integrating function, a person maintains satisfying and productive relations with others and with society-at-large. Continued failures here can lead to interpersonal conflicts, social isolation, or even to social deviance and delinquency. In addition, poor social relations during development can leave a person impoverished in cognitive skills and emotional responsiveness. Through the differentiating function, a person acquires a coherent identity and a feeling of control over her own destiny. Failure here can lead to a sense of confusion, paralysis, and despair.

Further, these two essential functions are deeply interconnected in the course of a person's development, often relying upon each other's achievements. Thousands of years ago, Aristotle wrote, "All friendly feelings towards others come from the friendly feelings that a person has for himself." Conversely, a shaky sense of self can impair one's social interactions, and a maladaptive history of social relations can bear unfortunate consequences for one's personal identity.

Together, these two functions penetrate into every area of life. Intellectual activity, for example, is frequently affected by one's social and personal adaptation. Both social and personal chaos can easily disrupt one's intellectual processes, just as confused thinking can disturb one's efforts to make sense out of problematic social and personal issues. There are, of course, unusual cases in which intellectual and social competence seem to become divorced from one another. One such example is the stereotype of the brilliant scholar who has great insights but who cannot manage the simplest of personal affairs. But for most individuals, their social and personality growth is closely reflected ·n their intellectual achievements.

Relations between Socialization and Individuation

In some ways, socialization and individuation are quite distinct processes, even at times operating in opposition to one another. Establishing one's individuality very often requires a different sort of activity from that required for "socialized" behavior in the traditional use of the term. Defining one's distinctness from others and staking out one's unique social position sometimes place one in an antagonistic relation to others. Conversely, being "socially acceptable" sometimes means forgoing personal wishes and habits in deference to the expectations of others.

Psychoanalytic writing has always emphasized this distinction between the individual and society. This was the subject of Sigmund Freud's (1930) treatise, *Civilization and Its Discontents*. Freud argued that to become civilized (his word for socialized) means renouncing some of one's most basic drives, in particular those of sex and aggression. But these drives do not simply go away once they are renounced: They remain as a source of conflict and discontent for the individual who has accommodated to civilized life. It is as if, in a far less extreme way, we are all seething Mr. Hydes contained within mild-mannered Dr. Jekylls, always in danger of bursting through our civilized veneers. Normally this universal conflict can be contained and even productively channeled without too great a toll on the individual's happiness. In less fortunate cases, it may lead to psychopathology or social deviance. But in all cases, according to classic Freudian analyses, it typifies the universal and constant tension between a person's individualistic and social needs. Freud may or may not be correct in his belief that "antisocial" drives like aggression are an intrinsic part of human nature. But the dichotomy that he described between individual and social tendencies, along with the conflict that the dichotomy sometimes produces, cannot be denied.

Yet there is a sense in which there are profound connections between socialization and individuation. Developmentally, the two often go hand in hand for important psychological reasons: As one learns more about others, one learns more about the self, and vice versa. This is because interactions between self and others simultaneously provide one with feedback about both the nature of the other and about the nature of the self. Such feedback includes information about relations with other people, about other people's view of the self, and about characteristics of persons that are shared by both self and other. In the course of conducting social relations with others, one learns simultaneously about how to get along with others, about what others are like, and about what the self is like. In this sense, socialization and individuation are really opposite sides of the same coin: They are the yin and yang of social development.

At the turn of the century, James Mark Baldwin (1902) introduced this two-directional notion of social development to the field of psychology. Baldwin wrote that children come to know themselves only as a consequence of social interactions with many others:

> The growing child is able to think of self in varying terms as varying social situations impress themselves upon him. . . . The development of the child's personality could not go on at all without the constant modification of his sense of himself by suggestions from others. So he himself, at every stage, is really in part someone else, even in his own thought of himself. (p. 23)

Just as the self is constructed through feedback received from others, Baldwin wrote, knowledge of others is constructed through feedback in the opposite direction: from the self projected outward. Thus, a young child who discovers that she gets angry when she is treated unfairly will assume that others also react this way to unfairness. An adolescent who learns that he can feel jealous of a rival becomes aware that people have a capacity for jealousy. In this manner, the child's sense of self and other grow simultaneously, inextricably woven together in the course of development. As both the self and other become clearly known, the child's thoughts of self are "filled up by thoughts of others" and the child's thoughts of others are "mainly filled up by thoughts of (the) self . . . but for certain minor distinctions in the filling" (p. 18).

Baldwin's theory perhaps goes too far in emphasizing the similarity between the processes by which the self and the other are known. In many respects, the construction of the self poses unique cognitive and affective problems not encountered by the child in other aspects of his social development. To claim that realizing one's individuality is identical in every way to learning about others and one's relations with others is clearly overstating the case. Individuality may in fact lead one into antisocial directions. Moreover, there are certainly more than "minor distinctions" between one's attitude toward the self and one's attitude toward others throughout the course of development. But despite its overstatement, Baldwin's argument has made social scientists aware of a fundamental connection between individual and social development, a connection based on the bidirectional process of understanding self and other.

In short, socialization and individuation are to a certain extent distinct from one another, and there is always the possibility that actions which will further one may not be in the service of the other, or may even stand in opposition to the other. But in the normal course of development, they go hand in hand, supporting each other's growth. There is a creative tension between the two, a dialectical interplay between the needs of the individual to maintain relations with others and the needs of the individual to construct a separate self. The individual can only construct the self in the context of relations with others, but at the same time, the individual must step beyond the confines of those relations and forge a unique destiny.

Socialization and the Active Child

As part of their integration into society, children are required to adopt certain behavioral standards. These standards vary somewhat from society to society, but generally they are the key regulators that guide the child toward prosocial and away from antisocial behavior. Adults spend a good deal of time and effort attempting to transmit such standards to their children, and they often feel directly responsible for the extent to which their children have understood and adopted the message.

In exerting their socializing influences, adults have many possible techniques at their command. They can tutor or lecture their children on the proper ways to behave, they can administer rewards for desired behavior and punishment for undesired behavior, and they can arrange their children's lives in order to expose them to certain experiences and restrict them from others. Adults, by their own behavior, can also set an example for their children to imitate. Through their many agents, such as the schools, the churches, the media, adults also control the information that is available to children. Perhaps most importantly, in their parenting roles, adults protect and nurture their children, and they maintain intensely emotional bonds with them. These bonds themselves may act as a powerful incentive for children to heed the directives of adults.

Yet, with all this, children do not always turn out exactly as the adults in their lives may wish. Sometimes they resist adult guidance, sometimes they fail to comprehend it, sometimes they simply may not be able to live up to standards that they do accept. Even in the normal cases of children who are destined to become well-adjusted citizens of their societies, conformity to adult standards is neither instantaneous nor uniform. By any measure, socialization takes years, and children of a new generation never exactly replicate their elders' social behavior. Despite the many tools of adult influence over children, transmission of standards and values from one generation to the next is a slow and uncertain process.

The main reason that children do not quickly become simple reflections of their elders is that children are not passive recipients of social input. A child's behavior cannot be explained by the sum total of social experience that the child has received, however detailed or complex a history we provide. Rather, children themselves are active agents in creating the social experiences that influence their development. They participate in determining the nature of their social relations, bringing their own dispositions and characteristics to any interaction in which they engage. They also process adult attempts at social influence in their own way. Whether a child comprehends or agrees with an adult directive is very much up to the child, as any parent instinctively knows. In addition, children can choose the persons that they will be influenced by; and often, they will choose peers rather than adults, or an idealized figure distant in time and place from their immediate families. Many a parent has been frustrated and bewildered by a child who adopts the mannerisms (and perhaps even some of the values) of a popular music star the child has never met.

The puzzle of socialization is how an active child comes to adopt behavioral standards consistent with the values embedded in the child's culture. Clearly, adults cannot directly transmit these standards to the child as if they were simply innoculating the child against disease. Nor do children passively copy what they see. Rather, socialization is a complex process of interaction between the child and others in the child's social network. This interaction has bidirectional effects, changing both the child and those with whom the child interacts. That this interaction occurs is now admitted by virtually all socialization theorists. The exact nature of this interaction, however, is the subject of much debate and controversy.

Biology, Culture, and Interaction

There is an old and a new form of the debate about the interaction between the child and others. The old form hinged on the opposition between "nature" and "nurture," or between "biology" and "culture." The key issue, as framed in this manner, is the extent to which particular behavior patterns can be explained by the child's inherent attributes, as opposed to the child's social experience. Is a tendency toward aggressiveness inherited or inculcated? Is communicative competence preprogrammed in the human species, or is it learned? How much of a particular child's talent is due to the child's genetic structure and how much is it due to a favorable upbringing? Are orderly developmental changes instigated by a natural "ground plan" evolved through the ages, or are they triggered by changes in the child's social environment as the child grows older? These and other nature–nurture questions have been traditional subjects for debate since the dawn of social science, and they show few signs of either being resolved or of losing their interest for social scientists.

A more recent, and more productive, form of this debate assumes that the child's biology and culture inevitably interact, but it questions the nature of this interaction. The focus of the debate, therefore, is neither on *whether* nature or nurture plays a role, nor on *how much* of a role either plays. Both are assumed always to work together in shaping every form of human behavior. The focus of the debate is now on *how* the two interact with one another to direct the child's behavior and development.

Answers to these questions have been offered by every socialization and personality theorist, but these answers often differ greatly from one another. Some theorists believe that biological endowment and early experience combine to shape a young child's personality in ways that remain stable throughout much of life. Other theorists believe that, as the child grows, biological and cultural influences on personality are increasingly mediated through the child's own cognitive (or "social–cognitive") processes, and therefore that persons always retain the potential to alter the course of their own development. As for the social influence processes responsible for the child's acquisition of behavioral standards, there is much debate about their exact nature. There is even dispute concerning whether one or many processes are implicated. Some believe that all cultural norms are learned in essentially the same manner, whereas others believe that certain kinds of behavioral standards are acquired in special ways. Finally, other theorists have offered innumerable modifications and variations on all of the foregoing positions.

In sum, persons are not simply products of society, but rather they are active participants in their own socialization. All aspects of social behavior and development result from an interaction between the person's own characteristics and the person's social experience.

References

Baldwin, James M. *Social and Ethical Interpretations in Mental Development*, 3rd ed. (New York: Macmillan, 1902).

Freud, Sigmund. *Civilization and Its Discontents*, James Strachey, transl./ed. (New York: W. W. Norton, 1962. First published in 1930).

2

Socialization and the Social Self*

Gerald Handel

One fundamental fact about the newborn human organism is that it is not prepared for the life that lies before it. The newborn baby is destined to live a life in society, a life in which it will be obliged to cooperate with others in order to survive and in which it will wish to cooperate with others in order to gain satisfactions. At birth, the baby is unable to cooperate; it has only the potentiality for doing so. Its inability derives from two related, but distinct, characteristics: (1) It is immature as a biological organism; it is biologically incapable of carrying out cooperative actions. (2) It is unsocialized; it does not know how to cooperate.

Maturation and Socialization

In the course of time, the baby will change as a biological organism, growing in size and capacities, undergoing changes in shape and proportions as it moves toward the adult form for its sex. These are known as *developmental changes* and referred to by the summarizing term *biological maturation* or, more briefly, *maturation*. The baby will also, over time, learn how to cooperate, and the processes through which this learning is accomplished are referred to by the term *socialization*. In the course of socialization, the infant develops into a person who is capable of functioning in society, particularly those parts of society that circumstance and, later, choice make available.

Although maturation and socialization are distinguishable, they are also interrelated in various ways. The newborn infant is dependent upon others for

*From: "Socialization and the Social Self" by Gerald Handel, in *Sociology: The Basic Concepts*, edited by Edward Sagarin. Copyright © 1978 by Holt, Rinehart & Winston. Reprinted by permission of Holt, Rinehart & Winston, Inc.

care. Neither maturation nor socialization can occur without it. A baby that does not receive care does not mature; it dies. In order to survive, it must, at the very least, be given food and it must be kept clean. Those who provide food and tend the baby are thereby simultaneously initiating *social interaction*, or responding in an interaction initiated by the baby's cry. Since true social interaction involves mutual taking account of the other person, the activities of infant and caregiver must be regarded, strictly speaking, as a forerunner or matrix of social interaction. Nevertheless, socialization is initiated in these care-giving activities; they provide the newborn's first experiences of the social world it has entered. Maturation cannot occur in the absence of these first socialization experiences. Throughout life, many activities require both maturation and socialization for their accomplishment. Socialization can, within limits, direct maturation. Contrariwise, maturation sets certain limits within which socialization can occur. Illustrating the first point, any neuromuscular activity such as writing with a pencil or climbing palm trees to pick coconuts requires a particular level of maturation, but many people go through their entire lives without knowing either how to write or to climb trees. Their socialization experiences have not provided them with the opportunities to learn these skills. As a result, the neuromuscular capacity for using a pencil or for climbing trees will not have developed to the level of which the human body is capable, for these biological potentialities develop through socialization.

That maturation sets limits to socialization is perhaps more obvious. A 5-year-old child may "play doctor," but there is no way in which the child can be taught to function as a doctor at that age; it is not mature enough. The developmental nature of the human organism thus sets certain limits to socialization; socialization experiences are generally limited by or geared to social judgments of maturation level.

Although the developmental nature of the human organism sets certain limits to socialization, it does not prescribe the process. A 5-year-old can do certain kinds of factory work, as was common before child labor laws were adopted prohibiting it, or a 5-year-old can be entered in a kindergarten to receive gentle instruction. This is possible because of the *plasticity* of the human organism, its potentiality for being shaped through socialization. What is expected of a five-year-old (or a child of any age) varies widely from one society to another or in the same society from one historical period to another. One of the questions of great public interest in recent years is whether a person's biological sex represents a real limit to plasticity or whether this has been exaggerated in explaining differences in social functioning of adult males and females. *Sex roles*, patterns of prescribed and preferred behavior for each sex, are to be found in every society. The question being raised today is whether socialization of the young to act in accord with society's sex roles is based on sound knowledge of the human organism or whether it is based on arbitrary interpretations of the relevance of biological sex for general social behavior.

Empathy and Communication

The persons who care for the newborn infant have three characteristics that are of particular importance to the infant's socialization, since the child will develop these characteristics during the course of socialization. First, the adult is able to know that the infant needs care because the adult has the ability to experience *empathy*, to place himself or herself imaginatively in the situation of the baby and to understand what needs to be done.[1] Empathy is one of the sentiments—perhaps the most basic one—that develops in the course of socialization. So far as is currently known, the ability to experience sentiments such as pride, courage, ambition, disillusionment, a sense of honor, consideration, contempt, hero worship, pity, sacrifice, cruelty, envy, appreciation, and many others is a distinctively human ability, developed in the course of socialization. All of these sentiments involve the capacity to put oneself imaginatively in the place of others in complex and differentiated ways.

Second, the adult has the ability to *communicate*. Other animals also have communication systems. However, the human use of language differs in a fundamental respect from the communication of other species (although some current research on chimpanzees raises new questions): Humans are able to make use of *significant symbols*—that is, the symbols (words) that a person uses in speaking (or writing) have the same meaning for the speaker as is intended for the hearer and as the hearer reveals by his response. Thus, when a parent says to a small child, "Get me the broom," the parent must first present those words to himself in an *internal conversation* before presenting them to the child. This inner conversation ordinarily occurs so rapidly as to take place outside awareness. The parent becomes aware of the internal conversation only in situations that are more problematic; for example, the parent might ponder: "I wonder if he is old enough to manage the broom without knocking over the vase." When the parent is first teaching the child to get the broom, the meaning of the words is not yet clear to the youngster. As the child works at understanding more fully, he can sometimes be heard to present the words to himself out loud, thereby directing himself to carry out the action that is meant. Eventually the child, too, is able to manage this aspect silently and speedily.

In the course of socialization, the child acquires language, both a vocabulary and a set of rules for combining words into sentences that are accepted as correct sentences in his social milieu. How these rules are acquired is not yet understood, and this problem is currently the focus of intense research activity. What is particularly intriguing is that the child apparently learns these rules at an early age so that he is able to speak sentences that he has never heard but that are nevertheless formed according to the rules. For example, the young child who says, "I throwed the ball" may never have heard that sentence, but he has in some fashion learned the rule about adding the "ed" sound to a verb to form the past tense, even though applying the rule incorrectly in the particular instance.

To be able to participate in social life requires the ability to use *significant symbols*. Each society embodies in its language an array of categories that help to organize its world; for example, Eskimos have many different words for snow, each referring to a distinctive condition of the snow. In our society the rough distinction between "snow" and "ice" is all the differentiation most people require. The Eskimo child learns to conceptualize snow in a more elaborate and more differentiated way than does the child in our society.

The Development of the Self

The use of significant symbols—the process of human communication—is, then, fundamentally different from communication in other species, with the distinguishing fact being that humans are able to know the meaning of their own words. They are able to present to themselves what they wish to communicate to others. This is possible only because the person has developed a *self*, which may be defined as the ability to take oneself as an object, *to be conscious that one is an object distinct from other objects*. So far as is now known, only the human being has the capacity to be aware of himself, to take himself as an object, to refer to himself. This characteristic—the third of the three referred to before—is not present at birth but develops in the course of social interaction. The newborn infant has no conception of itself as a separate and distinct being. The adults who care for the child, and others who engage in interaction with it, provide the child with a variety of sounds, sights, and tactile sensations. To the child, these are assumed to be, at first, "a buzzing, blooming confusion," as William James put it. Gradually, they gain form and definition, and a self becomes differentiated from the surrounding world. Only with the emergence of a self does the child become a person able to regulate its own conduct, to have that capacity for self-direction that is requisite for functioning in human society.

The emergence of a self is made possible by the interest that others take in the newborn, developing child. That interest may be perfunctory or enthusiastic, but interest on the part of others is both necessary and sufficient to stimulate the emergence of a self. These persons are the first in a succession of *significant others* who influence the course of socialization throughout the developing human's lifetime. The kind of interest a person takes in the child is, in effect, a kind of appraisal of the child, an expression of the child's importance or value to the adult. The child's self initially consists of these initial appraisals; the ideas he has of himself are, at first, ideas he gains from others about himself. In time, the child becomes able and does imagine how his appearance or his action affects a significant other so that the self he has is, in Charles Horton Cooley's celebrated metaphor, a *looking-glass self*, a reflection of what he imagines others think of him.

The I and the Me

George Herbert Mead (1934), who developed his ideas about the same time that Cooley did in the early years of the twentieth century, emphasized the two-part structure of the self. He represented this structure by the terms the *I* and the *me*. The me consists of the attitudes of others that the child adopts and makes his own. Language is important in bringing about this process. Thus a parent says things that communicate "good child" or "good behavior" and "bad child" or "bad behavior." Such communications from significant others (parents, siblings, playmates, teachers, relatives) become increasingly patterned or organized into that part of the self that Mead calls the me, the self as the object of others' attitudes. Along with language, participation in play is influential. In an early stage, known as the *play stage*, the child takes the role of another person, that is, imagines himself to be that other person and tries to do what he imagines that person does—perhaps a parent, a policeman, a workman in the neighborhood, an older child, or whoever. (In modern times, the movies and particularly television have enlarged the array of *models*, persons whose role the child assumes.) In time, the child becomes capable of participating in organized games. During this *game stage*, the youngster assumes the role not of a single other but of the organized group, or what Mead calls the *generalized other*. In order to play baseball, for example, the child must have within himself an organized conception of pitcher, batter, fielders, base runners as well as some knowledge of their attitudes toward the various things he might do as he plays his own part. This ability to assume the role of the generalized other has lifelong importance, for the same ability is required of the person in his capacity as member of a family, a work group, a friendship group, or any group or organization to which he might ever belong.

Through his concept of the I, Mead expressed the idea that the self is not merely the sum of others' attitudes but that it has, importantly, a subjective phase or aspect. The main source of this I, as explained by Mead, is the biological organism, the impulses that arise in one's own body; thus, while the self arises in social interaction, it is not merely a social product but includes, as well, one's own awareness of one's physical self. Mead was concerned with demonstrating the possibility of novelty in the world, something he judged to be impossible if persons were no more than individual replicas of the society that produced them. His concept of the I represented the idea that persons have individuality as well as social characteristics in common with others. Mead thus presented an early conception that helps guard against what Dennis Wrong (1976) has called "the oversocialized conception of man in modern sociology."

Two Perspectives on Socialization

A full study of socialization always requires that we consider the process from two complementary perspectives. One perspective—which we have adopted thus far—is focused on the child as he proceeds from unsocialized newborn to increasingly socialized participant in society. From this perspective, socialization is concerned with the *face-to-face social interaction* in which the child is engaged with significant others and with the outcomes of those interactions: the development of a self, the growth of human sentiments, and the acquisition of language. But it is equally necessary to consider socialization from the perspective of the society into which the child is being socialized. The persons who socialize the child are members of society, and their socializing actions are influenced by the positions that they occupy in society; thus, a child's significant others are also, from this second perspective, *socialization agents*. Stated briefly, the parents who love their child also act on behalf of the society of which they are members as they prepare the child for membership in the society. Parents have a certain amount of latitude in doing this, but they nonetheless have to observe specific limits. In our society, for example, parents may use a variety of punishments, but if their punishment of a child exceeds a certain degree of harshness, they may be legally charged with child abuse, which is, in effect, a charge that they are deficient in their performance as socialization agents. Child neglect and contributing to the delinquency of a minor are other offenses with which parents may be charged if they are judged by the agents of the society's legal order to be failing in their responsibilities as socialization agents, that is, not providing the kind of care that is deemed suitable for preparing a child for adult membership in society.

Parents (or their designated surrogates) and schools have legally defined responsibilities for socializing children, but this is not so for all socialization agents. A child's social participation with persons of his own age, at succeeding levels, is recognized as being highly significant in his socialization. It is in these *peer groups* that a child learns to function more independently, to acquire and test skills and beliefs that earn him a place among people of the same generation, to develop new outlooks that reflect youthful interests rather than adult ones. These groups, made up of age mates, form spontaneously in neighborhoods, playgrounds, schoolrooms, and schoolyards. The only authority they have over their members is the authority that the members themselves grant to the group. In groups with something of an age spread, the older members will often have more authority by virtue of larger size, greater skill, wider knowledge, or some combination of these. The effectiveness of peer groups as socializing agents derives primarily from three characteristics:

1. In these groups, the child participates in making the *rules* that govern the group, whereas in family and in school he learns primarily to abide by rules that are made by adults and handed down to him.
2. The peer group functions with a shorter time perspective than does the family or the school, so that the gratifications the group offers are likely to be more immediate.
3. The peer group provides an alternative to adult standards as well as to adult authority. Peer group, family, and school classroom are all *reference groups*, groups whose values, standards, and beliefs guide the child in carrying out his actions and in evaluating himself.

The peer group's authority is nonexistent early in life because the child is incapable of belonging to such groups. As he becomes more capable, the peer group's authority expands and becomes more encompassing. A child may experience conflict among the standards put forth by his diverse reference groups. A four-year-old, being urged by playmates to cross the street when his parents have forbidden it, is experiencing socialization conflict. Conflict between peer group and parental claims to authority may reach greatest intensity when a child approaches adolescence or youth; at that time, the developing person seeks to minimize or discard entirely the remaining vestiges of that dependence with which he began life. Experienced conflict between peer group and school standards and between family and school standards are fairly common also.

No child is simply born into society but rather into particular locations in society—a social class, an ethnic group, a type of neighborhood. The socialization agents in different social segments present different expectations to children, who will, accordingly, have different socialization experiences; for example, according to some studies, children growing up in Appalachia reach adulthood with less developed capacities for cooperating with others than is found in other parts of American society. While regional differences have received some attention, more interest has been focused on social class differences. Studies have shown, for example, that working-class parents in both the United States and Italy are more likely to train their children to obedience and conformity, whereas middle-class parents train their children to be self-directing.

When the child governs his own conduct by the same values and norms that his significant others hold out to him, he is said to *internalize* the values and norms. They are available within himself, so that they no longer need be presented by a socialization agent. Internalization takes place over an extended period of time and is accomplished through *identification* with significant others.

Adult Socialization

In recent years, it has been recognized that socialization is a lifelong process so that we now distinguish between *primary socialization* (of the child) and *adult socialization*. A person must learn to function in any group or organization that he enters: He must learn not only new practices, but also often new values and norms, a new and specialized vocabulary, new ways of interacting with others. When the person is making a major commitment, such as entering an occupation or converting to a new religion, he is also making such a significant change in his life that he can be described as developing a new self. Sometimes a person may aspire to belong to a group and, before actually entering the group, he may prepare himself by *anticipatory socialization*, taking on the attitudes and values of his prospective group (Merton, 1965). Adult socialization is usually thought of as building upon primary socialization since the basic human equipment of a self—human sentiments and language—have been fashioned during primary socialization. A satisfactory explanation of the relationships between primary socialization and adult socialization still awaits us; many ambiguities require further clarification.

Earlier it was pointed out that socialization inevitably involves conflict for the person being socialized because the agents doing the socializing differ in what they expect. Not only do parents and peers often have different expectations, but there are also many other conflicts—between parents and teachers, parents and other interested commentators such as aunts and uncles, two parents themselves. A question nevertheless arises as to whether, beyond these differences, there is some kind of convergence among socialization agents and agencies that leads to a general similarity among the members of a society. Alex Inkeles (1968) has proposed the concept of *societal demand*, that is, that each society has some conception of the kind of adult it would like its children to become. This is not yet an accepted concept in sociology and thus cannot be considered one of the acknowledged fundamental concepts. Still, if we consider revolutionary societies that seek to guide themselves by a systematic ideology, there is some reason to suppose that a concept such as societal demand is helpful in understanding socialization. Societies such as China, Cuba, or the Soviet Union have sought to change the socialization practices that prevailed before their respective revolutions. Each of these countries has the goal of developing a significantly different type of adult from what was typical of prerevolutionary times, one who is also different from the adults believed typical of other societies. But whether there are, in fact, society-wide *socialization outcomes* remains, at this time, an open question.

Note

1. This idea was first emphasized in modern sociology by Charles Horton Cooley (1964) who used the term *sympathy*, defining it as "the sharing of any mental state that can be communicated." He made clear that he was not using the term in the sense of pity or "other tender emotion." Nevertheless, this latter connotation clings to the word, and it has increasingly given way to and been replaced by *empathy* as the term that denotes the ability to understand what is going on in another's mind or feelings.

References

Cooley, Charles Horton. *Human Nature and the Social Order*, 2nd ed. (New York: Schocken Books, 1964).

Inkeles, Alex. "Society, Social Structure, and Child Socialization." In John A. Clausen, ed., *Socialization and Society* (Boston: Little, Brown, 1968), Chap. 3.

Mead, George Herbert. *Mind, Self, and Society* (Chicago: University of Chicago Press, 1934).

Merton, Robert K. *Social Theory and Social Structure* (New York: Free Press, 1965).

Wrong, Dennis. "The Oversocialized Conception of Man in Modern Sociology." In D. Wrong, *Skeptical Sociology* (New York: Columbia University Press, 1976), pp. 31–54.

PART II

Childhood in History

In one of the best-known passages from all of his plays, William Shake-speare gave, in 1599, a capsule summary of the human life course. Each of the "Seven Ages of Man" was identified by a few salient characteristics:

All the world's a stage,
And all the men and women merely players:
They have their exits and their entrances;
And one man in his time plays many parts,
His acts being seven ages. At first the infant,
Mewling and puking in the nurse's arms.
Then the whining school-boy, with his satchel
And shining morning face, creeping like snail
Unwillingly to school. And then the lover,
Sighing like furnace, with a woeful ballad
Made to his mistress' eyebrow. Then a soldier,
Full of strange oaths, and bearded like the pard,
Jealous in honour, sudden and quick in quarrel,
Seeking the bubble reputation
Even in the cannon's mouth. And then the justice,
In fair round belly with good capon lined,
With eyes severe and beard of formal cut,
Full of wise saws and modern instances;
And so he plays his part. The sixth age shifts
Into the lean and slipper'd pantaloon,
With spectacles on nose and pouch on side,
His youthful hose, well saved, a world too wide
For his shrunk shank; and his big manly voice,
Turning again toward childish treble, pipes
And whistles in his sound. Last scene of all,
That ends this strange eventful history,
Is second childishness and mere oblivion,
Sans teeth, sans eyes, sans taste, sans every thing.
(*As You Like It*, Act II, Scene vii)

21

Insofar as a few lines can summarize the whole life course, these are unsurpassed. The amount of information and insight given with such brevity is a stunning artistic achievement. Yet something is missing: we do not know whether woman's life has seven corresponding ages or consists of more or fewer. Shakespeare does not say.

Another limitation of the passage is the social and historical specificity of the ages. Although "mewling and puking" are universal features of infancy, they are not necessarily those that receive central attention in all historical periods or all societies. The ages of man and woman are more variable than a single Shakespearean passage can indicate. Twentieth-century social scientists have been looking at the human ages and finding that, within the broad constraints of a basic biological pattern—infancy, maturation, maturity, decline—there is great variation in how societies divide them up and what characteristics are featured in the ages that are recognized.

Modern awareness of this variability was greatly increased by anthropologist Margaret Mead's *Coming of Age in Samoa*, a study of adolescence published in 1928. In contrast to the storm and stress of adolescence in America, Mead found that Samoan adolescence was easy, conflict-free, untroubled.

A major landmark in the study of childhood was the research by historian Philippe Ariès, *Centuries of Childhood*, published in English in 1962, announcing surprisingly that childhood is not a universal stage of life. It did not emerge as a distinct stage in Western society until the end of the Middle Ages at the close of the fifteenth century. In fact, not until the seventeenth century, according to Aries, is the notion of childhood as a distinct period well established in western Europe. Before then, infancy was a long period lasting almost to the age of seven, at which time infants became little adults, mingling with older adults in an undifferentiated common stream of association and activity. As childhood was increasingly defined as a special period of life, it became the focus of increasing attention and thought, leading to the emergence of such fields of study in the twentieth century as socialization and child development.

In the following chapter, sociologist Anthony Synnott starts from Ariès's study and proceeds to review major variations in the definition of what childhood is over the past several centuries in Western society. His focus is on how influential writers thought about childhood, particularly in the early modern period (about 400 years ago). He finds five distinct beliefs about the nature of childhood and how children should be treated:

1. There are two kinds of children, some noble and some savage, but all should be treated kindly.
2. Children are born sinful and should be restrained and punished.

3. Children are born with little distinctive character and become whatever their education makes of them.
4. Children are born each with their own nature, not easily altered.
5. Children are naturally good.

Industrialization in the eighteenth and nineteenth centuries subjected working-class children to the same harsh work discipline in factories and mines as adults. At the same time, middle-class children were coming to be idealized as innocent angels. This view was significantly undermined in the early twentieth century by Freud who believed that strong impulses and passions existed in children. Still, the popular belief in innocence persisted, despite Freud. Synnott suggests, however, that childhood is changing significantly in the 1980s: Innocence is disappearing because children are being sexualized at younger ages. Synott maintains that confusion abounds today about what children are and what their place in society should be.

In the few short years since Synott wrote, the confusion has received a new twist from the spread of Acquired Immune Deficiency Syndrome (AIDS). Educators, physicians, clergy, parents, and others are disputing how much education children should receive about this life-threatening condition, what causes it, and how risk can be minimized. The principal dispute can be summarized in two contrasting viewpoints: (1) Inculcate children with the value of sexual abstinence until marriage and fidelity thereafter; help preserve their innocence by not going into specific descriptions of sexual activity; (2) It is necessary to assume that children may well begin to be sexually active in their early teens or even before, and therefore they need to be explicitly informed long in advance about the relative risks of various sexual practices, including the risk reduction provided by condoms. These two opposing positions involve very different assumptions about the nature of children, as well as about the relative efficacy of two very different socialization strategies of adults.

References

Ariès, Philippe. *Centuries of Childhood* (New York: Alfred A. Knopf, 1962. First published in 1960).

Mead, Margaret. *Coming of Age in Samoa* (New York: William Morrow & Company, 1928).

3

Little Angels, Little Devils:
A Sociology of Children*

Anthony Synnott

"Our world is obsessed by the physical, moral and sexual problems of child-hood," wrote Philippe Ariès in his well-known *Centuries of Childhood* (1962: 411). Obsessions may be too strong a word, but certainly concern is not new. Plato and Aristotle debated the subject of children at length.

In this chapter, we shall explore some of the themes in the development of thinking about children and childhood from the early modern age to the present, not as fixed paradigms of childhood reflecting specific interests, but as a set of interrelated themes, each composed of residual, dominant, and emergent elements. Certain elements appear, disappear, and reappear over time—yesterday's residual elements may become dominant tomorrow to be succeeded by new, emergent elements and so on. We shall describe the variations and explain why they changed over time.

Laslett has cautioned that "We know very little indeed about child-nurture in pre-industrial times" (1965: 104), but we do know a little about what people thought about children in general, and their own children in particular.

Indeed, the early moderns regarded children in five conceptually distinct ways or, to rephrase this, entertained five distinct beliefs about the nature of the child and, more broadly, about human nature itself (cf. Stone, 1979: 245 ff.).

Perhaps the most influential essayist of the Renaissance was Michel de Montaigne (1533–1592). He discussed children in two interesting essays, and perhaps a few brief excerpts will give the flavor of his extremely important ideas.

*Reprinted by permission of the author and the Canadian Sociology and Anthropology Association from *Canadian Review of Sociology and Anthropology*, 20(1): 79–95 (1983).

In one essay, "On the Affection of Fathers for Their Children," he discussed how to raise children: "I would try, by kindly dealings, to foster in my children a warm friendship and unfeigned good feeling towards myself; which from noble natures are not hard to win. But if they are savage brutes, such as our age produces in profusion, they must be loathed and shunned as such" (1978: 146).

This humanist believed that there are two kinds of children, some noble and some savage, some good and some evil, yet, on the whole, he believed in the former; his advice is for parents to treat their children openly and without violence. "I am open with my family, to the extent of my powers" (1978: 150), adding that "It is a very poor father that has no other hold on his children's affection than the need they have of his assistance—always supposing that this can be called affection at all. He should win their respect by his virtue and abilities, and their love by his goodness and sweetness of character" (1978: 141).

Unlike many who followed him in time (Locke, Calvin, Wesley, even Spock), Montaigne was opposed to violence: "I condemn all violence in the education of a tender soul" (1978: 142; cf. p. 72). And his essay "On the Education of Children" is a remarkable critique of the traditional, formal education system, which in many respects anticipated Montessori, Ivan Illich, and A.S. Neill by almost 400 years; Montaigne's essays first appeared in 1580.

Montaigne's urbane, reasoned, and almost modern views on children are in sharp contrast to those of the contemporary Calvinists, and then the Puritans, who regarded children as born with sin, prone to evil and requiring strict restraint, strong guidance, and salutary punishment. Calvin (1535) remarked concerning children: "Their whole nature is a certain seed of Sin, therefore it cannot but be hateful and abominable to God" (Muir and Brett, 1980: 3). And almost 100 years later the American Puritans Robert Cleaver and John Dod reiterated these views: "The young child . . . is altogether inclined to evil. . . . Therefore parents . . . must correct and sharply reprove their children for saying or doing ill" (deMause, 1975: 316–317; cf. Gordon, 1978: 158–159).

This view of human nature and children's nature had clear politial implications which were drawn by Thomas Hobbes in *Leviathan* (1651). His views on the nastiness of man in the state of nature and the necessity for strong government are well known. He was no Puritan, but his perception of people by nature as "in that condition which is called Warre; and such a Warre, as is of every man, against every man" was in line with the Puritan concept of children as, literally, "little devils." The Puritan view declined with Puritanism, and, in England, this can be dated to the Restoration of the Stuarts (1660).

A third view was environmentalist: The child is a "tabula rasa," a blank slate that is neither good nor evil intrinsically. The idea can be traced back to Aristotle, who was cited as stating: "The soul of a child is like a clean slate on which nothing is written; on it you may write what you will" (Beekman, 1977:

20). John Early repeated this in 1628: "A child is a man in a small letter, yet the best copy of Adam before he tasted of Eve or the apple. . . . His soul is yet a white paper unscribbled with observations of the world . . . he knows no evil" (quoted in Illick, *ibid.*: 317; and cf. p. 342, fn. 75).

This view was popularized by John Locke in his book, *Some Thoughts Upon Education* (1693). Locke's most famous saying, repeated in his *Essay on Human Understanding* (Book II, Chapter 1), is that a child's mind is like "white paper, or wax, to be moulded and fashioned as one pleases" (paragraph 216). He suggests that "the difference to be found in the manners and abilities of men is owing more to their education than to anything else" (paragraph 32); in his first paragraph he states: "I think I may say that, of all the men we meet with, nine parts of ten are what they are, good or evil, useful or not, by their education."

However, Locke was not a complete environmentalist. Even in the seventeenth century, the nature–nurture, genetic versus environmental determinism debate may be seen in embryonic form. Locke admits that "God has stamped certain characters upon men's minds. . . . Everyone's natural genius should be carried as far as it could, but to attempt the putting another upon him, will be labour in vain" (paragraph 66).

This biological determinism had been briefly anticipated by Francis Bacon (1561–1626), Lord Chancellor under King James I and a contemporary of Montaigne's. He rather dislikes children, regarding them, like wives, as "hostages to fortune; for they are impediments to great enterprises" (1957: 12). He half practiced what he preached for he was married but childless. However, where Montaigne had described the "age" (i.e., environment) as producing noble or savage children, Bacon stresses forces outside human control: "A man's nature runs either to herbs or weeds; therefore let him seasonably water the one and destroy the other" (Bacon, 1957: 72). Thus, in Bacon's view biological or theological determinism (it is not clear which) is not complete but may be modified.

The view that children's natures varied and were determined naturally (genetically, as we would say) or by divine will or by the stars also implies an element of fatalism. There was little or nothing that family or education (despite Locke) could do about it; and this view seemed to gain credence in the eighteenth century.

Lady Hervey (1744) explained that children "acquire arts but not qualities; the latter, whether good or bad, grow like their features; time enlarges but does not make them" (Stone, 1979: 255). A more direct statement came from Enos Hitchcock (1790) in the newly independent United States: "We must take children as they are, induced with a variety of humors, dispositions and propensities" (Beekman, 1977: 74). This was a far cry from Locke's *tabula rasa* theory of only 100 years before or the rigid controlling ideas of the Puritans and Calvinists.

Finally, some believed that children, and indeed all human beings, are intrinsically good. This Romantic view had been broached during the Renaissance but was given widest currency by Jean-Jacques Rousseau in the middle of the eighteenth century, particularly in his most acclaimed work, *Emile* (1762). "God made all things good, man meddles with them and they become evil," was the opening sentence to that work (1969: 5). He attacked the views of the Puritans and the fundamentalists, observing that "there is no original sin in the human heart" (1969: 56). He turned Hobbes on his head, arguing that the origins of war and other evils lie in society, not in man; and he disagreed with Locke, Bacon, and Montaigne on a number of points: "Use force with children and reasoning with men," he suggested (1969: 55) in a debate reminiscent of the ongoing discussion about permissiveness and discipline.

Unfortunately Rousseau was unable to practice what he preached and ended by dispatching his five children to an orphanage. Nonetheless his ideas on children and education exercised considerable influence, particularly over the English Romantics in the nineteenth century. The belief that man is naturally good, free, and equal was a powerful force in European and North American history, facilitating the American and French revolutions and reform in Britain.

Nonetheless, it was not unchallenged. There were, as we have seen, four other views about children circulating at the time. However, the principal contemporary challenge to Rousseau came from the Methodists, and a sermon of John Wesley's indicates that his ideas were close to Calvin's and the Puritans': "Break the will if you would not damn the child. . . . Let a child from a year old be taught to fear the rod and cry softly. . . . Let none persuade you it is cruelty to do this; it is cruelty not to do it. Break his will now and his soul will live" (Muir and Brett, 1980: 101).

William Wilberforce, the great abolitionist, states: "Remember that we are fallen creatures, born in sin and naturally depraved, Christianity recognizes no innocence or goodness of heart" (Thompson, 1968: 440). And Hannah More writes in 1799 that it is a "fundamental error to consider children as innocent beings" rather than as beings of "corrupt nature and evil dispositions" (Thompson, 1968: 440). These Puritan and Methodist views spanning two centuries hark back to the Biblical adage "He that spareth the rod, hateth his son" (Prov. 13: 24), more usually rendered in Butler's aphorism, "Spare the rod and spoil the child."

But both are a far cry from the words of Christ in the New Testament: "Verily I say unto you, except you be converted, and become as little children, ye shall not enter the kingdom of heaven" (Matt. 18: 3) and "Suffer the little children to come unto me, and forbid them not; for of such is the kingdom of God" (Mark 10: 14).

The early modern age, therefore, was not static and uniform but rich, varied, confusing, and moving fast. And the conflicting ideologies of various sages— the humanism of Montaigne, the repressiveness (as we would see it) of Calvin, the Puritans and Wesley, the environmentalism of Locke, the genetic determinism of others, and the romanticism of Rousseau—not only stimulated debate about the nature of children, and humanity generally, but also about the practices of raising children.

Perhaps the most important changes in the lives of children in the preindustrial era were: the rise of education, with the school creating modern childhood (Ariès, 1962: 369); the increasing transfer of functions to the state (notably education) (Stone, 1974: 27); and the growth of what Stone calls "affective individualism" (Stone, 1977; 221 ff.). This brings us to the question of love; Ariès warns us that the preindustrial family was an economic rather than a sentimental reality. "This did not mean that parents did not love their children, but they cared about them less for themselves . . . than for the contribution those children could make to the common task" (1962: 368). A delicate balance hesitated between the child as producer and as consumer.

There was a constant awareness of death that must have affected love; both fertility and mortality rates were higher, so love was "spread around" more children, who were more likely to die. Emotional involvement was likely to have been less, simply out of self-protection, but such things are impossible to measure. Perhaps children, and adults, were not loved any less, but differently.

A medieval villager in Montaillou cries out when his only son dies: "I have lost all I had through the death of my son Raymond. I have no one left to work for me" (Ladurie, 1980: 210). A modern father would not speak like this, but, of course, the implications of the death of an only son would be different. The thirteenth-century villager, without a son, was probably condemned to poverty and an early death. Nor would a woman console a new mother like this seventeenth-century woman does: "Before they are old enough to bother you, you will have lost half of them, or perhaps all of them" (Ariès, 1962: 38).

Among the wealthy and the secure, the gentry and the squirearchy, however, such seemingly cold attitudes were not so common. We can see Henry VIII playing with his son Edward with "much mirth and joy, dallying with him in his arms a long space" (1538) (deMause, 1975: 240). Mme de Sevigné writes about her 18-month-old granddaughter in 1670: "I am very fond of her. . . . She does a hundred and one little things—she talks, fondles people, hits them, crosses herself, asks forgiveness, curtsies, kisses your hand, shrugs her shoulders, dances, coaxes, chucks you under the chin: in short, she is altogether lovely" (deMause, 1975: 21).

Emotional attitudes varied, therefore, as did child-rearing practices. Swaddling clothes were being discarded, and babies were now dressed in looser clothes. As they grew older specific costumes were developed: children no longer dressed as miniature adults; mothers began to breast-feed their children instead of giving them to wet-nurses; control was maintained less by the rod and by breaking the will and more by sweet reason and sweet talk; formal distance between parents and children began to decline, as did a certain religious fatalism or acceptance of the Divine Will, to be replaced by a new practicality and eventually a scientific spirit. These gradually changing practices indicated gradually changing ideas about children. In sum, a world, or several worlds of childhood co-existed in the early modern period, with enormous variations by class and by philosophical or religious orientation.

Industrialization, in the conventional sociological wisdom, changed all this. The classical distinctions: Tonnies' Gemeinschaft-Gesellschaft typology and Redfield's folk–urban dichotomy emphasize the all-embracing impact of modernization on the family, specifically the shift from the extended family to the nuclear family. Neil Smelser states one consequence of modernization: "The direct control of elders and collateral kinsmen weakens. This marks in structural terms, the differentiation of the nuclear family from the extended family" (1964: 263).

Yet, obvious as this may seem in traditional sociology, many scholars have recently come to question this simple cause–effect relation. Laslett, for instance, has argued that the change from the extended to the nuclear family was not caused by industrialization, for the nuclear family was typical of life in seventeenth-century England, and industrialization did not begin until the second half of the eighteenth century. The change in the family (if any) therefore preceded, and did not follow, industrialization (1972: 1–89, 137–139).

Sidney M. Greenfield, a sociologist, has pointed out that industrialization and the nuclear family are not necessarily related: The extended family has persisted in urbanized, industrial Brazil, Québec, England (parts), and Japan, while the nuclear family exists in Barbados without either industrialization or urbanization. He argues that New England was founded by, and on, the nuclear family before industrialization (Greenfield, 1961; Schulz and Wilson, 1973: 46–60). Anderson has even shown that the extended family was strengthened, not destroyed, by industrialization in Lancashire (Anderson, 1975: 78–96).

Historians and sociologists may agree that childhood has changed, but while sociologists tend to favor dichotomous typologies, as Lee does, historians seem to emphasize that change has not been unilinear, has not been caused simply or primarily by modernization, and may proceed at different rates, in different directions, for different reasons, in different countries or parts of the country at different times.

Through industrialization and urbanization, modernization had tremendous, if varied, effects on children; many did not survive it. The infant mortality rate (0–1 year) soared from an English average in the second half of the seventeenth century of between 118 and 147 per 1000 to a rate of about 250 per 1000 in Sheffield in 1837–1842. The child mortality rate (0–5) was at least 506 per 1000. The situation was similar in Manchester. And these figures, in Thompson's view, "underestimate—and perhaps seriously underestimate—the actual child mortality rate" since they probably exclude deaths among the unregistered immigrant populations (deMause, 1975: 305; Thompson, 1968: 361).

These figures are averages only; a House of Commons Select Committee on the Protection of Infant Life reported as late as 1871 that the infant death rate in "baby farms" in large towns was "70, 80, and even 90 per cent" (1871: 610). This was attributed mostly to carelessness, but sometimes to criminal intent. Infanticide was not uncommon. The committee reported that 276 children, mostly under a week old, had been found dead in London in 1870, with another 105 up to 19 May 1871 (1871: 610).

Urban working-class life was difficult for children and adults, and perhaps no one documented this better than Henry Mayhew, who anticipated Studs Terkel and oral history by 100 years. He interviewed one 14-year-old lad—a "mud-lark" for 3 years:

> He worked every day, with 20 or 30 boys, who might all be seen at day-break with their trowsers tucked up, groping about, and picking out the pieces of coal from the mud on the banks of the Thames. He went into the river up to his knees, and in searching the mud he often ran pieces of glass and long nails into his feet. When this was the case he went home and dressed the wounds, but returned to the riverside directly, "for should the tide come up," he added, "without my having found something, why I must starve till next low tide." In the very cold weather he and his other shoeless companions used to stand in the hot water that ran down the river side from some of the steam-factories, to warm their frozen feet (Mayhew, 1968, vol. 3: 357).

It was quite normal for the young lads soon to turn to crime, their sisters to prostitution.

Industrialization also had a tremendous impact on children's lives. Children's labor was not new, but the *conditions* of labor were new. Conditions is the British coal mines, the cotton mills, and factories were appalling. Investigation after investigation, Blue Book after Blue Book documented atrocities of child labor and, as we shall see, ultimately generated a romantic reaction to capitalist reality. Yet reform was slow: The first Factory Act (1833) prohibited labor, but only for children under 6; children under 10 years were not permitted to work more than 16 hours a day.

The situation was similar in the United States and British North America, although there was considerable regional variation. The New England Working-men's Association declared in 1833 that "children should not be allowed to labor in the factories from morning till night without any time for healthy recreation and mental culture." The first child labor law was passed in Massachusetts (1842) limiting the number of working hours to 10 for children under 12; like much other legislation, however, it was more a statement of principle than reality for it contained the qualifier that only manufacturers who "knowingly" employed such children were to be fined (Lumpkin and Douglas, 1937: 247–248; cf. also Kaestle and Vinovskis, in Hareven, 1978: 138–139). Furthermore, slavery was not abolished in the United States until 1865.

Manufacturers in the days of high capitalism tended to regard children without romance or sentimentality as grist for the proverbial mill (i.e., as young adults); even into the 1920s some protested that they were against exploitation (which they presumably defined differently from the labor unions and the reformers): "We join in the condemnation of the exploitation of children . . . and we insist that our growing youth shall be taught the dignity, duty and necessity of labour" (National Association of Manufacturers, 1924). "The Savior has said, My Father worketh hitherto, and I work . . . May not the child follow the footsteps of the Savior in this?" (Lawyer, 1924, Lumpkin and Douglas, 1937: 219).

And yet, at the same time as the children of the industrial and agricultural proletariat died in North America and Western Europe, the middle classes of the Victorian era were building nests for their children. Mrs. Beeton, a popular advisor of the time, could write: "It ought . . . to enter the domestic policy of every parent to make her child feel that home is the happiest place in the world; that to imbue them with this precious home-feeling is one of the choicest gifts a parent can bestow" (Quoted by Robertson, in deMause, 1975: 413). Her contemporary, Mrs. Ellis, informed mothers in 1844 that the best preparation possible for the realities and hardships of life was a happy childhood (deMause, 1975: 413).

This was the Golden Age of Victorian childhood (for the middle class); childhood was the age of innocence. The child was idealized as pure, trusting, and carefree. The child was a little angel, despite Calvin, and was epitomized by the famous advertisement for Pears Soap, "Bubbles." Wordsworth's "Ode on Intimations of Immortality" captured the spirit of this innocent angel:

> Not in entire forgetfulness,
> And not in utter nakedness,
> But trailing clouds of glory do we come
> From God, who is our home:
> Heaven lies about us in infancy!

The idealized child of the Romantics and of Victorian sentimentality arose like Tiny Tim, Oliver Twist, Little Nell, and Pip from the debris of industrial labor. The Golden Age of Innocence and child labor, however, go ill together, and a contemporary of Queen Victoria and Charles Dickens, Karl Marx, observed in *The Communist Manifesto* (1848): "Society as a whole is more and more splitting up into two great hostile camps, Bourgeoisie and Proletariat," Bubbles and Tiny Tim.

The exploitation of child labor and the related sentimentality of the Romantics were two of the most salient features of childhood in the nineteenth century; in the second half of the century, Charles Darwin published, successively, *On the Origin of Man* (1859) and *The Descent of Man* (1871) which, although bitterly contested on theological grounds, soon transformed contemporary thought about humanity and, of course, children. To put it simply, perhaps too simply: Victorians had three perspectives on children—little workers, little angels, and little animals, especially little monkeys (still a favorite phrase today)—depending on whether they were high capitalists, Romantics, or scientists.

The Victorian age ended with the death of the old Queen in 1901; and much of what the age symbolized died with her or on the battlefields of World War I. A new world of childhood dawned with the new century. Certainly Freud tolled the death-knell on the ideology of childhood as innocence; little angels do not have Oedipus or Electra complexes; nor do they pass through successively oral, anal, and phallic phases of psycho–sexual development, with both sadistic and masochistic impulses! Freud's attitude to childhood, like Darwin's, was unsentimental and clinical. He introduced entirely new ways of regarding children, and if Wordsworth cannot be mistaken for Calvin, nor can Freud.

> Both sexes seem to pass through the early phase of libidinal development in the same manner. It might have been expected that in girls there would already have been some lag in aggressiveness in the sadistic–anal phase, but such is not the case. Analysis of children's play has shown our women analysts that the aggressive impulses of little girls leave nothing to be desired in the way of abundance and violence. With their entry into the phallic phase the differences between the sexes are completely eclipsed by their agreements. We are now obliged to recognize that the little girl is a little man (Freud, 1977: 151).

Little girls as aggressive, violent, anal–sadistic, and, even, little men! Calvin and Wesley might have recognized their aggressiveness and described it as sinfulness, and Hobbes would have felt vindicated; but none would have understood the sex change. And this was just the tip of the iceberg, to embrace an appropriate image. Freud's discussion of masturbation, castration complexes, erotogenic zones, and penis–equivalents in children created a total different view of childhood. Psychoanalytic theory, which has had such an impact on contemporary world views, was not the world of Bubbles or Tiny Tim or Emile. Thanks to Darwin and Freud, rather than to industrialization, I would suggest, the Victorian little angels became more like little sex-maniacs—devils, but not devils in the Calvinistic mode. Furthermore, in stressing the importance of the first 3 years of life, Freud reversed the traditional view of aging. Locke had argued that a person is 90% the product of education; Freud suggested people were principally the product of their first 3 years. Children were therefore no longer "only" mini-adults, to be seen and not heard. Adults were now "only" children grown older, merely *consequences* of their childhood.

Nonetheless, despite the impact of evolutionary and psychoanalytic theory in the nineteenth century, the later studies by sociologists and anthropologists on the socialization of children demonstrate that childhood in twentieth-century Western society is neither homogeneous nor static; nor is the thinking about childhood. Beekman (1977) and Stendler (1950) have reviewed the advice given to parents on how to bring up children and have shown the dramatic changes in advice over the century. After analyzing articles in such middle-class magazines as the *Ladies Home Journal, Women's Home Companion*, and *Good Housekeeping*, Stendler concluded that:

> Three different schools of thought have prevailed with regard to how children should be raised. The 1890s and 1900s saw a highly sentimental approach to child rearing; 1910 through the 1930s witnessed a rigid disciplinary approach; the 1940s have emphasized self-regulation and understanding of the child. These sixty years have also seen a swing from emphasis on character development to emphasis on personality development (quoted in Gordon, 1978: 150).

Each age seems to instruct its parents differently and to hold different beliefs about children. Reacting, perhaps, against the sentimentality of a Dickens or a Mrs. Beaton in Britain, or the "romance" of Tom Sawyer and Huckleberry Finn in the United States, the experts advised discipline and regularity in the 1920s. A typical work from 1921 states:

> If a young mother were to ask me what I consider the keynote of successful baby training, I should say, without hesitation, regularity.
>
> This means regularity in everything, eating, sleeping, bathing, bowel habits, and exercise. Each event in a baby's daily life should take place at exactly the same hour by the clock until the habit is established.
>
> It is quite possible to train the baby to be an *efficient little machine*, and the more nearly perfect we make *the running of this machine*, the more wonderful will be the results achieved and the less trouble it will be for the mother (quote in Beekman, 1977: 109–110; emphasis added).

This mechanistic view of the child not only ignored or denied the possibility of variability, which Locke had commented on so much earlier, but also made the mother's needs paramount over the child's.

The most popular book on child-care for years was Dr. Luther Emmett Holt's *The Care and Feeding of Children*, first published in 1894 and reissued dozens of times, even after his death, until 1943. Holt's attention was directed principally to the technical or "mechanical" aspects of child care—nutrition, formulas, schedules, hours of sleep, bowel movements, and so on. Physiology and routine were all. Emotional involvement was to be minimal: "Babies under six months old should never be played with, and the less of it at any time the better." Holt also recommended: "Never give a child what it cries for; let the child cry out and break the habit" (Beekman 1977: 117, 116). The idea of breaking takes us back to Calvin and Wesley.

Holt's ideas and beliefs were challenged by a behavioral psychologist, John B. Watson, who published *Psychological Care of Infant and Child it* 1928. The shift in emphasis from physiology to psychology is evident in the first two paragraphs of his book:

> Ever since my first glimpse of Dr. Holt's *The Care and Feeding of Children*, I hoped some day to be able to write a book on the psychological care of the infant. I believed then that psychological care was just as necessary as physiological care. Today I believe that it is in some ways more important Healthy babies do grow up under the most varied forms of feeding and bodily care. They can be stunted by poor food and ill health and then in a few days of proper regimen be made to pick up their weight and bodily strength.
>
> But once a child's character has been spoiled by bad handling which can be done in a few days, who can say that the damage is ever repaired? (quoted in Beekman, 1977: 147)

But equally evident and more ominous is the idea that the child is a problem—the threat of irreparable damage to the child due to "bad handling" is absolutely clear. The age of the expert, with all of his sanctions, has arrived. Indeed, Watson makes the astounding statement: "No one today knows enough to raise a baby." The implication, "except me," is obvious. He continues:

> Give me a dozen healthy infants, well-formed, and my own specified world to bring him up in and I'll guarantee to take any one at random and train him to become any type of specialist I might select—into a doctor, lawyer, artist, merchant-chief, and yes, even into beggar-man and thief, regardless of his talents, penchants, tendencies, abilities, vocations and race of ancestors (quoted in Beekman, 1977: 146).

Such promises were very American, congruent not only with Locke's "tabula rasa" theory, but also with democratic egalitarian theory, with the Horatio

Alger myth, and the Dale Carnegie ethic, although it was not the individual working virtuously for himself who achieved, but the parent who achieved for the children. "Treat them as though they were young adults," he advised; "never hug and kiss them, never let them sit in your lap. If you must, kiss them once on the forehead when they say good night. Shake hands with them in the morning" (Beekman, 1977: 151).

Watson's emphasis on training, discipline, and the minimum of emotional involvement—childhood as apprenticeship—was challenged by various doctors who focused increasingly on the needs of the child. None was more popular than Dr. Spock's *Baby and Child Care*, first published in 1946. It was comprehensive, inexpensive, well-written, and began reassuringly: "Trust yourself. You know more than you think you do" (1958: 15). Precisely the opposite of Watson, it showed that much had changed in only 30 years.

The fact that the dominant ideas in the middle class have changed over time does not necessarily mean that practice has changed equally, still less that family practices and the roles of children conform to the advice given. John and Elizabeth Newson conducted interviews in the 1950s with over 700 mothers in Nottingham, England, dealing with their manner of raising children; they found an enormous range of attitudes, and behavior, both by class and within class, with respect to weaning, spanking, sleeping patterns, toilet training, coping with temper tantrums, breast-feeding, permissiveness, the father's role, and so on (1965).

The Newsons, however, only interviewed parents. Devereux, Bronfenbrenner, and Rodgers surveyed children themselves in an extensive international comparison. Questions about 14 aspects of parental behavior were asked of 741 English children and 968 American children in matched samples. On 10 of these items the differences were significant. While these findings should be taken as indicative rather than conclusive, they are generally supported by other studies. Curiously, Harriet Martineau, an Englishwoman who visited the United States, described some of these same differences in 1837—a hint that practices have changed very little, despite increased industrialization, Queen Victoria, Darwin, and Freud (in Larson, 1976: 241–610).

Childhood in the 1980s may differ again from the 1950s or even the 1960s; most of us would agree that the difference is not only quantitative but qualitative as well. The innocence is shot. The "romance," as the Victorians would have said, has disappeared.

The lead article in *Homemakers' Magazine*, in a special issue to commemorate the Year of the Child, asks the extraordinary questions: "Why do we continue to fail children? Who listens to what the child has to say?" (Morris, 1979: 8). Even allowing for journalistic exaggeration and alarmism, these questions seem to indicate an amazing self-doubt, lack of self-confidence, and guilt. It is not just childhood that has changed; so has parenthood.

The lead article in a recent *New York Times Magazine* describes contemporary children as "children without childhood," arguing that children are now, in many ways, little adults, far more politically and emotionally aware than we, or their parents, ever were at their age (Winn, 1981). Such articles would have been impossible 20 years ago.

A symbol of the new child, or the new loss of childhood, is perhaps Brooke Shields. A high school student who has earned more than the president of the United States, she has appeared on the cover of *Time*, was featured in nine films, played a 12-year-old prostitute when she was 12, had worked for 16 years, by the time she was 16. Brooke Shields was not, of course, a typical 16-year-old, but 20 years ago she would have been impossible. Eileen Ford, head of the world's largest modelling agency, said of Shields: "She is a professional child and unique. She looks like an adult and thinks like one" (*Time*, 9 February 1981). There have been child stars before, like Shirley Temple; the earlier star was marketing innocence, however, while Brooke Shields is selling sexuality. And Shields is not alone. Jodie Foster played a child prostitute in *Taxi Driver* and a murdering nymphet in *The Little Girl Who Lives Down the Lane*. Kristy McNichol and Tatum O'Neal race to lose their virginity in *Little Darlings*, and Tatum O'Neal tries to seduce Richard Burton in *A Circle of Two*.

Pretty babies become cover girls; prepubescent girls become sex symbols, and while parents and school boards debate sex education in schools, their children identify with their "active" peers. Child sex is no longer taboo, at least in the movies. Kiddie pornographic magazines abound; pedophiliac organizations are springing up, the slogan of one being "sex before 8, or else it's too late" (*Time*, 7 September 1981).

Childen are being "sexualized" younger; adults are being socialized to children's sexuality. Children are the last sexual frontier, and the barriers are coming down—the taboos are being broken on the screen daily. The parents consent, indeed compete; the media, the fashion magazines, the garment industry (Calvin Klein jeans), the advertising industry cooperate in this redefinition of children as adults. Kids have money.

It is too early to see the consequences; crimes *by* children and crimes *against* children appear to be increasing, although this is not entirely the result of the sexualization process. However, the mass sex killings of children in Atlanta and British Columbia are a new phenomenon. The spillover of child sex and child violence from media fantasy to reality should be expected. Children are becoming sex objects—fair game and therefore potentially victims. One should not overestimate the media-hype, nor should one underestimate it. Brooke Shields is not typical, but there is a broad pattern of factors that affect the contemporary world of childhood.

Much has changed even since the 1950s. Enid Blyton and the Hardy Boys are light years away from Judy Blume and Norma Klein; Anne of Green Gables bears no resemblance to 12-year-old *Lolita* (1956); the Mad Hatter has been transformed into the satirical *Mad Magazine*. Television has exposed children of all ages not only to children's programs but also, and perhaps principally, to the adult world of soap operas, documentaries on famine, war, energy crises, and scandals, and adult fantasy worlds of explicit sex and violence, for hours at a time. In this sense, therefore, children are being socialized into an adult world prematurely.

Children's values and the structure of childhood have changed and so, naturally enough, have ideas about children. More couples want no children, and many want fewer children than they did in the past. The birthrate has fallen dramatically in the last 100 years and roughly halved since the baby boom of the 1950s in North America, to below replacement level. The abortion rate has increased steadily, doubling in the United States from 1973–1979 (*Time*, 6 April 1981).

Children are now being seen, perhaps for the first time in history, as unnecessary, both economically and psychologically. They are regarded as expensive luxuries or as hindrances to personal growth and career development, especially for women. (Shades of Bacon!) Indeed, Pogrebin refers to "the *flight* from motherhood" (1981: 143; emphasis in original). Even those who do have children are, like children themselves, under fire. Bronfenbrenner describes the major change in the family crisply: "Children used to be brought up by their parents" (1972: 95). Now schools, television, peer-groups, baby-sitters, and day-care centers more often do the job. Christopher Lasch argues that children are no longer the center of the family: With the "me" generation, parents no longer sacrifice themselves for their children, but sacrifice children for themselves (1979). Margaret Mead states firmly that "we have become a society who neglect our children, are afraid of our children, find children surplus instead of the raison d'être of living" (Gross and Gross, 1977: 154).

The pathology of childhood perhaps confirms these definitions of children as, increasingly, a social problem. Child homicide and suicide rates, alcholism, crime rates, and abortion rates are all rising. Child abuse is prevalent. A grim picture of childhood as violent, unhappy, and self-destructive is emerging— perhaps not accurate for all, but accurate for many and, more to the point, becoming increasingly prevalent.

In sum, ideas about the children and childhood are quite confused today. Children's liberationists claim that children have no rights, and some say that they never had it so bad (Gross and Gross, 1977). Others say children have never had it so good, with too many rights and not enough duties and responsibilities (the Tough Love Movement). Some describe children as bereft of childhood (Winn, 1981); others observe that children lack parents (Bronfen-brenner, 1972; Lasch, 1979). Some identify children as a social problem; others identify parents as the problem, one that is causal in nature. Still others identify other factors. However, despite the contradictions, there is very clearly a new trend emerging: The belief that children are not necessary, either psychologi-cally or socially, and that they are an increasing social problem. It is not a happy perspective.

Historically there has been little consensus. Both ideologically and struc-turally, many worlds of childhood have been constructed and many theories developed. Locke's theory of children as a *tabula rasa* contrasts strikingly with the beliefs of such contemporary fundamentalists as Calvin and, later, Wesley, who viewed the child as a little devil. The interests of high capitalists in children as little workers evoked the Romantics' description of children as little angels. Each construction of the nature of children (and, implicitly, humanity) may imply radically different theories of education, social control, politics, and so on.

Darwin's theory of evolution and Freud's theories of psycho–sexual devel-opment not only contradicted the Romantic view but added new and startling dimensions of thought—children as little animals and children as rampant ids. But not everyone changed their ideas. Durkheim entertained a sponge-theory of childhood, not far removed from Locke's *tabula rasa*:

> The child is naturally in a state of passivity quite comparable to that in which the hypnotic subject is found artificially placed. His mind yet contains only a small number of conceptions able to fight against those which are suggested to him; his will is still rudimentary. Therefore he is very suggestible (1965: 87).

On the other hand, Maria Montessori states that "children are human beings to whom respect is due, *superior* to us by reason of their innocence and of the greater possibilities of the future" (1965: 133; emphasis added). And she even compares the child to the child Jesus (1975: 67 ff.).

Not everyone agreed with Montessori: Dr Edward Glover, the distinguished British psychoanalyst, stated in 1922 that the normal baby is "a born crimi-nal" (Montagu, 1981: 118).

> Expressing these technical discoveries in social terms we can say that the perfectly normal infant is almost completely egocentric, greedy, dirty, violent in temper, destructive in habit, profoundly sexual in purpose, aggrandizing in attitude, devoid of all but the most primitive reality sense, without conscience or moral feeling, whose attitude to society (as represented by the family) is opportunist, inconsiderate, domineering and sadistic. And when we come to consider the criminal type labeled psychopathic it will be apparent that many of these characteristics can under certain circumstances persist into adult life. In fact, judged by adult standards the normal baby is for all practical purposes a born criminal.

This view is perhaps a logical development from Freud's ideas and is not far removed from the Puritan and Calvinist views of the child as a born sinner, although Glover's context is secular. But it is exactly the opposite of the Victorian view of the child as innocent and Montessori's view of the child as superior. Glover's views coexisted with those of other experts in the 1920s who compared the child to a little machine, insisting that "bad habits" be broken (a phrase reminiscent of the fundamentalists 250 years before who insisted that the child's "spirit" should be broken). Watson even said that children should be regarded as little adults (Beekman, 1977: 151). Contradictions abound. Of course, children could also be regarded as sponges, clean slates, little angels, little devils, little monkeys, unrestrained ids, or like the child Jesus. Romance, however, is not yet dead. Recall the Lord Mayor of London's remark when he heard that Lady Diana was pregnant: "Babies are bits of stardust blown from the hands of God" (*Gazette*, 6 November 1981). Calvin, Wesley, Darwin, and Freud would have shuddered.

Surely these constructions of childhood tell us more about the constructors than they do about childhood. Childhood is not a given; it is not a "natural" category. There are no natural categories, only social categories with different meanings imposed and developed by every age, and by different populations within every age. Educators, doctors, sociologists, religious leaders, parents, and philosophers have all put forward their ideas; no doubt it is trite to remark that none are likely to possess the truth, the whole truth, and nothing but the truth about childhood or, more broadly, humanity. Nonetheless, it is perhaps instructive to consider the scope and range of the views, the implications of these views for praxis, and some explanations for the variations. The emphasis on the range of historical perspectives should not blind us, however, to the range of our own personal and changing ideas, as John Wilmot, Earl of Rochester (1647–1680) so aptly commented: "Before I got married, I had six theories about bringing up children; now I have six children and no theories" (Muir and Brett, 1980: 99).

Acknowledgments

I would like to thank Michael Sullivan and Joseph Smucker for their critical comments. This chapter is a comment on "Paradigms of Childhood and Children's Sexuality," by John A. Lee, *Canad. Rev. Soc. Anthropol.* 19(4): 591–608.

References

Anderson, M. "Family, Household and the Industrial Revolution." In Michael Anderson, ed., *Sociology of the Family* (Harmondsworth: Penguin, 1975).

Ariès, Philippe. *Centuries of Childhood* (New York: Vintage Books, 1962).

Bacon, Francis. *Essays* (London: Frederick Warne, Chandos Classics, n.d.).

Beekman, Daniel. *The Mechanical Baby* (New American Library, 1977).

Bronfenbrenner, Urie. *Two Worlds of Childhood: U.S. and U.S.S.R.* (New York: Simon and Schuster, 1972).

Darwin, Charles. *The Expression of the Emotions in Man and Animals* (New York: Philosophical Library, 1955).

deMause, Lloyd (ed.). *The History of Childhood* (New York: Harper and Row, 1975).

Demos, John. "Infancy and Childhood in Plymouth Colony." In Michael Gordon, ed., *The American Family: Past, Present and Future* (New York: Random House, 1978).

Devereux, Edward C., Bronfenbrenner, Urie, and Rodgers, Robert R. "Child-Rearing in England and the United States: A Cross-National Comparison." In L. Larson, ed., *The Canadian Family in Comparative Perspective* (Scarborough: Prentice-Hall, 1976), pp. 240–260.

Durkheim, Emile. *Education and Sociology* (Glencoe, IL: Free Press, 1956).

Freud, Sigmund. *New Introductory Lectures on Psychoanalysis* (vol. 2) (Harmondsworth: Pelican Freud Library, 1977).

Gazette (London, 6 November 1981).

Gordon, Michael. *The American Family: Past, Present and Future* (New York: Random House, 1978).

Greenfield, Sidney M. "Industrialization and the Family in Sociological Theory." In David A. Schulz and Robert A. Wilson, eds., *Readings on the Changing Family* (Englewood Cliffs, N.J.: Prentice-Hall, 1973).

Gross, Beatrice and Gross, Ronald, eds. *The Children's Rights Movement* (New York: Doubleday, Anchor Books, 1977).

Hareven, Tamara K., ed. *Transitions: The Family and The Life Course in Historical Perspective* (New York: Academic Press, 1978).

Hobbes, Thomas. *Leviathan.* (New York: Macmillan, 1947. Originally published in 1651).

Hunt, David. *Parents and Children in History: The Psychology of Family Life in Early Modern France* (New York: Basic Books, 1970).

Illick, Joseph E. "Child-Rearing in Seventeenth-Century England and America." In Lloyd de Mause, ed., *The History of Childhood* (New York: Harper and Row, 1974).

Kaestle, Carl F. and Vinovskis, Maris A. "From Fireside to Factory: School Entry and School Leaving in Nineteenth Century Massachusetts." In Tamara K. Harevah, ed., *Transitions* (New York: Academic Press, 1978).

Ladurie, Emmanuel Le Roy. *Montaillou* (Harmondsworth: Penguin Books, 1980).

Larson, Lyle E., ed. *The Canadian Family in Comparative Perspective* (Scarborough, Ontario: Prentice-Hall, 1976).

Lasch, Christopher. *The Culture of Narcissism* (New York: Norton, 1979).

Laslett, Peter. *The World We Have Lost* (London: Methuen, 1965).

Laslett, Peter. *Household and Family in Past Time* (Cambridge: Cambridge University Press, 1972).

Locke, John. *Essay on Human Understanding.* (New York: Oxford University Press, 1979. Originally published in 1690).

Locke, John. *Some Thoughts Upon Education.* (Cambridge, England: Cambridge University Press, 1927. Originally published in 1693).

Lumpkin, Katherine Dupré, and Douglas, Dorothy Wolf. *Child Workers in America* (New York: International Publishers, 1937).

Marx, Karl and Frederick Engels. *The Communist Manifesto* (New York: Penguin, 1985. Originally published in 1848).

Mayhew, Henry. *London Labour and the London Poor* (first published 1861–1862) (New York: Dover Publications, 1968).

Montagu, Ashley. *Growing Young* (New York: McGraw-Hill, 1981).

Montaigne, Michel de. *Essays* (Harmondsworth: Penguin Books, 1979).

Montessori, Maria. *Dr. Montessori's Own Handbook* (first published 1914) (New York: Schocken Books, 1965).

Montessori, Maria. *Childhood Education* (New York: New American Library, Meridian Books, 1975).

Morris, Eileen. "A Child's Bill of Rights." In *Homemakers Magazine* (April 1979).

Muir, Frank and Brett, Simon. *On Children* (London: Heinemann, 1980).

Newson, John and Elizabeth. *Patterns of Infant Care in an Urban Community* (Harmondsworth: Penguin Books, 1965).

New York Times (New York, 25 January 1981).

Pogrebin, Letty Cottin. *Growing Up Free: Raising Your Children in the Eighties* (New York: Bantam Books, 1981).

Report from the Select Committee on Protection of Infant Life. British Sessional Papers, vol. VII: 607 (1871).

Robertson, Priscilla. "Home as a Nest: Middle Class Childhood in Nineteenth Century Europe." In Lloyd de Mause, ed., *The History of Childhood* (New York: Harper and Row, 1975).

Rousseau, Jean-Jacques. *Emile* (London: Dent, 1969).

Smelser, Neil. "Towards a Theory of Modernization." In Amitai and Eva Etzioni, eds., *Social Change* (New York: Basic Books, 1964).

Spock, Dr. Benjamin. *Baby and Child Care* (London: The Bodley Head, 1958).

Stone, Lawrence. *The Family, Sex and Marriage in England, 1500–1800* (Harmondsworth: Penguin, 1968).

Stone, Lawrence. "The Massacre of the Innocents." In *New York Review of Books* (14 November 1974).

Thompson, E.P. *The Making of the English Working Class* (Harmondsworth: Penguin, 1968).

Time (9 February; 7 September; 6 April 1981).

Tucker, M.J. "The Child as Beginning and End: Fifteenth and Sixteenth Century English Childhood." In Lloyd de Mause, ed., *The History of Childhood* (New York: Harper and Row, 1975).

Winn, Marie. "What Became of Childhood Innocence?" In *New York Times Magazine* (New York, 29 January 1981).

PART III

Families as Socializing Agents

Most children begin life in some kind of family. Whether the family is two-parent, single-parent, three-generational, or some other configuration, the earliest primary caretaker of a child is more likely than not to be its mother. Socialization begins at birth through caretaking. Caretaking involves interaction between mother and child (as well as, increasingly, father and child.) The first selection in Part III, by developmental psychologist H. Rudolph Schaffer, shows the central importance of social interaction in the earliest days and years of life.

After briefly presenting three influential psychological theories that do not recognize the importance of the mutuality of interaction, Schaffer rejects them and develops an explanation of how early socialization involves parental control techniques that are not implemented in an imposed manner but rather involve mutual influence, if parents are at all sensitive to their child's varying moods and states of being. As he says, "With very young infants, interactions are largely brought about by virtue of the adult's willingness to accept any action on the part of the infant as though it were a message that required some sort of reply." Also, he points out the value of a parent's talking to an infant not yet able to talk, and he discusses the ways in which parents try to influence children in the earliest months of life. In these various ways, infants begin to become participants in a meaningful social world.

A family's role in socialization is basic and broad. It introduces the infant to social relationships, and it fosters initial social skills. It introduces the child to language. It provides a child with its first notions of gender, what it means to be a boy or girl. Until thirty or forty years ago, there was wide agreement in

American society about ways in which boys and girls should be differently socialized. That changed with the rise of the women's movement. Women who identified themselves as feminists, often joined by male partners who agreed with them, regarded traditional gender norms as both antiquated and stultifying to girls and women. Parents with these views make efforts to socialize their children to believe in gender equality and in greater gender similarity than traditionally believed. The study by Barbara Risman and Kristen Myers is one of the few to date that seeks to understand how parents go about this and what the socialization outcomes are for the children. They briefly look at some theories of how children learn to be boys and girls, and they then present the procedures and results of their own study. It was not an easy study to do, and the results were somewhat surprising.

While some aspects of socialization are true of all families that raise a child from birth—for example, shaping initial social relationships, introducing language, initiating gender identity—other aspects are particular to families in particular situations. We illustrate this point by selecting from Shirley A. Hill's study of African American children her chapter on Racial Socialization. African American parents have the task of attempting to prepare their children for the realities of being Black in America. She examines the racial attitudes of parents that underlie their efforts. She concludes that all Black parents have the task of racial socialization of their children, whether they realize it or not.

In addition to these selections in Part III, other writings in this volume that include discussion of families as socialization agents are Chapters 13 and 14 in Part VII, Chapter 15 in Part VIII, and Chapters 17 and 18 in Part IX.

4

The Mutuality of Parental Control in Early Childhood*

H. Rudolph Schaffer

Introduction: Socialization and Social Influence

In what way do children change as a result of their encounters with other people and how is such change brought about? These questions pose a basic problem for developmental psychology; they form the core of the socialization issue.

There are three kinds of phenomena to which any complete account of socialization must address itself:

1. The end products of socialization (conscience, impulse control, sex role formation, etc.)
2. The intra-psychic mechanisms underlying these products (identification, role learning, internalisation, etc.)
3. The interactive experiences in the course of which children first encounter the expectations that other people have of them, as well as the means used to induce them to meet such expectations

The last mentioned of the three represents, of course, the first step in the sequence that eventually results in a fully socialized individual. It refers to the

*From Michael Lewis and Saul Feinman (eds.) *Social Influences and Socialization in Infancy* (Plenum Press 1991). Reprinted by permission of Kluwer Academic/Plenum Publishers and the author.

H. Rudolph Schaffer Department of Psychology, University of Strathclyde, Glasgow, Scotland G1-IRD, United Kingdom.

children's initial encounter with the aims and intentions that their social partners have with respect to the course of their behavior and it is here that a social influence orientation is applicable. Yet, curiously, this step has usually been omitted from direct empirical investigation. By and large socialization research has been preoccupied with long-term changes and with end-products and has paid little attention to the beginnings of the sequence. Socialization studies, that is, have not been firmly tied to a social interaction context.

Models of Socialization

The reason for this failure is to be found in the various theoretical models of the socialization process which have prevailed in the recent past and dominated our thinking. Each of these made certain assumptions about the role of children's original encounters with other people and the way these shaped their further development of socially acceptable modes of behavior. Although these assumptions differed radically from one model to the next no attempt was made to check them by means of empirical investigation. Indeed, each arbitrarily asserted that the child's crucial formative experiences were of a particular kind and then at once proceeded to the study of end-products and their underlying psychic processes. Three such models have been particularly influential (see Schaffer, 1984, for a more extensive discussion):

1. *Laissez-faire model.* According to this view, the precise nature of social encounters with caretakers plays little part in shaping the child's development. Basing their ideas on a belief in preformationism, proponents of this model (who included Rousseau and Gesell) asserted that adults ought to avoid all interference with the wholly natural and spontaneous process of development; if they played a more vigorous part they were likely to disturb the orderly unfolding of inherent capacities and prevent the processes of self-regulation and maturation from taking place. The task of parents is thus to provide a maximally permissive atmosphere in which children are allowed to grow as their nature dictates; any more active role in socialization is denied to caretakers.

2. *Clay molding model.* Rather than seeing children as preformed, this model views them as formless and passive. It is as though the child arrives in the world as an amorphous lump of clay which is then molded into any shape that caretakers arbitrarily decide upon. The end product is thus wholly explicable in terms of the adults' behavior: It is their schedules of rewards and punishment, their ways of habit training and the examples they set that wholly account for the course of the child's development. This view found

its most extreme expression in the writings of J. B. Watson (1928), with his faith in the wholly deterministic role of experience; it influenced much subsequent work that examined child-rearing practices from a behavioristic approach (Bijou & Baer, 1962). Socialization, according to Bijou (1970), is simply the product of the individual's reinforcement history. It follows that the child is regarded merely as a passive recipient of other people's stimulation and that the key influences which will account for the end result of socialization are to be found in the nature of that stimulation and the manner whereby it is applied.

3. *The conflict model.* This is probably the most prevalent view, powerfully backed as it was by Freud. Children, it is agreed, are not passive. From the beginning they are equipped with desires and response tendencies that impel them to behave in certain ways. These ways, however, are antithetical to the requirements of society; inevitably they will bring the child into conflict with caretakers, whose task it is to compel him or her to give up egoistic preferences and adopt the unnatural modes of behavior that they insist upon. Development is thus a painful process, for it requires the resolution of the basic antagonism between the child and the social group. The key experiences are thus conflict situations. Parent and child are seen as having different aims but, by virtue of being the more powerful partner, the parent is generally able to resolve the conflict by imposing her will on an antagonistic and resentful child. Hoffman's (1977) description of the way in which parents bring about the child's conformity to the moral requirements of society is one recent and influential expression of this view; in his account of the "discipline encounter" as the prototypical socialization situation the conflict element in the relationship between an egoistic child and a powerful parent is given prominence and is seen as providing the motive power for the child's eventual conformity.

Each of these three models makes assertions about the nature of early social interactions, but in each case these are based more on a priori considerations (derived respectively from the global theories of preformationism, learning theory and psychoanalysis) than from empirical study of those interactions. However, in the last 20 years a considerable amount of research has begun to shed light on the nature of early social development, and two general conclusions that are particularly relevant here have emerged:

1. Even in the earliest social encounters the child is by no means a passive recipient of adult stimulation; both parent *and* child play an active part in determining the nature and course of their interactions. The influence process is a bi-directional and not a unilateral one.

2. Mutual adaptation, not conflict, is the basic theme that runs through the course of parent-child interaction. The child arrives in the world preadapted for social encounters; from infancy on, both partners jointly construct their interactions. Conflicts occur, of course, but there is no indication that they constitute the key socialization episodes in a child's life. Rather than seeing the parent-child relationship as a never-ending battle investigators have come to be impressed by the "fit" of the two individuals' sets of behavior patterns. Far from starting off as an antisocial being who must be coerced into sociability, children share a common heritage with their caretakers that impels them to adopt the same social goals.

A model of socialization based on *mutuality* is thus indicated. Such mutuality is not an end-result to which children are driven by coercive pressures. Rather, it is a prerequisite without which the adult could not produce any effects in the first place. How this works out in practice has begun to be clarified in recent years.

Parental Control Techniques

Socialization does not begin with attempts to convey abstract values—of right and wrong, of the importance of honesty and respect for others, and of all those other qualities that one may regard as the hallmark of the "properly" socialized individual. It begins instead with adults' efforts to induce children to comply with requests referring to the ordinary, practical, very concrete minutiae of everyday living: to put a toy back into a box, do up a button, give the baby a kiss, refrain from shouting or from touching a valuable vase—in short, with any of those constantly occurring situations where a caretaker considers it necessary for one reason or another, to change the ongoing course of the child's behavior. We refer to these efforts as *control techniques*, using the term to describe all those behaviors employed by one person to channel another's activity in certain directions, inhibiting some tendencies but enhancing others. The emphasis is primarily on immediate and not long-term consequences, and though the controls used may be based on certain abstract values, the focus is on their overt content and not the underlying moral principles that they express. The interest for the investigator thus lies in the way in which a caretaker sets about the task of conveying an aim in her mind in such a way that the child comes to comply with it.

Control techniques take many forms. They are by no means confined to parade-ground commands but may be applied in indirect and subtle ways. They are also not to be considered in purely negative terms—as prohibitions, refusals, punishment, and discipline. There has been a tendency in the child-rearing literature to single out such didactic and negative techniques as though they were the only or at any rate the most effective means of dealing with young children, thus neglecting the many subtle and positive means parents have at their disposal for obtaining compliance from a child. Indeed, the first task confronting the investigator is to describe the range of control techniques parents and others use in their interactions with children of different ages and in various settings. Further tasks include relating the use of particular techniques to the child's condition and individuality, determining the circumstances under which controls are effective in obtaining the child's compliance, and investigating how, in the course of development, other-control gradually gives way to self-control.

One overriding conclusion that emerges from the relevant studies conducted so far (detailed in Schaffer, 1984) refers to the essentially interactive nature of control techniques. Controls, that is, are not to be understood as the arbitrary imposition of the will of one person upon another. By no means do they invariably take a bolt-out-of-the-blue form that descends on an unsuspecting and unprepared child. On the contrary, controls are to be understood in the same dialogic terms that are used for unstructured interactions in which neither partner is attempting to achieve any specified goal. Mutual influence, i.e., the effects of *both* partners upon each other, is just as evident in the one situation as it is in the other, even though one partner is more powerful and even though it may be the intention of that individual to induce the other one to conform to his wishes. This is seen particularly in the way in which the parent's control strategy is adapted to the characteristics of the child; the child's nature, that is, helps to determine the parent's behavior. We can illustrate this by referring to three kinds of child characteristics, namely the momentary state, the developmental level, and the individuality of the child.

Child's Momentary State

The now quite voluminous literature on adult-child interaction—whether concerned with face-to-face encounters or with object-centered interchanges, whether referring to infants in the very early months of life or to children in later years, and whether the adult involved is the mother or a less familiar individual—all points to one overriding conclusion, namely that the interactive quality of such encounters is largely derived from the sensitivity with which the adult integrates her behavior with the child's (Schaffer, 1977, 1984). Sensitivity takes many forms and subsumes a variety of phenomena (Ainsworth, Bell, & Stayton, 1971; Lamb & Easterbrooks, 1981; Schaffer & Collis, 1986)—it refers in particular to the *awareness* by the adult of the child's cues and communications, to the *appropriateness* of the nature of the adult's response to the child's behavior, and to the fineness of the *timing* of that response. With very young infants, interactions are largely brought about by virtue of the adult's willingness to accept any action on the part of the infant as though it were a message that required some sort of reply. A dialogue is thus set up—or to be more precise, a pseudo-dialogue, in so far as the interaction tends to be of an asymmetrical character, with one partner assuming major responsibility for converting the encounter into an interaction. Only with growing age will children gradually participate on a more equal basis; only with increasing cognitive capacity will they become capable of intentionally provoking the other person's behavior and of understanding the reciprocity that underlies all social exchanges (Schaffer, 1979).

These conclusions are largely derived from microanalytic studies of early social interaction. Much of the to-and-fro of any exchange between two individuals tends to take place at a split-second level: speaker-switch pauses, for instance, in adult conversations have been found to be around 0.6 sec. in duration (Jaffe & Feldstein, 1970); in the vocal interchanges of mothers and one-year-olds they are also frequently less than one second. Similarly, the integration of other interactional cues: of looking with vocalising (Schaffer, Collis, Parsons, 1977), of looking and vocalising with gestures (Murphy & Messer, 1977), of verbal labelling with manipulation (Messer, 1978) and with looking (Collis, 1977), and so forth. Both interpersonal and intrapersonal synchrony of responses tend to be so fine that videotaping or filming are required to record them, so that subsequent frame-by-frame or slow motion analysis may highlight the speed and precision of that synchrony.

This picture originally emerged from studies that placed adult and child in one particular context, namely in situations that were entirely unstructured and unconstrained, such as face-to-face situations in which the parent is merely told to amuse the child, or free play situations in which the two partners can do as they wish with whatever toys are available. Perhaps it is not surprising that under such circumstances mothers tend to carefully monitor the child's actions and sensitively attune their behavior accordingly, for they are under no pressure from external goals and can therefore let children take the initiative and merely follow their lead and adapt to their particular requirements. What is striking is that in more constrained situations, that is, in those where the adult does have some specific aim in mind that she must convey to the child and where she therefore sets out to direct the child's behavior in a particular direction, such adaptation also occurs. The interaction, that is, does not assume a unidirectional form in which the adult arbitrarily imposes her will on the child's. Instances of that no doubt do occur, but under most conditions adults go about the task of influencing their children in the same dyadic manner as described for unstructured situations, that is, by carefully monitoring the child's behavior in order to then intercalate their own appropriate responses at the appropriate moment of time.

This is illustrated in Schaffer and Crook's (1979, 1980) study of maternal control techniques applied to children in their second year. The sessions were conducted in a laboratory playroom and videotaped from behind a one-way mirror. To ensure that mothers took an active role in the interaction, they were instructed to make quite certain that the child played with all the toys available, not let him or her spend time with just one or two toys, and actively intervene in order to direct the child's play accordingly. As the results show, the mothers did indeed assume such a directive role: Approximately 45% of all their verbal utterances were found to have a control function, occurring at the average rate of one every 9 seconds. Yet the children were by no means overwhelmed by this seeming barrage, and a major reason for this is the way in which the mothers carefully timed their interventions. Controls, that is, rarely descended in bolt-out-of-the-blue fashion on the child but were emitted in such a manner as to ensure that the child's attention was appropriately focussed on a toy before some action on that toy was requested. Mothers tended to employ sequential strategies, whereby attention-directing devices (verbal and nonverbal) were used as a preliminary to action directives. The distinction between attention controls and action controls is thus a most useful one in any attempt to understand how mothers set about getting the child to perform some task. In many cases, however, the mother preferred to leave the first stage to the child's initiative, that is, she waited until the child's attention was spontaneously focused on a particular toy before issuing her action directive. In either case the mother did not leap in with such a directive without first establishing a mutual focus of attention. As shown by an analysis of the child's involvement state with the relevant object at the moment of time that the mother began to utter her action directive, in the great majority of cases the child was already visually attending to that object or even in physical contact with it. The success of this strategy is shown by the close association between the children's compliance rate and their involvement state: The probability of obtaining the required response was far greater when the child was already appropriately oriented to the toy. Again, the facilitative role of the mother's timing of her controls in relation to the child's ongoing behavior is highlighted.

A mother does not impinge on an inert child; the outcome of any attempt to influence behavior will depend (among other things) on his or her state and condition at that particular moment. By successfully manipulating this state the parent can avoid the clash of wills that the conflict model of socialization appears to regard as inevitable in any influence encounter (Stayton, Hogan, & Ainsworth, 1971), on the supposition that compliance is extracted from an invariably reluctant child. Parental regulation of child behavior can be accomplished relatively smoothly and without conflict under many conditions; a sensitive monitoring of the child's ongoing activity appears to be one of the more important pre-requisites for doing so. Such monitoring means that the parent does not merely react to undesirable behavior after the event but can also anticipate such actions and use suitable diversionary tactics. As Holden (1983) found during observa-tions carried out in supermarkets, mothers resorted to a great many such pro-active controls by, for instance, engaging their children in conversation, provid-ing them with some item of food, or diverting their attention with a toy or other object. The mothers who frequently employed this type of behavior had chil-dren who exhibited fewer undesirable actions. Proactive controls are not issued randomly; they reflect the mother's judgement that at a given moment of time it is necessary to employ such a tactic in order to attain a particular outcome with respect to the child's behavior. Again, the parent's action is seen to be influenced by the child's state.

Child's Developmental Level

That controls are adjusted to children's developmental level is hardly sur-prising. After all, as children get older their comprehensive abilities change, and as a result they become more competent in understanding a wide range of communicative messages. Thus, *how* an adult conveys directive requests can be expected to show progressive modification in the course of development, in the same way as adults' speech to children generally tends to undergo changes in the light of feedback information about the addressee's ability to compre-hend that speech (the "motherese" phenomenon). There is also one further change, namely *what* adults convey to children. With increasing cognitive and motoric competence children will be expected to comply with increasingly more complex and demanding requests, and the content of controls will there-fore change accordingly.

While conclusions are constrained by the rather limited age range covered by the various relevant studies, it does seem that the incidence of controls issued by parents to preschool children decreases over age (McLaughlin, 1983; Schaffer & Crook, 1979). However, though it may seem obvious at first sight that younger children require more guidance, there are several indications which suggest the need for caution in making such a generalisation. For one thing, Schaffer, Hepburn, and Collis (1983), in a study based on a number of set tasks which mothers had to convey to their children, found the mothers of 10-month-old infants giving out fewer verbal controls than the mothers of 18-month-old infants—presumably because the former did not yet have such serious expec-tations of success as the latter and also because they did not regard the verbal medium as particularly effective at this early age. For another, it appears that the nature of the task to be performed affects the adults' behavior. Power and Parke (1983) found that the incidence of socializing attempts changed between 11 and 17 months and especially so in the 14 to 17 months range; however, those aimed at self-care skills, household responsibilities, and participation in games increased whereas those concerned with independence and regulating attention decreased in incidence. Also relevant is a finding by Bridges (1979) who investigated mothers' behavior in an object retrieval game. When the object was familiar, 2-year-olds were provided with more directive clues than 2½-year-olds; when the object was unfamiliar there was no difference in the number of clues. Adjustment to the child's comprehension level presumably accounts for this pattern. And one further finding that affects conclusions about incidence refers to the distribution of attention controls and action controls over age: Schaffer and Crook (1979) noted that at 15 months attention-direction consumed more of the mothers' efforts; at 24 months, however, attention-direction had decreased and mothers then concentrated primarily on influencing the children's actions. Schaffer et al. (1983), though finding no significant change in the incidence of attention controls between 10 and 18 months, did find a doubling of action controls over this age range. Bearing in mind the sequential nature of attention-action strategies employed by parents, it appears that mothers of younger children felt it necessary to concentrate on the first stage of this sequence. At older ages, this aspect was more easily accomplished and the mothers were therefore able to focus their efforts on the children's actions.

Of particular interest are changes in the distribution of verbal and nonverbal communicative modes used by adults to convey directives to children of various ages, for the relationship between these two modes has implications for the understanding of early language development (Macnamara, 1972; Schaffer et al., 1983; Schnur & Shatz, 1984). Given children's initial linguistic incompetence, one might expect that adults would communicate to preverbal infants primarily by nonverbal means; as children become more able to comprehend language verbal messages would then gradually increase and replace these nonverbal behaviors. The evidence (at least for the first 2 or 3 years) indicates a somewhat more complex picture. In the first place, linguistically conveyed controls are by no means absent in the preverbal period: As Rheingold and Adams (1980) showed, even neonates have spoken commands addressed to them. Similarly, Hepburn and Schaffer (1983) found mothers of 5-month-old infants using verbal controls during a bathing situation—generally in association with relevant nonverbal signals but sometimes without such support. Thus from the beginning adults appear to use language to influence their children's behavior; as we shall see below, however, it is necessary to examine the whole dyadic situation prevailing at the time to appreciate the spirit in which these remarks are made.

An additional consideration refers to the subsequent course of the relationship between verbal and nonverbal modes. According to Schaffer *et al.* (1983), no crossover effect could be observed between 10 and 18 months, whereby verbal controls gradually begin to take over from nonverbal controls. It is true that there was an increase in verbally conveyed requests, though this was largely due to the rise in action controls, and especially those that specified the precise action to be performed on the toy (e.g., "push," "draw") rather than containing such general action verbs as "do" or "try"—once again a reflection of the child's growing competence to which the mothers adapted their demands. However, nonverbal controls remained at the same level for both ages; for that matter, the major groupings of nonverbal categories employed (object handling, gestures, and demonstration) showed no change during this period. It is only when one examines the two modes over a wider age range that the expected trend becomes evident: McLaughlin (1983) found fewer nonverbal concomitants to verbal controls at 2½ and 3½ than at 1½ years of age; Schaffer and Crook (1979) noted a decrease in nonverbal controls from 15 to 24 months, particularly in two categories labelled "manipulating accessibility" and "eliciting or prohibiting action," and interpreted this as a response by the mothers to the children's growing motoric competence; and Bridges (1979) observed that mothers used more gestures to their 2-year-old than to their 2½-year-old children even when the object referred to was familiar. By 2½ years gestures occurred only when the child could not be expected to know the name of the object. As has been documented repeatedly, younger children need to have verbal utterances embedded in a nonverbal context to be meaningful. The nature of adult input when conveying requests shows that parents are aware of this requirement and also that, in line with the child's growing verbal sophistication, they are prepared gradually to loosen this association.

Another respect in which one might expect to find changes occur over age is in the explicitness of adults' verbal requests. A number of writers (e.g., Bellinger, 1979; Schneiderman, 1983) have reported such changes, pointing to a general tendency for explicitness to be greater when in speech to children with relatively poor linguistic comprehension. The most common criterion employed to measure explicitness is a syntactic one, which contrasts the use of imperatives with rather less direct request forms such as embedded directives (in interrogative form) or hints and suggestions (in declarative form). However, explicitness can be assessed by various standards which may show different developmental trends. Thus Schaffer *et al.* (1983) found the syntactic criterion not to show any change in the 10 to 18 months age range. On the other hand, when the mothers' speech was examined for the extent to which both the name of the toy on which they wanted the child to act and the action he or she was to perform on the toy were explicitly named, it was found that an *increase* in explicitness occurred, reflecting largely the above mentioned rise in the use of specific action verbs. And just to complicate the picture further, yet another index showed a *decrease* in explicitness over age: At the younger age the mothers' object references were almost entirely to the toys immediately confronting the child (e.g., "put the *brick* on" or "scribble with the *pencil*"); at the older age, on the other hand, the mothers also introduced the consequences of the child's action by referring to their products (e.g., "build a *tower*" or "draw a *picture*"). The older child is thus taken out of the immediate here-and-now situation and a less concrete and therefore less explicit set of references is introduced. Thus, three different criteria appear to indicate three different trends; the danger, however, lies in thinking of explicitness as a unitary entity when in fact the three indices tap different aspects, each related to age in its own specific way.

Child's Individuality

At any given age children differ in a variety of characteristics that have implications for the type of treatment they receive from others. One such characteristic is the child's sex (Maccoby & Jacklin, 1974); however, as far as recent studies of early control techniques are concerned, the literature on sex differences is ambiguous. Minton, Kagan, and Levine (1971) found 2-year-old boys to be more often reprimanded by their mothers than was the case for girls; the fact that boys had higher rates of violation of parental standards and were more likely to disobey adult injunctions could well be held responsible for this difference. On the other hand, neither Schaffer and Crook (1979, 1980) nor McLaughlin (1983) found any differences in either the incidence or the type of control used for boys and girls, nor were there any differences in the rates of compliance by these children according to sex. However, Power and Parke (1983) found some sex-linked differences in *what* adults attempted to influence, e.g., parents of girls were more likely to engage in attempts to encourage prosocial behavior and to discourage aggression than were parents of boys. Such differences are, of course, notoriously lacking in robustness; they reflect cultural stereotypes that, especially nowadays, are in course of rapid change and, where they are found, may well be a function of temperamental characteristics that have only a tenuous association with sex and would be better investigated in their own right.

One such temperamental factor is activity level. In so far as some children are from the very beginning more active than others and in so far as such children can pose greater problems of restraint and attention focussing for their caretakers than less active children, it seems likely that parental control techniques will differ accordingly if they are to have the desired effect. More work is badly needed on the relationship between such temperamental characteristics and socializing practices within the "normal" range; an examination of the pathological extreme is, however, often particularly instructive. Thus, Cunningham and Barkley (1979) compared the interactions of normal and hyperactive boys with their mothers, and found that in both free play and task situations the mothers of the hyperactive children issued twice as many controls (in the form of commands and command-questions) as the normal children's mothers. Hyperactive children on the whole were less compliant, and this together with their transient and disruptive behavior might well have accounted for their treatment. Cause-and-effect statements are obviously difficult to make on the basis of such findings, but the authors' observation that the control exerted by the mothers of the hyperactive children usually followed the child's disruptive behavior is suggestive. Simply keeping a distractible child on task requires special measures, and the fact that these mothers tended to impose more structure on the child's play and social interactions seems plausibly to be in response to the child's particular characteristics. Such characteristics are, however, often difficult to specify. Thus Cunningham, Reuter, Blackwell, and Deck (1981), in a report on retarded children's interactions with their mothers, found compliance rate to be no different compared with normal children. The controls to which the former were subjected by their mothers were, however, significantly greater than was found for the latter, and here, too, the difference held for both free play and task situations. In so far as the mothers of the retarded children responded less positively to instances of compliance and cooperation it is possible that their control behavior expressed their generally more negative affective evaluation of the child. This does not rule out the possibility, on the other hand, that it was the less responsive and more solitary nature of these children that elicited such parental behavior.

Another pathological group on whom some information about control problems is available are deaf children. The very fact that adults cannot resort to the usual communicative channel when conveying messages to their children may well place an extra strain on both partners in the interaction. An unresponsive child is likely to elicit attempts to provide additional stimulation—hence presumably the report by several authors that the mothers of deaf children are by and large more intrusive, controlling, and didactic (Goss, 1970; Schlesinger & Meadow, 1972; Wedell-Monnig & Lumley, 1980). In a comparison of the interactions of deaf and hearing children with their mothers Brinich (1980) found the mothers of the deaf children to provide more instructions and to engage in more attention-controlling behavior, but suggested that this pattern (similar to that found among the mentally retarded) was unrelated to either deafness or to retardation as such; instead it represents a reaction to the breakdown in reciprocal communication. Thus, "when a mother finds it difficult to establish reciprocal communication with her child (whether this be because of deafness, mental retardation, or other disorders interfering with communication) she may adapt to that situation by emphasizing control in the relationship. . . . This situation might be compressed into an aphorism like 'when communication breaks down, the powerful take control' " (p. 81). Just as with younger children there is by and large a need for more control than with older children, so in cases of pathology the adult will make up for the child's deficiencies by assuming greater direction. The communication process does not simply disintegrate; rather it takes a different form in which the parent adjusts to the child's particular characteristics by suitably modifying the nature of her contribution to the child-parent system. However, one must acknowledge that this may not take place spontaneously. Professional help is needed which in turn is subject to scientific enquiry and sometimes controversy, as seen in the debate about the respective merits of oral-only and total communication modes (Greenberg, 1980). Meadow, Greenberg, Erting, and Carmichael (1981) found that deaf children provided with oral-only communication spend less time in social interaction with their mothers, receive more parental behavior requests, and have the highest incidence of noncompliance when compared with deaf children receiving total communication, deaf children with deaf mothers, and hearing children with hearing mothers—a finding that must surely be one very persuasive argument against the use of the oral-only mode.

Control during the First Year of Life

At all stages of the life-span, from birth to death, human beings are subject to social influence processes. No developmental period is exempt; only the content of the influence and the manner of its impact are likely to vary over age.

This point needs to be stressed in relation to the very beginning of life, for an impression is frequently given that infancy is a period when children are shielded from the demands of their social partners. Thus a dichotomy is made between the first year on the one hand and post-infancy development on the other; the earlier period is seen as one of nurturance and indulgence during which the parent's role is confined to that of comforter, and only on reaching the second year are issues of control and socializing said to arise. For instance, Hoffman (1977) has asserted that at the end of infancy "the parent's role shifts dramatically from primarily that of caretaker to that of socialization agent. His actions change from being facilitative and nurturant to disciplinary." Similarly Maccoby and Martin (1983) refer to "a major change that occurs during the second year," namely "the onset of socialization pressure." And in the same vein Hetherington and Parke (1976), while agreeing that socialization is evident in the first year of life, do not consider it to begin in earnest until the second year when the child achieves mobility and starts to speak.

Such assertions arise from an artificially narrow definition of the socialization process which equates the process with *verbal* influences on the part of the parent and with *voluntary* compliance on the part of the child. When either or both these aspects are missing the nature of interactive forces are thought to be of a completely different kind, requiring different labels and different explanations. Whether there are indeed such differences from one developmental period to another is at present an open issue; what needs to be recognized is that social influences do function from the neonatal stage on and that caretakers not only attempt to steer their children's behavior into socially approved channels from the very beginning but clearly succeed in doing so. In so far as socialization is a label used to designate the transformation of a biological organism into a social one, the process may be said to start at birth.

Let us consider some of the very earliest influences exerted by adults over infants' behavior. These concern the regulation of such basic functions as waking-sleeping states and feeding patterns. How effectively and how rapidly adults are able to regulate infants' states and impose socially acceptable form on them has been described in detail by Sanders (summarized in Sanders, Stechler, Burns, & Lee, 1979). Infants begin life with an endogenously determined pattern of state fluctuations; thus a newborn tends to sleep for many short periods, randomly distributed throughout the day and interspersed with even shorter periods of wakefulness. Such a pattern is inconvenient to caretakers; it does not fit into their own daily cycle and one of their earliest tasks therefore is to ensure that the infant's pattern conforms to their own timetable. As Sander has shown, the effects of this entrainment process are evident from the end of the first postnatal week on: more than half of the longest sleep periods of the 24 hours now occur during the night, whereas mobility and crying peaks have shifted to daytime periods. A coordination between infant state and caretaker activity is thus apparent. An *interpersonal* influence is clearly responsible for such changes in infants' behavior: As Sander was also able to show by means of "cross-fostering" experiments, different adults can produce different patterns in the same children. Individual specificity in the style of infant-caretaker adaptation is thus indicated, and the essentially social nature of the influences involved is further highlighted by cultural differences that occur in the development of waking-sleeping patterns (Super & Harkness, 1982). A similar picture emerges from studies of the feeding cycle during infancy: As the classical study by Marquis (1941) demonstrated, the adoption of either 3-hourly or 4-hourly schedules by caretakers will bring about correspondingly timed periods of restlessness in the infants. Once again, socially induced change has taken place; here too, as in the work by Sander, such change could be found to occur within the first 2 weeks of life. Whether the processes responsible for the change are basically different from those underlying change at subsequent developmental stages remains to be settled. Until this is done the use of socialization as an umbrella term to describe all adult-induced development is surely justified.

The manner whereby parents exert influence on such early functions as sleeping and feeding is, of course, very different from what one finds in later control episodes of the kind described in the previous section. In so far as verbal direction by the adult plays a major part in these controls it may be thought that such behavior would not become evident in the parental repertoire until the child is old enough to comprehend speech. That this is not so is seen in Hepburn and Schaffer's (1983) investigation of mothers' interactions with 5-month-old infants during a bathing session. A great many instances were found of mothers' attempts to change the infant's behavior, and a large proportion of these took verbal form. The mothers, that is, appeared to be requesting their infants to attend, to perform some action, or to refrain from some behavior in the same sort of way as has been described for older children. However, closer examination does reveal some differences. For one thing, a large proportion of verbal controls were accompanied by nonverbal actions, with the latter carrying the major communicative force. For another, mothers were often skilled in inserting their requests at points when the infant was about to perform the relevant action anyway; such anticipation is, of course, particularly easy in the context of a well-established routine such as bathing. And finally, many of the controls were in fact "pseudo-controls," in that they referred to an action that either the mother or the child was already carrying out at that moment. In addition, some requested an action that, given the child's developmental level, was totally unrealistic (e.g., "put on your socks," said laughingly to one of the 5-month-old infants) and therefore not expected to achieve a result.

That the compliance rate on the part of the infants approached 50% may at first sight seem surprising for so immature a being; given the fact that mothers tended to select those circumstances under which it would be easiest for the infant to comply, and that they did so by appropriately incorporating their requests into the sequence of the routine rather than have them impinge as isolated controls on an unprepared child, the *apparent* conformity of the child becomes rather more comprehensible. In any case, the highest compliance rates were found for nonverbal controls, the vast majority of which succeeded in their aim of eliciting some change in the child's behavior. Interestingly, the addition of verbal utterances to nonverbal controls seemed to detract from the effectiveness of the latter.

Why do adults indulge in such apparently unrealistic behavior as verbal requests addressed to preverbal infants? According to Rheingold and Adams (1980) even neonates are spoken to in this fashion—a tendency that seems to argue against the notion of parental adjustment to the child's competence level.

Such apparent lack of realism is, however, by no means confined to the control function; it occurs, for instance, with respect to speech generally, which is found in almost all of adults' interactions with infants of any age. Why this is so can only be a matter of speculation. One consequence, however, is that infants have obtained a massive amount of experience of language input by the time they themselves reach the point of linguistic competence, and it is certainly conceivable that such experience in the previous phase will have played its part in enabling the infant to get to this point. The same applies to the control function: Being involved in such interactive formats right through the early months provides infants with plenty of opportunity to become acquainted with the demand characteristics of other people's requests, including the association of word and action, thus enabling infant, in due course, to enter such formats relatively rapidly and efficiently. And as far as the parent is concerned, it has the advantage that she can repeatedly test out the infant's ability to participate in control-compliance sequences and judge when the child is becoming capable of acting independently. At that point she can begin to hand over responsibility to the child. Up till then she herself may complete the sequence on his or her behalf.

Parental control of one kind or another is thus very much a feature of children's social experience during the first year of life. Indeed Power and Parke (1982), observing infants aged 8 to 10 months, found that the vast majority of interactions could be classified as parental attempts to influence the infants' behavior, either with regard to their attentive, their exploratory, or their social behavior—a conclusion that held for both laboratory and home settings and for both mothers and fathers. Power and Parke, moreover, make the valuable point that parents not only influence their children's behavior *directly* by means of the controls which they impose in play and other social interaction situations but also *indirectly* by the way in which they organise the child's physical environment. This latter, "managerial" function is exercised by setting limits to the number of home settings to which the child is given access ("floor freedom") and by determining the kinds of objects that the child can explore. In view of the fact that young children spend a greater part of their daily lives interacting with their inanimate environment than with other people (White, Kalsan, Shapiro, & Attanucci, 1977), such a managerial function is likely to play a most important role and deserves greater attention in any attempt to understand socialization processes than it has received so far.

Conclusions

Controls are thus a regular feature of parent-child interaction. They are not confined to any particular age range, nor are they reserved for such traditional areas of study as the socialization of toileting or of aggression. They are evident even in playful encounters, constituting an inevitable part of adult-child interaction under a wide range of circumstances. The greater the asymmetry of power between the two partners is, the more evident they are likely to be. This means that they are most prominent in the early years of childhood and gradually diminish as the child becomes more capable of regulating his or her own behavior. How eventually other-control comes to be replaced by self-control is one of the most important problems in developmental psychology that still needs solution. Work on this issue has begun (Kopp, 1982; Vaughn, Kopp, & Krakow, 1984; Wertsch, McNamee, McLane, & Budwig, 1980) and, once satisfactory definitions of self-control have been agreed on, the antecedent conditions which give rise to this development can then be determined. Do children whose parents are particularly skillful in adapting their controls to the individual child achieve self-control early? Are the conditions that foster compliance (an immediate reaction) identical to those that give rise to moral internalisation (a long-term product)? Do different types of parental control strategies result in varying patterns of self-control? Answers to questions such as these will take one a considerable step further along the road to understanding how parents come to play a part in affecting the course of children's development.

The main thesis advanced here is that social influence cannot be understood unless conceived as a mutual, reciprocal process to which both partners contribute. This applies to all types of social situations and all types of individual— the mother and her newborn baby in a feeding situation, the teacher and student in a classroom, the captor and his prisoner in a "brainwashing" session, or any other interaction in which, at first sight, one partner appears to be more powerful than the other and can therefore exert pressure on him and control his behavior. Closer examination invariably shows that the nature of that pressure and control needs to be adapted to the characteristics of the less powerful individual if there is to be any chance of success. This applies equally to the content, the manner and the timing of the influence being applied: In each case the recipient affects the sender's behavior and in this way becomes a sender also.

References

Ainsworth, M. D. S., Bell, S. M. V., & Stayton, D. J. (1971). Individual differences in strange-situation behavior of one-year-olds. In H. R. Schaffer (Ed.), *The origins of human social relations* (pp. 17–57). London: Academic Press.

Bellinger, D. (1979). Changes in the explicitness of mothers' directives as children age. *Journal of Child Language*, 6:443–458.

Bijou, S. W. (1970). Reinforcement history and socialization. In R. A. Hoppe, G. A. Milton & E. C. Simmel (Eds.), *Early experiences and the processes of socialization* (pp. 43–58). New York: Academic Press.

Bijou, S. W., & Baer, D. M. (1962). *Child development*. New York: Appleton-Century-Crofts.

Bridges, A. (1979). Directing two-year-olds attention: Some clues to understanding. *Journal of Child Language*, 6:211–226.

Brinich, P. H. (1980). Childhood deafness and maternal control. *Journal of Communication Disorders*, 13:75–81.

Collis, G. M. (1977). Visual coorientation and maternal speech. In H. R. Schaffer (Ed.), *Studies in mother-infant interaction* (pp. 355–375). London: Academic Press.

Cunningham, C. E., & Barkley, R. A. (1979). The interactions of normal and hyperactive children with their mothers in free play and structured tasks. *Child Development*, 50:217–224.

Cunningham, C. E., Reuter, E., Blackwell, J., & Deck, J. (1981). Behavioral and linguistic developments in the interactions of normal and retarded children with their mothers. *Child Development*, 52:62–70.

Goss, R. N. (1970). Language used by mothers of deaf children and mothers of hearing children. *American Annals of the Deaf*, 115:93–96.

Greenberg, M. T. (1980). Social interaction between deaf preschoolers and their mothers: The effects of communication method & communication competence. *Developmental Psychology*, 16:465–474.

Hepburn, A., & Schaffer, H. R. (1983). Les controles maternels dans la prima enfance (Maternal controls in early infancy). *Enfance*, 1–2:117–127.

Hetherington, E. M., & Parke, R. D. (1976). *Child psychology: A contemporary viewpoint*. New York: McGraw-Hill.

Hoffman, M. L. (1977). Moral internalisation: Current theory and research. In L. Berkowitz (Ed.), *Advances in experimental social psychology*, (Vol. 10, pp. 85–133). New York: Academic Press.

Holden, G. W. (1983). Avoiding conflict: Mothers as tacticians in the supermarket. *Child Development*, 54:233–240.

Jaffe, J., & Feldstein, S. (1970). *Rhythms of dialogue*. New York: Academic Press.

Kopp, C. B. (1982). Antecedents of self-regulation: A developmental perspective. *Developmental Psychology*, 18:199–214.

Lamb, M. E., & Easterbrooks, M. A. (1981). Individual differences in parental sensitivity: Origins, components, and consequences. In M. E., Lamb & L. R. Sherrod (Eds.), *Infant social cognition: Empirical and theoretical considerations* (pp. 127–153). Hillsdale, N.J.: Erlbaum.

Maccoby, E. E., & Jacklin, C. N. (1974). *The psychology of sex differences*. Stanford, CA: Stanford University Press.

Maccoby, E. E., & Martin, J. A. (1983). Socialization in the context of the family: Parent-child interaction. In P. H. Mussen (Ed.), *Handbook of child psychology*, (4th ed.) Vol. IV: *Socialization, personality, and social development* (pp. 1–101). New York: Wiley.

McLaughlin, B. (1983). Child compliance to parental control techniques. *Developmental Psychology*, 19:667–673.

Macnamara, J. (1972). Cognitive basis of language learning in infants. *Psychological Review*, 79:1–13.

Marquis, D. P. (1941). Learning in the neonate: The modification of behavior under three feeding schedules. *Journal of Experimental Psychology*, 29:263–282.

Meadow, K. P., Greenberg, M. T., Erting, C., & Carmichael, H. (1981). Interactions of deaf mothers and deaf preschool children: Comparisons with three other groups of deaf and hearing dyads. *American Annals of the Deaf*, 126:454–468.

Messer, D. J. (1978). The integration of mothers' referential speech with joint play. *Child Development*, 49:781–787.

Minton, C., Kagan, J., & Levine, J. A. (1971). Maternal control and obedience in the two-year-old. *Child Development*, 42:1873–1894.

Murphy, C. M., & Meser, D. J. (1977). Mothers, infants and pointing: A study of a gesture. In Schaffer, H. R. (Ed.), *Studies in mother-infant interaction* (pp. 325–354). London: Academic Press.

Power, T. G., & Parke, R. D. (1982). Play as a context for early learning: Lab and home analyses. In I. E. Sigel & L. M. Laosa (Eds.), *The family as a learning environment.* New York: Plenum Press.

Power, T. G., & Parke, R. D. (1983). Patterns of mother and father play with their 8-month-old infant: A multiple analyses approach. *Infant Behavior and Development*, 6:453–459.

Rheingold, H. L., & Adams, J. L. (1980). The significance of speech to newborns. *Developmental Psychology*, 16:397–403.

Sanders, L. W., Stechler, G., Burns, P., & Lee, A. (1979). Change in infant- and caregiver variables over the first two months of life. In E. B. Thoman (Ed.), *Origins of the infant's social responsiveness* (pp. 349–407). Hillsdale, NJ: Erlbaum.

Schaffer, H. R. (1977). *Mothering*. London: Fontana; Cambridge, MA: Harvard University Press.

Schaffer, H. R. (1979). Acquiring the concept of the dialogue. In M. Bornstein & W. Kessen (Eds.), *Psychological development from infancy: Image and intention* (pp. 279–305). Hillsdale, NJ: Erlbaum.

Schaffer, H. R. (1984). *The child's entry into a social world*. London: Academic Press.

Schaffer, H. R., & Collis, G. M. (1986). Parental responsiveness and child behavior. In W. Sluckin & M. Herbert (Eds.), *Parental behaviour in animals and humans* (pp. 283–315). Oxford: Blackwell.

Schaffer, H. R., Collis, G. M., & Parsons, G. (1977). Vocal interchange and visual regard in verbal and preverbal children. In H. R. Schaffer (Ed.), *Studies in mother-infant interaction*. London: Academic Press.

Schaffer, H. R., & Crook, C. K. (1979). Maternal control techniques in a directed play situation. *Child Development*, 50:989–998.

Schaffer, H. R., & Crook, C. K. (1980). Child compliance and maternal control techniques. *Developmental Psychology*, 16:54–61.

Schaffer, H. R., Hepburn, A., & Collis, G. M. (1983). Verbal and nonverbal aspects of mothers' directives. *Journal of Child Language*, 10:337–355.

Schlesinger, H. S., & Meadow, K. P. (1972). *Sound and sign: Childhood deafness and mental health.* Berkeley: University of California Press.

Schneiderman, M. H. (1983). "Do what I mean, not what I say!" Changes in mothers' action-directives to young children. *Journal of Child Language*, 10:357–367.

Schnur, E., & Shatz, M. (1984). The role of maternal gesturing in conversations with one-year-olds. *Journal of Child Language*, 11:29–41.

Stayton, D. J., Hogan, R., & Ainsworth, M. D. (1971). Infant obedience and maternal behavior: The origins of socialization reconsidered. *Child Development*, 42:1057–1069.

Super, C. M., & Harkness, S. (1982). The infant's niche in rural Kenya and metropolitan America. In L. K. Adler (Ed.), *Cross-cultural research at issue* (pp. 47–55). New York: Academic Press.

Vaughn, B. E., Kopp, C. B., & Krakow, J. B. (1984). The emergence and consolidation of self-control from eighteen to thirty months of age: Normative trend and individual differences. *Child Development*, 55:990–1004.

Watson, J. B. (1928). *Psychological care of infant and child*. New York: Norton.
Wedell-Monnig, J., & Lumley, J. M. (1980). Child deafness and mother-child inter-action. *Child Development*, 51:766–774.
Wertsch, J. V., McNamee, G. D., McLane, J. B., & Budwig, N. A. (1980). The adult-child dyad as a problem-solving system. *Child Development*, 51:1215–1221.
White, B. L., Kalsan, B., Shapiro, B., & Attanucci, J. (1977). Competence and experi-ence. In I. C. Uzguris & F. Weizmann (Eds.), *The structuring of experience* (pp. 115–152). New York: Plenum Press.

5

As the Twig Is Bent:
Children Reared in Feminist Households*

Barbara J. Risman and Kristen Myers

This is a study of children in families in which both the responsibility for income production and the household division of labor is actually post-gendered. Our data come from a larger study of privileged white parents who intentionally organize their households fairly, sharing housework, child care, and emotion work. These parents deconstruct gender not only by encouraging their daughters and sons to develop free from stereotypes but also by modeling such behavior in their own social roles. The data reported here are based on interviews with the children themselves and home observations. We have drawn two main conclusions. First, children do seem to adopt, uniformly, their parent's non-sexist attitudes but then they must negotiate serious inconsistencies between their beliefs and their lived experiences with peers. They resolve this with a dichotomy: men and women are similar and equal, but boys and girls are different and unequal. Second, personal identities seem to be forged more from lived experiences than from ideology.

In recent years, sociologists have come to define gender as a social construct to be negotiated rather than as a fixed entity (West and Zimmerman 1987; Connell 1987; Risman and Schwartz 1989; Howard et al. 1996). In this view, gender is neither simply an attribute of individuals, nor a constraint of the social structure. Instead, when people interact in their daily lives, they "do gender" which helps to reproduce the larger, gendered social structure. West and Zimmerman (1987) argue that individuals are actors working within structural constraints rather than passive pawns. The conceptualization of gender as behavior that may or may not be enacted allows those concerned with inequality to hope

*Reprinted from *Qualitative Sociology*, Vol. 20, No. 2, 1997 by permission of Kluwer Academic/Plenum Publishers and Barbara J. Risman.

Direct correspondence to Barbara Risman, Department of Sociology and Anthropology, Box 8107, North Carolina State University, Raleigh, NC 27695-8107; e-mail: Barbara_risman@ncsu.edu.

for change: What would happen if we decided *not* to do gender, or to do it differently? Would we radically alter the social structure as we know it, or are larger social pressures strong enough to override individual insurgency?

In this paper, we are concerned with these possibilities. In particular, we examine children whose parents deliberately reject gender stratification in the family, and who consciously divide their household labor without regard for traditional gender-based roles. How does this affect the children they are raising? And if parental models and beliefs do affect their children, how do these processes actually work? While our research project is broader in scope than this interest in children, this paper focuses specifically on the experiences of children living in egalitarian households, specifically their gender performances, ideologies and attitudes. We know of no other research precisely on this topic, and so we begin with a brief review of the more generic literature on children and gender. We then present data from our study of feminist families, concentrating particularly on the children's management of the gendered selves and ideologies. We explore the effects of being raised in a feminist household with regard to the children's own gendered identities, and their gendered enactments in and out of the home. Finally, we speculate about the future consequences of such an approach to child-rearing.

Learning How to Behave: Acting Versus Reacting

Sociologists have only rarely—and quite recently—studied children's gender. Therefore, much of the literature to be reviewed originates in other disciplines. When children are studied, in both sociology and psychology, the predominant questions center around the ways in which children learn to be boys or girls. We organize this literature analytically, for purposes of discussion, based on the presumptions about children's role in their own socialization. We divide this scholarship into three categories: that which sees children as the primary *actors* in the gendering process, or cognitive theories; that which sees children's gender as something that is *imposed* by the larger culture, and that is reinforced through structural constraints, or socialization theories; and that which argues that children are constrained by long-standing gender norms, but which sees children as *participating in and negotiating* the enactment of gender or social constructionist theories.

We briefly summarize these analytic categories. First, theories where children are the primary actors [including Piaget (1932); Kohlberg (1966); Maccoby (1992); and Martin (1993)] are theories of cognitive development, which argue that children play an active role in gender acquisition, rather than passively absorbing appropriate information from their parents and peers. Instead, children seek relevant information, and they organize it into predictable patterns.

They begin to do this at a young age in order to make sense out of their worlds. This perspective puts undue emphasis on the child as rational actor freely picking and choosing among the available options, and selecting gender as the most salient organizing force in society (Bem 1993).

The second category—which conceptualizes gender as structurally imposed upon children—includes Parsons and Bales (1955); Inkeles (1968); Bandura (1962, 1973); Cahill (1987); Deaux (1984); Fagot et al. (1992); Hutson (1983); and Stern and Karraker (1989); and Eisenberg et al. (1985). This perspective sees the socialization process as a one-way conduit of information from adult to child. Beginning at birth, people in society (parents, teachers, and peers) reward children for learning the behavior of the same sex. Because they receive positive feedback for "correct" behavior, children imitate same-sex behavior, and "encode" it into their behavioral repertoires. Once encoded, the child's gender is set. This socialization perspective offers a static picture of gender with the child as a relatively acquiescent recipient of appropriate models of behavior, which in turn offer little room for improvisation and change. This is typical of role theorists in general (Kreps et al. 1994). It also does not allow for the enactment of multiple masculinities and femininities (Connell 1992), thereby reifying and valorizing a gender dichotomy.

The last category is more consistent with a social constructionist perspective. In recent years, sociologists have taken a more critical look at the gender socialization of children, arguing that socialization is not a one-way conduit of information, with adults providing role models and sanctions, and with the children hitting, missing and eventually getting it "right" [for more, see Corsaro (1985), Alanen (1988), and Giddens (1979)]. Instead, the children participate in the process as social actors. Research in this tradition is quite new. For example, Borman and O'Reilly (1987) find that kindergarten children in same-sex play groups initiate play in similar manners, but that the topics for play vary by gender. That is, boys and girls play different types of games, thereby creating different conversational and negotiation demands. Thorne (1993) examines groups of children in classrooms and school yards, illustrating how "kids" actively create and police gender boundaries, forming various strata among themselves. She asserts that gender relations are not invariant, but instead can change according to the context and the actors involved. Thorne criticizes most socialization and development frameworks for presupposing a certain outcome: that boys will learn appropriate masculinities, girls will learn appropriate femininities; and if they fail to do so, they will either be punished or labeled 'deviant.' She argues that this future-oriented perspective distorts the children's every day realities, which are crucial to their on-going gendered negotiations. As she says, "children's interactions are not preparation for life, they are life itself" (p. 3).

Bem (1993) improves upon both cognitive and socialization theories by linking them. Bem argues that children try to make sense of the world by forming categories, or "schema," but these categories are shaped by the ubiquitous presence of existing gender categories in society. She argues that learning gender is subtle, transmitted to children by adults both consciously and unconsciously, so that the dominant way of understanding the social world is seen as the only way to understand it. Existing gender divisions are hegemonic and therefore usually unquestioned by both children and adults. Therefore, calling into question the taken-for-granted gendered organization of society is difficult and unlikely, though not impossible.

It seems quite reasonable that all three processes occur. Children who live in gendered societies do, no doubt, develop gender schema and code themselves as well as the world around them in gendered terms. But this seems much more likely to be the result of their lived experiences in patriarchal societies and not the consequence of some innate drive for cognitive development. While children do indeed develop cognitive gender schema, adults and older children also treat boys and girls quite differently. Gender socialization is apparent in any observation of children's lives. And, while children are being socialized, they react, negotiate, and even reject some of the societal pressures as they interact with each other, and adults. Children are actors in the gendering process, but that does not mean that we must ignore the impact of differential reinforcement of gender-appropriate behavior on them. The cognitive effects of living in a gendered (and sexist) society, the reality of gender socialization, and the active efforts of boys and girls to negotiate their own worlds interact to affect their future options and constraints.

Unequal Outcomes: Reproducing Gender Inequalities

Even when we recognize that children both act and react throughout the gendering process, we cannot overlook the strong empirical data which suggests that boys and girls are differentially prepared for their adult roles. Boys are still routinely socialized to learn to work in teams and to compete; girls are still routinely socialized to value nurturing (just notice the relative numbers of boys and girls in team sports versus those dedicated readers to the very popular book series, *The Babysitters Club*). Thorne (1993) has shown very convincingly that there is much more cross-over gender play than dichotomous thinking presumes; and yet other research continues to indicate the consequences of gender socialization on children (Lever 1978; Luttrell 1993; Hawkins 1985; Wilder et al. 1985; Signorelli 1990; Maccoby 1992; Hutson 1993). There is also much evidence that gender socialization differs by social class, ethnicity and religion (Peterson and Rollins 1987; Hill Collins 1990).

Lever's (1978) classic study of boys' and girls' play offers insight into the ways in which boys and girls are differentially prepared for their futures: men are presumed to belong in the public, competitive sphere and women in the private, nurturing sphere. Boys' games were more likely to be outside, involve teams and be age-integrated. Girls were more likely to play "makebelieve" games with one or two others, and to break up a game rather then work through conflict. After interviewing two groups of working class women about their gendered experiences in school, Luttrell (1993) suggests that school is politically embattled, and femininity is used to undermine working class girls' academic confidence and success in school. Hawkins (1985) argues that girls often do not receive sufficient support with regard to learning computer skills; they are thereby somewhat handicapped in an increasingly computer-reliant world. Wilder et al. (1985) echo this argument, examining the ideology that technology is a male domain. In surveys of 1600 children in kindergarten through twelfth grade, they find that girls like computers less than boys and therefore use them less. In a survey of first year college students, they find that women students feel less competent with computer technology, regardless of their skill or experience.

Gender specific experiences aren't limited to play and school. Because human beings are helpless at birth and, in our society, adulthood may not arrive for more then two decades, children are dependent upon families for a very long time. Therefore, parents and the immediate family are one source of transmission of existing gendered expectations (Maccoby 1992). The research we have discussed above points to the negative impact of gender-typing on their psyches, their acquisition of competitive market skills, necessary nurturing skills, and their interaction with each other. Research indicates that parents participate in gender-typing by often rewarding gender-typical play and punishing gender atypical-play (Hutson 1983). In order to help combat gender inequality, we must carefully attend to both gendering processes and the negotiation of gender among children. While several scholars have documented that some families in our society are moving in the direction of shared parenting, we have as yet little information about how effective such changes in parenting style might be in a society in which gendering processes continue to occur in other social realms (Coltrane 1996; Marsiglio 1995; Schwartz 1994; Segal 1990).

In this paper, we examine children whose parents have attempted to break the chain of gender inequality that begins at birth. We focus particularly on the ways in which children grapple with and enact gender. The children in this study are living in a different context than children in more mainstream families: these are children whose parents make a conscious effort *not* to replicate what Connell (1987) calls hegemonic masculinity and emphasized femininity in their everyday lives. They have an ideological and practical commitment to organizing their homes and families in an egalitarian manner. Whereas main-stream parents may react with delight when their daughter wants to be Barbie for Halloween and their son wants toy guns for his birthday, the parents in this study are likely to be dismayed. Rather than receiving reinforcement from their parents when they enact hegemonic behavior, these children are likely to encounter disappointment or concern. So, how do these children negotiate gender given their atypical parents?

There has been no previous research that we know of pertaining to children who are raised in egalitarian households. Therefore, we have little informa-tion from other studies with which to compare the findings about children from what we call "fair" households. We discuss the actual criteria for inclusion in this study below, but we first address our use of the term, "fair." We use this term to summarize the parents' ideological and actual commitment to and actual success at dividing household labor and child care equally. These fami-lies do gender more fairly than typical American families (Hochschild 1989). They are a small, unusual group of families. Our "fair" families are similar to those studied by Ehrensaft (1987) in her research on politically radical parents who shared a commitment to egalitarian household labor and child care. She finds that men did help, but the women worked harder to keep the boat afloat. "Fair" families in our study differ from Ehrensaft's in that a criterion for inclu-sion is a more equal division of labor. Another major difference is that we inter-viewed the children, and Ehrensaft did not.

This paper, therefore, is exploratory; we can not know whether the patterns identified here are true or not for all upper-middle-class white children raised by heterosexual[2] parents in contemporary America. We believe they are not. On a personal level, one of us has directly observed her own children's friends and their families, and the patterns we identify in this study simply do not apply to most of them. However, we can and do compare these patterns to some new gender research on children, per se, and we make some educated guesses about what makes these children different.

"Fair Family" Study Research Design

A team of researchers collected these data over a five year period. Inter-viewers included Stephen Blackwelder, Sandra Godwin, Steven Jolly, Jammie Price, Margaret Stiffler, Danette Johnson-Sumerford and the authors. In 1990, our team spent an entire semester writing and revising interview formats for heterosexual couples and their children. This was particularly challenging because we wanted to include in the study children as young as four and as old as eighteen. We finally decided on three separate formats: an interview schedule with questions resembling stories for the 4 to 6 year olds; an interview format which included some questions, some poetry writing and free-play for 7 to 11 year olds; and a format which included open-ended questions and some paper-and-pencil items for teenagers. Here, we address only the findings from our home observations and open-ended yet structured interviews with the children, although we also interviewed the parents separately.

Our hardest challenge was to *find* "fair" families. We advertised widely—in every PTA newsletter in Wake County, North Carolina. We posted signs or mailed advertisements to every day care center in the city of Raleigh, many libraries and fitness centers, on grocery store bulletin boards, and in the staff publication of our home institution, North Carolina State University. We advertised in the Women's Studies Programs of Duke University, the University of North Carolina at Chapel Hill and NCSU, in local feminist group newsletters (NOW and NARAL) and in newsletters of local churches and synagogues. In addition, we asked everyone we knew for referrals. All told, we sought families in Raleigh, Durham, Chapel Hill, and Greensboro, North Carolina. Many people responded, wanting to participate.

We had specific, though not especially stringent, criteria for inclusion in this sample. Our first requirement was that the couples must report that they equally shared the work of earning a living and raising their children. Only couples who reported this to be true in a short telephone conversation were eligible to receive a survey, another screening device. We sent short surveys to both husbands and wives in those families where one spouse appeared eligible based on the short telephone call. We included only families in which both parents independently reported on the survey that (a) they spent approximately equal hours per week in the paid labor force; (b) the household labor and child care, as reported task by task, averaged at least a 40/60 split overall; and (c) both spouses described their marriage as "fair" on a series of dimensions. Overall, we wanted to make sure that we were studying couples who did family life fairly and not second-shift families where women did more than their fair share. This survey was our first stage of data collection, designed merely to select appropriate families for interviews and home observations.

The Families

Seventy-five families volunteered to participate, and they all *believed themselves to be* eligible based on our stated criteria. Because they all passed the telephone pre-screening stage, we sent all of them the short survey. We wanted to be absolutely sure to identify "fair" families before taking a team out to interview an ineligible family. The survey worked well—only once did our screening device let through a family in which the woman did more than her share. Unfortunately, this pre-screened group of 75 families yielded us only

15 families which met all four criteria for inclusion. Only one out of five—20% of those who claimed to be fairly sharing-really were, as measured by their own responses to our survey! That alone tells us much about the invisibility of gender inequity in contemporary American marriage.

The 15 families who met our criteria were not "regular folks;" they were the educationally elite. Over half of the parents (8 men and 9 women) had Ph.D.'s or MD's. Another 8 parents had Master's degrees (usually in education or business). Three fathers and one mother had only a bachelor's degree, and only one mother had never completed college. These families were not necessarily wealthy; indeed, many had given up higher paying occupations to co-parent their children. Others were college professors, a group with a notoriously high educational attainment relative to their incomes. Nevertheless, these were the only families that met our predetermined criterion. The question is, Why?

The sample characteristics may reflect our local population. Local mythology reports—inaccurately—that the Triangle area of North Carolina has more Ph.D.'s per capita than any other part of the country. Nevertheless, with three major universities and several colleges, and the research divisions of multinational corporations in Research Triangle Park, there are a disproportionate number of highly educated persons in our region. But there are also many less educated persons in our region as well—some of whom sent in questionnaires that we later eliminated because the couple did not really "do it fairly." Perhaps women in our society do not have the clout or self-assurance to seek a peer marriage unless they are highly educated income-producing professionals. Or, perhaps the pool of men who practice non-hegemonic masculinity, to the extent that they would not be threatened by a "fair" marriage, is so small that most women who desire a "fair" relationship are unlikely to find a suitable partner. Regardless, we know that high education and the ability to earn a good living is not a sufficient condition to create a peer marriage (or we'd have many more by now), but those pre-conditions seem necessary.

The women in this sample were self-assured, strong-willed, committed to their work, and had eagerly sought parenthood. Such women tend to marry equals with regard to cultural capital, and so their husbands were also highly educated, income-producing professionals. The men tended to be easy-going, family-centered, unattached to John-Wayne style, hegemonic masculinity, and they worked in jobs with some built-in flexibility.

The one unusual pattern was the number of couples in the same sort of work: there were three academic couples in the same fields (two even in the same departments) and two couples in similar fields but different work places. Another pattern quickly became obvious: many of these wives (6 of 15) had occupations with either higher earnings or higher prestige than their husbands' occupations. Only two husbands so out-ranked their wives. The norm, however, was for the spouses to hold relatively equally prestigious jobs and earn comparable incomes. In slightly over half the families (8 of 15), the wife followed tradition and assumed her husband's name upon marriage, and they gave the children his name also. The remaining families had either both kept their birth names upon marriage, or they hyphenated one or both names. Their children's surnames also took a variety of traditional and nontraditional forms. In this analysis, we gave each family a code name.[3] We also changed identifying characteristics such as occupation and worksite to protect the respondents' anonymity.

Another noteworthy pattern was that all of the families were white. Because we are unable to compare the gendered experiences of these white children with those of children of color, we can only speculate on the importance of white privilege for these children's gender lenses. As members of the dominant group, these children wear an invisible, taken-for-granted knapsack of privileges (McIntosh 1992), which affects all of their experiences—including their experiences with gender advantage or disadvantage. Attacking gender stratification may have a different priority for families of color who are not insulated by white privilege (hooks 1995). The fact that the children in this sample are white is important; they are free from the ideological and material oppression experienced by people who are systematically disenfranchised due to race or ethnicity (Feagin 1991). Although some of these children are Jewish in a predominantly Christian area, most of these children are free from racist oppression in their everyday lives. This affords them and their families the luxury and resources to challenge gender stratification. Most of these parents are able to do things fairly because they can hire outside help when internal conflict arises. We recognize this economic advantage, and address it more fully elsewhere (see Risman, forthcoming). This sample bias is yet another reason that we consider this study to be exploratory.

The Children

There were 26 children in these 15 families, but five were under four years of age, which was too young to interview. The children's sample included 12 boys and 9 girls. We interviewed 10 children in the four to 6 year old category, 7 children between 7 and 10 years of age, and four children 11 years old and older. Three of the four teenagers, however, were from one family, so we refrain from making any generalizations about that group. In addition to the data from the interviews, we used our field notes to document the decor of the children's rooms; the toys, books and games with which they played; and the character of our interaction. Taken together, we began to piece together an understanding of how these children negotiate their lives.

The Complicated Worlds of Fair Children

In examining the stories, poems, and conversations of the children, we have drawn two main findings. The inconsistencies between the children's egalitarian beliefs and their experiences with peers is the major and consistent finding in these data. The second finding, also consistent, is that identities seem to be forged more from lived experiences than from ideology. The disjunction between ideology, experience, and identity seems to be a common thread woven through all these children's stories. In discussing the findings and providing the words of the children themselves, we refer to the gender of the child. We recognize that, in focusing repeatedly on gender, we may be reinforcing the notion of gender differences rather than similarities; that is not our intention. It is simply a necessary means of distinguishing subjects and the differential experiences.

We divide our findings into three major categories: ideology, experiences and identities of the children. In analyzing the data, we realized that gender operates on several levels for these children. They all espouse a certain rhetoric of gender which they have learned in part from living in "fair" families. We find that this rhetoric is not always in sync with the children's gendered experiences and behaviors, so we address them separately. And, last, we find that the children have internalized notions of gender which affect their identities as girls and boys.

Ideology

Approximately 80% of the children (16 of 21) entirely adopted their parents' egalitarian or feminist views on gender. Two of the children without such views were four year olds whose answers were better described as inconsistent than traditional. These children knew that occupations were currently sex-segregated but believed they shouldn't be. They didn't see any jobs in families that ought to be either for men or women. One 10 year old boy actually became annoyed as we questioned him about what men and women should do. He retorted in an irritated voice and rolled his eyes: "I told you I think anybody can do these jobs. . . . I think that saying just men or just women could do these jobs isn't being equal." The children over 6 years of age didn't have any problem differentiating what was true from what should be so.

Most of both boys and girls not only believed that men and women should be free to work in any occupation and share the family labor, they also understood that male privilege existed in contemporary society. This 9 year old girl told us that she believed very much in feminism because "I don't think that it is the least bit fair that in most places males have the main power. I think that women play an important part and should be free to do what they want to do." Similarly, a 15 year old told us, in response to a question about what he liked about being a boy, "It's probably easier being a guy at least it is now because of stereotypes and prejudices and everything." Overall, most of these children were sophisticated, true believers in gender equality and the capabilities of men and women to be in the same jobs and family roles. The influence of their parents as ideological conduits and role models was evident in these children's attitudes.

Experiences

These children may have had "politically correct" attitudes about gender equality for men and women, but when that ideology contradicted their experiences as boys and girls, the experiential data won hands-down. Despite their answers to what should be for grown-ups, these children gave remarkably typical answers about the differences between boys and girls. In order to find out their "gut" beliefs about boys and girls, we probed their experiences with a variety of techniques. We asked them how their lives would be different if a magician turned them into a girl/boy. We provided them short scenarios using stereotypically male and female adjectives (e.g. weak, strong, fearful, adventuresome) and asked them to circle a male or female diagram, and then asked why. We asked what they liked and disliked about being a girl or boy. We asked them to write poems which began with the line "If I were a boy/girl" using the opposite sex category. We showed them different pictures of a boy and a girl (similar in the fact that both sat on the same sofa), and we asked them to tell us a story about each child. We followed up every comment which would help us assess their experiences.

None of the four, five or six year olds had yet begun to believe that boys and girls were different. These egalitarian parents managed to exert some insulation for their pre-schoolers from typical American norms—perhaps by choice of paid care giving arrangements and selection of friends. This finding differs from theories based on developmental psychological research (e.g. Kohlberg (1966), Kohlberg and Ullian (1974)), which suggests that children necessarily begin sex-stereotyping as early as four years old.

Once children hit 7 years of age, however, their non-familial experiences have broadened considerably, as have their ideas about differences between the sexes. We found the descriptions of school age children remarkably consistent—and stereotypical—across sex and age categories. Girls were sweet and neat; boys were athletic and disruptive. The list of adjectives which follow are representative direct quotes about boys. The age and sex of the speakers who use each adjective at least once are indicated. Notice that of the 16 adjectives used to describe boys, half are socially disruptive personality traits, often considered aspects of masculinity. The rest are more neutral descriptors, but still very stereotypically masculine. The world these school-aged children knew—and the boys and girls agreed—was one in which boys as a group were athletic and mean.

When they talked about girls (which was notably less often), the children described girls almost as a different species. Although we elicited more comments about boys than girls, the comments were remarkably consistent. The age and sex of each speaker who used this precise language is included in the table. All of these adjectives describe traditional feminine stereotypes. Six of the 10 adjectives used to describe girls are socially valued personalities traits, the others more neutral yet still stereotypically feminine traits. These children offered unequivocal support for the belief in major sex differences between boys and girls within minutes of having parroted their parents feminists' views about the equality and similarity of men and women.

Three of these children qualified these stereotypical answers. An 8 year old boy made a point of telling us that he knew girls could be into sports or computers, he just didn't personally know any who were. A 7 year old girl was sure that girls were better behaved and boys were mean, but she also sometimes wanted to be a boy because they seemed to have more playful and active games. A 10 year old boy knew that some girls were "like boys," and he even let such a girl try out for his spy club. And one 6 year old boy made the very acute observation that girls played different games on the playground but the same games as boys in the neighborhood [Thorne (1993) finds the same thing]. This little boy had a close neighborhood girl friend, but we observed that when the other boys came around, he left her alone. Crossing gender for play was fine with him, but not at the expense of ridicule from the other boys. Our observation was reinforced by his parents independently mentioning this pattern.

When family experiences collided head-on with experiences with peers, the family influences were dwarfed. For example, one 6 year old boy told us that if a magician were to turn him into a girl, he'd be different because he'd have long hair. This boy's father had a long straight black ponytail which went to the middle of his back, and his mother's hair hardly reached below her ears. A four year old boy told us that if a magician were to turn him into a girl, he'd have to do housework—despite his father's flexible work schedule, which allowed him to spend more time in domestic pursuits than his wife. Children knew that *women and men* were equal; it was *boys and girls* who were totally different. It almost seemed as if these children believed that boys and girls were opposites, but men and women magically transformed into equal and comparable people.

Table 5.1
Adjectives Used by the Children to Describe Boys and Girls

Adjective for Boys	Speaker	Adjective for Girls	Speaker
Active	girl, age 7	Nice	girl, age 4 boy, age 10 boy, age 12
Into sports	girl, age 7 girl, age 9 boy, age 10 boy, age 10 boy, age 12	Well behaved	girl, age 7 boy, age 10
Mean	girl, age 4 girl, age 7 boy, age 15	Quiet	girl, age 7 boy, age 10 boy, age 10
Bad	girl, age 7 girl, age 9	Cooperative	girl, age 9
More free	girl, age 11	Good	girl, age 9
Sarcastic	boy, age 15	Sweet	girl, age 7
Cool	girl, age 4	Not into sports	boy, age 10
Aggressive	girl, age 9 boy, age 10 boy, age 12	Not sneaky	boy, age 12
Athletic	boy, age 10 boy, age 12	Nicer to friends	boy, age 12
Tough	boy, age 12	Less free	girl, age 11
Stronger	boy, age 6 boy, age 10		
Into fighting	girl, age 9 boy, age 10		
Troublemaking	girl, age 9 boy, age 10		
Competitive	girl, age 9		
Bully	boy, age 10		
Into computers	boy, age 4		

Seven of these children spoke explicitly about male privilege among peers or at school. A 9 year old girl told us that sometimes she wished to be a boy because when

> teachers need help like to carry a box to their classroom, they always come in and say, like, can I borrow a couple of your boys, and never say, "can I borrow a couple of your students?" And so the girls never get to do any of the stuff and leave the classroom. . . . it's always the boys that get to leave. And like, little trips and stuff, when we need to go on field trips, the boys would always have to carry a basket of lunches, and go ahead, and like, when they had stuff to bring from the car, it'd always be boys that'd get to go to the car and eat and the girls, like, had to stay on the bus and just sit there and wait while some boys got to go there and the girls never got to do it, do that stuff . . . you get left out because you're a girl. . . . But I'm not wimpy.

The 7 year old girl told us that she was "more hyper" than most girls and many of her friends were boys because they were more active and playful. A 10 year old boy mentioned "racism against women" in sports. One 9 year old girl was an avowed feminist who also espoused implicitly essentialist notions about girls' innate cooperativeness versus boys' innate combativeness. She thought girls ought to have more power in the world because they were better people. The following paragraph written by an 8 year old boy was an articulate statement about male-privilege, but such an understanding of such privilege was widely shared by all of the children, though not usually so well articulated.

> If I were a girl I'd have to attract a guy—wear makeup; sometimes, wear the latest style of clothes and try to be like-able. I probably wouldn't play any physical sports like football or soccer. I don't think I would enjoy myself around men in fear of rejection or under the pressure of attracting them.

Therefore, while boys and girls shared the perception that boys were troublemakers, sarcastic, and athletic, they also sensed that boys had advantages. Only a few of the boys were, in fact, conscious that they belonged to a group for which they had internalized negative characteristics. One aware boy answered our question about how he was different from other guys this way, "I think I'm taller. I don't like bullying people around that much. When one of my friends starts fighting somebody or arguing with somebody. I don't join in. I steer clear of them. I try to get in as few fights as possible." This boy built his identity in sports (his room was a baseball shrine and his activities were sports, sports, and more sports), but tried to distance himself from the violent aspects of peer group masculinity. Another boy told us that if he were magically transformed into a girl, he would be nicer to his friends. These boys had internalized very negative attitudes toward their own group—and at some level, themselves. In no case did any girl tell us how bad girls as a group were. When girls talked about how they were similar and different from other girls, their answers were idiosyncratic. These children "knew" that boys and girls were very different; they "knew" that boys had advantages; but they also "knew" that girls were nicer people.

Identity

These boys and girls were consistent when they explained how boys and girls were different. The unanimity dissolved when we began to look at how they forged their own identities. Only 6 of these children seemed to have fashioned selves which unambiguously fit into their own stereotyped notions of childhood gender. The interview and observational data collected in these families identified 6 children (the 11 year old Germane girl, the 12 year old Potadman boy, the 8 year old Pretzman boy, the 10 year old Stokes girl, the 6 year old Green girl, and the 9 year old Sykes girl) who described themselves in consistently gendered fashion, and who were so identified in observational data. The first obvious finding was that these children's attitudes and identities were not consistent. The Pretzman boy, Stokes girl, Green girl, and Sykes girl are very self-consciously egalitarian, even feminist. The Germane girl and the Potadman boy, however, were two of the children with more traditional beliefs about gender. The Pretzman and Potadman children were "all-boy;" the Sykes, Stokes, Green and Germane children "all-girl."

What does "all-boy" or "all-girl" mean? In this instance, we refer back to the list created by the children themselves. The children suggested boys were active, into sports, mean, bad, freer than girls, sarcastic, cool, aggressive, athletic, tough, stronger than girls, into fights, troublemakers, competitive, bullies, and into computers. These 6 children could indeed be described exclusively by characteristics in this list, with no reference to those traits which were used to describe girls. Now, this doesn't mean that every characteristic was applicable, only that no characteristics from the opposite sex list fit at all. For example, there was no indication that the Pretzman boy was mean or a troublemaker, just the opposite. He was an academically gifted child who took school very seriously, and followed directions impeccably, yet all his interests were masculine—sports, leggos, star-trek, computers. He described himself as "strong" and used that criterion to differentiate boys and girls. He didn't play much with girls, and there was simply no indication of cross-gender behavior or traits either in the interview or as we watched him at home. The Potadman boy was similar. His main interest and identity seemed to be attached to sports. He was interpersonally instrumental, answering us with short, not-too-reflective comments. In traditionally masculine fashion, his friendships were described almost entirely in terms of sharing activities.

The four girls who were "all-girl" could be described by using the characteristics the children provided for us about girls: nice, behave well, quiet, cooperative, good, sweet, not into sports, not sneaky, nice to friends, less free. While none of these girls embodied every one of these traits, it is unlikely that these girls would be described by any of the traits in the "boy" list. One shared characteristic was their distaste for competitive sports. The Germane girl provided an easy comparison to the Potadman boy discussed above. Her very favorite games were make-believe fantasies, and her favorite activity was dance. Her favorite possessions: dolls and stuffed animals. The Stokes 10 year old was similarly gendered. Her very favorite activities were reading, writing poems and art. She was adamant about disliking sports, and she knew why: she didn't like any activity where you had to be pushy or aggressive. The Green daughter had three doll houses, and not a "boy" toy in the house. Because we interviewed the entire family, we knew that this child preferred girl toys in spite of her parents' teaching. Her parents were very conscious of encouraging her to make her own choices and develop her own potential; the mother told us she "was working on" trying to get her daughter to be willing to play some sports, at least at school during recess.

These 6 children, raised by egalitarian parents and often holding feminist attitudes themselves, nevertheless fashioned selves which are unambiguously gendered. The following poem sums up what these children thought when they imagined being the opposite sex. The essay was written by the Sykes girl in response to our request to write a verse which began with the phrase, "If I were a boy". She wrote,

> If I were a boy, I'd know my parents had made a mistake, and that I should have been a girl. I'd always feel that I didn't belong because the girls were who I wanted to play with; but they wouldn't let me, and I didn't want to be with the boys.

This 9 year old girl provided an interesting and stark example of the disjunction between identity and ideology. She lived in one of our most self-consciously feminist and progressive families. They saw themselves as living outside the mainstream, with no television so their daughter avoided excess materialism. All three Sykes were avowed feminists. And yet, the daughter was one of the most feminine in the sample—her long wavy hair flowed below her waist. She loved and collected china tea cups, hated competitive sports, and loved nature and hiking. She saved a bug from destruction during a home observation, and she carried it tenderly outside. In honor of the interview, she put on her favorite pajamas, a long nightgown with a pink bow. This child was very smart, and knew it. She intended to succeed professionally, maybe in a scientific career. So perhaps she too, despite her feminine self-presentation and dislike for most things male, was actually more actively crossing over gender boundaries than we could determine in our limited access to her life.

The other 15 children had also fashioned gendered selves. The boys were much more likely to enjoy sports, the girls to enjoy dance. Despite their parents role-modeling, despite their own ideologies, all of these girls were more feminine than masculine. All of these boys were more masculine then feminine. But all of the rest of these children, to varying degrees, crossed over gender lines in interests and interpersonal style. All but one of the girls was either involved in at-least one competitive sport or expected to be when she got older. All of the boys stood out some way as exceptions to hegemonic masculinity. An interesting sex difference existed, however. All the girls told us in quite explicit terms just how they were different from other girls, but the boys often denied any differences from other boys, differences that our interview and observational team noted. For example, one girl knew she was different from other girls because she loved team sports and would like to be a boy, except that she knew "they aren't always very nice." A four year old liked to climb trees, as well as play fantasy games about babies. She knew she was "nice, like other girls" but wanted to be "cool" like boys. She told us her future goal was to "be a mommy so I can work hard and like my job." In seeing this child in public settings in the last few years, we know that she has become an enthusiastic baseball player with a square and chunky frame. She looks tough on the field. Another child believed she was more active then other girls, but she was also "real sweet," liked horses, and was nice to her friends (all characteristics she sees as different from boys). Yet another child told us she was "not like other girls particularly." She had friends who were boys, although her best friend was another girl. But she liked being a girl because she could do whatever she wanted.

The boys whom we coded as portraying some cross-over behaviors and interpersonal style were much less likely to notice it themselves. While some of the data reported here came directly from the interviews, much of it also relied on subtle inconsistencies in their own words, body language, and, to some extent, the "gut" feelings of the interview and observational team as recorded in field notes. Both of the older Potadman boys (15 and 17 years of age) told us some hopes and dreams which seemed to cross-over gender stereotypes. The 15 year old babysat and loved domestic work, to vacuum and cook. He would like to stay home with his children if his wife could earn a high enough income. His very tall older brother, whose long pony tail reaching below his waist was his most distinctive visual characteristic, hated to work out, and found it unfair that women can be considered sexy without being muscular but that men can't. He wrote poetry and never has been into sports, although he did like volleyball. He described himself as an intellectual outsider, and seemed comfortable—if somewhat vulnerable—with the status.

Four little boys—all aged four or five—also told us their androgynous preferences. One liked lots of boys games, particularly baseball. But he also wanted to be like his sister, played housekeeping at day care, and enjoyed playing "dress-up" in his sister's clothes. Another boy's favorite movie characters were Aladdin and the Little Mermaid, and he had shoes adorned with the likenesses of both. A four year old boy thought being "silly" was the best part of being a boy. While he liked guns and had mostly boys as friends, his answers to most questions seemed gender-neutral. Similarly, one five year old boy liked boys' toys and baseball, but many of his favorite activities seemed gender-neutral, board games, and playing out of doors with both boys and girls. His body language and self-presentation, his greater enthusiasm for non-gendered subjects, brought to mind the characteristic "gentle." One 6 year old boy preferred stereotypically boy toys, and he took Tae Kwon Do, but like the 15 year old above, he too would like to not work at all, to "spend more time with his children." Even when these boys talked about their stereotypical behaviors, they never seemed rough or tough; they seemed warm and caring.

There were two boys whose words contradicted their behavior (as reported by parents) and our observations. One 10 year old boy seemed to try too hard at his self-presentation. He wanted us to think he was tough, mean, and sneaky— a real boy. But the boy we met was warm, kind and soft-spoken, even as he told us about his war games. This son of two nonfiction writers wanted a blue-collar job where he could wear "lots of armor" and be tough. But all of these words did not square with what we found—a ten year old who played gently with his sister. He came back from the bathroom, interrupted our interview and his four year old sister's interview to bring her to look out the bathroom window. He wanted to make sure she didn't miss the full moon. He talked to her quietly, handled her gently. When we noticed some Barbie-dolls in his closet and asked what kind of games he played with them, he answered, "Oh, I mostly kill them. They're my sister's." His mother told us otherwise, that both children played fantasy games with the dolls. He alluded to this himself later on: "I like the Ken doll because he is a basketball star." This boy twitched, visibly, when he spoke about gender preferences. The interview was poignant: he knew that boys were "supposed" to be mean and sneaky, and he wanted very much to fulfill those expectations, or at least to make us believe that he did. But we could not believe it; he gave too many contradictory signals.

We had a similar experience with the 10 year old Woods boy. He was a baseball fanatic and his room was entirely in Carolina Blue, rug and all. He talked about liking to compete. Both of these characteristics are hegemonically masculine, and they were clearly central to his identity. And yet, he described his baby brother in loving terms, and in three straight losses in an UNO card game with his interviewer, he never once showed any competitive spirit nor disappointment in losing. He emanated warmth, as did his father. He also differentiated himself from other boys because he wasn't a bully and didn't like to fight. These children's behavior challenged the boundaries of a rigid gender dichotomy, redefining athletics and competition as less hegemonically masculine.

Summary

The children in fair families have adopted their parents' egalitarian views. They believe men and women are equal, and that no jobs—inside or outside the family—ought to be sex-linked. But beyond these abstract statements concerning beliefs, these children depend on their own lived experiences for understanding gender in their childhood worlds. And they "know" that boys and girls are different—very different. The children—including the boys themselves—describe boys as a group as not only athletic, but also mean and troublesome. Girls are described as sweet, quiet, and well-behaved. Six of these children met their own criteria for being "all-boy" or "all-girl," while the rest portrayed some examples of cross-gender behavior. The girls knew and reported how they were different from other girls, the boys didn't.

One way to interpret the inconsistencies that we observed between children's ideology and their behavior and identities is that gender socialization has many sources, which are sometimes contradictory. Parents may be the primary socializing agents, but children are influenced by myriad social pressures outside of the family to conform to existing gendered norms. We think this is part of the story. While these parents have struggled to raise their children without oppressive gendered categories, the parents are unable to completely cloister their children. They go to school, synagogue or church, and to their friends' homes—places where gender is done differently.

The closest we came to finding a case where the parents had completely controlled their children's gendered environment was with a family whose two children were under four years old. The children were too young to be interviewed, but one interviewer played with them and observed them for three hours while other team members interviewed their parents. What we saw was remarkable. The parents and their private child care worker had carefully eliminated gender distinctions from their children's lives: they changed pronouns in books to be gender neutral; they never referred to their children as "girls" but as people; and they concentrated instead on teaching love for all people, flora and fauna. In talking with the older child (who was three years old—her sister was an infant), the interviewer asked her if she was a boy or a girl. The child proudly responded that she was a person. She did not yet differentiate along gendered lines. We wondered what life would be like for this child when her parents could no longer shelter her and her sister from the hegemonically gendered organization of larger society. Nevertheless, she was the only child we observed who lived this seemingly non-gendered life.

Another way to look at these inconsistencies is to see them as a gradual process of gender revolution. These children may be challenging the rigid proscriptions of a gender dichotomy. Sociologists have begun to recognize (see especially Connell 1987 and 1995), that there are multiple masculinities and femininities, but most of society still wholly adopt and enforce a simple dichotomy. These children's actions challenge the existing gender structure of society in that they reject the dichotomy. Being competitive and into-sports does not impede a boy's ability to be tender and loving. Girls can wear hair bows and pink dresses and still be feminists. One set of characteristics does not preclude the co-existence of the other. They straddle the boundaries. The straddling makes some children nervous—like the 10 year boy who twitched—because they know they're unusual. But many consider their duality to be normal. These children are not post-gendered in that they obliterate the differences between boys and girls; on the contrary, they embrace and occasionally celebrate them. They are post-gendered because they do not use these differences as dichotomies nor to be used as a basis for ranking each other. What all of these children have in common is a focus on kindness and gentleness. They can be masculine or feminine or both, but they are all humanitarian.

Conclusion

How does this inform the larger literature on gender and children? We can only speculate, but it seems as if these children have much more complicated, and less consistent gender schemes then do other children. They see that boys and girls are different, but men and women are believed to be much the same. These children's gender schemes seem much less dichotomized than studies of children from more mainstream families (Lewis 1972; Renzetti and Curran 1992). This supports Bem's argument that children raised with less gender stereotyping will develop weaker gender schemes.

The continued reports from these children about tough boys and sweet girls also indicate the concurrent importance of gendered experiences which are omnipresent in social arenas outside of their families. The variety and inconsistencies in how these children construct their identities supports Thorne's (1993) notions about the active negotiation of gender in children's lives. These children from "fair" families encounter more inconsistencies in gender meanings than most children because they are more likely to recognize them in the first place. They pick and choose gendered meanings and identities; some conform without knowing it, others crossover dramatically, and most do a little of each. Life for these children is one in which they must negotiate new meanings. They not only "do gender" they must "make" it too.

These children are the product of a gender structure in flux. While clearly developing gendered selves, most of them cross gender boundaries even as they subscribe to the folk knowledge—the ruling cognitive images—that define boys and girls as opposites in their own culture. Each time a girl admits she's not like other girls because she likes sports, and each time a boy differentiates himself from boys as a group because he doesn't like to fight, or he does like to babysit, we can see the cognitive image begin to blur. And the children know they are blurring the lines through their own behavior. Eventually, perhaps, with some adult intervention, those childhood cognitive images might crack and dissolve, to be re-created in a post-gender society.

But does this child-rearing approach offer a *viable* threat to the existing social structure? Are these children going to help revolutionize gender meanings? At this point, the answer is no. While parenting styles and philosophies have great impacts on children, these children live in multiple social realms with often conflicting social pressures. Schools, churches, peers, media, and public policies provide children with stereotypical pictures of men and women, and offer rewards for compliance. If children do indeed both act and react to the gendering process, then we must recognize the limit to parental influence, for children live both within and outside of their parent's home.

This is not to say the egalitarian philosophies and behaviors learned by the children at home will be lost forever in a cacophony of injustice. But we need longitudinal data to discover how these children negotiate gender as they grow up. The question remains, of course, what impact such a few children raised in such unusual homes could possibly have on the larger social structure. Still, these are pioneers, chipping away a legacy of patriarchal inequality. As the twig is bent, we can only hope that, as these boys and girls may become men and women, they remain committed to doing it fairly at home, at work, and in political and religious arenas.

Notes

1. Acquiring the label of "deviant" is, of course, a form of punishment in and of itself.
2. All of the parents were heterosexual, and all but one couple were married. The findings would be different if we included gay families. Because we were interested in the ways men and women negotiate and challenge traditional patriarchal arrangements, we focused on heterosexual couples. Gay couples must negoti-

ate these same constraints, but the dynamics are quite different. Future research should include more alternative family arrangements.

3. This rule—while not faithfully representing the family's naming policy—will provide the reader with a better understanding of which husbands and wives, parents and children, are in the same family.

References

Alanen, L. (1988). Rethinking childhood. *Acta Sociologica*, 31, 53–67.

Bandura, A. (1962). Social learning through imitation. In M. Jones (Ed.), *Nebraska symposium on motivation*, volume 10, (pp. 211–274). Lincoln: University of Nebraska Press.

———. (1971). *Psychological modeling: Conflicting theories.* Chicago: Aldine-Atherton.

Bem, S. L. (1993). *The lenses of gender.* New Haven: Yale University Press.

Borman, K. M., and P. O'Reilly. (1987). Learning gender roles in three urban U.S. kindergarten classrooms. *Child and Youth Services*, 8:43–66.

Cahill, S. E. (1987). Language practices and self-definition: The case of gender identity acquisition. *Sociological Quarterly*, 27:295–311.

Coltrane, S. (1996). *Family man: Fatherhood, housework and gender equity.* Oxford: Oxford University Press.

Connell, R. W. (1987). *Gender and power.* Stanford: Stanford University Press.

———. (1992). A very straight gay: Masculinity, homosexual experience, and the dynamics of gender. *American Sociological Review*, 57:735–751.

———. (1995). Masculinities. Berkeley: University of California Press.

Corsaro, W. A. (1985). *Friendship and peer culture in the early years.* Norwood: Ablex Publishing.

Deaux, K. (1984). From individual differences to social categories: Analysis of a decade's research on gender. *American Psychologist*, 39:105–116.

Ehrensaft, D. (1987). *Parenting together. Men and women sharing the care of their children.* New York: Free Press.

Eisenberg, N., S. A. Wolchik, R. Hernandez, and J. F. Pasternack. (1985). Parental socialization of young children's play: A short-term longitudinal study. *Child Development*, 56:1506–1513.

Fagot, B. I., M. D. Leinbach, and C. O'Boyle. (1992). Gender labeling, gender stereotyping, and parenting behaviors. *Developmental Psychology*, 28:225–230.

Feagin, J. R. (1991). The continuing significance of race: Anti-black discrimination in public places. *American Sociological Review*, 56, 101–116.

Giddens, A. (1979). *Central problems in social theory.* Berkeley: University of California Press.

———. (1984). *The constitution of society.* Berkeley, CA: University of California Press.

Hawkins, J. (1985). Computers and girls: Rethinking the issues. *Sex Roles*, 13:165–180.

Hill Collins, P. (1990). *Black feminist thought.* Boston: Unwin Hyman.

Hochschild, A. R. (1989). *The second shift: Working parents and the revolution at home.* New York: Viking.

Hooks, bell. (1995). *Killing rage: Ending racism.* New York: Henry Holt and Company.

Howard, J., B. Risman, M. Romero, and J. Sprague. (1996). *The gender lens book series*. Thousand Oaks, CA: Forge and Sage Publishers.

Hutson, A. H. (1983). Sex-Typing. In E. M. Hetherington and P. H. Mussen (Eds.) *Handbook of child psychology*, volume 4, New York: Wiley.

Inkeles, A. (1968). Society, social structure and child socialization. In J. Clausen (Ed.) *Socialization and society*. Boston: Little, Brown.

Kohlberg, L. (1966). A Cognitive-developmental analysis of children's sex-role concepts and attitudes. In E. E. Maccoby (Ed.) *The development of sex differences*. Stanford: Stanford University Press.

Kohlberg, L., and D. Z. Ullian. (1974). Stages in the development of psychosocial concepts and attitudes. In R. C. Friedman, R. N. Richart, and R. L. Vande Wiele (Eds.) *Sex differences in behavior*. New York: Wiley.

Kreps, G. A., and S. L. Bosworth; with J. A. Mooney, S. T. Russell, and K. A. Myers. (1994). *Organizing, role enactment, and disaster: A structural theory*. Newark: University of Delaware Press.

Lever, J. (1978). Sex differences in the complexity of children's play and games. *American Sociological Review*, 43:471–483.

Lewis, M. (1972). There's no unisex in the nursery. *Psychology Today*, 5:54–57.

Luttrell, W. (1993). The teachers, they all had their pets: Concepts of gender, knowledge and power. *Signs*, 18:505–546.

Maccoby, E. E. (1992). The role of parents in the socialization of children: An historical overview. *Developmental Psychology*, 28:1006–1017.

Marsiglio, W. (1995). *Fatherhood: Contemporary theory, research, and social policy*. Thousand Oaks: Sage.

Martin, C. L. (1993). New directions for investigating children's gender knowledge. *Developmental Review*, 13:184–204.

McIntosh, P. (1992). White privilege and male privilege: A personal account of coming to see correspondences through work in women's studies. In M. Anderson and P. Hill Collins (Eds.) *Race, class and gender: An anthology*. Belmont, CA: Wadsworth.

Merton, R. K. (1948). The self-fulfilling prophesy. *Antioch Review*, 8:193–210.

Parsons, T., and R. Bales. (1955). *Family, socialization and interaction process*. Glencoe: Free Press.

Peterson, G. W., and B. C. Rollins. (1987). Parent-child socialization. In M. Sussman and S. Steinmetz (Eds.) *Handbook of marriage and the family*. New York: Plenum.

Piaget, J. (1932). *The moral judgement of the child*. London: Kegan Paul.

Renzetti, C. M., and D. J. Curran. (1992). *Women, men and society: The sociology of gender*. Boston: Allyn and Bacon.

Risman, B. (Forthcoming). *Gender vertigo: American families in transition*. New Haven: Yale University Press.

Risman, B., and P. Schwartz, (1989). *Gender in intimate relationships: A microstructural approach*. Belmont, CA: Wadsworth.

Rosenthal R., and L. Jacobsen. (1968). *Pygmalion in the classroom: Teacher expectations and pupil's intellectual development*. New York: Holt.

Schwartz, P. (1994). *Peer marriage: How love between equals really works*. New York: Free Press.

Segal, L. (1990). *Slow motion: Changing masculinities, changing men*. New Brunswick: Rutgers University Press.

Signorelli, N. (1990). Children, television, and gender roles. *Journal of Adolescent Health Care*, 11:50–58.

Stern M., and K. H. Karraker. (1989). Sex stereotyping of infants: A review of gender labeling studies. *Sex Roles*, 20:501–522.

Thorne, B. (1993). *Gender play*. New Brunswick: Rutgers University Press.

Vander Zanden, J. W. (1985). *Human development*. New York: Knopf.

West, C., and D. Zimmerman. (1987). Doing gender. *Gender & Society*, 1:125–151.

Wilder, G., D. Mackie, and J. Cooper. (1985). Gender and computers: Two surveys of gender-related attitudes. *Sex Roles*, 13:215–228.

6

Racial Socialization*

Shirley A. Hill

Black folks aren't born expecting segregation, prepared from day one to follow its confining rules. Nobody presents you with a handbook when you're teething and says, "Here's how you must behave as a second-class citizen." Instead, the humiliating expectations and traditions of segregation creep over you, slowly stealing a teaspoonful of your self-esteem each day. . . . By the time I was four years old, I was asking questions neither my mother nor grandmother cared to answer: "Why do white people write 'Colored' on all the ugly drinking fountains, the dingy restrooms, and the back of the buses?"
—Melba Patillo Beals, *Warriors Don't Cry* (1994, p. 136)

One of the most pernicious outcomes of slavery has been an almost intractable denigration of blackness in American society. Although slavery evolved because of the need for a stable, cheap, controllable labor force, its ideological linchpin was the alleged innate inferiority of Africans. Kitano (1991) argues that slavery has been the single most important factor defining the status of African Americans because it classified black people as subhuman in ways that continue to shape race relations. Despite numerous success stories and role models, and a great deal of socioeconomic progress, African Americans as a group are still stigmatized as less intelligent, less attractive, and less capable than white people. This makes child socialization doubly challenging for black parents who, as Billingsley (1968/1988) has pointed out, have always had to teach their children not only how to be human but also how to be black in a white society. That children must be taught the meaning of being black speaks to the socially constructed nature of the meaning of race.

*Reprinted from Shirley A. Hill, *African American Children*, pp. 89–102. Copyright ©1999 by Sage Publications, Inc. Reprinted by permission of Sage Publications.

Racial socialization has been defined as parents' "attempt to prepare their children for the realities of being Black in America" (Taylor et al., 1990, p. 994). These realities are socially defined by parents based on their own personal experiences and their education, income, religious beliefs, and expectations for their children. Most see black-white relations as contentious and white hostility as widespread; for example, nearly 25% believe that most white Americans accept the racial views of the Ku Klux Klan, and nearly half do not believe that blacks will ever achieve social and economic equality with whites (Sigelman & Welch, 1991). As many as two-thirds of blacks feel that they simply do not, as a group, have the same opportunities as whites, and most believe that whites do not want to see them get ahead (Billingsley, 1992, p. 228). These attitudes, and their own personal experiences, underlie the need for racial socialization.

Many of the parents in this study grew up during the civil rights era of the 1960s and 1970s and vividly recall the difficulties they faced with racial integration. Melba Brown, a 35-year-old social worker and mother of two, was among a few blacks selected to be bussed to a predominantly white school in the 1970s, and this experience shapes her constructions of the realities of being black. Her strong religious orientation leads her to teach her children to be tolerant and forgiving of racism. Yet, as was the case with many black parents, her message also conveys a strong underlying racial sentiment: She tells her children that if they are not tolerant, they will "be as bad as some white people are." She draws on her own experiences to show her children that race is an important issue:

> I want them to be aware that they are black in a white world where there are people who may possibly treat you badly just because of that. But when people have a problem, you're not to hold that against them—so we've had those little lectures—to keep their minds open, and not be as bad as some white people are. . . . My racial experiences were real negative. I was one of the first few [blacks] bussed [to a white school]back in the 1970s, and I had some real negative experiences behind it. . . . I was the black girl in the class and then had the audacity to have a brain in my head and how dare me—and I mean I was really treated badly. Some of the stuff that happened to me was life-changing. . . . I had several teachers cheat, lie, lose my work . . . like I said, this is life-changing.

Although many parents like Melba have had negative racial experiences, there are very few who teach children messages of racial hatred. Michael Beard, a 35-year-old sales representative, tries to temper what he describes as the "black militancy" he felt in his earlier years with a more moderate position based on his current Christian orientation:

> Quite naturally, just being the era I grew up in and the stance that I believe—I'm quite pro-Afro American, but when you become a Christian you try to overlook

that . . . a friend used to say that I hate white people, but it's not that I hate white people: I dislike people who dislike me. . . . I can understand how Marcus Garvey felt
when he said, Let's just go back to Africa, because . . . I guess my frame of mind is,
Why can't we have our own stuff? But I think if you use being black as a crutch, it
becomes a crutch. I'm more than the media say that I am. . . . I think if I can instill
in my son some of the values I have, then race really won't make any difference.

Like most parents, Michael sees racism as something that is real but under-
stands that it can also be used as a "crutch" to explain failure. Racial socialization can be a difficult task as parents walk a fine line between telling their
children that racial discrimination and hatred do exist and may well affect the
opportunities that are available to them, while assuring them that they can
overcome these racial barriers with the right attitude and hard work. By engaging in racial socialization, parents are challenging the dominant society's depictions and assessments of black people; as Michael has pointed out, they want to
teach their children that they are "more than the media" say they are.

In this chapter, I examine the racial attitudes of parents that underlie their
efforts to racially socialize their children, specifically whether they think their
children have already been victimized by racial discrimination and how they
think race will affect their children's futures. As we will see, the attitudes of
black and white parents are more divergent on racial issues than on any other
aspect of child rearing. Second, I examine the issue of self-esteem among black
children, specifically the common assumption that racism, negative stereotypes, and poverty result in low self-esteem among blacks. Although my findings are based solely on parental assessments of their children's self-esteem,
they do not support the view of diminished self-esteem among black children.
Finally, included in this chapter is an examination of the racial socialization
messages parents give their children. While the majority of parents see racial-
ethnic socialization as important, most adopt a rather reactive stance in discussing race with their children: They respond to the issue of race after their
children become aware of its significance and start to ask questions. Parents
strive to create a balance between acknowledging the importance of race and
allowing their children to racialize every negative encounter with whites.

Parental Perceptions of Racial Barriers

I asked parents if they felt being a racial minority makes it more difficult to
get a good education and a good job: 45% of black parents felt that being a
racial minority makes it more difficult compared with about 29% of white parents (Table 6.1). Asked whether they felt their child had ever experienced
unfair treatment because of his or her race, white parents (29%) were significantly more likely than black parents (19%) to report unfair treatment based on

Table 6.1

Racial Attitudes of Parents by Race

Questions/Issues	PARENTS BY RACE		BLACK PARENTS BY INCOME LEVEL		BLACK PARENTS BY EDUCATION LEVEL	
	Black (N = 525)	White (N = 204)	Low (N = 201)	High (N = 117)	Less (N = 220)	More (N = 300)
1. Being a racial minority makes it more difficult to get a good education and a good job.						
Agree	45.3	28.9***	36.3	36.8	42.3	47.3
Disagree	50.1	67.6**	51.2	43.6*	51.8	49.0
No response	4.6	3.5	2.5	5.1	5.9	3.7
2. Children are better off being taught by teachers who are of the same race as the child.						
Agree	22.7	10.8***	17.9	30.8***	19.5	24.7**
Disagree	73.0	87.7**	79.1	63.2**	75.5	71.3
No response	4.3	1.5	3.0	6.0	5.0	4.0
3. Has your child experienced unfair treatment because of his or her race?						
Yes	18.6	23.5*	10.1	25.4*	13.1	21.6**
No	79.6	56.4	89.1	71.2	85.4	75.8*
No response	2.2	2.5	.8	3.4	1.5	2.6
4. How will your child's race affect his or her future?						
Will have no impact	52.3	60.8*	61.2	42.2**	58.5	48.4**
Make it more difficult	40.9	6.9***	27.9	55.9***	31.5	46.8**
Make it easier	4.0	13.2***	7.0	1.7	4.6	3.7
No response	2.8	.1	3.9	.2	5.4	1.1

*p < .10; **p < .05; ***p < .01.

Note: Questions/issues 1, 2, and 4 are based on responses from the entire sample. Question/issue 3 is based on responses from a subsample of 323 blacks and 166 whites (N = 489).

race. The higher percentage of white parents reporting racial unfairness no doubt stems from the fact that those in this study were attending predominantly black schools and perceived the exclusion that comes from being a racial minority. Among black parents, both income and education were positively related to having children who experienced unfair racial treatment. Parents earning more than $30,000 per year were more than twice as likely as low-income parents to say their child had experienced racism. High-income parents, because they have more education, are often more sensitive to racism and more confrontational in addressing racial insults.

Asked how they felt race would affect their child's future, 41% of blacks indicated that they thought their child's race would make things more difficult, compared with only 9% of whites. The sex of the focus child shaped parental beliefs about the impact of race on their children's future: The parents of sons (47%) were more likely than the parents of daughters (36%) to say that race would adversely affect their children's future (this information is not shown in the tables). Here again, we find that high-income parents are more aware of the barriers imposed by race than are low-income parents. Low-income parents attribute their status primarily to their own failure to get a better education, and they believe that education will allow their children to succeed despite racism. I asked 22-year-old Shawn Branson, whose 6-year-old daughter is currently in a special education class for slow learners, whether she thought being black would affect her daughter's success:

> No, not really. You just have to be determined, have a goal in life. If you have a goal in life or what you want to do and what you want to become, you can do it. She shouldn't have any problem, especially if she does well in school—that's the most important thing. You have to do well in school, and get a scholarship, or whatever.

More educated and affluent parents doubt that it's quite that simple. They have often experienced career mobility and often hold jobs in racially integrated settings, yet they find that race shapes their acceptance and progress. Their expectation of overcoming racial inequality through success and hard work has not always been realized; in fact, their occupational positions and education heighten their awareness of the gap between striving and achieving, and place them in social environments where they are even more likely to experience rejection or exclusion. They expect their children will also be achievers but feel that race will still make it more difficult.

Education and Racial Integration

Because African American parents believe strongly in the importance of education, the racial integration of schools was once held by many civil rights activists to be the key to economic mobility, social inclusion, and the end of racial stereotypes. Efforts to integrate schools, however, have never been completely successful: In 1988, nearly two-thirds of blacks attended schools where the majority of the students were nonwhite (Armor, 1992). Moreover, while the majority of blacks still firmly support racial integration, a significant minority have reconsidered the value of a racially integrated society, especially in terms of education. After three decades of efforts toward racial integration, which have included notable victories and failures, blacks are beginning to assess what they have lost in their efforts to become a part of mainstream society. In terms of education, it is common to hear blacks express the belief that white teachers and schools care very little about the education and well-being of their children, and that the lack of a common cultural background impedes the ability of teachers to understand or teach children. In a recent study, Wilkinson (1996) suggested that racial integration has been harmful for many black children. She argues that although the U.S. Supreme Court was correct to argue in 1954 that separate racial facilities are inherently unequal, forced integration and bussing have been psychologically and culturally destructive for African American children.

One result of this disenchantment has been the growth of independent black schools in urban areas, which differ from traditional schools in that African American culture and history are the bases of the curriculum. In her study of the impact of an Afrocentric transformation on the choice of a black school, Shujaa (1992) quotes one mother as saying:

> I want my son to have a very positive self-concept about himself and about Black people in general and what they can do. And I think to give him that positive self-image for him to be around Black professionals, to be around Black students and see that achievement is, indeed, possible. So, because I believe that, I live in a Black community, I work with community organizations . . . I shop in a Black community. I don't go across town because I believe that by supporting our community we make it strong and I want that positive self-image to also be fostered in my son. So, I chose a Black school. In fact, I never considered going to a White school. (p. 155)

In my study, I asked parents whether they thought children were better off being taught by a teacher who was the same race as the child: 23% of black parents felt that their children would be better off with a black teacher, with low-income parents less likely to support this view than high-income parents (see Table 6.1). Afrocentric schools are now becoming an option in the school districts of the parents in this study, yet only one mother indicated that her child had attended such a school. Asked about the racial socialization of her child, Candy Corbin, a low-income single mother of a 6-year-old, said,

> Well, he goes to an African-centered school . . . so Black pride and African pride is one of the things that they teach there, but we don't blow it all out of proportion.

[*Why did you choose this school?*] Well, it was chosen for me. It wasn't the first thing on my list . . . but when I found out what kind of school it was, I thought it might be interesting. I went to one of the programs, and was interested to see that they pray before their programs. They sing songs of worship. . . . They have a good principal, and you can see she's very cultural. And she teaches them to be proud of being Black. I want him to be proud, but I don't want him to be overwhelmed with that every day . . . just be a good boy.

Despite the concerns of a significant minority of parents, most blacks are still in favor of an integrated education (Billingsley, 1992). Toni Cason, for example, rejects the idea of a racially segregated school for her 13-year-old daughter, Taylor. Because we live in a racially integrated society, she thinks it's important to learn to deal with other races throughout one's education. She teaches her daughter about race by telling her

to respect herself but not to exclude [segregate]herself from other races. That's one of the reasons she's going to the school she goes to—there are a lot of different races who go there. I want her to know who she is, and her history, but I want her to also be able to deal with people of other races. She went to a predominantly black junior high . . . and I didn't care for that too much. Because what happens when you grow up in a black neighborhood, and go to a black grade school, junior high school, high school, college—then you hit the workforce, and you really don't know how to deal with them [whites], and they don't know how to deal with you.

Self-Esteem

The historical denigration of blackness in American society and the conviction among parents that their children will encounter racial discrimination, hostility, and rejection links the emphasis on racial socialization to the issue of self-esteem. Most parents agree that it is extremely important for their children to develop a positive self-concept, and it has conventionally been held that racism, negative stereotypes, segregation, and poverty all have a corrosive effect on the self-esteem of black children. Early researchers uniformly reported that these factors had damaged the self-concepts of black children, diminishing their sense of value and worth and even leading to self-hatred.

In 1940, Davis and Dollard examined the impact of race and racism on the personality development of southern black adolescents. They found stereotypes of black people as lazy, childlike, criminal, sexually promiscuous, and unfit for most employment firmly intact nearly a century after slavery had ended. Low self-esteem and self-hatred were common among the children they studied. A similar study by Kardiner and Ovesey (1951) also argued that the self-concept was shaped by the social conditions of one's life. They concluded that slavery, the destruction of the African culture and the black family, along with the idealization of whiteness, had taken a devastating toll on the self-esteem of children.

Much of the evidence for the self-hatred hypothesis rested on the assumption that black people had actually internalized the dominant value system to the extent that they preferred whiteness to blackness. Black parents were described as greatly concerned about the skin color and hair texture of their children. Davis and Dollard found that special advantages and status were often conferred on children with light skin and relatively straight hair. Such children were more likely to have their basic material needs of food, clothing, and shelter met—especially when having light skin was the result of having a white father. Although these fathers rarely openly acknowledged their black offspring, they did often provide them with some privileges and resources, especially when they had an ongoing relationship with their mothers. Light skin also meant higher social status and a greater opportunity for mobility through class barriers (Kardiner & Ovesey, 1951, p. 2).

The best known early research on racial identity among young black children was conducted by Kenneth and Mamie Clark (1939, 1947) in the late 1930s and 1940s. They presented 253 black children between the ages of 3 and 7 with a white doll and a colored doll, and asked the children a series of questions about the dolls. Most of the children could identify their own race and the race of each doll, but having to identify themselves as black elicited extreme negative emotions in some children who, according to the Clarks, sometimes left the testing room in tears. The majority of black children preferred to play with the white doll and, perhaps even more distressing, explained their preference by saying that the white doll was prettier and nicer. These studies were used to document the detrimental impact of racial segregation on the self-identity and self-esteem of black children, and they seemed to be supported in the writings and experiences of blacks who grew up during the pre-civil rights era. Studies supporting the devastating impact of segregation on the self-esteem of blacks were crucial in abolishing de jure racial segregation in schools in the *Brown v. Board of Education of Topeka* decision of 1954. Of interest, however, the Clarks also discovered a regional difference in the responses of children: Those from southern racially segregated schools were less likely than those from the northern region to show a preference for the white doll.

Theorizing About Self-Esteem

According to social theorists, the self-concept develops as children learn to distinguish themselves from others with whom they interact and incorporate the values, attitudes, and expectations of others into their personalities. Self-esteem, the more evaluative component of the self-concept, is based on feelings of competence, worth, and self-approval. It consists of either a positive or a negative attitude toward the self, with a negative self-attitude implying self-rejection and self-dissatisfaction (Rosenberg, 1965). Charles Horton Cooley's (1902/1964) concept of the looking-glass self captures both the interpretive and the evaluative aspects of self-concept formation. He explains that the self is socially constructed based on one's imagination of his or her appearance to others and of the evaluations others are making about that appearance. Self-esteem, one's estimation of one's value and worth, derives from the role-taking process in which others are used as mirrors and their appraisals are internalized. As a result, young children are typically capable of describing themselves as attractive, popular, academically talented, or well loved.

Social psychologists view the self-concept primarily as a product of early socialization within the family. Given that the self is created at an early age, special significance is placed on the evaluations of significant others, such as family members and reference group members, who interact intensively with children during the early years. Thus, the impact of families and other primary groups is implicitly seen as more important than larger social structural factors that come into play later. As Meltzer, Petras, and Reynolds (1975) explain,

> Social experiences, as mediated through the early social groups, the primary groups, begin to shape the child into a moral entity and give a particular direction to the development of the self-concept. While there are certain overriding expectations, patterns of behaviors, values, etc. which are dictated by the society at large, their influence upon the individual is, for the most part, tempered by the early social and primary groups. (p. 13)

Parents and other family members do play a vital role in the development of a child's self-concept. Being reared in a loving, nurturing family where one receives attention and emotional support is important for developing a positive self-concept. Studies of school age children have found that those with high esteem had more verbal communication with parents than others, and perceived that communication to be positive (Enger, Howerton, & Cobbs, 1994). Joseph (1994) emphasizes the value of spending quality time with children, as attentive listening and personal interest are effective ways to say to children that they are important and valuable. Positive self-esteem is related to accepting responsibility for what happens in life rather than feeling that events happen by chance (Enger et al., 1994). Parenting styles that foster success in other areas of life also enhance the self-esteem of children. Steinberg (1992) has pointed out that regardless of race, age, or social class, parental warmth, strict supervision, and allowing psychological autonomy tend to foster confidence and success.

Although most black parents rank their children's happiness and self-esteem as their number one value (see Chapter 3), they vary in their ability to instill a positive self-concept in their children. The majority of black children grow up in families where they are loved and the center of a great deal of attention from their parents and extended family. A significant minority, however, live with poor parents who are socially isolated, depressed, and often unable to attend to the emotional needs of their children. Young teenage parents often lack parenting skills and do not understand the importance of talking and interacting with their children; rather, they invest their meager resources in material things in an effort to please their children.

Children's self-perceptions are also influenced by the larger social environment as children eventually learn to see and evaluate themselves from the perspectives and standards of the "generalized other," or the community. Thus, we judge and compare ourselves with others in the broader society, and it is in that society that we expect to receive affirmation. Coopersmith (1967, p. 37) concurs that although self-esteem is shaped primarily by the respect and acceptance we receive from significant others, it is secondarily affected by our status, position, and success in the world. Recent research has found that self-esteem is diminished among those who physically do not fit society's cultural ideal (Brenner & Hinsdale, 1978; Hendry & Gullies, 1978) and those who live in environments where they are different (e.g., in terms of race or class) from the majority group. Low self-esteem has also been found to lessen academic success and achievement (Harter, 1987) and may be related to crime, drug abuse, and adolescent pregnancy (Berns, 1993).

There are at least three reasons to assume that racial minority children will have lower self-esteem than majority children, according to Rosenberg and Kaplan (1982, p. 212). One is the idea of reflected appraisals, the tendency to see ourselves from others' point of view. While parents labor to instill in their children ethnic pride, their children also see that African Americans occupy the low-status position in virtually every arena of the larger society. They also note that blacks are often not adequately represented in the media, schools, or other nonfamily institutions and are often negatively stereotyped. Second is the social comparison principle, in which we compare ourselves with others. Black children not only have much higher rates of poverty than white children, they are more likely to live in families that are stigmatized as dysfunctional and in communities with high rates of crime and drug dependency. These factors contradict parental messages that they are "just as good as anybody else." Finally, Rosenberg and Kaplan discuss the self-attribution principle, which holds that we evaluate ourselves on the basis of behavioral outcomes. Black children often see themselves as not performing as well as whites in certain arenas, such as school.

Challenging Definitions of Blackness

Theories of how the self is socially constructed, the second-class citizenship of blacks in the United States, and the plight of many low-income African Americans make the notion of diminished self-esteem among black children seem plausible. Yet there is a great deal of evidence that black people have consistently rejected messages of racial inferiority. Racial socialization dates as far back as slavery when black parents, according to Blassingame (1972), tried to "cushion the shock of bondage" for their children and "give them a referent for self-esteem other than their master" (p. 79). Early research by Davis and Dollard found that the behavior of black people refuted the dogma of black docility and acceptance of racist norms; rather, blacks often defended themselves against the indignities of second-class citizenship, even when the penalty for doing so was high.

Black Americans have historically struggled to define and defend themselves, to validate their cultural heritage and family experiences, and to instill pride and positive self-esteem in their children. Historical research shows that although families could not always prevent verbal and physical assaults on their children, they could provide them with the inner resources needed to fight against racism. Gordon Parks (1992), a well-known writer, movie director, and photographer, described his experiences as a young teenager growing up in Kansas in the early 1900s:

> Our parents had filled us with love and a staunch Methodist religion. We were poor, though I did not know it at the time; the rich soil surrounding our clapboard house had yielded the food for the family. And the love of this family had eased the burden of being black. But there were segregated schools and warnings to avoid white neighborhoods after dark. I always had to sit in the peanut gallery (the Negro section) at the movies. We weren't allowed to drink soda in the drugstore in town. I was stoned and beaten and called "nigger," "black boy," "darky," "shine." These indignities came so often I began to accept them as normal. *Yet I always fought back.* (p. 26, italics added)

Fighting back has been a common response of blacks since the institutionalization of slavery. By the early twentieth century, this resistance was taking the form of northward migration and black nationalism. Marcus Garvey organized the largest black nationalist movement in history, with an emphasis on taking blacks back to Africa. According to Pinkney (1993), Garvey also emphasized "pride in blackness, racial solidarity, and respect for the African heritage of black people" (p. 217). The ideology of black nationalism was also emphasized again during the 1960s by Malcolm X, the Black Muslims, and the Black Panthers. More mainstream efforts to challenge the negative portrayals of African Americans came from civil rights leaders and the black popular culture, such as leading black crowds to chant, "I am somebody." The widespread cultural endorsement of the value of black people, a growing emphasis on black pride, and the initiation of black studies programs no doubt elevated the self-esteem of many African Americans. The civil rights movement and racial integration expanded opportunities available to black people and helped parents talk with their children more openly and positively about issues of race.

This emphasis on racial-ethnic pride in the broader culture during the 1960s coincided with a greater emphasis on racial socialization in families. Racial socialization, defined as giving children positive messages about being black and coping with racism, is more common today than in the past: About two-thirds of black parents racially socialize their children but only about 50% of parents say they were racially socialized by their own parents (Billingsley, 1992). Educated and middle-class black parents, perhaps because they live and work in settings that require more racially integrated social interactions, and expect that their children will do the same, are more likely than other parents to focus on racial socialization (Taylor et al., 1990). Marshall (1995) found that nearly 90% of middle-income parents felt that ethnicity was important in raising their children.

Racial Socialization Messages

Studies of racial socialization messages have identified several major themes, which often vary based on parents' own socialization experiences, socioeconomic status, and integration into the mainstream society (Demo & Hughes, 1990). Parents usually teach their children about racism—that they should expect it and learn to cope with it—and they try to instill in their children messages of self-acceptance, racial pride, and racial solidarity. Racial socialization also includes the growing emphasis among African Americans on teaching children about their heritage and history (Billingsley, 1992; Thornton et al., 1990). Bowman and Howard (1985) found that parents emphasized ethnic pride, self-development, awareness of racial barriers, or egalitarianism. Some parents involve their children in distinctively African American cultural events, such as Kwanza, an African American Christmas tradition, or the Juneteenth celebration, which commemorates the end of slavery. Billingsley (1992) found that racial socialization is often expressed in terms of teaching children African languages and supporting black businesses. Racial socialization themes often resonate with the dominant societal ideology of success, although the underlying message is one of overcoming racism. For example, Thornton and associates (1990) found that hard work and a good education were the most common messages. More broadly, the ideology of success is combined with ideals of morality: Marshall (1995) cites studies showing that parental emphasis on education, hard work, humanism, religiosity, and equality are all part of their racial socialization messages. Bowman and Howard (1985) pointed out that the sex of the child may influence racial socialization messages: Parents are more likely to emphasize racial barriers with their sons but to emphasize racial pride and commitment with daughters.

My study concurs with earlier research in finding that the majority of parents believe race is important and say that they discuss it with their children. Yet parents do not focus inordinately on it; few, for example, select in advance a specific racial script to share with their children or a particular appropriate age frame. Rather, they tend to wait until their children become aware of racial issues and then they provide age-appropriate information. In the meantime, they simply make sure that their children are exposed to environments that emphasize the importance of black people, especially successful role models. Considering his previous self-professed "militancy" on the issue of race, I asked Michael Beard what he was teaching his 11-year-old son about race:

> I really don't come out and teach him anything about race . . . he's seen movies like *Malcolm X*, he knows about Martin Luther King and some of his stances, so I try not to preprogram him at this juncture. The thing that I found is that you have to deal with each person as an individual. So if I instill anything in him, it would be to evaluate each person based on their receptivity to you.

Similarly, Mary Haney emphasizes creating and participating in environments where the achievements and diversity of blacks are highlighted:

> When it's time to get books, I try to get books about blacks. And if they're not about blacks, they have pictures of blacks in them, okay. At church we do black history month programs, and at the day care center—that's when he really started—they just go through the whole thing, "Black Americans are thinkers, Black Americans are nonthinkers." That's why I really loved the day care . . . and we always kept him out of school for Martin Luther King's birthday. We explained who King was, a famous black American, and that this is a holiday for us, and so he could stay home and celebrate his birthday with us.

Parents believe that children learn about racial differences in school, and they then try to address the questions their children bring home. Yadira Bright, mother of three children, said,

> I think race is taught to kids because it never became a factor until they went to school. The only time I talk to them about it is if they have a problem. I try not to make it a big deal—I want them to be proud of who they are—that's why I have black pictures in my house—I want them to be proud. I don't want them to feel that because they're black, they're bad. . . . But it's not something that's discussed often.

As mothers address the concerns their children have about race, many of which stem from contact with white students, it becomes apparent that children are learning about the preference given to whites in American society. Another mother said,

> We talk often about race, ever since he started school. He would come home and describe children by their color—everybody was brown or pink or white. He didn't know it was a different race at that time, but soon he started focusing on white and black. He'd ask why all the kids in a commercial were white, and they show only one black. He'd say they ought to show more blacks. He asks a lot of questions about why things are the way they are. . . . He's gotten now when he colors pictures, he makes all the faces brown, even Raggedy Ann and Andy. And he asked why Jesus was [white] and if you colored him brown, would that be wrong, and I told him it wasn't wrong. If it made him feel okay, do it.

As parents acknowledge to their children that racism and racial barriers exist, they face the risk of having their children explain their own problems and failures in terms of race. Thus, parents often challenge their children's tendency to racialize every event. Practically speaking, they teach their children to accept responsibility for their own behaviors rather than using racism as a ready excuse:

> [My son] had a problem at school, and the first thing he said was that they [the teachers] only agreed with the girl because she's white and he's black. But I had to talk to him and make him understand that sometimes that's easy to say but sometimes it's a cop-out, that not everything is black and white. If you're wrong, you're wrong; if she's wrong, she's wrong. They have black and white friends. I'm not real radical about black power, or whatever, but I want them to have pride in who they are.

Carrie Gaines, mother of 13-year-old Tiera, said,

> She's quick to do a thing, and then say that the other person doesn't like her because she's black. So I have to get the whole story to know if she's telling the truth or if she's just using race to get out of trouble for mouthing off.

At the same time, parents teach their children that in a predominantly white society, it is likely that they are going to have to learn to accept white authority. One black mother, teaching her daughter how to survive in the "real world," suggested that blacks are and will always be in a subordinate position:

> I tell her that she has to learn . . . that white people are going to be here, wherever she goes, and they're *always* going to tell her what to do. No matter what, there is always going to be some white person telling you what to do, and 9 times out of 10 you're going to have to do it, and do it with the right attitude.

Racial socialization for many black parents, as indicated earlier, means work-ing hard and getting a good education. Although parents understand the impor-tance of race and want their children to learn about their own history and heritage, they primarily want their children to prepare themselves for success by getting a good education. Paula Jackson, mother of 12-year-old Manual, pointed out,

> I like for children to know their culture, as far as their roots, our history, but I don't want them to dwell on that. . . . I know prejudice is out there, and I told the children that prejudice is out there, but don't use prejudice as an excuse. I try to teach my kids how to react, and to react, you need to be prepared, to have some kind of ammuni-tion. And that's where their education comes in, to have something to go forward with. If you get your proper education, and you get real good at what you want to do, and pray—I really do believe they should have a good spiritual base—the doors will open for them. So don't use prejudice as an excuse.

Many parents feel faith in God can help overcome racial barriers. They want their children to know they can succeed if they combine hard work and faith in God:

> I'm trying to teach him work ethics, how he can mesh being a God-fearing child, a Christian, with some of these other things he wants to be. . . . So I'm trying to instill in him that if he puts God first, he can be whatever he wants to be. That not every-thing is going to come easy, that there are some things you have to work hard for. And things that come easier often really aren't worth anything. So those things that you work hard for, those are the things that you appreciate more.

Redefining Physical Attractiveness

Recent years have witnessed a resurgence in the issue of skin color as the basis of self-esteem. Reddy (1994) has argued that colorism, an aspect of racism, is still powerful among both blacks and whites in American culture, where light skin, straight hair, and European features are the standards for beauty. This colorism dates back to slavery, when light-skinned blacks were often given greater privileges than dark-skinned blacks. Creating divisions among people of color is a common strategy for domination and social control; in fact, due to widespread colonialization by Europeans, light skin is almost uni-versally accepted as superior to dark skin. Black Americans have often inter-nalized these European standards of beauty and tried to imitate white Ameri-cans. In 1965, Clark argued that hair straighteners and skin bleaches were evidence that blacks had come to accept their own inferiority; in fact, he argued that "few if any Negroes ever fully lose that sense of shame and self-hatred" (p. 65). A recent study by Robinson and Ward (1995) of African American adolescents found that a relationship existed between satisfaction with skin color and self-esteem. They concluded that students described as either "lighter" or "darker" in skin color were less satisfied that those who were in between. bell hooks (1992) speaks of being "painfully reminded" of the skin color/hair texture issue while visiting friends on a once colonized black island:

> Their little girl is just reaching that stage of preadolescent life where we become obsessed with our image, with how we look and how others see us. Her skin is dark. Her hair is chemically straightened. Not only is she fundamentally convinced that straightened hair is more beautiful than curly, kinky, natural hair, she believes that lighter skin makes one more worthy, more valuable in the eyes of others. (p. 3)

Racial socialization includes black parents' effort to help children redefine beauty, or at least question why they consider the characteristics of Europeans to be more physically attractive than those of blacks. Darrick Donaldson, father of 7-year-old Eric, said,

> He's just beginning to notice racial differences. We try to focus on the positive, point out black role models, blacks who are achieving. We did the test where you have two dolls, one black and one white, and ask the child which is the prettiest. He chose the white one, so we talked about that.

Given the common designations of races by skin color, children often have some difficulty identifying themselves as black, as few people are literally black or white, and the skin tones of blacks are especially varied. Blacks co-opted the once-derogatory label of "black" and imbued it with pride, yet young children do not so easily embrace the label. Asked what she told her 13-year-old daughter, Jazmine, about race, Sharon Booker said,

> I don't make it [talking about race] a regular thing; just occasionally. She used to not like being black, or at least she always thought she was white. I had to go to great lengths to convince her that she was not white. [*Why did she think she was white?*] I think because when she started school she had white instructors, and there were only a few black kids, but for some reason she decided she was white. I had to convince her that she was a black kid, just light-complexioned.

Hair texture is another concern among African American children. Sherry Davis talked about her 7-year-old son's sudden interest in having hair that was like that of the white children, although he was going to a predominantly black school:

> He started with his hair—he wanted his hair to be curly . . . in big curls, and I told him we could go get a kit for him to make it curly. So I told him if that makes him feel better about himself, I'm all for it. But I told him I wanted to let him know that however his hair looked, I still loved him and he was still beautiful. But he said it would make him feel good, so he wanted his hair to grow so it could be curled.

Laura Raymond's 13-year-old son also worries a lot about his overall appearance—a situation not uncommon among adolescents—but he is especially preoccupied with his hair:

> His cousin has this humongous wave thing in his head [hair] and so my son begged me to get [the same thing]. . . . I told him his hair wasn't horrible. I said, " . . . Your hair is beautiful; you have Black hair. There's nothing wrong with your hair that a haircut won't cure." But he kept begging me and begging me, so I finally put it [a hair straightener] in there. . . . But I try to make him realize that whatever features he has, he's black. And I'm black, his daddy's black, his sister's black, his family's black, and to be proud of that.

Self-Esteem Revisited

The common contention that black children have poor self-esteem was challenged during the 1960s. Despite racism, discrimination, and the fact that African Americans as a group occupy low positions in most institutions, it is quite difficult to determine whether race diminishes the self-esteem of black children. In their 1982 overview of self-concept research, Porter and Washington describe the theories of the 1950s and early 1960s as the "mark of oppression" approach, where blacks were "assumed to internalize negative racial images of themselves with a devastating effect on comprehensive self-esteem" (p. 225). They noted, however, that actual research findings on self-esteem are quite mixed.

Some argue that black children's self-esteem has never been adequately measured, and that the self-esteem of black children is as high or higher than that of white children (Crain, 1996; Cross, 1985; McAdoo, 1983; Staples & Johnson, 1993; Whaley, 1993). Cross (1985) has been especially influential in analyzing the black self-hatred hypothesis generated by the doll studies conducted by the Clarks. According to Cross, these studies were not direct measures of self-worth, as racial group preference is not a proxy for self-identity. Black children are more likely than whites to grow up in a multicultural society, to be exposed to both white and black dolls, and to be more accepting of both. In a review of more than 100 studies conducted between 1939 and 1977, Cross noted that most (72%) reported black self-esteem to be equal to or higher than white self-esteem. McAdoo (1985) also rejected the notion involved in the self-hatred hypothesis among young black children:

> These children felt that they were competent and valued individuals and believed that they were perceived positively by their mothers. They felt that they were as highly regarded by their teachers. These findings of positive feelings of self-worth . . . cause one to question the commonly held view of a lower value that minority children place upon themselves because of the negative messages communicated to them in the environment. (pp. 238–239)

The interviews conducted for this study also found little evidence of children with low self-esteem, at least based on the views of their parents. Parents over-whelmingly felt their children had high levels of self-esteem, although they worried about certain aspects of their self-esteem, such as satisfaction with their personal appearance or shyness. They did, however, link positive self-esteem with their children's accomplishments. I asked Sherry Davis how her 7-year-old son Harry felt about himself:

> I think he feels pretty good about himself. He says that he's smart, and he asks about getting good grades—[asking] does he have to get all As. But he likes school, he thinks he's a good person. I asked him if he knows I love him, and he said, "Yes," so he knows everybody loves him. I don't think he has any problem with self-esteem. His school performance is excellent.

Speaking of his 9-year-old son, Deitrich, Norman Rodney notes that he does very well in school and was one of a few students chosen to participate in an expanded class including fourth through sixth graders:

> He's very creative and inquisitive—he likes to know what's going on and why did things happen. He's a pretty intelligent young man. He thinks very highly of him-self when he accomplishes things. He likes to show off what he does. He has good self-esteem, very high.

Similarly, Kim Cole described her 11-year-old son, Van, as

> creative and competitive; he has a quick temper, cooperates most of the time, and performs well in school. He seems to have a high level of self-esteem, I guess you would call a big ego—I forgot to mention too he has a very sharp sense of humor; he's very witty. . . . He's very artistic, too, and he can take things he's never seen and figure out how to use them or do something interesting with them.

The relationship between race and self-esteem continues to be controversial. Although some researchers have rejected the view of low self-esteem among black children, others continue to see this as an important issue. For example, the belief that black children have high levels of self-esteem is contradicted by psychologists Powell-Hopson and Hopson (1990) in their replication of the self-esteem research done by the Clarks in the 1940s. These researchers found that, nearly 40 years later, 65% of black children chose a white doll instead of a black one (compared with 67% in the Clark study), with 76% say-ing that the black dolls "looked bad" to them. Black children continue to live in a world where blackness is disparaged in the toy and game market (Wilkin-son, 1974) as well as the media. Powell-Hopson and Hopson suggest that the words parents' offer to build positive self-esteem in their children may be inadequate to overcome dominant cultural messages. Their research raises the question of whether teaching children to verbally affirm pride in their race translates into high self-esteem, as noted by Arthur Dozier:

> Authority, beauty, goodness, and power most often have a white face. Most of the heros, from He-man to Rambo, are white. In the '60s we were naive, too, in thinking that saying "Black is Beautiful" was enough. The change has to permeate society. (Powell-Hopson & Hopson, 1990, p. xx)

Many studies of self-esteem are, in fact, seriously flawed. For example, age, gender, and social class are rarely considered to be important factors in the development of black children's self-esteem. As is the case in studying other aspects of African American life, black children are viewed as a monolithic, undifferentiated group. Many studies focus on young children and assess whether they feel good about themselves and loved by others. Yet research shows that young children often lack a distinctive view of themselves (Whaley, 1993), and that they tend to make finer distinctions in how they view themselves as they grow older (Pallas, Entwisle, Alexander, & Weinstein, 1990). Research by Branch and Newcombe (1986) found that older children were significantly more pro-black and anti-white in the multiple choice doll test.

Gender norms also shape children's appraisals of their self-esteem. Because of a cultural emphasis on gender-appropriate behavior, boys and girls tend to evaluate themselves on the basis of different criteria as they grow older: Boys tend to emphasize their athletic abilities, and girls, their appearance (Pallas et al., 1990). In assessing the self-esteem of black children from northern and southern regions of the country, McAdoo (1985) found that boys initially had higher levels of self-esteem than girls, although boys in the South lost this advantage over time.

Research rarely examines intragroup variability or the impact of social context. For example, social class affects self-concept: McAdoo (1983) reported that upper-middle-income children felt more positive about themselves than did low-income children, while Crain (1996) suggested that social class is an even more powerful predictor of self-concept than is race. Pallas and associates (1990) found that advantaged children gave themselves higher evaluations in terms of academics and character than did less advantaged children.

Finally, it appears that a host of psychological and behavioral characteristics are indicative of having positive self-esteem. Yet self-esteem is rarely measured in terms of black children's sense of mastery, competence, self-control, or aspirations, and the studies that exist are contradictory. For example, blacks often appear to have high self-esteem but rank low on feelings of self-efficacy and adequacy, control over their environment, and satisfaction with life (Porter & Washington, 1982), all of which are important components of esteem and of feeling like a worthwhile and productive person. Crain (1996) pointed out that black students tend to have higher global self-concepts than other racial groups, but significant dimensions of the self-concept are often not measured. A study by Walter Allen (1981), comparing black and white male adolescents between the ages of 14 and 18, also raises doubts about the connection between self-esteem and more tangible attitudinal and behavioral characteristics. He found that while black sons had higher educational expectations than did white sons, they had lower self-esteem, a lower academic self-concept, and significantly lower occupational expectations. Expressing pride in being black and embracing the African-oriented cultural styles do not necessarily translate into a sense of self-confidence, mastery, or achievement.

Despite the recent research on racial socialization, few studies have assessed the impact of changing racial beliefs and racial socialization on children. The assumption is that racial socialization benefits children by fostering a positive ethnic identity and teaching them to cope with the stress of racism and rejection. In fact, examining the consequences of racial socialization in itself is extremely difficult, especially given the diversity of racial socialization messages and differences in the extent to which parents emphasize race. Demo and Hughes (1990) found that blacks who said they were racially socialized during childhood, compared with those who were not, had stronger feelings of closeness to other blacks, more concern over black issues, and a stronger commitment to black separatism.

Bowman and Howard (1985) examined the effects of racial socialization on adolescents and young adults in three-generation families. They found that making children aware of racial barriers led to a greater sense of personal efficacy, better academic performance, and higher levels of motivation. Racial socialization may make children less reactive to racial insults and derogatory remarks: Phinney and Chavira (1995) found that the children of parents who had discussed racial discrimination were more likely than other children to ignore incidents of prejudice and less likely to use verbal retorts. In a study of ethnic socialization among middle-income African American parents with children who attended predominantly white schools, Marshall (1995) found that ethnic socialization was actually predictive of lower classroom grades, although the issue of directionality is unclear. Overall, there is much work to be done in assessing self-esteem among black children, delineating the multiple variables that affect it, and determining the role played by racial socialization in the construction of the self.

Conclusions

In this chapter, I have expanded on current research on two important issues: racial socialization and self-esteem. I argue that although the concept of racial socialization is relatively new, black parents have always racially socialized their children. In the past, those messages included teaching the customs and racial dissimulation required of blacks for survival in a racial caste system, but today racial socialization more commonly refers to teaching pride and self-acceptance. Although quantitative studies typically report that about two-thirds of black parents engage in racial socialization (Billingsley, 1992), I would argue that racial socialization is nearly universal among black parents, who can scarcely escape talking about racism and racial pride and who engage in myriad subtle strategies to challenge the denigration of blackness. At the same time, I point out that black parent-child relations are not consumed with the issue of race, and that black parents rarely make precise plans about when and what they will tell their children about race. I describe how the racial socialization messages grow out of parents' own experiences and the broader cultural images of black-white relations, and how they support black pride, the dominant society's ideology of success, and themes of morality. I also relate racial socialization to changing self-concepts, a seemingly obvious but rarely explored connection. Much research work still needs to be done to understand the complex nature of self-esteem among black children, especially how it varies based on age, race, and social class. My personal observations and research lead me to conclude that black children do typically have a positive global self-esteem; indeed, black children are often explicitly taught to accept blackness and *say* that they are proud of their race and of themselves. A much deeper and enduring sense of esteem, however, must be linked to real achievements. In this study, blacks who were most confident of their children's positive self-esteem were quick to enumerate their success experiences. In the next chapter, I explore how gender affects child rearing.

References

Allen, W. R. 1981. "Moms, Dads, and Boys: Race and Sex Differences in the Socialization of Male Children." pp. 99–114 in L. E. Gary (ed.) *Black Men.* Beverly Hills, CA: Sage.

Beals, M. 1994. *Warriors Don't Cry: A Searing Memoir of the Battle to Integrate Little Rock's Central High.* New York: Pocket Books.

Berns, R. M. 1993. *Child, Family, Community: Socialization and Support.* (3rd ed.) Fort Worth, TX: Harcourt, Brace, Jovanovich.

Billingsley, A. 1992. *Climbing Jacob's Ladder: The Enduring Legacy of African American Families.* New York: Simon and Schuster.

Blassingame, J. W. 1972. *The Slave Community: Plantation Life in the Antebellum South*. New York: Oxford University Press.

Bowman, P. J. and Howard, C. 1985. "Race-Related Socialization, Motivation and Academic Achievement: A Study of Black Youths in Three-Generation Families." *Journal of the American Academy of Child Psychiatry*, 24:134–41.

Branch, C. W. and Newcombe, N. 1986. "Racial Attitude Development among Young Black Children as a Function of Parental Attitude: A Longitudinal and Cross-Sectional Study." *Child Development*, 57:712–21.

Brenner, D. and Hinsdale, G. 1978. "Body-build stereotypes and Self-Identification in Three Age Groups of Females." *Adolescence*, 13:551–61.

Clark, K. B. and Clark, M. P. 1959. "The Development of Consciousness of Self and the Emergence of Racial Identification in Negro Preschool Children." *Journal of Social Psychology*, 10:591–9.

Clark, K. B. and Clark, M. P. 1947. "Racial Identification and Preference in Negro Children." Pp. 169–78 in Committee on the Teaching of Social Psychology (ed.) *Readings in Social Psychology*. New York: Holt.

Cooley, C. H. 1964. *Human Nature and the Social Order*. New York: Schocken. (Original work published 1902.)

Coopersmith, S. *The Antecedents of Self-Esteem*. San Francisco: Freeman.

Crain, M. R. 1996. "The Influence of Age, Race, and Gender on Child and Adolescent Multidimensional Self-Concept.: Pp. 395–421 in B. A. Bracken (ed.) *Handbook of Self-Concept: Developmental. Social, and Clinical Considerations*. New York: John Wiley.

Cross, W. E. 1985. "Black Identity: Rediscovering the Distinction between Personal Identity and Reference Group Orientation." Pp. 155–71 in M. B. Spencer, G. Kearse-Brookins, and W. R. Allen (eds.) *Beginnings: The Social and Affective Development of Black Children*. Hillsdale, NJ: Lawrence Erlbaum.

Davis, A. and Dollard, J. 1940. *Children of Bondage: The Personality Development of Negro Youth in the Urban South*. New York: Harper and Row.

Demo, D. and Hughes, M. 1990. "Socialization and Racial Identity among Black Americans." *Social Psychology Quarterly*, 53(4):364–74.

Enger, J. M., Howerton, D. L. and Cobbs, C. R. 1994. Internal/External Locus of Control, Self-Esteem, and Parental Verbal Interaction of At-Risk Black Male Adolescents." *Journal of Social Psychology*, 134(3):269–74.

Harter, S. 1987. "The Determinants and Mediational Role of Global Self-Worth in Children." In N. Eisenberg (ed.) *Contemporary Topics in Developmental Psychology*. New York: John Wiley.

Hendry, L. B. and Gullies, P. 1978. "Body Type, Body Esteem, School, and Leisure: A Study of Overweight, Average, and Underweight Adolescents." *Journal of Youth and Adolescence*, 7:181–95.

Joseh, J. M. 1994. *The Resilient child: Preparing Today's Youth for Tomorrow's World*. New York: Plenum.

Kardiner, A. and Ovesey, L. 1951. *The Mark of Oppression: Explorations in the Personality of the American Negro*. New York: World.

Kitano, H. H. L. 1991. *Race Relations*. (4th ed.) Englewood Cliffs, NJ: Prentice-Hall.

Marshall, S. 1993. "Ethnic Socialization of African American Children: Implications for Parenting, Identity Development, and Academic Performance." *Journal of Youth and Adolescence*, 24(4):337–96.

McAdoo, H. P. 1985. "Racial Attitudes and Self-Concept of Young Black Children over Time." Pp. 213–42 in H. P. McAdoo and J. L. McAdoo (eds.) *Black Children: Social, Educational, and Parental Environments*. Beverly Hills, CA: Sage.

McAdoo, J. 1983. "Parenting Styles: Mother-Child Interactions and Self-Esteem in Young Black Children. Pp. 135–50 in C. P. Obudo (ed.) *Black Marriage and Family Therapy*. Westport, CT: Greenwood.

Meltzer, B., Petras, J. W., and Reynolds, L. 1975. *Symbolic Interactionism: Genesis, Varieties., and Outcomes*. London: Routledge and Kegan Paul.

Pllas, A., Entwisle, D., Alexander, K., and Weinstein, P. 1990. "Social Structure and the Development of Self-Esteem in Young Children." *Social Psychology Quarterly*, 53(4):302–25.

Parks, G. 1992. "A Choice of Weapons." Pp. 26–31 in J. David (ed.) *Growing up Black*. New York: Avon.

Phinney, J. S. and Chavira, V. 1995. "Parental Ethnic Socialization and Adolescent Coping with Problems Related to Ethnicity." *Journal of Research on Adolescence*, 5(1):31–53.

Pinkney, A. 1993. *Black Americans* (4th ed.) Englewood Cliffs, NJ: Prentice-Hall.

Porter, J. R. and Washington, R. E. 1982. "Black Identity and Self-Esteem: A Review of Studies of Black Self-Concept, 1968–78." Pp. 224–34 in M. Rosenberg and H. B. Kaplan (eds.) *Social Psychology of Self-Concept*. Arlington Heights, IL Harlan Davidson.

Powell-Hopson, D. and Hopson D. 1990. *Different and Wonderful: Raising Children in a Race-Conscious Society*. New York: Prentice-Hall.

Reddy, M. T. 1994. *Crossing the Color line: Race, Parenting, and Culture*. New Brunswick, NJ: Rutgers University Press.

Rosenbeg, M. 1965. *Society and the Adolescent Self-Image*. Princeton, NJ: Princeton University Press.

Rosenberg, M. and Kaplan, H. B. 1982. *Social Psychology of the Self-Concept*. Arlington Heights, IL: Harlan Davidson.

Shujaa, M. J. 1992. "Afrocentric Transformation and Parental Choice in African-American Independent Schools." *Journal of Negro Education*, 61:148–59.

Sigelman, L. and Welch, S. 1991. *Black Americans' Views of Racial Inequality: The Dream Deferred*. Cambridge, MA: Harvard University Press.

Staples, R. and Johnson, L. B. 1993. *Black Families at the Crossroads: Challenges and Prospects*. San Francisco: Jossey-Bass.

Steinberg, L. 1992. "Impact of Parenting Practices on Adolescent Achievement: Authoritative Parenting, School Involvement, and the Encouragement to Succeed." *Child Development*, 63:1266–81.

Taylor, R. J., Chatters, L. M., Tucker, M. B., and Lewis, E. 1990 "Developments in Research on Black Families: A Decade Review." *Journal of Marriage and the Family*, 52:993–1014.

Thonton, M. C., Chatters, L. M., Taylor, R. J., and Allen, W. R. 1990. "Sociodemographic and Environmental Correlates of Racial Socialization Black Parents." *Child Development* 61: 401–9.

Whaley, A. L. 1993. "Self-Esteem, Cultural Identity, and Psychosocial Adjustment in African American Children." *Journal of Black Psychology*, 19(4):406–22.

Willkinson, D. Y. "Racial Socialization through Children's Toys: A Sociohistorical Examination." *Journal of Black Studies*, 5(1):96–109.

Wilkinson, D. Y. 1996. "Integration Dilemmas in a Racist Culture." *Society*, 33:27–31.

PART IV

Day Care and Nursery School as Socialization Agents

Until well past the middle of the twentieth century it was normal (i.e. most usual) for mothers of very young children to stay out of the paid labor force and to remain home with their children, at least until the children began school, and often longer. While it was not possible for all mothers to adopt this pattern, it was the widely shared ideal. The strength of that ideal began to fade in the last quarter of the century and, whether or not it is widely desired today, fewer and fewer mothers live by it. There are probably three main reasons for this changed situation: (1) Changes in the economy made it harder for one (usually male) breadwinner to earn enough to support a family. Many more families had to become two-job families, with both husband/father and wife/mother in the paid labor force. (2) The rise of the women's movement, beginning in the mid-1960's, led to profound changes in women's self-concepts. Well educated women wanted to use their education in productive work, which became an important avenue of self-fulfillment. They also wanted to lessen their economic dependence on men, and this was true of less well educated women as well. (3) Increases in single motherhood, primarily due to increased divorce rates and increased out-of-wedlock births, mean increased numbers of women who had to work to gain an income.

All of these changes that led to an increase in mothers of young children working also led to an increase in the number of children placed in day care centers at younger and younger ages and in nursery schools. These organizations are significant in the lives of the young children who attend them, and scholars have been studying them. (Some children of working mothers are placed in home care arrangements with a relative or with someone who takes care of a few children at home, but those situations are much harder to study.) The two selections in Part IV provide important sociological insights into these organizations.

Robin Leavitt's study of a dozen infant-toddler day care centers over several years yields some illuminating, and perhaps unexpected, results. She reveals how the staff exercises power over the children, more for staff convenience than for consideration of the children's wellbeing. She finds staff members focused on *managing* the children and seldom concerned with trying to understand what a particular child needs at a particular time. She also discusses children's resistance to the power that is being exercised over them. The theme of children's resistance to adult authority is gaining increased attention in recent years. In later reports from her study, Leavitt has described and analyzed how toddlers' emotions are socialized (Leavitt 1995) and how day care centers socialize children's use of their bodies (Leavitt and Power 1997).

Day care and nursery school are somewhat different institutions, although the distinction is sometimes blurred. One difference is a difference in age range: while some day care centers take children soon after birth, nursery schools are mostly geared for children between the ages of three and five. Both these institutions play a significant part in the lives of the children who attend. Catherine C. Lewis's study of fifteen Japanese nursery schools presents a picture of adult-child authority relationships that is dramatically different from that in Leavitt's study. While Lewis makes clear that her study cannot claim to be a study of *the* Japanese nursery school, she also makes clear that the teachers in these schools make some psychological assumptions about young children that are significantly different from what is common in American nursery schools and in American psychology. The teachers in her study downplay their authority and make skillful use of children's peer groups in achieving classroom management.

Chapter 10 in Part VI also includes material on nursery schools., including a focus on how children develop social skills in resisting teacher authority.

References

Leavitt, Robin L. "The Emotional Culture of Infant-Toddler Day Care." Pp. 3–21 in J. Amos Hatch (ed.) *Qualitative Research in Early Childhood Settings* (Westport, CT and London: Praeger, 1995).

Leavitt, Robin L. and Martha Bauman Power. "Civilizing Bodies. Children in Day Care." Pp. 39–75 in J. Tobin (ed.) *Making a Place for Pleasure in Early Childhood Education* (New Haven: Yale University Press, 1997).

7

Power and Resistance in Infant-Toddler Day Care Centers*

Robin Lynn Leavitt

In the last two or three decades the milieu of child care has changed with the increasing number of working mothers. The process by which the child is socialized is no longer primarily through the institution of the family. In 1950, 12% of women with children younger than 6 worked outside the home. In 1988, the percentage rose to 57%. More than half of all new mothers return to work before their child's first birthday (Child Care Action Campaign 1988). The most dramatic growth in the child day care population has been that of our youngest children—infants and toddlers, defined as those under three years of age. Most of these children are cared for in family day care homes, but an increasing number are being enrolled in group care centers (Neugebauer 1989). It is the plight of these children which is addressed in this paper.

Child care is not simply a pedagogical or technical issue, it is a political and social issue whose character has changed throughout history and varied according to culture and society.[1] This paper explores how the child's world is shaped, controlled, and constrained by the decisions and actions of the adults who care for them. Specifically, I illustrate the ways in which day care centers are sometimes sites of struggle and contestation, where children often "lose" as their own meanings and constructions of the world are undermined, as their identities are constructed within relations of power. Further, I contend that these

*Reprinted from Spencer Cahill (ed.), "Perspectives On and Of Children," in *Sociological Studies of Child Development*, Volume 4, pp. 91–112. Copyright ©1991 by JAI Press Inc. Used by permission of Robin Lynn Leavitt.

child care practices reflect and reproduce the dominant values and principles of positivist rationalist thought, particularly those of control, predictability, objectivity, and efficiency. In an effort to go beyond description and interpretation, to provoke efforts directed toward social change, I conclude with an exploration of the concepts of freedom and empowerment as they might apply to infants and toddlers in day care centers.

Assumptions and Method

Two major assumptions are guiding my approach to this exploration. The first is that young children's daily experiences are as important as the outcomes of these experiences, thus the necessity of looking at their experience *as it is lived*. Infants and toddlers have few means and little power to make their "voices" heard, therefore a great deal of attention and interpretive effort is involved in understanding their experiences. This effort attempts to view experience as much as possible from the child's perspective.

My second major assumption is that a primary goal of child rearing is to empower children by responding to their needs for attention and security; by supporting their developing capacities to think, communicate and act competently; and by providing opportunities for them to act autonomously, to make choices and to be self-directed. This process of empowerment, I contend, begins in infancy.

The theoretical and methodological perspective of this paper, then, in keeping with these assumptions is phenomenological and interpretive, as well as deconstructive.[2]

> Phenomenological research tries to understand the experiences of other people as they are constituted in actual everyday situations and to record the themes which may be found there. The goal is awareness, appreciation of the other's situation. . . . where the child's world is of utmost importance, phenomenological research can be used to make us aware of the experiences of the powerless and of the powerful (Barritt, Beekman, Bleeker, and Mulderij 1983, p. 189).

Interpretive studies seek to reveal and disclose "the world as felt, lived, and experienced by those studied" (Denzin 1982, p. 22), to make meaningful and understandable their situated lived experience. Recognizing that "social acts and events have meaning in a specific context or social setting" (Packer 1987, p. 2),[3] an interpretive approach allows the examination of child care as an ongoing process in the setting in which it occurs.[4] This requires immersion into the everyday life-worlds of those being studied, observing and recording ethnographic or "thick descriptions" (Geertz 1973). Thick description involves the detailing of the language, emotions, expressions, behaviors, and actions of those being studied in their natural settings. The criterion for thick description is verisimilitude, achieved when the reader is able to feel and sense the flow of interaction, that is, when the experiences of those being studied come alive in the mind of the reader. Such descriptions provide the accounts necessary for the "progressive uncovering and explication (never fully completed) of the researcher's practical understanding of what is being studied" (Packer 1985, p. 1089).

The deconstructive process involves the examination of the theories, concepts, and understandings surrounding the phenomenon (Denzin 1989a) of infant-toddler day care, illuminating the values made primary, and those made secondary, in the everyday practices of caregivers. As Ryan (1982) noted, deconstruction makes one aware of the interrelationship between theory and practice, how each influences and produces the other. Thus, this paper is an exploration of the relevance and application of contemporary political, philosophical, and social theory to an understanding of a specific locale—the child care center.

My immersion into the worlds of the infants and toddlers consisted of five to ten hours a week over the past several years observing in about 12 infant and toddler classrooms in six local, licensed day care centers. Two of these centers are privately-owned, enrolling about 55–75 children each. In one of these, the clientele tends toward the "professional," two-working-parent family; the other serves a broader range, including low-income and single parents; this last one has recently gone out of business. Two other centers are nonprofit and housed in churches; they serve a variety of families and are partially subsidized by federal funds. This includes one of the largest local centers, enrolling as many as 176 children, and a more average-sized center, with a capacity of 71. The larger of these two centers has more children from low-income, culturally diverse and single-parent families, while the smaller serves a considerable number of academic and professional families, although it is the only one of the six with a sliding fee scale. The fifth center is the newest, a corporate-sponsored program with a capacity for 142 children. The last center is a for-profit program affiliated with a national chain, with a capacity for 123 children. Four of these centers accept infants at six weeks of age, the other two between 15 and 24 months. All are open for a 10–12 hour day.

All but one of these centers have a local, "word-of-mouth" reputation for being the "best." Both the University and the two-year Community College place students in these centers for practicum experiences. I first began observing in these programs in 1983, as I supervised child care practicum students at their placement sites. This involved approximately one hour visits to each classroom every other week. Caregivers and students usually knew in advance when to expect me. While there has been some variation in student assignments, these same placements have been repeatedly used over the years, as alternative (model) infant-toddler care programs are not locally available. Over the years, some of the caregivers have changed, but at two centers (the largest and the for-profit) there has been unusual long-term staff retainment.

Collection and interpretation of field notes has been an ongoing interrelated process of pattern recognition (Smith and Robbins 1982) or a search for emerging themes. In addition to my own observations, a considerable number of field notes were recorded by practicum students enrolled in the University's child care training program, who each average nine hours per week a semester working in local centers. These student accounts have been in some sense "verified" by my own visits to these classrooms, as I noted similar incidents visit after visit, year to year, as I reconstructed and recorded my own observations. Indeed, while the practicum students have changed each semester, accounts of their observations and experiences have varied little.

The organization of this paper is meant to provide concurrent illustration and discussion. Thus, there is not "data," then subsequent analysis—rather, description and interpretation are interwoven and inseparable. The field notes herein represent repeatedly observed situations, within and across all these centers over the years, and provide the foundation for my interpretations and understandings. In the tradition of Coles (1967) and Suransky (1982), I often have drawn composite pictures, combining two or three similar incidents in order to emphasize and highlight the issues for the reader. In this process, I have attempted to be faithful to the words and gestures of these observed. Field notes are presented as they illustrate the themes discussed. "Theory" will be introduced likewise, as it helps to illuminate what I am trying to describe and understand.

This inquiry is situated within my own personal experiences and convictions (Bernstein 1978; Denzin 1989a; Mills 1959). In my endeavor to understand a phenomenon which has long been troubling me, I draw from multiple theoretical perspectives, selecting theorists whose writings seem to speak to the themes as they have emerged in the process of description, interpretation, and understanding. Typically the works of these authors have been applied exclusively to the *adult* social and political world. I wish to explore what their theories can offer an understanding of the life-worlds where adults and children are placed together.

Disciplinary Time

> *Time is not a line but a network of intentionalities.*
> —Merleau-Ponty (1962, p. 417)

In the average day care center, one or two caregivers may have responsibility for about 8 to as many as 16 infants and/or toddlers each day. For a major portion of their day (up to 10 hours or more) all the aspects of children's lives—sleeping, playing, and eating—are conducted in one place and according to the shared authority of the caregivers. In what Goffman (1961, p. 6) described as "collective regimentation," children's daily routines are tightly scheduled, with one activity leading at a prearranged time into the next, the whole sequence of activities being imposed above by a system of formal rulings. Infant schedules are typically organized according to "custodial" routines: eating, sleeping, and diaper changing. Sometimes an "activity" is planned, for example, water play. As children get older (about 15 months) more is added to the schedule, typically adult-directed activities, such as story time, art, or music. A schedule, or what Foucault (1979, p. 149) referred to as a "timetable," is often posted on the wall, as was this one:

Toddler Daily Schedule

7:30–8:30	Arrival/Free play in the room
8:30–8:50	Group time (calendar, story, fingerplays)
8:50–9:20	Breakfast
9:20–9:30	Clean up/Toileting
9:30–10:30	Park or Gym
10:30–11:00	Teacher activity (art, small and large motor activity, blocks)
11:00–11:20	Stories/fingerplays/music
11:30–12:00	Lunch
12:00–2:30	Naptime
2:30–3:00	Toileting
2:50–3:15	Teacher activity
3:15–3:30	Snack
3:30–3:40	Grouptime
3:45–4:40	Park/Gym
4:40–5:00	Toileting/fingerplays/stories/music
5:00–5:30	Free play

These daily activities are carried on within a shared group setting; children are always in the company of other children, all of whom are treated alike and required to do the same thing together. As Goffman (1961) noted in his description of "total institutions," the organization and management of daily routines reflect an underlying rationale, in this case, the securement of children's compliance for an orderly day and the supposed benefits to their development. Consider the following field notes.

> Before the children (two year olds) were permitted to sit at the table and eat their lunches, the caregiver had them identify their names, written on large nametags she had made. All the children sat on the rug while the caregiver randomly selected and help up a name tag directly in front of the child who's name it was. That child then was to identify him or herself by saying his or her name and then was permitted to sit down at one of the tables (and wait again for lunch to be served). The other children had to remain sitting on the carpet and wait for their nametags to be shown. They were told to sit on their "bottoms." If they stood, or began to walk over to the tables on their own initiative, they were told to sit down; their names were then called last. Today the caregiver mistakenly held out the wrong nametag in front of one little boy. He called out his own name and jumped up to sit down at the table. Another little girl said "me" when the caregiver held out her nametag.

The preceding field notes reveal how the children are not "reading" their names, but have merely learned the "procedure." But some of the necessary dispositions for participation in this culture, that is, waiting, turn-taking, and compliance, are secured.

As the schedule indicates, children are often required to go through 15 or more transitions, or change of activity, each day. The ways in which caregivers manage these activities, routines, and transactions often reveal an absence of flexibility, intersubjectivity, and spontaneity. Some ways in which schedules dictate children's experiences are described in the field notes below.

> Many of the toddlers had already eaten when they arrived this morning, yet breakfast was served immediately. All the children were required to sit at the table.

> The children appeared sleepy about a half hour before lunch time, at least an hour still to go before the scheduled nap time, yet they were forced to stay awake through the lunch period.

> The transition from play time to snack time was managed by gathering the toddlers together in a group for a story. The children were dismissed one by one, as the story-reader called each toddler by name and excused him or her to the snack table. As they waited, the children often expressed puzzlement as to how it was decided who could go next.

> The caregiver insisted that all the infants have an afternoon nap. Six month old Kim had only a one-half hour nap early this afternoon, so without any visible indication that she was sleepy or fussy, the caregivers decided Kim should take a nap. Kim's play was interrupted and she was put in her crib; she lay there quietly with her eyes wide open, sucking on a blanket. When she started whimpering about half-an hour later, the practicum student went to get her out of her crib, but was told, "No, she'll go to sleep eventually." Kim started crying and screaming 10 minutes later. The student went again to pick her up and was told to leave Kim, that she'd go to sleep eventually. After 20 more minutes of her crying, one of the caregivers gave her a

bottle and then Kim stayed up the rest of the afternoon. Kim was in her crib for one hour total—without closing her eyes once.

In the field notes thus far, it can be seen how scheduled routines were given primacy over the children's inclinations; their understandings and expressions of their own feelings of fatigue, hunger, and energy were denied, and subordinated to adult imposed schedules. Suransky (1977, p. 74) described this as the imposition of "temporal rigidity"; Foucault (1979, p. 151) labeled it "disciplinary time."[5] As infants are subjected to this discipline and rigidity, their lived-time world is refashioned into the metacategories of institutional time (Suransky 1977, p. 79).

Managing Routines and the Exercise of Power

The schedule serves to tell the day care staff what they will be doing at any given moment and implies that children, left on their own, could not initiate and organize their own actions (Denzin 1977). Thus, caregivers' adherence to the schedule serves as the "stipulations of norms" (Philp 1985, p. 67) for the children's behavior. Foucault (1979, p. 147) has described the imposition of routinization as the organization of "serial space." Moreover,

> The seriation of successive activities makes possible a whole investment of duration by power: the possibility of a detailed control and a regular intervention . . . in each moment of time (p. 160).

The following field notes illustrate the nature of the caregivers' power over children, as they are made to conform to the norms stipulated by the schedule.

> During lunch time the toddlers were tired. Today a child started to droop into slumber at the table. He was roused and encouraged to eat, as the adult said, "*it's not time* to sleep yet." When this was not enough to wake the child, his chair was jostled in an attempt to awaken him. When that didn't work, the child was removed from the chair and stood up in another attempt to awaken him. Only after the lunch period was over was the child cleaned up and permitted to nap on his cot.

> One day, one little boy was falling asleep the minute he sat down for lunch. The caregiver tried to get him to stay awake and eat, but he responded by crying. After only a minute of crying, he started to fall asleep again, food in his mouth. At this point, one of the caregivers tried to get him to stand up, but his legs just folded underneath him. She sat him back on his chair, and turned her attention to another child. Before anyone had time to prevent it, the little boy fell out of his chair. He was definitely awake then!

In these situations, the schedules appear to be arbitrarily planned and implemented, in the absence of any observation and interpretation of the children's experiences. By enforcing the schedule above all else, and rigidly managing transitions, caregivers exercise their control and power. As the children's "time controllers" (Suransky 1977, p. 80), they make children do what they would not otherwise—sleep, eat, line up, be silent, sit, wait, be still.[6]

> When the toddlers were done eating their lunch, they were to stay seated until called to wash their hands and brush their teeth. They were called in the order they finished eating. Several children finished eating about the same time, so some of them waited a long time to be called, doing nothing but sitting. When a child got out of his or her chair, he or she had to go back and sit down for a little while before being called. Carrie, on her own initiative, got out of her seat and waited by the sink. When the caregiver refused to let her wash her hands and brush her teeth, Carrie began to cry; it was clear that she was quite upset. The caregiver told Carrie she needed to sit down until she was called. Neither caregiver tried to comfort her or help her back to her seat. After about five minutes of crying, the caregiver irritatedly told Carrie to go lie down on her cot, without washing or brushing.

> After breakfast, the babies were placed on the rug for "free play." Then, one by one, the caregiver interrupted their play, picking an infant up and taking him or her over to the table to do an "art" project. When it was his or her designated turn, the child had to go with the adult, regardless of whether he or she was already involved in play. As each child sat at the table, the caregiver dipped a brush into paint, placed the brush in each child's hand, and held the child's hand while he or she "painted." When the caregiver felt the picture had been painted enough, the picture was considered finished. In spite of the adult direction, some children showed quite a bit of interest in the painting activity, and were upset when told they had to stop. Each child was allowed to do only one painting.

In these situations, the concept of allowing children to initiate and carry out their own handwashing, or to continue in self-directed activity, was subordinate to the adult's prearranged schedule and implementation procedures.

In situations such as those described thus far, the experience of childhood is not, as conventionally perceived, "a time of carefree disorganized bliss" (Denzin 1977, p. 182). "Time is not experienced as a spontaneous part of the lived-world but rather as an external force" (Suransky 1977, p. 80). Very early children experience power as "an inherent feature of social relations" as power operates to constrain or otherwise direct their actions (Philp 1985, pp. 74–75). The following field notes illustrate again the nature of the caregivers' control and power over the children in their care.

> After playing in the large motor room the toddlers were allowed to get drinks of water. When a child asked for a drink but hadn't lined up "right," however, a drink was prohibited. Only the children that lined up were allowed a drink. Henry and Matt were still on bikes when the other children lined up for drinks. When they got to the fountain they were told to go into the classroom, without a drink.

The toddlers were required to be quiet, and sit with their hands in their lap before they were served breakfast or lunch. They were not allowed or encouraged to serve themselves. Some children were refused food until they stopped making "noise." Some had been crying, others were talking. The adults talked to each other while they served the food and during lunchtime. No reason was given to the children about why they shouldn't talk. When the children's plates were empty, they were given more food, without being asked first. Afterwards, their plates were taken away, also without consulting them.

Objectification

The exercise of power, in these situations, reveals how (or requires that) children are managed as objects.[7]

To be *objectified* by the Other is to be totalized, defined, judged, limited—incorporated into a system of ends that one has not chosen—and at the mercy of an alien consciousness (Schroeder 1984, p. 176).

Throughout this text, the field notes describe how caregivers literally "take over" and direct these children's lives. The child's presence, for the caregivers, is of instrumental, rather than existential significance. The child becomes objectified because it is not the *being* of the child that is looked to, but his or her management (Suransky 1977, p. 289). The following field notes provide another illustration.

The toddlers were playing in the large motor area. Three caregivers sat on the floor watching the children play. Two-year-old Vicki arrived with her mom, who told the caregivers Vicki had been awake since 3:30 this morning. Vicki sat and absently watched the others; she did not respond to the adults' initiations. Her eyes started to close. A caregiver said if Vicki fell asleep before lunch, she wouldn't sleep during nap time. Suddenly, this caregiver grabbed Vicki from behind and shook her, saying, "Wake up, Vicki, wake up!" Vicki began to cry. The caregiver told her, "but Vicki, if you sleep now, you won't take your nap." Vicki continued to scream and cry. The caregiver said, "Vicki, stop it now, no reason to cry."

Vicki was at the "mercy" of her caregiver who failed to recognize and respond to Vicki's physical and emotional state. Vicki was to be managed according to the "system of ends"—the daily schedule—which had little relation to her own individual needs and choices. In this way, she was objectified.

Although individual in their development and personality, these children's individual differences and preferences appear to have no influence in the management of scheduled routines and the exercise of control. Each child, in his or her management, seems interchangeable with any other. Indeed, changes in classroom grouping are typically made according to quantitative criteria such as maximum group size and children's chronological age. Every six or twelve months children move into the next (older age) group and assume the routines of those children previously there. The structure remains unchanged by the particular children present.

Cultural Context and Historical Precedent

The experience of children in programs organized in accord with an ideology of objectivity, efficiency, discipline and authority is not new. What *is* new, is the increasing number of our "littlest ones"—infants and toddlers—in group care programs for a significant number of hours each day, subjected to the same disciplinary control found in schools, factories, prisons and other institutions (Cahill and Loseke 1990). How has this phenomenon come to be imposed upon our youngest children? Is it intrinsic to grouping and institutionalization? Or, looking outside the child care center for explanations, is it yet another expression of the scientifically inspired and rationalistic discipline of the modern age (Cahill and Loseke 1990)?

> [T]he discipline of professionalized and standardized group care prepares children for the discipline of the school, and thereby for modern life—a life lived within a great carceral network of disciplinary mechanisms (Cahill and Loseke 1990, p. 31).

I believe the necessity of organizing children's lives from their earliest moments according to an efficient time plan reflects the influence of our Enlightenment heritage.[8] The well-intentioned philosophers of the Enlightenment prepared the way for the domination of modern culture by instrumental, technical rationality (Giddens 1978a; Ryan 1982). Deeply embedded in our society is a commitment to science and technology, with a special affection for efficiency (Kessen 1983). The increasing rationalization of society was noted by Weber (in Gerth and Mills 1946) and Mills (1959, p. 169), who saw it as "the most important feature of the contemporary problem of freedom and reason."

Giroux (1981, p. 8) has characterized this dominant rationality as "the culture of positivism."[9] This culture is the legacy of the Enlightenment, a legacy which includes those convictions and concepts related to control, prediction, objectivity and certainty, and which exercises a powerful and pervasive influence on contemporary life. As the field notes illustrate, our Enlightenment heritage is not just a set of ideas, "it is a set of material practices that are embedded in the routines and experiences of our daily lives" (Giroux 1981, p. 44). The pervasiveness of technical rationality in our everyday lives was noted by Eddy (1975, p. 22):

> No longer is [technology] confined merely to the production of material goods. It has penetrated virtually all man's activities in one way or another. There seems to be

no limit to the technical imperative to find the most efficient means. Given "scientific management" . . ., technique penetrates not only economic but all political, administrative and social life, including education.[10]

This phenomenon of technical rationality is also apparent in the care of our youngest (*pre*-school) children, most particularly in the organization of children's time and the management of their bodies in time, as caregiver practices attempt to make child rearing "scientific," and children subject to "objective" laws. Moreover, it is intricately tied to the power relations manifested in group care settings.[11]

Rigidly prescribed schedules and routinized caregiver practices have a long history. Early in this century, behaviorists Watson and Thorndike advised parents to be objective and detached, that obedience should always be expected. Bulletins published by the Children's Bureau of the Department of Labor emphasized the importance of early training and discipline by "establishing a daily schedule and sticking to it" (Lomax 1978, p. 130).[12] An excerpt from one particular bulletin descriptively titled "Lesson Material in Child Management," published in 1930, gives a flavor of the message:

> *Begin when he is born.*
> Feed him at exactly the same hours every day.
> Do not feed him just because he cries.
> Let him wait until the right time.
> If you make him wait, his stomach will learn to wait.
> His mind will learn that he cannot get things by crying.
> You do two things for your baby at the same time. You teach his body good habits and you teach his mind good habits
> (Weill, cited in Lomax 1978, p. 135).[13]

For several decades now, though, the advice to child rearers from pediatricians and child psychologists, among others, has been to abandon rigid schedules, and recognize individual inclinations and differences, and respond accordingly (Murphy, Heider, and Small 1986; *Tufts University Diet and Nutrition Letter* 1989). Regardless of the change in professional advice, rigid child care practices persist (as illustrated in this paper), reflecting pervasive characteristics of our contemporary society from which they cannot be separated. My concern is that these practices are becoming institutionally embedded in group care programs enrolling an increasing number of our most vulnerable children—infants and toddlers—and subjecting them to disciplinary time for as long as 10 or more hours a day.

While children are active agents in their own constructions of the world, they come to understand themselves in the mirror of what others have constructed as a world (Wartofsky 1983). While Wartofsky (1983) cautions us not to underestimate the extent to which children create, differentiate, and individuate themselves in the face of what some mistakenly take to be a totalistic construction from without, I contend that the parameters allowing children their own activity, their intentionality, are severely constrained in child care centers. The implications of this skewed constraint at such early ages demands serious consideration. In what ways will children be able to join and participate in the definitions of their childhoods? The particular ways children live the world of day care may amount to Sartre's "unsurpassable childhood" (Sartre [1960] 1963, p. 65), as children attempt to make meaning and construct their worlds within the constraints described in this paper.

Resistance

Foucault posited that power is not completely controlling, that there is always resistance where there is power. I now ask what freedom the child has to project him or herself into the organization of the day care world. The following field notes describe what happens when children resist routinization.

> Today at naptime Emily (19 months) was having trouble getting settled. She often has a difficult time falling asleep, tossing and babbling. Once she is sleeping, though, she'll sleep a long time. Today, the caregiver walked over to Emily's cot, grabbed her arm and very roughly turned her on her stomach. She then rubbed Emily's back very hard, while Emily cried. When Emily tried to move, the caregiver pushed down on her back a little harder to stop Emily from moving.

> Everyday after lunch the children brush their teeth. Only two children can fit at the sink at a time, so the others that are waiting are expected to sit still and quietly until it is their turn to brush their teeth. Everyday the same children get in trouble for not sitting "nicely" until their turn comes. Children who do not sit "nicely" are refused help.

> There are times when a toddler resists sitting in his or her chair during mealtime. Several of them like to get up in the middle of snack and leave the table, so the caregivers decided to strap the toddlers to their chairs during meals and snacks. The caregivers used either a blanket or an elastic cord to wrap around the child and the back of the chair. Or, they took the child's shirt and put it over the back of the chair while still worn by the child; this put the chair between the child's skin and shirt. Within a week after they started strapping the infants in, 15-month-old Troy deduced that being belted to the chair didn't mean that he and the chair couldn't move, and he and his chair walked away (or scooted away) from the table. Troy and the other children thought this was really funny, and it got even harder to get the toddlers to stay at the table during snack time.

> If a toddler doesn't go to bed "cooperatively," the caregiver will put him or her on the cot, face down, and put one arm across the back of the child's neck, and the other arm over the child's ankles, holding the child down. The caregiver remains in that position until the child falls asleep. No reasons are given to the children for why this is done. They are simply told they have to stay on their cots.

The repression of children's efforts at resistance, critical to the development of their autonomy, leaves them in a kind of "culture of silence" where the oppressed are mute, prohibited from "naming" and transforming their world (Freire 1970). Insofar as children's expressions of their physical and emotional needs and inclinations are subordinate to the adult-imposed schedule, they are "silenced." Indeed, a degree of violence can be seen in the physical management of children when the adults tie them to their chairs or use force.[14] The control of time and children's bodies in time and space amounts to "a systematic negation of self-affirmation and an education toward conformity and docility" (Suransky 1977, p. 136).

I do not deny that child rearing involves coercion.[15] Child-centered as he was, Rousseau's (1979) benevolent manipulation of Emile was a coercive strategy, as his wants and actions were shaped by his "tutor." As Suransky (1977) noted, "the social reality of child care is such that it is the adults who are imbued with the use and abuse of power in the world of the child" (p. 251). But it is helpful here to consider Smith's (1983) distinction between "developmental" and "extractive power." Developmental power supports a child's ability to develop his or her own capacities—this is the ideal aim of those concerned with cultivating a generation of human beings. Developmental power emphasizes interdependence and recognition of individuality, as children are regarded as developing persons. Extractive power, on the other hand, treats children as property or things to be managed, directed and controlled.

So, on the surface, the management of these child "inmates" (Goffman 1961) might be rationalized in terms of child rearing aims—that is, helping children learn to live in society, therefore their compliance is an indication of developmental progress. In the situations described in this paper, however, it is extractive, not developmental, power which is exercised; control appears to have become the operative and primary goal for caregivers, rather than a means to achieve developmental goals, such as health, safety, and competence. Indeed, the field notes illustrate how the exercise of control often operates to the children's detriment. Yet the assumptions of efficiency, control, authority, and objectivity underlying caregivers' management of children are accepted as given, and then pointed to as a rationale. Caregiver practices may reflect what Gramsci has called "contradictory consciousness" in that they are somewhat rooted in "common sense," but at the same time influenced by the scientific philosophy and ideals which have entered ordinary life (Giroux 1981).

The challenge that center based group care presents to well-intentioned caregivers must also be recognized. Caregiver practices evolve in attempts to resist the practical constraints imposed on *them*—responsibility for at least 4–15 children, confinement to one room with rarely a break, inadequate professional training, extremely low financial compensation, lack of administrative and structural supports, and little respect from the parents they serve and society in general. The caregivers employed in these centers vary widely in their experience and professional training—most states have minimal or no requirements for caregivers. Caregivers' implementation of the daily schedule is intended to make the day easier, more manageable and efficient for *them*, as well as the children. They may be doing the best they can, given the situations within which they find themselves, unprepared, and from which they can find no way out (Mills 1959, p. 170).

The caregivers' inflexibility, then, may stem partly from their own needs for control and predictability. They fail to see how their strictly enforced routinization works against them, pitting them in struggles with the children, which they respond to, in turn, with more rules and disciplinary punishment. The caregivers themselves undoubtedly experienced the same "discipline" as grade school children. It is "a machine in which everyone is caught, those who exercise power just as much as those over whom it is exercised" (Foucault 1980, p. 156). More attention, then, beyond the scope of this paper, needs to be given to caregivers' own understandings of their practices, as well as the meanings children are constructing out of these experiences.[16]

Freedom and Empowerment in the Child Care Center

Negative accounts of day care are not new. I am not concluding that we abolish infant-toddler day care centers. Neither am I suggesting we abandon our responsibility and allow a laissez-faire system of child rearing. What I have attempted to do in this paper is articulate how these "stories" reflect the prevailing "terrain of politics," and document some specific ways in which infant-toddler day care is a microcosm of the cultural, political, social, ethical, and moral values embedded in our society since the "Enlightenment." The belief in the values of efficiency, control, and objectivity, and their saturation into our collective practices and routines, has developed historically. We cannot make significant changes in child care practice without such recognition. The present crisis in the quality of child care is a political and social problem that goes beyond the day care center, permeating every sphere of our social existence. Specifically, it speaks to the scant value our society places on children and their lived experience, and the insufficient value we place on child rearing and nurturance.

Postmodern theory, while helpful in deconstructing (or undermining) contradicting cultural values in our society, is inadequate in the construction of alternatives. Turning to critical theory, I find that most critical pedagogy (for example, Freire 1970; Giroux 1987; McLaren 1989) focuses on school-age children or adults who are able to participate in the "unmasking" or deconstruction of the hegemony they experience. These students are considered to be competent dialogic participants. The experience of infancy, early childhood and early institutionalization of care has been virtually left out of these "border" pedagogy philosophies, with the notable exception of Suransky (1977, 1982). We have neglected to apply the concepts of resistance and empowerment to infants and toddlers. It is as if child care is not relevant to the practice of freedom. Under what conditions can their autonomy flourish? What follows is an initial exploration of the concepts of freedom and empowerment as they might apply to our very youngest children in day care centers.

> The child as a conscious *becoming* being pursues a 'project' of freedom in order to become some-one himself and not a being for others (Vandenberg, cited in Suransky 1977, p. 262).

The condition of freedom for children in day care, as Vandenberg suggests, is the appreciation of the child for him or herself. This means recognizing children as Subjects—active, reflective, interpreting participants in the day care environment (Packer 1987). As Suransky (1982, p. 173) wrote:

> [Children] are in the world; they act upon the world; they discover things in the world; and in so doing and acting, they are fulfilling a fundamental human activity of intentionality and purposiveness.

If we look to the child, attempt to see the world from the child's perspective, and allow the child the "freedom to create and construct" (Freire 1970, p. 55) *sharing* power with children, it *is* possible to humanize the child care center. This is what Suransky (1977) has called child care "grounded in the being of the child" (p. 291). It contrasts directly with a positivist ethic that does not allow for a child who is able to construct his or her own meanings.

The empowering caregiver, then, attempts to enter and participate in the child's world, to understand her lived experience and the meanings she negotiates and assigns to experience. Caregivers then can validate children's lived experience, learn from it, and respond to it with flexibility and sensitivity. I have described this elsewhere as "following the child's lead," and as "responsive caregiving" (Leavitt and Eheart 1985). A daily schedule is not in itself necessarily oppressive, provided the desire for efficient management does not take precedence over the development and needs of the children. The postmodern assertion that "there is no absolute to guide action which is not . . . provisional" (Ryan 1982, p. 81) suggests possibilities for spontaneity and flexibility. If we attend to the child and the child's experience of lived-time, then perhaps the *process* of managing daily routines will be as important as accomplishing them. Children are then empowered as their experiences and voices are recognized, validated, taken into account, and allowed expression.

The following field notes reveal the challenge to caregivers that flexibility represents, when a change in routine was suggested by a practicum student.

> Today was a warm, sunny day. The children had been involved happily in outdoor play for about 45 minutes. The caregiver said that it would be time to go inside for snack in a few minutes. The practicum student suggested that since the weather was so nice the group could have snack outside, perhaps lay down some blankets and have a picnic. One caregiver said that they hadn't done it before and she would have to check with the director. The other caregiver seemed very disturbed by the idea and looked at the student skeptically and said, "You've got to be kidding." She went on, "Well, what about washing their hands? How are we going to get them to sit still? What if . . .? What are you going to do when . . .? How will . . .? They both seemed very flustered by the suggested changes in routine, but agreed to give it a try.
>
> The caregivers brought wet washcloths outside and helped the children wash their hands. They sat with the children while they ate their snack, and engaged in conversation with them. The children were not restrained or reprimanded, and were allowed to take their time eating. As soon as a child was finished, he or she was washed and allowed to resume outdoor play immediately.

In this situation, the children appeared to respond to the change in routine without difficulty. No one had to sit and wait for a turn at the sink, adult permission to eat or talk, or to resume play. Thus, there were no struggles between the children and the caregivers.

In an article calling for a blend of scientific and personal knowledge in the practice of child care, Bowman (1989) stressed the critical necessity of empathy in understanding young children. The empathic capacity involves connecting one's own experience to that of others, and through that connection, gaining understanding of their feelings. Empowering caregiving requires the integration of feeling, subjectivity and intersubjectivity, intimacy, involvement, connection, care, compassion, respect, empathy, comfort, and nurturance—realms of experience excluded from science-driven practice (Denzin 1989b) and neglected in our dominant (positivist) culture, but given primacy in most contemporary feminist theory.[17] Kuykendall (1983, p. 264) has suggested that

> Two principles, at least, are necessary to the development of a feminist ethic of nurturance. The first is that the power exercised by the nurturer toward the nurtured (as by mother toward child) be not merely dominant or controlling, but primarily healing, creative, and transformative. The second principle, which complements the first, is that the relationship between the nurturer and the nurtured be not merely symmetrical, but at least potentially mutual and reciprocal.

I acknowledge the challenge involved in expecting the child care environment, as also a work environment, to reflect values and practices which run contrary to those of, and lack credence in, the workplace (Leach and Page 1987). But the following field notes demonstrate that it is certainly possible for caregivers to become more child-aware, and more self-aware and reflective in their everyday practices, and consequently more responsive within their existing settings.

> It was lunch time and all the toddlers were starting to eat, except Micha who was sitting in his chair not eating. The practicum student tried, unsuccessfully, to find out what was wrong. The caregiver sat near Micha, expressing her concern, and offered to hold him. Realizing he was sleepy, the caregiver helped him to lie down on his cot. A little while later, on his own initiative, he came back to the table. He seemed to feel better and finished eating his lunch.

This situation demonstrates how simple and satisfactory flexibility and responsiveness can be, as a caregiver, recognizing and understanding this child, allowed his needs to have primacy over the schedule. In this way, the care of the individual and care of the group can become two sides of the same coin with infants, toddlers and their caregivers in group day care settings.[18]

Conclusion

This interpretation of only one aspect of infant-toddler day care is, of course, unfinished, to be taken up again (Denzin 1984). I have tried to make visible some of the everyday life experiences of infants and toddlers in day care centers. I did not set out to prove that all day care centers resemble those depicted here, but I believe what has been described is "symbolic of the larger child care milieu" (Suransky 1977, p. 9). Moreover, in this exploration of the lived experiences of these children, I have tried to develop preliminary groundings for understanding and emancipatory action.

This is the place to start, for this is where the children are. For only a hard look at the world in which they live—a world we adults have created for them in large part by default— can convince us of the urgency of their plight and the consequences of our inaction. Then perhaps it will come to pass that, in the words of Isaiah, "a little child shall lead them."
—Bronfenbrenner (1970, p. 165)

Acknowledgments

I am indebted to Belden Fields, Norman K. Denzin, Martha Bauman Power, Ralph Page, Walter Feinberg, and Carolyne White for their helpful comments. I also wish to acknowledge the contributions of students enrolled in the University's Developmental Child Care Program. Finally, I would like to express my gratitude and appreciation to Carolyn Casteel for her patient and skillful assistance in the preparation (and multiple revisions) of this manuscript.

Notes

1. See, for example, Clarke-Stewart's (1982) historical overview, as well as Liljestrom (1980), Suransky (1977, 1982), and Weber (1984).
2. For elaboration on the theoretical and philosophical foundations of hermeneutic phenomenology; and its applications, see Bleicher (1980), Denzin (1983, 1989a, 1989b), Gadamer (1976), Packer (1985), Sartre ([1932] 1967), Schutz and Suransky (1977, 1982) among others.
3. See also Blumer (1969) on the premises of symbolic interactionism.
4. The importance of studying children within their natural settings has been noted by many (e.g., Bronfenbrenner 1979; Clarke-Stewart 1982; Coles 1964, 1967; Denzin 1977; Damon 1977; Scarr 1979; Suransky 1977, 1982).
5. Foucault's concept of disciplinary time parallels Weber's definition of discipline: "the 'practiced nature' of uncritical and unresisting *mass* obedience" (Weber 1962, p. 117).
6. Weber (1962) also defines power as the imposition of one's will on the behavior of others, even against their will.
7. See Leavitt and Power (1989) for another description of children regarded as objects, or nonpersons, by caregivers during emotional interactions. This lack of emotional identification and reciprocity is discussed in the context of postmodernism. See also Leavitt (1990) for elaboration on the lack of reciprocity and responsiveness in infant day care centers.
8. It is also from the Enlightenment that the moral primacy of individual freedom is derived, as well as the virtues of charity, kindness, and humaneness. Thus, the assumptions underlying my interpretations and concerns in this paper also derive from the Enlightenment heritage. I suggest we need to reinterpret the dialectic of these conflicting values on individual and societal levels.
9. For critiques of positivist science, see Bernstein (1978), Giddens (1978a, 1978b), Giroux (1981), Guba and Lincoln (1985), Habermas (1971), Pirsig (1974), Sartre ([1960] 1976), and Shils and Finch (1949) regarding Max Weber's views. By my thesis I do not intend to blame all the ills of society, and those related to child care, on scientific, technical rationality, but to illustrate it as *one* definite and primary influence on everyday life on individual and institutional levels. Certainly, our culture is constructed out of weaves of old and new and counter currents, as well as local and personal philosophies. "The child is an invention of not one, but several of the cultures embodied within a modern society" (White 1983, p. 14).
10. See Giroux (1987) and Bowles and Gintis (1976) for more discussion of the relationship between technocratic, rationalist ideology and schooling.
11. Mills (1959, p. 16) also asserted that "rationally organized social arrangements . . . often . . . are a means of tyranny and manipulation, a means of expropriating . . . the very capacity to act as a free [being]." Hellesnes (1982) also posited that the interest in control and domination is inherent in the positivist tradition, and that its application in practice, makes such practice authoritarian.
12. I find the fact that child care advice was distributed by a federal department of labor extremely illuminating with regard to the parallels between the organization of the workplace and the caregiving practices within child care institutions.
13. These recommendations parallel the distancing and discipline advocated in even earlier times, based on religious convictions: "[T]he trainer of the young must first break or chastise their self-will . . . children must be strictly treated. . . . The

self-will must be broken" (Liljestrom 1980, p. 6). Emphasis on the child's submission to authority is not new, then, but rephrased in a different framework of rationalization, that of "science." The old is woven into the new, which may help explain the persistence of these practices, contemporary advice notwithstanding. The balance between restrictive and permissive philosophies of childrearing seems to cycle historically (Kagan 1984). A thorough historical analysis of patterns of child rearing, however, is beyond the scope of this paper.

14. By no means do I intend to imply that the "culture of silence" for children in day care centers in the United States is comparable to the extreme physical, political, and economic oppression and violence experienced in Central and South America and other "Third World" societies to which Freire typically refers. Looking at the ways in which children are enculturated from early infancy, however, enables us to see how the imposition of oppressive ideologies, whatever the degree, are ingrained in our everyday, taken-for-granted practices. An analysis informed by Freire helps us to see how "hegemony is produced in the everyday routines and rituals of the social encounter" (Giroux 1981, p. 74), including those situated in day care centers.

15. It is worthwhile to note here that I strongly disagree with the following statement by Neill which, in his supposed empathy for children, ignores the reality that society constructs childhood and children regardless of its intentions; he also evades a value stance about what is a desirable childhood:

I'm not trying to produce any kind of person here. I'm only trying to let people be themselves without outside interference. No one should dare say they are trying to produce a certain kind of person. Nobody is good enough to try to tell a child how to live or what to do (Neill, cited in Suransky 1977, p. 234).

16. For example, consider the following episode:

The caregiver entered the darkened room at 2:30. The babies were just awakening from their naps; some were still asleep. The caregiver announced to the room in general, "You guys are so *good!*" She turned to me to explain, "They usually wake up at 1:00."

In this situation the children were considered "good" because they stayed asleep until the end of scheduled nap time, a physiological state of being not under their control. In this way, children construct understandings about their behaviors and themselves through caregiver practices.

17. See for example, Cook and Fonow (1986), Farganis (1986), Gilligan, Ward, Taylor, and Bardige (1988), Keller (1985), Kuykendall (1983), Martin (1981, 1988), and Smith (1983). In my suggestion to turn to feminist theory, I acknowledge that, historically, the existentialist also rejects science as a model, largely because scientific thinking is concerned with objectification, "cool neutrality," and excludes intuitive awareness, experience, subjectivity, self-reflection and passionate engagement (Green 1973, p. 137).

18. See Gonzalez-Mena and Eyer (1989) for an excellent elaboration on responsive infant care.

References

Barritt, L., T. Beekman, H. Bleeker, and K. Mulderij. 1983. *A Handbook for Phenomenological Research in Education.* Ann Arbor: The University of Michigan School of Education.

Bernstein, R. 1978. *The Restructuring of Social and Political Theory*. Philadelphia: University of Pennsylvania Press.

Bleicher, J. 1980. *Contemporary Hermeneutics*. London: Routledge & Kegan Paul.

Blumer, H. 1969. *Symbolic Interactionism: Perspective and Method*. Englewood Cliffs, NJ: Prentice-Hall.

Bowles, S., and H. Gintis. 1976. *Schooling in Capitalist America: Educational Reform and the Contradiction of Economic Life*. New York: Basic.

Bowman, B. 1989. "Self-reflection as an Element of Professionalism." *Teachers College Record*, 90:444–451.

Bronfenbrenner, U. 1970. *Two Worlds of Childhood: U.S. and U.S.S.R.* New York: Russell Sage.

———. 1979. "Contexts of Childrearing: Problems and Prospects." *American Psychologist* 34:844–850.

Cahill, S. E., and D. R. Loseke. 1990. "Disciplining the Littlest Ones: Popular Day Care Discourse in Post-War America." Paper presented at the annual meetings of the Society for the Study of Symbolic Interaction, Washington, D.C.

Child Care Action Campaign. 1988. "Child Care: The Bottom Line." *Child Care ActionNews*, 5(September–October), pp. 1–6.

Clarke Stewart, A. 1982. *Day Care*, Cambridge, MA: Harvard University Press.

Coles, R. 1964. *Children of Crisis: A Study of Courage and Fear*. Boston: Little, Brown. 1967. *Children of Crisis: Migrants, Sharecroppers and Mountaineers*. Boston: Little Brown.

Cook, J., and M. Fonow. 1986. "Knowledge and Women's Interests: Issues of Epistemology and Methodology in Feminist Social Research." *Sociological Inquiry*, 56:2–29.

Damon, W. 1977. *The Social World of the Child*. San Francisco: Jossey-Bass.

Denzin, N. K. 1977. *Childhood Socialization*. San Francisco: Jossey-Bass.

———. 1982. "Contributions of Anthropology and Sociology to Qualitative Research Methods." Pp. 17–26 in *New Directions for Institutional Research: Qualitative Methods for Institutional Research*, edited by E. Kuhns and S.V. Mortorana. San Francisco: Jossey-Bass.

———. 1983. "Interpretive Interactionism." Pp. 129–424 in *Beyond Method: Strategies for Social Research*, edited by G. Morgan. Beverly Hills: Sage.

———. 1984. *On Understanding Emotion*. San Francisco: Jossey-Bass.

———. 1989a. *Interpretive Interactionism*. Newbury Park, CA: Sage.

———. 1989b. *The Research Act: A Theoretical Introduction to Sociological Methods*, 3rd ed. Englewood Cliffs, NJ: Prentice-Hall.

Eddy, W. 1975. "Of Techne and Humanitas." *Phi Kappa Phi Journal*, 55:17–25.

Farganis, S. 1986. "Social Theory and Feminist Theory: The Need for Dialogue." *Sociological Inquiry*, 56:50–68.

Foucault, M. 1979. *Discipline and Punish: The Birth of the Prison*. Translated by A. Sheridan. New York: Vintage.

———. 1980. *Power/Knowledge: Selected Interviews and Other Writings, 1972–1977*. Edited by Colin Gordon and translated by C. Gordon, L. Marshall, J. Mepham, and R. Soper. New York: Pantheon.

Freire, P. 1970. *Pedagogy of the Oppressed*. Translated by M.B. Ramos. New York: Seabury.

Gadamer, H. G. 1976. *Philosophical Hermeneutics*. Edited and translated by E. E. Linge. Berkeley: University of California Press.

Geertz, C. 1973. *The Interpretation of Culture: Selected Essay*. New York: Basic.

Gerth, H. H., and C. W. Mills, eds./trans. 1946. *Max Weber: Essays in Sociology*. New York: Oxford University Press.

Giddens, A. 1978a. "Positivism and Its Critics." Pp. 237–286 in *A History of Sociological Analysis*, edited by T. Bottomore and R. Nisbet. New York: Basic.

————. 1987b. *Positivism and Sociology*. London: Heinemann Educational Books Ltd.

Gilligan, C., J.V. Ward, J. M. Taylor, and B. Bardige, eds. 1988. *Mapping the Moral Domain*. Cambridge, MA: Harvard University Press.

Giroux, H. 1981. *Ideology, Culture, and the Process of Schooling*. Philadelphia: Temple University Press.

————. 1987. "Citizenship, Public Philosophy, and the Struggle for Democracy." *Educational Theory*, 37:103–120.

Goffman, E. 1961. *Asylums: Essays in the Social Situation of Mental Patients and Other Inmates*. Garden, City, NY: Doubleday.

Gonzalez-Mena, J., and D. W. Eyer. 1980. *Infancy and Caregiving*. Palo Alto, CA: Mayfield.

Green, M. G. 1973. *Teacher as Stranger: Educational Philosophy for the Modern Age*. Belmont, CA: Wadsworth.

Guba, Y., and E. Lincoln. 1985. *Naturalistic Inquiry*. Beverly Hills: Sage.

Habermas, J. 1971. *Knowledge and Human Interests*. Translated by J. Shapiro. Boston: Beacon Press.

Hellesnes, J. 1982. "Education and the Concept of Culture." Pp. 335–369 in *Knowledge and Values in Educational Research*, edited by E. Bredo and W. Feinberg. Philadelphia: Temple University Press.

Kagan, J. 1984. *The Nature of the Child*. New York: Basic.

Keller, E. F. 1985. "Contending with Masculine Bias in the Ideals and Values of Science." *The Chronicle of Higher Education* (October): 96.

Kessen, W. 1983. "The Child and Other Cultural Inventions." Pp. 26–39 in *The Child and Other Cultural Inventions*, edited by F. S. Kessel and A. W. Siegel. New York: Praeger.

Kuykendall, E. H. 1983. "Toward an Ethic of Nurturance: Luce Irigaray on Mothering and Power." Pp. 263–274 in *Essays in Feminist Theory*, edited by J. Trebilcot. Totowa, NJ: Rowman and Allanheld.

Leach, M., and R. Page. 1987. "Why Home Economics Should be Morally Biased." *Illinois Teacher* (May/June): 169–174.

Leavitt, R. L. 1990. "The Objectification of Infants and Toddlers in Day Care Centers." Paper presented at the Midwest Sociological Society Meetings, Chicago.

Leavitt, R. L., and B. K. Eheart. 1985. *Toddler Day Care: A Guide to Responsive Caregiving*. Lexington, MA: D.C. Heath.

Leavitt, R. L., and M. B. Power. 1989. "Emotional Socialization in the Postmodern Era: Children in Day Care." *Social Psychology Quarterly*, 52:35–43.

Liljestrom, R. 1980. *Children and Culture*. Strasbourg: Council of Europe.

Lomax, E. 1978. *Science and Patterns of Child Care*. San Francisco: W.H. Freeman.

Martin, J. R. 1981. "The Ideal of the Educated Person." *Educational Theory*, 31(2):97–109.

————. 1988. "Science in a Different Style," *American Philosophical Quarterly*, 25(2):129–140.

McLaren, P. 1989. *Life in Schools: An Introduction to Critical Pedagogy in the Foundations of Education*. White Plains, NY: Longman.

Merleau-Ponty, M. 1962. *Phenomenology of Perception*. London: Routledge & Kegan Paul.

Mills, C. W. 1959. *The Sociological Imagination*. New York: Oxford University Press.
Murphy, L., G. Heider, and C. Small. 1986. "Individual Differences in Infants." *Zero to Three*, 8(2):1–8.
Neugebauer, R. 1989. "Surveying the Landscape: A Look at Child Care '89." *Child Care Information Exchange*, 66 (April):13–16.
Packer, M.J. 1985. "Hermeneutic Inquiry in the Study of Human Conduct." *American Psychologist*, 40:1081–1093.
———. 1987. "Interpretive Research and Social Development in Developmental Psychology." Paper presented at the Biennial Meeting of the Society for Research in Child Development, Baltimore, MD.
Philp, M. 1985. "Michel Foucault." Pp. 65–81 in *The Return of Grand Theory in the Human Sciences*, edited by Q. Skinner. Cambridge: Cambridge University Press.
Pirsig, R. 1974. *Zen and the Art of Motorcycle Maintenance*. New York: Bantam.
Rousseau, J. -J. 1979. *Emile or On Education*. Translated by Allan Bloom. New York: Basic.
Ryan, M. 1982. *Marxism and Deconstruction: A Critical Articulation*. Baltimore, MD: The Johns Hopkins University Press.
Sartre, J. P. (1956) 1966. *Being and Nothingness*. Translated by H.E. Barnes. New York: Simon and Schuster.
———. (1960) 1963. *Search for a Method*. New York: Knopf/Vintage.
———. (1960) 1976. *Critique of Dialectical Reason*. Translated by A. Sheridan-Smith. London: WLB.
Scarr, S. 1979. "Psychology and Children: Current Research and Practice." *American Psychologist*, 34:809–811.
Schroeder, W.R. 1984. *Sartre and His Predecessors*. London: Routledge & Kegan Paul.
Schutz, A. (1932) 1967. *The Phenomenology of the Social World*. Translated by G. Wals and F. Lehnert. Evanston, IL: Northwestern University Press.
Shils, E., and H. Finch, eds. 1949. *Max Weber on the Methodology of the Social Sciences*. New York: The Free Press.
Smith, A., and A. Robbins. 1982. "Structured Ethnography: The Study of Parental Involvement." *American Behavioral Scientist*, 26:45–61.
Smith, J. F. 1983. "Parenting and Property." Pp. 198–212 in *Mothering: Essays in Feminist Theory*, edited by J. Trebilcot. Totowa, NJ: Rowman and Allanheld.
Suransky, V. P. 1977. "The Erosion of Childhood: A Social Phenomenological Study of Early Institutionalization." Unpublished Ph.D. dissertation, University of Michigan, Ann Arbor.
———. 1982. *The Erosion of Childhood*. Chicago: University of Chicago Press. *Tufts University Diet and Nutrition Letter*, 1989. 7(4):1–2.
Wartofsky, M. 1983. "The Child's Construction of the World and the World's Construction of the Child: From Historical Epistemology to Historical Psychology." Pp. 188–215 in *The Child and Other Cultural Inventions*, edited by F. Kessel and A. Siegel. New York: Praeger.
Weber, E. 1984. *Ideas Influencing Early Childhood Education: A Theoretical Analysis*. New York: Teachers College Press.
Weber, M. 1962. *Basic Concepts in Sociology*. Translated by H.P. Secher. Secaucus, NJ: Citadel.
White, S. 1983. "Psychology As a Moral Science." Pp. 1–25 in *The Child and Other Cultural Inventions*, edited by F. Kessel and A. Siegel. New York: Praeger.

8

Cooperation and Control in Japanese Nursery Schools*

Catherine C. Lewis

Phenomena as diverse as nonverbal communication and commitment to permanent employment have been attributed to Japanese child rearing. Yet, there is remarkably little English-language evidence on early socialization in Japan. This article provides observational data from 15 Japanese nursery schools. It is not my intention here to draw generalizations about Japanese nursery schools or to demonstrate differences between Japanese and American schools. The substantial variability in nursery schools within each country makes such systematic comparison an ambitious undertaking. Rather, the behavioral and ethnopsychological data of the present chapter are intended to identify potentially interesting areas for future research on nursery school socialization and to stimulate American thinking about two aspects of early education: school practices that influence the development of cooperative behavior in children and adult strategies for controlling children's behavior.

Japanese Early Education

Nearly two-thirds of the 5-year-olds in Japan attend nursery school (*yochien*).[1] Researchers have studied the early Japanese parent–child relationship and the socialization of values by Japanese elementary and secondary schools.[2] Studies seeking the roots of Japanese educational achievement have investigated the period between ages 2.5 and 6,[3] but social development during

*Reprinted from *Comparative Education Review*, Vol. 28, no. 1, pp. 69–84. by permission of the author and The University of Chicago Press. ©1984 by the Comparative and International Education Society. All rights reserved.

this period remains largely unstudied. This is a tantalizing gap. Accounts suggest that Japanese children must make a transition from the undisciplined, "indulgent" child rearing of the home[4] to an elementary school classroom where 40–50 children share one teacher and where subordination of personal needs to group goals is the dominant norm.[5] For most Japanese children, nursery school is that transition. Nursery school generally commences at age 3 or 4 and continues until age 6, when elementary school begins. Of the almost 15,000 nursery schools in Japan, approximately 60% are private, 40% public (city, ward, etc.), and fewer than 1% national.[6] Of the 15 schools in the present study, 6 were private, 7 public, and 2 national.

The Development of Cooperative Behavior: A Brief Review of Literature

The reader is referred elsewhere for an extensive discussion of theoretical and operational definitions of cooperation.[7] In this chapter, cooperation refers to an orientation to seek mutual benefit rather than individual benefit when the two conflict. Japan presents an interesting arena for studying socialization to cooperate. In Japan, as in other highly industrialized countries, a large number of individuals compete on objective examinations for a limited number of educational and occupational opportunities.[8] Yet, contemporary Japanese institutions often preserve traditional sanctions against face-to-face interpersonal competition.[9] For example, Japanese workers' willingness to subordinate individual goals to group goals is frequently cited as a reason for the success of Japanese work groups.[10]

Numerous studies employing various cooperative board games and tasks have documented large, replicable cross-cultural and subcultural differences in cooperative behavior.[11] These studies demonstrate, for example, that while Mexican or Israeli kibbutz children quickly work out a cooperative style that allows all children to win prizes in a board game, American children maladaptively compete in a way that prevents all children from winning prizes. While cross-cultural differences in cooperation as early as age 5 are well documented, we know very little about why these cultural differences emerge. What aspects of early education promote in children a willingness to cooperate? While the research and theoretical literature is sparse, it suggests several hypotheses.

The Opportunity to Learn the Rewards of Cooperation

In the framework of learning theory, cooperation may be viewed as a behavior that is elicited and reinforced within the classroom. Experiences of shared positive arousal, such as sharing a group reward or a sense of accomplishment, may condition empathy among children who cooperate. Empathy, in turn, may promote cooperation in a circular process. Research designed as a laboratory analogue of empathy conditioning has been carried out.[12] Classrooms may differ in the extent to which cooperation is elicited and reinforced. Competitive situations may decrease children's opportunities to learn an association between positive affect and cooperation. Research suggests that competitive situations that focus children's attention on individual rewards tend to undermine, for example, children's attention to creative aspects of a task.[13] Other research suggests that a seemingly trivial manipulation of game instructions (e.g., describing a game goal using the "we" versus "I") significantly influences cooperation. These various findings suggest that children's tendency to cooperate may be increased by providing classroom activities that elicit cooperation and enable children to learn associated positive rewards and reducing competitive activities that focus children's attention on individual achievement and consequently undermine attention to cooperative aspects of tasks.

The Use of Small Constant-Membership Groups

A single experimental study found that children who learned to perform a cooperative block-building task in groups of constant (rather than changing) membership were subsequently more cooperative when paired with new children.[14] The authors of the study speculate that membership in a constant group may facilitate children's ability to recognize and avert maladaptive competition.

Competition for the Teacher as a Resource and for Other Classroom Resources

As anyone will attest who has observed frantic hand waving by children seeking a teacher's attention, competition for the teacher's recognition can be a major classroom force. It stands to reason that minimizing competition for the teacher's attention (either by having the teacher interact with the class as a whole or by having a high adult–child ratio) would reduce classroom competition. Similarly, reducing competition for symbols of the teacher's attention (honors, awards, conferred positions) and for classroom resources may increase children's attention to the cooperative and interpersonal aspects of tasks.

A shortcoming of experimental studies of cooperation is the questionable ecological validity of the tasks (e.g., board games) used to study cooperation, particularly with respect to cross-cultural comparisons. This chapter provides some data on the natural contexts in which cooperation may be socialized (and studied) in the classroom.

Adult Strategies for Controlling
Children's Behavior: A Brief Literature Review

Until recently, psychologists widely accepted the view that firm control by parents (i.e., consistent enforcement of clear rules) promotes internalization of values by children.[15] Accounts of Japanese child rearing challenge this American view of firm control. Japanese mothers apparently do not make explicit demands on their children and do not enforce rules when children resist;[16] yet, diverse accounts suggest that Japanese children strongly internalize parental, group, and institutional values.[17] The nursery school observations reported in this chapter were designed to stimulate American thinking about firm control by providing preliminary data on Japanese teachers' control strategies and beliefs regarding control.

Recent psychological research suggests that children are most likely to internalize rules when they receive the least external pressure in the course of obeying these rules.[18] Presumably, children who obey rules under strong external pressure can "attribute" their obedience to the external pressure, while children who obey rules without salient external pressure must "attribute" their obedience to some internal factor, such as believing in the rules or being a good child. According to this attribution theory, control strategies will maximize children's internalization of rules if they minimize the external pressure necessary to exact children's compliance, and reinforce the "good child" identity, that is, the child's tendency to think of himself or herself as someone who obeys rules.

Method

Observations of 15 Japanese nursery schools were conducted during May through July of 1979. At each school, one class of 5-year-olds was observed for 2 days. During the first day, the author noted the materials and equipment in view at the school, the schedule of activities engaged in by the children, and any incidents related to control or cooperation. Initially, the major purpose of the first day's observation was simply to accustom children and teachers to the presence of a foreigner in the classroom. However, these unstructured observations, and teachers' subsequent interpretations of what occurred, proved remarkably interesting and are the primary data of this report. On the second day, the author conducted spot observations every 20 min, noting the locations and activities of all children and teachers. In addition, a 10-min running account of teachers' behavior was dictated into a small hand-held tape recorder every 20 min. After observations on both days 1 and 2, teachers were interviewed about specific incidents which had been observed, about usual classroom practices, and about the concepts of child development which lay behind teachers' practices.

Observations

Setting. The teacher–child ratio was noteworthy: almost all classrooms contained one teacher and 30–40 children. In only 2 of 15 schools was a second adult (a student teacher) present. All 15 teachers observed were female. No schools permitted parents to visit the nursery school classroom, except for special parent programs which occurred several times a year. In the nursery schools studied, children attended school between 2½ and 5½ hours per day.

The sections which follow topically organize information from the unstructured observations, interviews with teachers and school directors, spot observations, and transcribed dictations of teacher behavior. Since interview questions and observational categories were added to the original format in the course of the observations, data from fewer than 15 schools are sometimes reported.

Small groups within the classroom. Small fixed-membership groups were a striking feature of most nursery schools visited; 13 of 15 classrooms had such groups. Groups had their own tables and were frequently the units for chores, teacher-initiated special projects, lunch, and children's own informal play. Groups of six to eight children were most common, with group size ranging from four to ten. Teachers selected the groups. Nine of 11 teachers reported that they based the groups on children's own friendships, choosing as a core for each group children who "played well together." Only one of 11 teachers mentioned that best friends were split up in constructing groups. Distributing "able" children among groups was a second strategy for constructing groups, spontaneously mentioned by six of 11 teachers. Abilities mentioned as important to distribute among groups included leadership and social skills, athletic skills, and artistic ability. Same-sex and mixed-sex groups were both seen. The tenure of the small groups depended on how well children played and carried out tasks together. Teachers planned to maintain the same groups for periods ranging from 1 term (4 months) to 2 years; most teachers expected to maintain the groups without major changes for at least 1 year. When teachers made changes in the groups, it was sometimes a de facto recognition that children were not functioning together as a group: "We don't change the groups; the groups change." Children were frequently referred to collectively by group name. Dismissal and other rewards were sometimes conferred by group, and group murals with the names of each group member were in evidence in many classrooms. Teachers planned activities which required children to elicit and accommodate other children's intentions. For example, in one classroom, the teacher asked each group to make a *kamishibai* (paper theater) by having all children in the group make pictures that fit together in a continuous story. This task required children within the group to agree on a story line and to divide up the story among group members. The teacher in this classroom used an interesting technique for physically orienting group members toward one another. Before starting the activity, all groups were asked to find their members, hold hands in a circle, lie back in a pinwheel, and then sit up. As the groups planned the paper theaters, the teacher circulated through the room, physically orienting toward their groups any children who were turned outward. In addition, the teacher deflected children's questions to their fellow group members, telling children, "Ask the other children in your group what they want to make" and "Remember to make pictures that fit together in a story, not the same picture."

Play materials and cooperation. Foreign visitors to Japan are accustomed to seeing familiar objects miniaturized to fit an environment where space is a precious resource. An interesting exception to this was the oversized heavy wooden blocks, of 3 feet or longer, which were observed in eight of 12 schools. Such blocks are extremely difficult or impossible for one child to manipulate without help. These large blocks would seem to demand cooperative play.

Observation notes suggest also that classroom materials may be distributed in a way that facilitates cooperation. For example, a teacher in one classroom placed paints on each group's table, providing fewer brushes than children and asking the children to consult each other about paint use so the paints would not be spilled. A subsequent interview with the teacher confirmed that the teacher had deliberately chosen to provide fewer brushes than children and to place the paints in a location (the center of each group's table) where they would be spilled if children failed to confer about their use. Other teachers spontaneously mentioned that they withdrew toys as children became older, to help children learn cooperation. In some respects, these findings ran counter to the original hypotheses: teachers viewed scarce, not plentiful, resources as a means for promoting cooperation among 5-year-olds.

Minimizing competition for the teacher's attention. With 30 to 40 children per classroom and only one adult, teachers could hardly minimize competition by giving close personal attention to all children. During interviews, several teachers commented on the use of aides and parent helpers in American nursery schools and expressed envy of the greater flexibility this would allow classroom teachers. However, these teachers also remarked that the presence of parents in the nursery class could undermine children's formation of friendships with other children.

Neither did teachers choose to minimize competition by interacting with the class as a whole. In only 22% of spot observations did teachers interact with the class as a whole. However, hand waving and other forms of competition for the teacher's attention were not in evidence, perhaps because much classroom authority was delegated to children. As we will see below, children were encouraged to consult other children, not the teacher, on matters ranging from what to draw to how to settle a playground fight.

Strategies for controlling children's behavior. How is a transition made from the indulged, undisciplined early child rearing at home to a nursery school structure which must, at the very least, ensure the safety of 30 to 40 children? As noted above, a growing research literature suggests that salient external control—beyond that necessary to elicit compliance with a request—tends to undermine children's internalization of the norm in question. On the other hand, control strategies which elicit compliance using minimal pressure tend to foster internalization of norms. From this point of view, four aspects of teachers' control strategies were particularly interesting: (1) minimizing the impression of teacher control; (2) delegating control to children; (3) providing plentiful opportunities for children to acquire a "good girl" or "good boy" identity; and (4) avoiding the attribution that children intentionally misbehave.

Minimizing the impression of teacher control. One way to minimize the salience of teacher control in the classroom is simply to tolerate a wide latitude of child behavior. The observations suggest that Japanese nursery school teachers may do just that. In view of previous suggestions that the behavior of Japanese children in nursery school is somewhat regimented,[19] the noise and chaos level of the Japanese nursery schools was perhaps the single most astonishing aspect of the observations. Very high levels of spontaneous background noise from children (shouting, laughing, etc.) partially obscured almost half of the dictations of teacher behavior, even though the tape recorder was held directly to the observer's mouth and the children were rarely within 2 feet of the observer. One possibility is that Japanese adults relatively value children's *genki* (vigor) and that considerable classroom noise does not necessarily reflect negatively on the teacher.[20]

The spot observations also suggest that teachers kept a low profile as classroom authorities. In only 53% of the spot observations were all children even within the teacher's sight. In 13% of the spot observations, none of the children in the classroom were within the teacher's sight. These percentages do not include situations in which another adult was responsible for teaching the children, or all children were in an area, such as the playground, where supervision was not required. (Subsequent questioning affirmed that teachers did not expect the observer to watch the children in teacher's absence.) Nor was it the case that classrooms had been child proofed to obviate the need for adult presence. In six of 10 schools one or more of the following were within reach of the children: sharp scissors, razor blade knives, leather punches, or nails. Teachers recognized that children could hurt themselves with these objects but believed children would only use them under supervision. My questions about whether children would purposely use these objects to hurt other children elicited puzzlement. Perhaps, as we shall see below, the puzzlement centered on differences in attribution about intent. Teachers stated that the children were capable of self-supervision on occasions when the teacher was called out of the room. Beliefs about children's capacities for self-control and self-regulation have received some attention but deserve further research in the future.[21]

A low profile as classroom authorities was suggested, also, by teachers' responses to misbehavior. The dictated descriptions of teacher behavior and the observation notes include numerous incidents, such as the following in which teachers made requests but did not enforce the requests or did not check to see whether children complied:

> Yuki is throwing sand and calling it "snow." Teacher asks Yuki to stop throwing sand. Yuki continues. Teacher repeats request two more times. Yuki continues. Teacher tries to turn child's attention to building a race track, but he brings more sand to throw. Teacher, "If you fill up the tunnel with snow you can't have a race." Teacher turns to student teacher and says, "It's no use. They want to make it snow no matter what you do."[22]

Interviews with teachers about these incidents and others suggested that their goal was not necessarily to make children comply but, rather, to make them understand what was proper behavior. (Other investigators provide further evidence on this point.)[23] In another incident described in the field notes, boys had been dropping clay "bombs" on the fish in an aquarium. The teacher explained that the clay would hurt the fish but did not specifically tell the boys to stop (nor did they). In her announcements to the whole class at the end of the school day, the teacher explained that some boys in the class thought they were "helping" the fish by throwing in clay "food," but that actually the boys were harming the fish. When I subsequently interviewed the teacher about the incident, our exchange was as follows:

INTERVIEWER: Did you really think the children were trying to help the fish by throwing the clay pellets?

TEACHER: Yes.

INTERVIEWER: Don't you think the boys understood they might hurt the fish by throwing the clay pellets?

TEACHER: If they *understood* it was wrong, they wouldn't do it.

An incident from the observation notes suggests that understanding may sometimes also take precedence over performance as a teaching goal.

> Child is sitting on steps, having just put his shoes on in order to play outside. Shoes are on wrong feet. Teacher notices and says to child, "Do you feel anything funny?" Child fails to recognize problem. Teacher says, "Do your shoes feel funny?" Child

still doesn't understand. Teacher says, "Look at Taro's shoes. Do they look the same as yours or different?" Child still does not understand. Teacher continues this line of questioning for approximately three minutes. Child still doesn't understand. Teacher says, "Oh well, just go ahead and play," Child goes off to play with shoes on the wrong feet.

While systematic evidence is needed on teachers' monitoring and enforcement of requests, the preceding interview material suggests a philosophy of child development coherent with minimal use of control; if children understand what is proper behavior, compliance will naturally follow. Thus, understanding, not compliance, becomes the teacher's primary goal.

Delegating control to children. Frequently, children were responsible for calling the class together, overseeing class projects, and even managing disagreements. For example, in one class 38 children initiated preparations to go home on the basis of one quiet remark made by the teacher to a few children playing near her. When interviewed, the teacher indicated that ideally she should not need to mention going home even to a few children since they should keep an eye on the clock and remember it spontaneously. Similarly, when classes assembled for some program (such as a puppet show or singing) it was common for the teacher to make only one quiet statement to a few children. Sometimes children would be asked to check and see if their friends or group members had assembled; frequently teachers themselves did not attempt to find or involve children who did not appear for lunch, dismissal, or other class activities. Children were frequently seen searching for missing classmates, reminding isolated or distracted classmates about class activities, and improvising noisemakers to summon or quiet classmates for an activity.

Examples from the observations and interviews suggest that teachers often encouraged children to manage their own and other children's problems without teacher intervention. For example, when a child reported to the teacher that members of the "tulip" group were throwing stones out of the playhouse window, the teacher did not herself investigate the situation, but said, "Tell the tulips it's dangerous." In another example from the field notes, a teacher asked two girls to encourage a boy to finish his lunch. The girls sat with the boy, helped him assemble scattered grains of rice and exhorted him to eat, and finally reported to the teacher that the boy had eaten. Interview and observational data also suggest that teachers preferred not to intervene directly in classroom aggression but to have the children themselves manage aggression.

When I see kids fighting, I tell them to go where there isn't concrete under them or where there are mats. Of course, if they're both completely out of control, I stop it Fighting means recognizing others exist. Fighting is being equal in a sense.

We let them fight a bit, not to the point of biting, etc. We have to let them experience pain to a small extent, but not to the extent of hurting themselves. I tell children to cry if they're being hurt, because the opponent will bite or pull until they cry. If they work hard to keep from crying, they'll get hurt more in the end.

If children can solve fights on their own without people getting hurt, I let them do it themselves and ignore it. Kids start out rooting for the weak kid if the teacher stays out of it. If I can, I let them solve it.

The fact that there isn't more fighting among children is considered a problem by many teachers and parents. Teachers plan things so that there will be more fighting, like decreasing the number of toys for 5-year-olds. We try and get kids to take responsibility for each other's quarrels. We encourage children to look when someone's crying and to talk about what the child is feeling, thinking, etc.

In one of the few aggressive episodes recorded in the field notes, two boys had a fight which progressed from sand throwing to hair pulling and hitting. The teacher did not directly attempt to stop the fight; in fact, she cheered on the smaller boy, saying, "Give it your best" and "Look, Taro's gotten strong; now he can fight without crying." When asked by a child why the two boys were fighting, the teacher said, "You'd better ask the fighters." The teacher encouraged two bystanders to question the fighters about the problem and then asked each bystander to report what he had learned. After eliciting the reports, the teacher said, "You're the caretakers, so you should decide what to do" and turned her back. The caretakers tried to get each fighter to apologize but failed. The caretakers then became frustrated and abandoned their mediation efforts. The fighting then resumed, and the teacher asked a girl watching the fight to help the two fighters make up. At the same time, the teacher said, "I am washing my hands of this" and walked away. The girl and a second nearby girl each began to question the fighters, saying, "Are you mad? If not, say 'I'm sorry.'" Meanwhile, the teacher drew a circle around the fighters and children solving the fight and asked the rest of the children to start cleaning up to go home. The two girls succeeded in getting the fighters to apologize to each other. Each girl held hands with one fighter and brushed the sand off him, and then the two girls joined hands, forming a chain with the two fighters. From a distance, the teacher said, "Great! The problem has been solved, due to the two girls." Noticing that one boy was still crying, the teacher said, "Now it's your problem alone, if you've already made up." Although class dismissal time had already been delayed by about 15 min by the fight, the teacher discussed the incident with the whole class, assembled for dismissal. The teacher named the fighters and described in detail how they had thrown sand, pulled hair, and hit. She also named all four mediators and praised them for helping solve the class's problem. Parents picking up their children were kept waiting for about 20 min beyond the normal dismissal time.

The number of aggressive episodes observed was too small to permit generalization. However, the limited data available suggest that teachers are less interested in stopping aggression than in developing children's own ability to stop aggression. Seemingly, teachers preferred not to isolate or hide incidents of aggression but to involve other children, using aggressive episodes as grist for fostering peer management skills.

Providing opportunities to develop a good-child identity. In addition to children's informal involvement in classroom management, 14 of 15 schools had a formal system of daily rotating *toban* (monitors). Toban were responsible for such visible leadership roles as leading the class in greetings and distributing tea at lunch. The toban's authority might include deciding which group to dismiss first, deciding which group was quiet enough to have lunch, giving permission to individual children to go outside after lunch, and finding children who were missing at lunch time or other assembly times. Toban were addressed as "san," a higher honorific than that normally used to address kindergarten children.

Some schools had a toban from each group, while others had one or two toban from the class as a whole. The toban changed daily, and picture charts showed when each child's turn would come up. Although all children became toban automatically in turn, considerable pomp and circumstance were attached to the position. In most schools, at the beginning of each day, a song or ceremony identified the new toban and a badge was conferred. At the end of the day, the toban received formal thanks from the whole class. The honor was keenly appreciated by children: teachers reported parents had difficulty keeping ill children home from school if it happened to be their toban day. The toban system afforded each child an opportunity to develop an identity as a classroom leader and authority figure.

Although the toban system existed in 14 of 15 schools, individual teachers took pains to explain how the system emerged "naturally" from the children's wishes.

> Toban grows naturally out of children's helping. It is not required for 3-year-olds; for them, the children who want to help do help. For the older children, the toban system allows even a child who can't normally be a leader a chance to be a leader. The children who are least able to lead others in daily encounters are often the ones who work the most carefully when they are toban.

> Children think up the jobs that need to be done in the classroom; then, they decide who will do them. Usually they take responsibility to do them, since they've mentioned the job themselves. If they don't, the teacher may do the job for awhile.

In the view of the teachers, the toban system and the chore groups (which were often the same as the children's fixed groups) helped children learn cooperation:

"You understand how hard people can make it for you and how much better it is to have help."

One teacher recounted her ongoing efforts to encourage the children to adopt a new chore. Each day for several months the teacher had asked the class to thank Ken for closing the classroom door. She mentioned that this prevented neighborhood cats from entering the classroom at night. So far, the children had not picked up the teacher's hint to make door closing a regular chore. The teacher justified her plan to continue hinting, rather than making an open request: "Children can't be told those things; they must learn them by doing."

Similarly, teachers took pains to see that classroom decisions "naturally emerged" from the children; if even one child objected, teachers might refrain from enforcing a new policy:

> Boys are putting blocks in a box and carrying it to another class. About six boys are all carrying the box together, and several boys are complaining that the other class gets the blocks. The teachers says, "We've had them for a long time, so we'd like to lend them to the other class. Do you think that's a bad idea?" Most of the boys says it's not a bad idea; one boy says it's a bad idea. Teacher says, "Then please stop moving them. We need to ask how the whole class is feeling about this."

A further incident from the field notes suggests that teachers helped children find peer-based, not teacher-based, methods for dealing with breakdowns in cooperative work. In the course of asking groups to report to the class on their chores, a teacher was told by the bird group that they did not finish their chore because they "began playing in the middle." The teacher solicited suggestions from the whole class about what to do if a group could not get its members together to work. The teacher passed over suggestions that the group members be punished, saying, "It's not a good situation when people work because they are forced to." The teacher appeared satisfied when one child finally suggested that the group members ready to do chores could "get together and shout to call the people who aren't there." The solution focuses not on punishment or reward of behavior but on a pragmatic strategy for eliciting cooperative behavior.

Avoiding the attribution that children intentionally misbehave. As illustrated in the case of the boys who did not "understand" not to bomb the goldfish, teachers frequently attributed children's misbehavior to something other than malicious intent. For example, children had "forgotten their promises" or did not "understand" what was right. Misbehavior was often described as "strange" behavior. Frequently, discipline by teachers took the form of a simple explanation of appropriate behavior or of a series of questions which assumed that the child would not knowingly commit wrongdoing. For example, a boy who hid the shoes of a boy washing his feet was questioned as follows: "Did Ben ask you to move his shoes?" "What happens when you finish washing your feet and your shoes aren't there?" "Do you know it would be nicer to help Ben?" The teacher's questions concluded with, "This time is over, but remember these things next time." Similarly, a boy with his hand cocked back about to throw a large rock was asked to "lend" the rock to the teacher who demonstrated, by touching the child's head with the rock, how he could be hurt if such a rock hit the back of his head. The teacher then returned the rock to the child, asking him to carry it carefully. The teacher did not ask the child to put down the rock or imply that the child intended to throw it. Parenthetically, it is interesting to note that teachers' use of naive questions as a form of discipline may shape children's responses to interviewing. On the occasions when I was not carrying out observations and was free to interact informally with children, they apparently interpreted my (genuinely naive) questions about game rules as a signal that they were behaving improperly.

When questioned about children's misbehavior, teachers frequently volunteered that enjoyment of school was the key to good behavior for children. An emotional attachment to the teacher and friendships with children were considered critical elements in the child's enjoyment of school. Techniques for building the teacher-child relationship included keeping the same teacher for 2 or more years (seven of nine schools) and teacher visits to the children's homes (four of eight schools). Some schools offered special preparatory classes for children who had cried during their nursery school interviews; prior to the school year, these children visited a nursery school as frequently as was necessary to adjust to the new setting. Teachers' elaborate efforts to construct children's groups that "successfully" played together were described above. One school even held regular meetings of the mothers' groups corresponding to the children's small groups. These parallel maternal networks were intended to strengthen the children's groups.

Discussion

Whether the observations set forth here are generally representative of Japanese nursery schools and whether they indicate differences from practices in American nursery schools remain to be documented by future research. Elements of the observations corroborate existing research on Japanese adults' control strategies, including the maternal verbal reports obtained by Conroy *et al.* and the home observations conducted by Vogel.[24] The concluding paragraphs identify, from the observations, aspects of early education worthy of future systematic comparison in Japan and the United States and perhaps in other countries as well.

The role of small groups in socialization. While previous accounts of Japanese nursery schools have focused on the likely restrictiveness of group activity, the role of small groups in promoting cooperation, empathy, and self-management among nursery school children is largely unexplored. The literature review notes a lone experimental finding that children trained in constant membership groups are more cooperative when grouped with new children than are children trained in changing membership groups. The present observations suggest two possible interpretations of this finding. First, retributive justice may more often prevail (e.g., children who commit aggressive acts may be punished, children who shirk work may be discovered, etc.) in groups that continue over time. This may be particularly true if group activities demand cooperation and accommodation, and if children focus attention on ways of achieving cooperation rather than on extrinsic goals such as avoiding punishment or obtaining rewards for the group. Second, repeated long-term interaction with a constant small group may accelerate children's understanding of other children's intentions, affect, needs, etc. These hypotheses need to be tested by future research that more fully explores the role of long-term small-group membership in children's early socialization.

Concepts of the child that may underlie socialization. Interviews with teachers revealed conceptions of child development that deserve systematic comparison with concepts held by Americans. The observations revealed some concepts that are strikingly similar to those described historically for the Japanese: for example, that children younger than age 6 or 7 are incapable of intentional wrongdoing.[25] The child's capacity for self-management, the child's capacity for willful misbehavior, and the child's responsiveness to peer versus adult disciplinary sanctions were all suggested as potential areas of interest. The consequences of these concepts for teacher behavior also represent a key area for future research.

Delegating authority to children. Children in Japanese nursery schools appear to receive considerable encouragement to be their brother's keeper. Peers, not teachers, may have authority to manage aspects of classroom life ranging from participation in class events and finishing one's lunch to fights with other children. While interesting evidence exists on peer management of classroom behavior by older students,[26] little is known about consequences of peer management in nursery schools. Research on children's moral judgments suggests that peer justice may be unduly harsh,[27] but little is known about how these moral judgments translate into actual behavior.

What are the likely effects of peer versus adult enforcement of rules on children's internalization of rules and their attitudes toward authority? Several speculations are in order. First, delegating authority to children enables teachers to make few behavioral demands on children. In the Japanese schools observed, peers assume much of the authority for checking that children complete their chores, finish their lunches, behave nicely toward other children, and so forth. This delegation of authority may enable the teacher to remain a benevolent figure to whom children have a strong, unconflicted positive attachment. A second speculation is that delegation of authority allows children to experience negative sanctions as intrinsic consequences of their acts. When the toban fails to realize it is time for lunch and is hit on the back by hungry group mates attempting to redirect his attention (to take an actual example from observations), the child may experience this very differently from a teacher's reprimand. Children's sanctions may appear less contrived and external and more like the direct, natural consequences of the child's own acts, thus fostering greater behavioral change. Finally, it may be that peer criticism, in comparison with adult criticism, poses less of a threat to the child's identity as a good child. Research on moral judgment suggests that, in the mind of a 5-year-old, morality and adult authority are inextricably linked.[28] Thus, criticism by adults may, to a much greater degree than peer criticism, cause the child to feel like a bad child. The "good child" identity may, in turn, be a critical determinant of the child's subsequent willingness to obey rules.[29] The fragile "good child" identity may fare better in an environment in which peers, not adults, bear messages that the child has misbehaved.

An earlier section of this report poses the question, How is a transition made from the indulged, undisciplined early child rearing at home to a nursery school structure which must, at the very least, ensure the safety of 30–40 children? The present data suggest several answers. Teachers may tolerate, at least initially, a wide latitude of behavior by children. Compliance, orderliness, and classroom harmony may be viewed as consequences that naturally follow when children understand what is proper behavior, not as behavioral goals that must be quickly achieved. Since it is frequently the peers, not the teacher, who are responsible for eliciting proper behavior, there is reduced need for the teacher to exercise authority. Further, teachers provide plentiful opportunities for children to shape classroom rules and formally to assume positions of authority. The attribution theory discussed here suggests that providing children with opportunities to cooperate and act in accordance with classroom rules, without salient external pressure from the teacher, will promote strong internalization of classroom values. Thus, these Japanese nursery school practices may promote strong internalization and, ultimately, high compliance, while maintaining the role of the teacher as a benevolent, though perhaps not quite indulgent, figure.

Acknowledgments

This work was carried out while I was a postdoctoral fellow of the Social Science Research Council. The observations could not have been made without the considerable help of Shigefumi Nagano in setting up nursery school observations and providing background on the Japanese educational system. I am also indebted to Fukumi Ichikawa, Hiroko Yano, and the teachers and directors of the 15 schools. Special thanks are due to Robert LeVine for nurturing and broadening my interest in cross-cultural comparisons.

Notes

1. *Nihon Kyoiku Nenkan* (Tokyo: Nihon Kyoiku Nenkan Hanko linkaihen Gvosel 1982). Statistics are as of April 1980.
2. W. A. Caudill. "Tiny Dramas: Vocal Communication between Mother and infant in Japanese and American Families." In W. P. Lebra, ed., *Mental Health Research in Asia and the Pacific* (vol. 2) (Honolulu: East-West Center, 1972). William Caudill and Carmi Schooler. "Child Behavior and Child Rearing in Japan and the United States: An Interim Report." *Journal of Nervous and Mental Disease*, 1973, 157: 323–38; Nancy Shand. "Cultural Factors in Maternal Behavior: Their Influence on Infant Behavioral Development in Japan and the U.S., "Progress Reports I and II (Meninger Foundation, 1978); William Cummings. *Education and Equality in Japan* (Princeton, N.J.: Princeton University Press, 1980).
3. Robert Hess and Hiroshi Azuma. "Family Effects upon School Readiness and Communication Skills of Preschool Children in Japan and the United States," Data Reports 1–6 (Stanford University Graduate School of Education and University of Tokyo Faculty Education, n.d.); Robert Hess *et al.* "Maternal Expectations for Early Mastery of Developmental Tasks in Japan and the United States." *International Journal of Psychology*, 1980, 15:259–271; L. Taniuchi, "The Creation of Prodigies through Special Early Education: Three Case Studies" (paper of the Van Leer Project, Harvard University Graduate School of Education, n.d.).
4. Takeo Doi. *The Anatomy of Dependence* (Tokyo: Kodansha International, 1973); Hiroko Hara and Hiroshi Wagatsuma, *Shitsuke* (Tokyo: Kobundo, 1974); Ezra Vogel, *Japan's New Middle Class* (Berkeley: University of California Press, 1963).
5. Cummings.
6. Figures as of May 1, 1981, from Gakko Kihon Chosa survey, reported in *Japan Statistical Yearbook* (Tokyo: Statistics Bureau, Prime Minister's Office, 1982).
7. Harold Cook and Sandra Stingles. "Cooperative Behavior in Children." *Psychological Bulletin*, 1974, 81:918–33.
8. Ezra Vogel. *Japan as Number One: Lessons for America* (Cambridge, Mass.: Harvard University Press, 1979).
9. Chie Nakane. *Japanese Society* (Berkeley: University of California Press, 1972).
10. Robert Cole. *Work, Mobility and Participation: A Comparative Study of American and Japanese Industry* (Berkeley: University of California Press, 1979).
11. Spencer Kagan and Millard Madsen. "Cooperation and Competition of Mexican-American and Anglo-American Children of Two Ages under Four Instructional Sets." *Developmental Psychology*, 1971, *5:* 32–39; Millard Madsen and Ariella Shapira. "Cooperative and Competitive Behavior of Urban Afro-American, Anglo-American, Mexican-American and Mexican Village Children." *Developmental Psychology*, 1970, 3:16–20; Ariella Shapira and Millard Madsen. "Cooperative and Competitive Behavior of Kibbutz and Urban Children in Israel." *Child Development*, 1969, 40:609–17.

12. J. Aronfreed. "The Socialization of Altruistic and Sympathetic Behavior: Some Theoretical and Experimental Analyses." In J. Macaulay and L. Berkowitz, eds., *Altruism and Helping Behavior* (New York: Academic Press, 1970).
13. Teresa Amabile, William DeJong, and Mark Lepper. "Effects of Externally-imposed Deadlines on Subsequent Intrinsic Motivation." *Journal of Personality and Social Psychology*, 1976, 34:92–98.
14. Moses Goldberg and Eleanor Maccoby. "Children's Acquisition of Skill in Performing a Group Task under Two Conditions of Group Formation." *Journal of Personality and Social Psychology*, 1965, 2:898–902.
15. D. Baumrind. "The Development of Instrumental Competence through Socialization." In A. D. Pick, ed., *Minnesota Symposia on Child Psychology* (vol. 7) (Minneapolis: University of Minnesota Press, 1973); Eleanor Maccoby. *Social Development: Psychological Growth and the Parent-Child Relationship* (New York: Harcourt Brace Jovanovich, 1980); Catherine Lewis. "The Effects of Parental Firm Control: A Reinterpretation of Findings." *Psychological Bulletin*, 1981, 90:547–63.
16. Hara and Wagatsuma; Vogel, *Japan's New Middle Class.*
17. Vogel, *Japan as Number One: Lessons for America;* Nakane.
18. M. Lepper. "Social Control Processes, Attributions of Motivation, and the Internalization of Social Values." In *Social Cognition and Social Behavior: Developmental Perspectives*, E. T. Higgins, D. N. Ruble, and W. W. Hartup, eds., (San Francisco: Jossey-Bass, 1981).
19. Leslie C. Bedford, "Rakuto Kindergarten: Observations on Japanese Preschooling," *Harvard Graduate School of Education Association Bulletin* 23 (Spring 1979): 18–20; Ruth Bettelheim and Ruth Takanishi, *Early Schooling in Asia* (New York: McGraw-Hill, 1976).
20. Christena Turner, personal communication, July 1979 (diss. in progress), Stanford University.
21. Robert Hess *et al.* (n. 3 above).
22. All translations are mine.
23. Vogel, *Japan's New Middle Class* (n. 4 above). Mary Conroy *et al.*, "Maternal Strategies for Regulating Children's Behavior in American Families," *Journal of Cross-cultural Psychology*, 1980, 11 [no. 2]:153–72.
24. Conroy *et al.;* Vogel, *Japan's New Middle Class.*
25. Hara and Wagatsuma (n. 4 above); Hideo Kojima. "Childrearing Concepts as a Belief-Value System of Society and Individual" (paper presented at the Conference on Child Development in Japan and the United States, Center for Advanced Study in the Behavioral Sciences, April 1983).
26. Urie Bronfenbrenner. *Two Worlds of Childhood: U.S. and U.S.S.R.* (New York: Pocket Books, 1973).
27. R. Johnson. "A Study of Children's Moral Judgments," *Child Development*, 1962, 23:327–354.
28. L. Kohlberg. "Morals and Moralization: A Cognitive Developmental Approach." In T. Lickona, ed., *Moral Development and Behavior* (New York: Holt, Rinehart & Winston, 1976).
29. Lepper (n. 18 above).

PART V

Schools as Socialization Agents

In the thirteen original British colonies that later banded together to become the United States of America and during the early decades of the new country itself most children did not go to school, and many who did went for only a year or two or three. Children were socialized in their families and communities (which usually included church attendance.) Most families lived on farms, and children learned to work alongside their parents, as did children who lived in the towns and small cities of the time and whose parents had small shops or workshops. Only a relatively small elite could afford to send their children to school for an extended school education.

As the country became more urbanized, and businesses increased in scale and complexity, more schooling was required in order for people to know how to function in the new, more complex society. Reading, writing, and arithmetic—"the three R's"—became essential knowledge for almost everyone. Eventually, a specified number of years of schooling became compulsory. Parents were no longer free to keep children out of school on the ground that their work was required to contribute to the family income.

Not all parents were pleased with the new requirements. As sociologist Viviana Zelizer observes in her study of the social reevaluation of children, "The exclusion of children from the marketplace involved a difficult and prolonged battle lasting almost fifty years from the 1870s to the 1930s. . . . Two groups with sharply conflicting views of children struggled to impose their definition of children's proper place in society. For child labor reformers, children's early labor was a violation of children's sentimental value . . . On the other hand, opponents of child labor reform were just as vehement in their support of the productive child." (Zelizer 1985: 57). Thus, two different trends were making schools important: (1) A more complex society required better educated people; (2) A cultural trend was underway that led to a redefinition of what a child is. The older notion that children should be productive workers contributing to the family income was being replaced by the belief that children are emotionally priceless and should be spared the hardships of working in factories, mines, and other workplaces that were unsafe physically and morally. Parents with low incomes resisted this change of outlook, but many eventually accepted it, if reluctantly. Not many believe children don't need much schooling.

Sociologist Steven Brint presents a discussion that shows that schools are more than institutions for teaching school subjects. They play an important part in shaping children's ability to fit into society. He argues that schools and teachers try to train children in three different kinds of conformity: behavioral conformity, moral conformity, and cultural conformity. He recognizes that these efforts are not always successful. Further, in addition to describing the formal socialization that takes place in the classroom Brint also presents a discussion of the informal socialization that takes place on the playground. Here, adults play a minimal role; children are in control, and they have much to learn from interacting with each other.

Chapter 19 in Part IX also deals with schools as socialization agencies and shows how social class differences result in differential socialization in classrooms.

Reference

Zelizer, Viviana. *Pricing the Priceless Child*: *The Changing Social Value of Children* (New York: Basic Books, 1985).

9

Schools and Socialization*

Steven Brint

The early-nineteenth-century American school reformer Horace Mann observed that it is easier to create a republic than to create republicans (Mann, quoted in Cremin 1957:14). By this, Mann meant that the self-restraint and virtuous conduct that make representative government possible do not necessarily come naturally to those born into republics and must therefore be created by society's institutions, particularly its schools. Mann's observation suggests the important role schools have long played in the socialization of children.

Sociologists use the term *socialization* to describe the efforts of powerful members of a society to shape the behavior and values of less powerful members of the society. School authorities do not always succeed in their efforts to socialize their students, any more than they always succeed in their efforts to teach the official curriculum, but the effort to socialize is undoubtedly one of the major activities of schooling. Think of how often students' attention and behavior is organized in school around explicit or implicit norms of conduct. Every time a teacher says "I need your attention," she is socializing students to be responsive to authority. Every time she hands back a paper with a smile or a frown, she is socializing students to value work well done in the eyes of the school.

Schools play a secondary role to families in socializing children. The powerful mix of emotional intimacy and consistent attentiveness typical of family life cannot be duplicated by the more impersonal institutions of society. Families create the capacity for trust and self-control out of which healthy egos develop. Even so, schools are organized in ways that are particularly conducive to the formation of personalities for a public world in which intimacy and attentiveness are not always in generous supply. Schools specialize in the creation

*Reprinted from Steven Brint, *Schools and Societies* pp. 136–39 and 150–63. Copyright © 1998 by Pine Forge Press. Reprinted by permission of Pine Forge Press.

of people who can adapt to impersonal work environments and who can pursue their interests in action with and against people who are neither kin nor intimate friends. Without lengthy exposure to the socializing environments of the school, most children would not be as well prepared as they are for adult life.

This chapter begins by describing the three types of socialization that can take place in schools and then sketches the historical development of schools' socializing role. The remainder of the chapter analyzes two distinct sites of socialization in contemporary schools: the classroom and the "playground." By playground, I mean all school spaces outside the classroom—the hallways, playgrounds, lunch rooms, and extracurricular activity rooms. Classrooms are the spaces in which lessons of industry and work-related achievement are principally taught. Playgrounds are the spaces in which friendships and coalitions are formed and broken, status hierarchies are expressed and challenged, and children learn to balance self-assertion and self-control in informal social life. If teachers are the primary socializers in the classroom setting, the dominant boys and girls are the primary socializers in these outside spaces.

Three Dimensions of Socialization

Socialization is more than instilling values and standards of conduct. Think of socialization as involving three dimensions: efforts to shape behavior, moral values, and cultural styles. The differences in these dimensions become clearer when we consider how students who conform primarily on one of these dimensions are characterized. Students are described as "well disciplined" by authorities if they conform behaviorally, "good" if they are seen to conform morally, and "well adjusted" if they conform culturally.

Behavioral conformity. Training for behavioral conformity involves activities related to the body, its mechanical actions, and its accessories. In schools with strict disciplinary environments, students may, for example, be required to sit erect with their eyes on the teacher, to raise their hands before talking, to stay in their seats unless they are excused, to have their pencils sharpened at all times, and to have their textbooks with them in class. If students are punished for failing to comply with these requirements, the school is attempting to use its powers of control to socialize for behavioral conformity.

Moral conformity. Training for moral conformity involves activities related to the production of an internalized sense of "right action." Teachers may talk about the importance of such virtues as honesty, kindness, courage, hard work, or fairness. They may also assign reading materials that illustrate the consequences of not being guided by these virtues. At higher levels, more complex moral issues may be raised, involving the collision of two "goods" or finer judgments of others' actions. Clearly, training for behavioral and moral conformity are overlapping in practice. Most schools expect a movement from external discipline based on behavioral control to self-discipline in conformity with key moral values. Nevertheless, it is possible to have a high level of behavioral conformity without much in the way of moral conformity, as the various cheating and harassment scandals in the military academies demonstrate.

Cultural conformity. Training for cultural conformity, or acculturation, is more a matter of learning approved styles and outlooks. In the better Parisian secondary schools, for example, students are expected to express themselves vividly, with memorable phrases and sharp wit (Bourdieu 1988). If a student makes a very witty remark in class, the teacher will smile in appreciation or attempt an equally witty riposte. By contrast, in secondary school in a Central European republic, it may be more important for students to demonstrate conspicuous thoughtfulness: to probe beneath the surface appearances and to ask questions that get to the heart of a difficult problem. These styles and outlooks reflect the cultural logic of a particular group or time or place. It is, for example, reasonable to expect that centers of learning in cosmopolitan capitals like Paris will reflect the quick pace and brilliant surfaces of archetypal urban life, whereas those in relatively isolated regions show a gravity that frequently appears unduly stiff to urban sophisticates. Students of acculturation tend to be cultural relativists; they try to understand the social logic that produces distinctive cultural styles, but they do not necessarily think that cultural styles and outlooks have any universal validity.

Even when schools emphasize all three types of conformity, they may be more successful in one area than others. For example, military cadets are required to conform to an enormous number of behavioral rules. If they don't salute in a crisp fashion, they can be sent back to barracks. If their boots don't show a "spit shine," they can be forced to clean out latrines. Because well-executed response to orders is vitally important in the military, behavioral conformity is a top priority. By contrast, faculty in art schools may expect students to take pride in thumbing their noses at behavioral and moral conventions, as the famous battle cry of bohemia, *"épater les bourgeois"* (literally, shock or flabbergast the middle class), demands. But acculturation is unavoidable even in this nonconformist environment. To be accepted by other bohemians, would-be bohemians will necessarily conform to the expressive style and outlooks typical of their set. They may need to be able to talk knowledgeably about obscure poets or musicians and to shift smoothly between attitudes of enthusiasm for the offbeat and worldweariness in the face of the familiar. A would-be bohemian who does not act in these ways is not very well suited for bohemian life.

Discussions of the role of schools in socialization are often muddled by the failure to keep these three dimensions distinct. Many contemporary conservative critics, for example, suggest that schools are failing in the area of social-ization because they have stopped emphasizing moral virtues. In the introduc-tion to his best-seller *The Book of Virtues* (1993), former U.S. Secretary of Education William Bennett wrote:

> Where do we go to find the material that will help our children in [the] task [of devel-oping moral literacy]? The simple answer is we . . . have a wealth of material to draw on—materials that virtually all schools and homes and churches once taught to stu-dents for the sake of shaping character. That many no longer do so is something this book hopes to change. (p. 11)

Although he raises an important issue in this passage, Secretary Bennett is highlighting one dimension of socialization while playing down the other two.

Schools need to develop a certain minimum level of behavioral conformity, and they can't help but acculturate students in some way. Nor have they aban-doned the field of moral instruction as completely as Bennett and other critics contend. The specific socialization messages and the techniques used to social-ize have, however, changed greatly over time.

Socialization Inside the Classroom

Today's schools continue to buzz with socializing messages in the classroom and on the playground. But some of the most effective means of socialization are not part of the verbal buzz. Instead, they either frame the boundaries of acceptable behavior or are embedded in the very fabric of school routines. I will now look in greater detail at the practices of classroom socialization in contemporary schools and the extent to which these practices are successful in channeling behavior, belief, and orientations along school-approved lines.

Techniques of socialization. It is helpful to think of classroom socialization as organized around a core of relatively effective rules and routines surrounded by rings of less insistent (and therefore less effective) moral instruction.

The core consists of rules backed up by sanctions and routines of schooling that acculturate students to the worlds of impersonal organization and con-sumer choice. These embedded routines include such everyday features of schooling as lining up, working independently, choosing among electives, and taking tests. Sociologists have sometimes used the term *hidden curriculum* to describe lessons of socialization that are embedded in the very fabric of school-ing: in its official categories and constantly repeated routines.

Surrounding this core are rings of moral instruction. One ring consists of explicit moral instruction—the overt teaching of moral virtues that is found mainly in the elementary grades. Another ring consists of less explicit moral instruction. Some of this instruction occurs through exposure in later grades to the moral lessons of literature and history. Some occurs through observation of the exemplary actions of teachers and principals. Figure 9.1 diagrams this conception of classroom socialization.

The Core: Impersonal Rules and Embedded Practices

Teachers and principals do not force today's students to behave by whacking them across the bottoms or pulling the short hairs on their necks. Instead, students are socialized into an impersonal order in which rules and routine practices construct the boundaries of legitimate conduct; within those boundaries, students are relatively free to act as they wish. Because these rules and practices are built into the very fabric of schooling, they are taken for granted. They therefore direct students' orientations to the world through a powerful, if largely invisible, force—not unlike a magnetic force field.

School rules. School rules define the serious infractions that require punishments: hurting other children, insulting teachers, being disruptive in class, cheating, and the like. School rules may also prescribe where students can be at different times during the day, and the conditions under which they may leave their classrooms. Rules represent the prerequisites of bureaucratic life: being where you are supposed to be, doing your job, interacting in a peaceful way with co-workers, and accepting the authority of bosses.

Figure 9.1
Zones of Socialization in Contemporary Classrooms

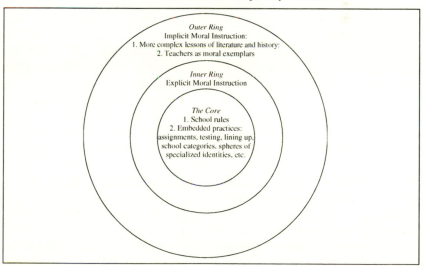

Outer Ring
Implicit Moral Instruction:
1. More complex lessons of literature and history:
2. Teachers as moral exemplars

Inner Ring
Explicit Moral Instruction

The Core
1. School rules
2. Embedded practices:
assignments, testing, lining up,
school categories, spheres of
specialized identities, etc.

The number of socializing rules in schools varies by society and level of instruction. In the United States, primary schooling is very heavily encased by rules. Secondary schooling depends, to a greater degree, on the internalization of these earlier experiences with rules. This pattern is the norm in most of the developed world. In Japan, however, children remain strongly embedded in group-centered moral life through primary school and emerge into an impersonal, rule-bound setting only with the arrival of secondary schooling (White 1993). In the developing world, rules are frequently equally elaborate in primary and secondary schools.

Embedded Practices. In addition to explicit rules, sociologists have uncovered a number of embedded practices that also play a role in socialization for the world of consumer choice and bureaucratic regulation.

The routine practices of offering choices are the key to the consumer side of classroom socialization. The trend toward consumerism may have been reaching its outer limit at the time Powell, Farrar, and Cohen published their study of shopping mall high schools (Ravitch 1995:48–58). Even so, the choices available to students at secondary schools do continue to resemble the variety of choices they face on a Saturday shopping expedition: dozens of extracurriculars, scores of electives, hundreds of social networks and possible identities, and only a relatively small number of common requirements.

Many other routine practices of schools are relevant to socializing students for life in bureaucratically organized settings. These encourage students to renounce their immediate impulses and gain patience; value individualism and individually earned achievements; deal effectively with authority and evaluation; and orient themselves to bureaucratic ways of seeing the self and others. These begin in primary school and continue to be embedded in schooling throughout secondary school.

Children are naturally egocentric and inclined to demand the regard of others and the freedom to pursue their own interests as they see fit. Schools as institutions are just as naturally opposed to allowing the natural egoism of children free expression. All of the "lining up" at school—for a turn at the water fountain, in anticipation of lunch or recess, for dismissal at the end of the day—requires students to learn patience. Because groups at school are relatively large, more patience and waiting for others is usually required than at home. Things happen at school not because students want them to happen but because it is time for them to occur. The denial of desire that schools require is "cumulatively important." The crowded condition of classrooms makes delayed gratification inevitable, as well as requiring students to deal with delays, denials, interruptions, and distractions (Jackson 1968).

School practices also socialize students into a life of evaluation based on individual performance. The three-step pattern of assignment, performance, and evaluation—repeated over and over in schools—reinforces the disposition to distinguish one's own efforts and feeds directly into the value of "success" in modern societies. Evaluations at school are more formal, more performance based, more public, and more consequential for adult status than those at home. Rewards are also generally for individual rather than group achievements. Because evaluation is so important in school, it teaches not only the norms of hard work and individual achievement but also various stratagems for managing evaluation while protecting the ego. As Philip Jackson (1968) pointed out, students learn how to enhance praise, how to publicize positive evaluations, and how to conceal negative ones (p. 26). Those who are evaluated poorly may learn to disengage, to "play it cool," to not get involved, and to mask cheating.

School practices also socialize acceptance of authority. Every time a teacher invokes a rule, makes an assignment, or calls for an answer, her or his authority is reinforced. Obedience and even docility are part of the life of labor, and the transition from classroom to factory or office is made easily by "those who have developed 'good work habits' (which is to say responsiveness to authority) in their early years" at school (Jackson 1968). The spatial and temporal organization of schools itself expresses authority relations. Students are not allowed free access to certain spaces: the principals' offices, the teachers' lounges, the counseling rooms. Even their access to classrooms is controlled by the staff. Students are required to be out of hallways and off the grounds at certain times.

At least two other modes of orientation required by bureaucratic life are also taught in schools. One is the habit of considering oneself a member of some larger category of people. Another is the habit of expressing only a facet of one's total personality. These can be thought of as norms of orientation toward *categorical statuses* and *specialized competencies*, respectively (cf. Dreeben 1968).

In schools, categories of people often matter more than individual personalities. Members of the "red group" may be first in line to use the computer during a particular week, and members of the "blue group" the next week. Third graders as a group may be given certain rights and responsibilities, such as the right to use certain equipment on the playground and the responsibility to clean up the playground on certain days. Through these repeated processes of grouping, schools give students experience in making social comparisons in categorical rather than particular terms. Pupils learn to distinguish between persons and the social positions they occupy. This orientation is important in bureaucratically organized societies, where people are constantly being asked to view themselves as members of particular categories—such as those with a particular level of taxable income or having a similar job grade—and to accept the duties and privileges consistent with those categories.[13]

Students also learn to express only specific, situationally relevant parts of their personalities. The whole person rarely matters in the school classroom. What counts is how good a math student the person is, or how good a social studies student. The whole personality is divided into parts, and students learn that only one or a few features of their whole personalities may be relevant. This type of understanding, too, is important in bureaucratically organized societies. It is not, for example, very important to a passenger whether a pilot is good company or likes sports as long as he or she can fly a plane properly.

Schools and Families as Sites of Socialization. Schools are suited structurally to prepare people for impersonal bureaucratic environments in ways that most families are not. In particular, school classrooms have two advantages over families for this purpose:

• Classrooms are the first performance-oriented bureaucracies in which children spend a good deal of time. Unlike families, classrooms are explicitly defined as performance-oriented places, and they are typically organized by relatively distant and titled authorities. Teachers are, in this respect, children's first "bosses" and schoolwork their first "job."

• Classrooms include many more children than families do, and the relationships that develop are broken at the end of the school year. Children do not have the same teacher every year or continue with exactly the same children. The large groups in classrooms and the annual discontinuity of classroom life limit the deep emotional attachments characteristic of families. The interest of teachers is, by necessity, limited to specific aspects of the child and is somewhat more distant emotionally. This impersonality becomes more true as children progress from the early primary grades to the later primary grades, and it is more or less completely true by the time children reach secondary school.

Table 9.1 shows these differences between families and classrooms. Because parents are usually more concerned with the whole child and have a personal, direct authority in the household, "families lack the resources and competence to effect the psychological transition to adult life" in impersonally organized settings (Dreeben 1968:85).

The Outer Ring: Moral Instruction

It is often assumed that moral instruction has been completely drained out of public schooling. No doubt, some schools have become leery of stepping on toes in a pluralistic society, and others may feel that the traditional types of moral instruction are old-fashioned. Nevertheless, moral instruction has not

Table 9.1
Structural Differences between Classrooms and Families

Classrooms	Families
Yearly promotion	No yearly promotion
Relatively large size	Relatively small size
Heterogeneous composition	Homogeneous composition
Broken relationships	Unbroken relationships
High child to adult ratio	Low child to adult ratio
Narrow, homogeneous age grouping	Mixture of several ages
Narrow range of activities and events	Wide range of activities and events
Little privacy	Some privacy
Specific treatment of individuals	Diffuse treatment of individuals

Source: Adapted from Dreeben (1968).

disappeared from the public schools. Most primary schools continue to be full of moral exhortation—to work hard and plan well, to be honest and faithful, to be courageous and kind, and so on. And many continue to use stories involving well-known heroes (such as George Washington and his apocryphal cherry tree) or familiar fables (such as the ant and the grasshopper) to inculcate traditional moral virtues. Teachers (by overwhelming majorities) say that schools should teach common core moral values, such as honesty, punctuality, responsibility, and industriousness (Farkas and Johnson 1996). And social studies and reading textbooks continue to emphasize such traditional values as "honesty, courage, compassion, persistence, bravery" (Sharp and Wood 1992).

At the same time, traditional moral instruction has been augmented by at least two values that have become more important in American society over time. One is the value of "fairness," which connects directly to the tensions between sharing, equality, and merit that schools must try to resolve. The question, "Is that fair?" has become central to the moral life of many a school classroom. The other new value is "respect for diversity." Some 96 percent of teachers say they believe in "teaching respect for others regardless of their racial and ethnic background," and nearly every schoolroom now includes posters of famous women and minorities, along with the white men who once presided almost exclusively. Textbook studies confirm a dramatic increase in concerns with pluralism and the contributions of the many groups that make up American society (Fitzgerald 1979; Wong 1991; Elson 1964). This is not to say that the balance between the old and the new has always been worked out perfectly. When schoolchildren are asked to choose a famous person to research, men such as Abraham Lincoln and Thomas Edison may be left off the list altogether in the name of diversity.

Oddly, we do not yet have a definitive study of changes in moral instruction over time. The educational historian David Tyack (1996) suggests it is possible that "the national [identifying symbolism] has been enlarged rather than abandoned." But it is also possible that moral education supporting the old Protestant-republican-entrepreneurial culture has grown significantly thinner over time while respect for group differences has grown significantly thicker. Such a change would be a near-perfect demonstration of Émile Durkheim's thesis that societies move from states of cohesion based on a common and obligatory moral order (which he termed *mechanical solidarity*) to states of cohesion based on pluralistic and balance-oriented moral orders (*organic solidarity*), as their social structures grow more complex.

Cross-national variations. Some important cultural variations exist in the organization and content of moral education provided by schools. One of these differences is the extent to which schools create curricular boundaries around moral education. In most of the developed world, moral instruction is interlaced with the regular curriculum. In the United States, for example, discussions of Abe Lincoln's honesty take place in relation to lessons in American history. By contrast, many developing countries, as well as many developed Asian countries, devote explicit time every day to moral or religious education. Imagine an American student taking a test on morality in public school, which is commonplace in Singapore, Hong Kong, and elsewhere in East Asia. Separate periods for moral instruction presumably produce more commitment to moral norms, although they may create more transparent forms of hypocrisy as well.

Another important difference has to do with the location of control over moral instruction. In a few countries, the primary responsibility for enforcing behavioral and moral conformity is the student group, rather than the teacher. In Japanese nursery schools, for example, teachers do not pull children out of the group for misbehaving. Nor do they talk to children about behavior problems. Instead, they rely on other children in the class to censure those who are misbehaving. As Catherine Lewis (1995) notes: "[These] practices may promote strong internalization and ultimately high compliance while maintaining the role of the teacher as a benevolent, though perhaps not quite indulgent, figure" (p. 84). In other words, group-based authority may increase the legitimacy of behavioral norms while allowing teachers and school administrators to be seen in a more sympathetic light than they might otherwise be.

A similar emphasis on peer authority can still be found in British public schools (called private schools in the United States). Sixth-form leaders (students of 16 to 17 years old) are selected to help the staff organize and discipline younger students. These "prefectures" both train selected students in habits of command and encourage student leaders to use their energies on behalf of the staff rather than on behalf of their potentially rebellious classmates. At Eton College, for example, the most famous of the British public schools, prefects are members of the Eton Society, also known as "Pop." The members of Pop wear fancy waistcoats, braided tailcoats, stick-up collars with white bow ties, check trousers, and a floral buttonhole. They enjoy tremendous prestige among the younger boys. In the past, members of the Eton Society could hand out whippings without the authorization of any housemaster, but corporal punishment by boys was banned in 1970. Today, members of the Eton Society must rely on the "symbolic violence" of words to keep their charges in line. Nevertheless, as one observer has noted, "Boy power is still strong and anyone coming [to Eton] from another school is struck by the weight and importance of boy opinion," represented at its pinnacle by the members of Pop (McConnell 1985:212). Just as in the case of Japanese peer authority systems, the prefectorial system has long been credited as one of the hidden reasons for the cohesiveness of British elites.

The content of moral instruction also varies considerably around the world in response to particular political, religious, and pedagogical traditions. In the former Soviet Union, for example, respect for manual work, a centerpiece of Communist ideology, filtered into moral instruction in numerous ways. Heroes of labor were celebrated, special times were set aside for manual labor, and the moral virtues of workers and peasants were celebrated (Bronfenbrenner 1970). In Japan, "principles of the Shinto and Confucian moral order, such as loyalty, filial piety, the discipline of group life, industry, cleanliness, physical strength and perseverance" are reinforced "by means of school rituals, courses of study and extracurricular activities" (Fujita 1986:330). In Israel, the rabbinical tradition of aggressively questioning what one reads, exploring paradoxes, and commenting on commentaries shows up in the qualities of mind that leading academic secondary schools try to cultivate. Singular individuals are also sometimes important. In areas of Europe (particularly Italy and Germany), for example, the progressive pedagogy of the Swiss school reformer Pestalozzi encouraged moral teaching based on a sense of the splendor and balance of nature.

Secondary Schooling and Moral Complexity. As students move up the ladder of formal schooling, moral instruction either diminishes greatly or becomes increasingly implicit and complex. It diminishes most completely for students who enroll in general or vocational programs in secondary school. Industrial work values may continue to be stressed (Oakes, Gamoran, and Page 1992), but otherwise moral instruction fades from the official curriculum. By contrast, moral instruction increases in complexity for students who enroll in the academic programs, particularly those who take a large number of courses in humanities. Exhortations to be honest, hard working, courageous, and kind are replaced by far more challenging lessons, just as simple addition is replaced by more complex mathematics.

The moral instruction of the humanities works at a higher level than the illustrated lists of virtues that today's critics of schooling wish to add to the curriculum. Not every student has the capacity to take moral lessons from literature and history, but these lessons are the stuff out of which the higher forms of moral judgment are created. The widely assigned George Eliot novel *Middlemarch*, for example, expresses several of the more demanding perplexities of moral life: how, for example, a dedicated scholar, for all his knowledge and hard work, can suck the blood out of life, and how an otherwise admirable doctor can desire to please his beloved wife so much that he goes deeply into debt to support her expensive tastes. Through examples such as these, motivated students can learn that even widely proclaimed virtues can at times go too far or fail to be sufficiently balanced by other virtues. Students may also learn that many situations in life involve not a choice between right and wrong, but between two rights. In *Huckleberry Finn*, for example, the meaning of civilization is debated from many sides. Is it obedience to the law and cultivated manners? Or the ability to empathize with the personality and situation of others, regardless of reigning conventions? What happens when the two come into conflict?

Teachers as exemplars. Most schoolteachers are aware of their role in socializing the young and try to express values through their actions in the classroom. In the primary grades, for example, they usually express the values of kindness and empathy. They have, as Phillip Jackson (Jackson, Boorstrom, and Hansen 1993) observes, "a knack for discerning latent grace in the awkward gesture" and "applaud those who try no matter how slight their success" (p. 259).

Teachers have different strengths as exemplars, and what they have to teach is therefore more evident to some students than to others. One teacher may make precision and clarity important values in her classroom and express respect for these values through the carefulness of her handwriting, the persistence of her correction of imprecise language, her attention to detail in the working through of a proof. Another teacher may express the moral importance of truly engaged activity by throwing his whole body into a lecture, by beaming with pride when a student gives a good answer to a difficult question, or by cheerfully brushing off an annoying interruption. Another may express the moral importance of digging beneath the surface by patiently leading students ever deeper into a short story, by suggesting alternative interpretations, or by engaging in Socratic questioning of students' answers.

Dramatic gestures frequently aid in the expression of moral values. An erect posture, a concentrated energy, a poised piece of chalk at eye level—all can express a kind of heightened respect for precision. A thoughtful stroking of the chin, a dramatic "aha!" and a long pause before sweeping away a shallow interpretation—all can convey a heightened respect for digging deeper.

How successful is moral instruction? Moral conformity is not as easily gained as behavioral conformity or acculturation into bureaucratic/mass consumption ways of life. If moral teachings support the practices and social circumstances of students' families and local communities, they are likely to be accepted. If they do not, they may be treated with a good deal of skepticism, or even flatly rejected. The dominant moral culture of schools reflects the social conditions of people who have some authority in society (or identify strongly with those who do) and who are, in addition, not extremely cosmopolitan or worldly in outlook. It is, therefore, most congenial to those who are upwardly striving or located in the broad middle of the social structure. At a minimum, it always confronts opposition on at least two fronts: from the practical opportunism of the "have-not" classes and from the worldliness of upper-class sophisticates (see Bourdieu 1984; Collins 1988:208–25).

Even where the moral teachings of the schools are accepted in principle, they may not have a strong impact on behavior, because the temptations of selfishness, dishonesty, laziness, and cowardice are always great. Moreover, the organizational side of schooling sometimes undermines even simple moral lessons. Schools, for example, subscribe to the value of honesty, but often inadvertently reward cheats who are motivated by the equally high importance schools attach to achievement. Schools preach equality of opportunity, but are notorious for tamping down the ambitions of lower-status children. Many schools proclaim the importance of sturdy independence, but they do not generally approve of nonconformity that upsets the staff's authority.

Socialization Outside the Classroom

The school playground is an enormously important part of childhood socialization, and it is perhaps too little appreciated. If classrooms are an introduction to bureaucratic life, the playground is an introduction to informal social networks. School experiences outside the classroom prepare children for adult life by teaching them about self-assertion and self-control among friends and colleagues. The values of the classroom and the playground often coexist peacefully, but in some secondary schools, adolescent values crowd out school values.

Like the classroom, the playground has important structural features that are different from those found in students' homes:

• On the playground, adult authority is present in the form of monitors, but this authority is in the background. Adult presence prevents anarchy, but adult distance allows a maximum opportunity for group-directed activity.

• Many children mix on the playground, and freely chosen interactions with a relatively large number of children are, therefore, theoretically possible. The members of school play groups are usually similar in age, but are usually not close neighbors or family members. Age similarity limits the social distance between children, but the aggregation of many acquaintances creates a wide opportunity for cementing, altering, and breaking relationships. The variety of possible contacts allows children to develop increasingly refined judgments about the possibilities and problems of social interaction.

Because they are spheres of monitored, but largely self-directed, activity involving a variety of interaction possibilities among others who are neither very close nor very distant, playgrounds have advantages over close friends and family for the development of skills in informal social relations.

The Playground and Informal Social Life

On the playground, children must learn to deal with bullies, tag-alongs, tattletales, false friends, snobs, and other familiar childhood types. Deciding how to react to these types refines judgment. How does one deal with aggression from another child—by confronting the child, raising a coalition, or trying to avoid the harassment? Under what conditions should a higher authority be appealed to, and when is this action interpreted as failing to stand up for oneself? When does friendship fall over the line into dependency? How much should acquaintances be trusted with valuable information—when does such information cement a friendship and when does it increase one's vulnerability? How much effort should one make to win the friendship of an aloof but desirable child? When should one speak out and when should one wait to assess the situation further? How can one express pride in abilities and achievements without fostering resentment among others? Through confronting these issues, children may become skillful navigators of relationships.

Without a great many experiences in dealing with these issues, children would be less well prepared for adult life. These lessons clearly apply to informal relationships with friends, potential mates, and other community members. But they are no less applicable to informal social relations at work. Much occupational activity can be thought of as "political labor," in which people take and avoid taking stands and in which they maneuver to make useful alliances, to avoid encumbering connections, and to defuse potential conflicts (Collins 1979, chap. 2).

Some sociologists have long seen the experiences of the playground as an important socializing complement to the experiences of the classroom. Talcott Parsons (1959), for example, pointed out that not all important jobs in industrial societies require high levels of academic ability. Social skills are particularly important in many managerial and sales jobs—and also in promotional and public service work. In Parsons's view, those who gain status on the playground but not in the classroom form the pool of future occupants of all jobs that require high levels of social skill and emotional labor (e.g., salespeople, public relations people, entrepreneurs, actors and actresses). They are also the future central organizers of adult friendship networks. Those who gain status in the classroom but not the playground form the pool of future occupants of jobs that require high levels of scholarly and analytical ability (e.g., scientists, engineers, professors, print journalists, civil servants, technical managers). Those who gain status both in the classroom and on the playground are future achievers in elite spheres of occupational and public life (e.g., corporation executives and upper-level managers, college presidents and deans, doctors, lawyers, research entrepreneurs, politicians). Finally, those who lack status in both domains are unlikely to become socially dominant personalities (unless they are unusually late bloomers).

Although it provides opportunities for experimenting with identity, the playground is far from an unstratified domain. Indeed, some inequalities are more apparent on the playground than in the classroom. Although teachers usually try to mix boys and girls, for example, boys and girls overwhelmingly separate along gender lines on the playground. In primary schooling, the dominance of boys is evident in their ability to control large, open play spaces, to label girls as ritually polluting (girls are primarily responsible for "cooties" on most playgrounds), and to invade spaces occupied by groups of girls. Thus, the playground can be a space in which some social relations—particularly gender and gender-related aggressiveness—are reproduced in a more faithful way than in the classroom (Thorne 1995). Status systems based on skills and attributes prized by the dominant children rule the social order of the playground. The social divisions of the playground—cool/uncool, jock/brain, tomboy/sissy— overlap with meaningful divisions in adult informal social life. Because these social divisions draw a high level of verbal attention from children, they exalt some children more regularly and wound others more deeply than adult social divisions usually can.

For all of its verbal violence, the playground is nevertheless an arena of experimentation and change. It is a place where children practice making and breaking friendships and where they try out new identities, which may prove rewarding. It is a place where children watch on the border of socially organized spaces and make forays across the borders at times, as when a popular boy decides to play with the girls for a day or girls join the boys' kickball game. It is a place where children learn to use verbal aggression to fight unwanted labels, as much as to enforce the existing status hierarchy.

Adolescent Society and the Schools

As children grow into teenagers, friends become an increasingly central part of the incentives to attend school. Because of the nonacademic interests of most adolescents, many adults fear that the influence of adolescent culture undermines adult authority and does not adequately prepare children for adult life. It is a worry that goes back to the 1950s as a research concern (see sidebar) and may indeed be a perennial issue. These worries, however, are prone to overstatement. Most adolescent friendship groups are not as deeply alienated as adults fear. Even those teenagers who are deeply alienated may not stay that way; many alienated adolescents grow up into well-adjusted adults once they take on the responsibilities of jobs and families. In addition, adolescent friendship groups reinforce many of the same values as adults. For example, adolescents socialize emotional control by criticizing those who do not show it and calling them "crybabies." And, in most cases, if teenagers do not act with acceptable honesty or show up at appointed times, they will be loudly criticized until they conform or are forced to find new friends.

References

Bennett, William J. 1993. *The Book of Virtues*. New York: Simon and Schuster.
Bourdieu Pierre. 1984. *Distinction*. Cambridge, MA: Harvard University Press.
Bourdieu Pierre. 1988. *Homo Academicus*. London: Polity.
Bronfenbrenner, Urie. 1970. *Two Worlds of Childhood: U.S. and U.S.S.R.* New York: Russell Sage.
Collins, Randall. 1979. *The Credential Society*. New York: Academic Press.
Collins, Randall. 1988. *Theoretical Sociology*. San Diego: Harcourt, Brace, Jovanovich.
Cremin, Lawrence. A. ed. 1957. *The Republic and the School: Horace Mann on the Education of Free Men*. New York: Teachers College Press.
Dreeben, Robert. 1968. *On What is Learned in School*. Reading, MA: Addison-Wesley.
Elson, Ruth. 1964. *Guardians of Tradition: American Schoolbooks of the Nineteenth Century*. Lincoln: University of Nebraska Press.
Farkas, Steve and Jean Johnson. 1996. *Given the Circumstances: Teachers Talk about Public Education Today*. New York: Public Agenda.
Fitzgerald, Frances. 1979. *America Revised: History Schoolbooks in the 20th Century*. Boston: Little, Brown.
Fujita, Hidenori. 1996. "A Crisis of Legitimacy in Japanese Education—Meritocracy and Cohesion." *Bulletin of the Faculty of Education, Nagoya University* 32:117–23.
Jackson, Philip W. 1968. *Life in Classrooms*. Troy, MO: Holt, Rinehart, and Winston.
Lewis, Catherine C. 1995. *Educating Hearts and Minds: Reflections on Japanese Preschool and Elementary Education*. Cambridge, UK: Cambridge University Press.
McConnell, James. 1985. *English Public Schools*. London: Herbert.
Oakes, Jeannie, Adam Gamoran, and Reba N. Page. 1992. "Curriculum and Differentiation: Opportunities, Outcomes, and Meanings." P. 570–608 in Philip W. Jackson (ed.) *Handbook of Research on Curriculum*. Washington, DC: American Educational Research Association.

Parsons, Talcott. 1959. "The School Class as a Social System: Some of its Functions in American Society. *Harvard Educational Review*, 29:297–318.

Powell, Arthur G., Eleanor Farrar, and David K. Cohen. 1985. *The Shopping Mall High School: Winners and Losers in the Educational Marketplace.* Boston: Houghton Mifflin

Ravitch, Diane. 1995. *National Standards in American Education.* Washington, DC: Brookings Institution.

Thorne, Barrie. 1995. *Gender Play: Girls and Boys in School.* New Brunswick, NJ: Rutgers University Press.

Tyack, David B. 1996. "Preserving the Republic by Educating Republicans." Unpublished paper presented at the Conference on Common Values and Social Diversity, Center for Advanced Study in the Behavioral Sciences, Stanford University, Stanford, CA.

Wong, Sandra. 1991. "Evaluating the Context of Textbooks: Public Interest and Professional Authority." *Sociology of Education*, 64:11–8.

PART VI

Peer Groups as Socialization Agents

Since children begin life in some kind of family setting that provides initial socialization, and since a fundamental goal of socialization is to enable children to become capable of functioning independently of the family in the larger society, some means are necessary to enable children to separate from their families. The school is one such means; it brings children under extrafamilial supervision and authority, and it is significant in defining wider values, norms, and loyalties, as well as imparting skills and knowledge that empower children.

Probably at least as important is the peer group, the group of children that forms in street, playground, or classroom and constructs activities that, although influenced in some degree by adult expectations, nonetheless has an autonomous authority of its own. As Iona and Peter Opie (1959, 1969) convincingly documented, children sustain a culture of their own alongside the adult culture that is being imparted to them. The norms, values, and symbols of this culture are distinct from and sometimes in opposition to those of adult society.

The importance of peer groups in adolescence has long been recognized and studied. Their importance at younger ages has not been quite so well established. The three chapters in Part VI are valuable contributions to our understanding of early childhood and preadolescent peer relationships and their socializing impact. In the first, William Corsaro delineates some aspects of peer group functioning in an American nursery school. In contrast to the Japanese nursery schools observed by Lewis, where peer groups were actively fostered by the teachers, Corsaro finds spontaneous group organization, through which

175

the children are able to fashion cooperative strategies for temporarily evading adult rules. The reader should be extremely cautious (i.e., should refrain) from treating this contrast as indicating any cultural difference between Japanese and American societies because the studies are not designed for such a purpose, and they do not permit justifiable statements of that kind. Each focuses on a quite different aspect of socialization. Lewis is concerned with how nursery school teachers work to achieve their socialization goals. Corsaro here focuses on how children acquire and use social knowledge and communicative and interactive skills; further, he shows how the children's peer culture contributes to these socialization outcomes. Lewis is concerned with teacher strategies, Corsaro with children's group-generated strategies.

Different kinds of group formation take place in a carpool. The growth of sub-urbs in American society following the end of World War II in 1945 and the consequent increased reliance on automobiles led to a new phenomenon, car-pooling, in which a group of parents take turns driving their children to schools either too distant to walk to or not served by adequate public transportation. Patricia and Peter Adler recognized that carpooling is not just a transportation arrangement but a socialization context. They report the results of 40 inter-views with carpool parents and 23 interviews with carpooled children between the ages of 4 and 10. They also observed their own child's carpool. There are two categories of social relationship in a carpool (1) The relationship between the adult driver and the children; (2) The relationship among the children. There are several variations within each category. In addition to reporting and classi-fying their observations, the authors show how these can be understood in the light of the two main theoretical approaches to socialization found in sociol-ogy, the *normative* approach that emphasizes children's internalization of adult norms and values (originating with Emile Durkheim), and the *interpretive* approach that emphasizes children's interpretations through taking the roles of others in interaction (originating with George Herbert Mead and Charles Horton Cooley). By role-taking, children see things in new perspectives and they exper-iment with these roles and perspectives. Through this process they develop greater interactional competence and become increasingly self-regulating.

Gary Alan Fine's study of the socializing effects of friendship among pread-olescent (ages 7–12) boys takes a largely interpretive approach, which is also known as *symbolic interactionist*. (Mead's student, Herbert Blumer, coined the term symbolic interaction in the 1930s to characterize Mead's work. Symbolic interactionism has since been developed and expanded by many sociologists and some psychologists.) After setting forth its basic assumptions and con-trasting it with other approaches, Fine focuses on two aspects of social com-petence that children are in the process of developing. One is learning how to display the social self in public—learning how to act appropriately in different social settings. The other is learning how to use rules in social interaction. He then shows how peer friendship contributes to developing these social skills. First, friendship serves as a staging area for action, a context in which children explore ways of expressing sexual attitudes, aggression, and attitudes toward school and work. Second friendship is an institution in which cultural information is transmitted, information that children need for their growing up, information that adults usually cannot provide. Third, friendship shapes a person's self-image, providing the child with a context in which s/he can learn an appropriate self-image to present in social situations.

References

Blumer, Herbert. *Symbolic Interactionism* (Englewood Cliffs, NJ: Prentice-Hall, 1969).

Cooley, Charles Horton. *Social Organization* (New York: Scribner's, 1962. First published in 1909).

Cooley, Charles Horton. *Human Nature and the Social Order* (New York: Scribner's, 1964. First published in 1902).

Durkheim, Emile. *Moral Education: A Study in the Theory and Application of the Sociology of Education* (New York: Free Press of Glencoe, 1961. First published in 1925).

Mead, George Herbert. *Mind, Self, and Society* (Chicago: University of Chicago Press, 1934).

Opie, Iona and Peter. *The Lore and Language of Schoolchildren* (Oxford, England: Oxford University Press, 1959).

Opie, Iona and Peter. *Children's Games in School and Playground* (Oxford, England: Oxford University Press, 1969).

10

Children's Conception and Reaction to Adult Rules: The Underlife of the Nursery School*

William Corsaro

In a brilliant essay in his book *Asylums*, Erving Goffman argued that, without something to belong to, individuals have no stable self, but total commitment to any social unit implies a kind of selflessness. For Goffman, "our sense of being a person can come from being drawn into a wider social unit; our sense of selfhood can arise through the little ways in which we resist the pull" (1961:320).

In pursuing this view of the individual in society, Goffman introduced the notion of "secondary adjustments." Secondary adjustments are "any habitual arrangement by which a member of an organization employs unauthorized means, or obtains unauthorized ends, or both, thus getting around the organization's assumptions as to what he should do and get and hence what he should be." According to Goffman, "secondary adjustments represent ways in which the individual stands apart from the role and self that were taken for granted for him by the institution" (1961:189).

Secondary adjustments are seen by Goffman as forming the *underlife* of social establishments. Goffman identified a number of types of secondary adjustments in his documentation of the underlife of an asylum, a highly restrictive institution. Goffman argued, however, that his work in an asylum led to findings regarding the individual's relationship to organizations that apply in some ways to all institutions. Furthermore, Goffman believed that the individual's

*From William Corsaro, *Friendship and Peer Culture in the Early Years*, pp. 254–270. © Copyright Ablex Publishing Corporation, 1986. Reproduced with permission of Greenwood Publishing Group, Inc., Westport, Ct.

tendency simultaneously to embrace and to resist institutional rules and expectations is a central feature of personal identity or self.

But is Goffman's work useful for understanding peer culture? Surely the nursery school is not a total institution as is an asylum or a prison. Further, it is difficult to argue that preschool children have developed the cognitive skills necessary to define their emerging selves in regard to both their embracement of and resistance to the organizations to which they belong. On the other hand, the nursery school, like all other organizations, involves a set of goals, rules, procedures, and expectations for its members. In this sense, Goffman's work has implications for understanding how children conceptualize and adapt to the rules and procedures of this particular social institution. And, although preschool children do not have a stable sense of self or the cognitive skills necessary to infer the implications of both embracement and resistance of organizational rules for personal identity, *they do have a clear notion of the importance and restrictiveness of the adult world as compared to children's worlds*. At this age, children have made a distinction between adults ("grown-ups") and children. In fact, they can, and often do, distinguish between the adult world and their own peer world.

Although membership and participation in the adult world is important to nursery school children, their developing sense of who they are is also strengthened through their active resistance of certain adult rules and expectations regarding their behavior. In this sense, the children's joint recognition of adult rules, and their mutual resistance of certain of these rules, can be seen as stable elements of peer culture.

Nursery School Rules and Children's Secondary Adjustments

The university school, like all nursery schools, had a set of rules that embodied expectations regarding the children's behavior. Given my interest in peer culture, my concern is less with the rules themselves than with the children's conceptions of the rules and their strategies for evading them (i.e., their secondary adjustments). Therefore, I will not attempt to cover all the school rules. Instead, I will concentrate on those rules that were most burdensome to the children and that motivated them to invest a great deal of energy in devising evasive strategies.

Rules Regarding Play Areas and Materials

Early in the school year, the children learned that certain behaviors could occur in some areas and not in others, and that some play materials were to be used only in the areas in which they were stored and available.

One rule regarding the use of play areas in the school centered around the teachers' distinction between inside and outside play. Running, chasing, and loud shouting were defined as inappropriate behaviors inside the school and were restricted to the outside yard. Problems in adherence to this rule were most apparent when children became overly excited while playing indoors, or when disputes turned more physical and resulted in running and chasing. Normally, the teachers and TAs reacted quickly to such violations, and the children seldom resisted correction except to deny that they were indeed involved in the behavior ("I wasn't running!") or to claim that another child was responsible ("Peter was chasing me.").

The rule restricting more physical play to the outside yard was most troublesome to boys, especially the older boys in the afternoon group. The boys enjoyed physical play and often attempted to include physical activities (running, etc.) in play that normally did not involve gross motor behavior without breaking the general theme or frame of the ongoing activity. Before describing some of these attempts, which can be seen as secondary adjustments, I should note that the boys in the afternoon group faced an additional rule. Since the boys seldom played indoors during the first month of the school term, the afternoon teacher designated the outside area as "closed" for the first 45 minutes of the afternoon session. The teacher hoped that the rule would encourage the boys to become more involved in play activities inside the school. The rule was successful in this regard, but it also led to the emergence of a number of secondary adjustments as the boys attempted to get around the rule which limited running, chasing, and similar physical activities to the outside yard.

One type of secondary adjustment I observed in the afternoon group involved attempts to extend family role play. Boys who felt confined in the inside of the school would sometimes join other children engaged in family role play in the playhouse area. After joining the other children, the boys would often suggest new directions for the role play. For example, the boys would propose that the house was being robbed and take the roles of robbers and police. The police would eventually chase the robbers from the house and throughout the inside of the school. When the teacher or TAs reminded the boys that there was no running inside, the boys would claim that they were not running and explain that the playhouse had been robbed. When faced with this sort of explanation, the TAs would often compromise and allow the children a bit more latitude, but ask that they confine the chase to an area near the playhouse. On another occasion, I saw the role play extended when some boys suggested that the playhouse was on fire, and, more imaginatively, in another case a family was threatened by a wild lion which escaped from the zoo. In this instance, one boy exuberantly adopted the lion role while another boy became a lion trainer, chased the lion from the playhouse, and eventually captured him.

On other occasions, boys who felt confined inside the school entered the playhouse and, finding it unoccupied, were at a loss what to do. In one instance, two boys (Graham and Peter) decided to play house and, after some negotiation, one boy became a father and the other an uncle. But, after adopting these roles, the boys seemed to have no idea what an uncle and father might do together. So they roamed around the playhouse and eventually overturned the kitchen table. To their surprise, they saw that the table was an overturned waste can with a round piece of plywood attached to the top. Now, upside down, the table became a race car as Peter climbed inside the waste can and Graham pushed him across the floor of the playhouse. Neither the teacher nor the TAs noticed this unusual bit of family interaction involving the uncle and father.

These types of secondary adjustments were not confined to the afternoon group. On one occasion, two boys (Denny and Martin) and one girl (Leah) from the morning group were in the upstairs playhouse but soon became bored with family role play. Denny found a piece of string and, lying flat on the floor of the house, dangled the string through the bars and announced that "he was fishing." Leah and Martin ran downstairs, got some string, and soon joined Denny at his fishing hole. Soon other children and several TAs noticed the trio. The TAs were so impressed with this ingenious use of the upstairs playhouse that they overlooked this mild violation of proper inside behavior. In fact, the TAs helped some of the children in the downstairs playhouse tie toy animals to the dangling fishing lines. Denny, Leah, and Martin ended up catching a lot of fish.

These secondary adjustments were quite complex in that they involve the active cooperation of several children, and they can be seen as extensions or elaborations "of existing sources of legitimate satisfactions" for private ends. They are what Goffman has referred to as examples of "working the system" (1961:210).

There were other secondary adjustments regarding use of play materials that were less complex, but just as effective. For example, children often violated the rule about moving play objects (blocks, dishes, toy animals, etc.) from one area of the school to another simply by concealing them on their persons during transport. On one occasion in the afternoon group, Daniel took a suitcase from the playhouse, carried it to the block area, and filled it with blocks and toy animals. He then carried the suitcase outside, dumped the blocks and animals in the sandpile, and buried them. Shortly thereafter, a TA noticed the suitcase in the sandpile and told Daniel to return it to the playhouse. He did so, but then quickly returned to the sandpile to play with the blocks and animals. At clean-up time, Daniel abandoned the secretly transported objects and went inside. When a TA discovered the objects in the sand during clean up, she asked two children in the area how they got outside. They responded with a typical preschooler answer: "We don't know." Which in this case was true, but not believed by the TA.

The concealment strategy was also used consistently to evade the rule about not bringing toys and other personal objects from home to school. This rule was necessary because personal objects were attractive to other children just because they were different from the everyday play materials in the school. As a result, the teachers were constantly settling disputes about sharing the personal objects. Therefore, the rule specified that objects should not be brought and, if they were, they must be stored in one's locker until after school. Early in the school term, the children began to evade this rule by bringing small personal objects that they could conceal in their pockets. Particular favorites were small toy animals, along with candies and chewing gum. While playing, a child would often show his or her "stashed loot" to a playmate, and they would carefully share the forbidden objects without catching the attention of the teacher or TA. Although such small deceptions may seem insignificant to an adult, as they were to the TAs who would often chuckle and ignore them, they were not trivial to the children and were important moments in the sharing of peer culture.

Rules against Guns and Shooting

There were no toy guns in the school, nor were the children allowed to bring guns and similar toys to the school. There was also a general rule against the use of pretend guns and shooting. However, many of the children, in almost all cases boys, would employ what Goffman has termed "make-dos" to get around the no-guns rule. That is, the children would use "available artifacts in a manner and for an end not officially intended" (Goffman, 1961:207). For example, boys would often shoot at each other from a distance simply by pointing their finger and cocking their thumbs. The "hand gun" was just one of many weapons created by the children. They also often used shovels, blocks of wood, and broomstick horses as rifles. The children would go to great lengths to avoid detection in evading the rules about guns and shooting. For example, when the children played "hunter," the boys created rifles by flipping over their broomstick horses, used crackers for bullets, and shot at objects that could not shoot back (targets and children from the adjoining school). As a result, they almost avoided detection, and, when they were discovered by a TA, they received only a mild warning. A warning they promptly ignored and continued with their hunter play.

I should note here that I am in no way negatively evaluating the school rules regarding guns or shooting or the teachers ability to enforce the rule. My point is that the children's strategies to evade the rule, their secondary adjustments, *can become as important aspects of peer culture as the children's original interest in guns themselves*. In fact, the children's resistance of the rules is another symbolic marker distinguishing the adult world from peer culture.

Rules Prohibiting Bad Language

Many of the rules the children encountered in the nursery school were the same as those they followed at home. At school as well as in the home, the children were expected to obey adults, share their toys with others, and were not to fight or swear. The children seldom used bad language in school. But there were occasions when a child would become upset and say "damn" or "shit" or some other swear word. There were also instances where verbal disputes would escalate into cursing and name calling. In every instance where swearing occurred, the children involved or nearby would look around and check to see if an adult were present. If a teacher or TA was in earshot of a child who said a bad word, the child would always be corrected and told not to repeat the word again. In short, the children knew that swearing was bad and, therefore, refrained from the behavior or were careful to confine their swearing to places in the school where adults would be unlikely to hear them.

However, just because swearing was bad or taboo, it had a certain appeal to the children. This attraction to bad or taboo words was shared by the children and was thus an element of peer culture. The appeal of swearing was best expressed through routines where children rattled off strings of bad words. The bad words were spoken, not because the children were upset or arguing, but just in a sense "to be bad." However, in these instances the children wanted more than to be bad, they wanted to *be bad and not be caught*—in short, to put something over on their adult caretakers, and, in Goffman's view, maintain a sense of self through secondary adjustments.

I observed several of these swearing routines in both groups over the course of the school year. In every case, there were two to four children involved, and the routines always occurred in peer-dominated areas of the school (e.g., in the climbing house, climbing bars, or upstairs playhouse). One instance was especially interesting and involved two girls in the morning group.

The two girls, whom I will just refer to as A and B, had been playing in the outside yard. We were videotaping their play, which involved climbing up on a large wooden spool and jumping to a mat on the ground below. I was sitting near the spool holding a microphone. After several jumps to the mat, A walked behind the spool and then called out: "B, hey, B! Look here!" B came around to look and I followed close behind with my microphone. When we found A, she was ducking into a small opening in the back of the spool. She then sat down inside the hollow center of the spool.

"Come on in," she said to B. B quickly joined her and, as I appeared in the opening, A said: "Not you! Go away and leave us alone." I said: "Ok, but can I leave my microphone?" B responded: "Ok, but you get out of here!" I set the microphone inside the spool and quickly left to join my assistant, who was operating the camera and monitoring the audio.

I was anxious to hear what the girls were talking about, so I motioned for my assistant to let me use one half of the headset and we listened together. The first thing I heard was a banging of the microphone as A picked it up and said: "I'll talk first." She then said "you !!XX, XX, XX!!, !!XX, !X!X,_____!" The string of curses was 14 words long and contained some words I had heard only a few times, and two or three I had never uttered in my life. I should add here that I am not a prude. I have been known to cuss every now and then. Many of these words were references to sexual activity and curses which had to do with the legitimacy of one's parentage. When A finished, B said: "Let me talk to 'he dummy!" B, who seemed to be referring to me, took the microphone and said: "You !X!X, XXX,_____!" Her string repeated several of the bad words A had produced, but she also added a few of her own. I must admit that I was a bit shocked that these two little girls could repeat such words, but I was sure that they had no idea what most of them meant. They simply knew that they were bad words.

The routine continued for three more rounds, with the girls producing many of the words over and over and giggling at their bit of naughtiness. They then emerged from the spool and I approached and asked them why they were calling me bad names. "You couldn't hear us," said A. I said that I had, and B said: "We weren't talking to you, anyway!" "Yeah," said A, "you didn't hear us anyway." They both turned and walked away, but B looked back and said: "Don't tell teacher!"

It is not clear whether the girls knew that I could hear them or not. They probably did not. It is clear that the main aim of this routine was to be naughty. The children found themselves a hideaway, a hideaway in which they were momentarily concealed from the adult world. In this situation, they decided to engage in forbidden behavior and commenced to enunciate every bad word they had probably ever heard. In doing so, they were not really being bad. They were producing a ritual that they would repeat many times in their youth, a ritual that symbolizes one of children's most cherished desires: *to defy and challenge adults, share the experience, and not be detected.*

Clean-up Time

Of all the rules of nursery school, the ones most actively resisted by the children pertained to proper behavior during clean-up time. Shortly before meeting time in both the morning and afternoon groups, the teacher and TAs would move throughout the school calling: "Clean-up time!" When the clean-up announcements were made, the children were expected to do three things: (*a*) stop their ongoing play activities; (*b*) help the TAs return the school to its proper order by replacing all the materials they were using in their proper places; and (*c*) move to the back room of the school for meeting time. Although the children enjoyed meeting time, they often did not want to stop playing, and they frequently resisted cleaning up. During the first half of the school term, when clean-up time was announced in the morning group, the children would often ask if they could keep playing for a while longer. The following excerpt from field notes is a typical example of the children's attempts to prolong play activities.

Example 5.18*

October 22
Morning Episode 1
Scene: Inside, Block Area
Participants: Cindy, Ellen, and Jack

FN: Cindy, Ellen, and Jack have been building in the block area for around 20 minutes when a TA, Catherine, comes over and announces clean-up time. "Oh, no, not yet!" Jack protests. "We're not finished," says Ellen. "Well, you still must clean up now," says Catherine, and then adds: "It's almost time for our meeting." "We don't want to go to meeting yet," says Cindy. "We have a special story today. You like stories, don't you, Cindy?" asks Catherine. "Yes, but we want to finish our building first!" Cindy responds. "No, you can build another one tomorrow, now let's start putting the blocks away," says Catherine as she picks up several blocks from the floor and places them on the shelf. Catherine then asks Jack: "Come on and help me. Hand me that block there by your foot. We have to hurry." Jack hands her the block, and all three children begin placing the blocks on the shelf. The children move slowly, but soon the area is in order and the three children run to the back room to hear the promised story.

PN: The children seem to want to continue playing and go to the meeting as well. They do not seem to understand why the meeting cannot be delayed. The adult notion of time and scheduling seems arbitrary to the children. It seems to me that Catherine was successful because she simply initiated clean up rather than continuing to discuss "why" the children should stop playing.

Example 5.18 illustrates both the children's apparent lack of understanding of the rationale for "why" they are asked to stop their play and the common strat-

---

*Example number reflects author's original usage in previous publication. FN, field-note; PN, personal note.

egy of verbal resistance. The example also illustrates how the TAs successfully overcame such resistance. In the second half of the school term, children in the morning group seldom verbally resisted the implicit request in the clean-up time announcement to cease their play activities. Having learned the futility of asking to play longer, the children virtually abandoned verbal resistance, and, like their counterparts in the afternoon group, they immediately employed one of several strategies to evade clean-up time.

Before considering these secondary adjustments to the rules of clean-up time, it is useful to consider how the children conceptualized and felt about the rules. The children seldom discussed the rules of the school among themselves, but they did talk about cleanup much more than any other adult rule. From their discussions, it is clear that the children felt clean-up time was dumb and redundant. Consider the following example from field notes.

Example 5.19

November 9
Afternoon Episode 10
Scene: Outside, Sandpile
Participants: Peter and Graham

FN: Peter and Graham had been shoveling sand into their dumptrucks in the sandpile. They then hear a TA, Willy, announce clean-up time in another part of the yard. Anticipating Willy's arrival, Peter looks at Graham and frowns. Graham says, "Clean-up time! Ain't that dumb! Clean-up time!"

"Yeah," responds Peter, "we could just leave our dump trucks here and play with 'em tomorrow."

"Yeah," says Graham as he turns over his truck and shakes out the remaining sand, "clean-up time is dumb, dumb, dumb!"

Just then Willy arrives, makes the announcement to the boys. They seem to ignore him, but after a brief delay they put away their trucks and go inside.

PN: There is a certain logic to the boys' complaints. The rule does seem dumb on the surface, but there are very good reasons for clean up. The children are thinking about the reasons. But are they thinking about them in the right way?

After I recorded my notes on November 9, I was careful to listen for other comments about clean-up time and other adult rules. I heard similar comments to those in Example 5.19 espoused by children in both groups on several occasions. One boy from the morning group, Richard, extended Graham's point by arguing that putting the toys away meant that we would "just have to take 'em out all over again." From the children's point of view, clean up is just not work that they don't want to do. It was not that the children were lazy. To them, clean up was unnecessary. It was dumb work that interfered with fun play.

Given the children's conception of clean up, it is not surprising that they had some fairly elaborate strategies to evade it. In the first part of the school term, the children in both groups often relied on what I will call the "relocation strategy." When employing this tactic, children would move from one area of the school to another immediately after hearing the clean-up time announcement. When asked to clean up in the new area, the children would claim that they had not been playing there and that they had already cleaned up elsewhere. Since the children had indeed not been in the new area and may have worked elsewhere, the TAs would often soften their demands. They would not insist the children clean up, but they would suggest that the children help. The children would often agree, but do very little, and the TAs and children who did not relocate would do the bulk of the work. Although a successful tactic in the first part of the school year, the TAs soon figured out the ruse or were informed of it by the head teacher. From that point on, children who employed the relocation strategy were told that everyone had to clean up regardless of where or what they played during the day. If children insisted that they had cleaned up elsewhere, the TAs merely said "good for you, but you must work here too." Not surprisingly, the "relocation" strategy was employed much less frequently during the second part of the school term.

The children employed a second strategy to evade clean up which I will refer to as the "personal problem delay." When using this strategy, children claim they cannot help clean up for one of a number of personal reasons. The problems include such things as feigned illness or injury (e.g., "I got a stomach ache," "I hurt my foot," etc.), pressing business (e.g., helping another TA clean up in another part of the school, or role play demands). Although these strategies are seldom completely successful, they do delay the start of work. As a result the children involved often have less work to do once they do begin to clean up. Some of the most interesting personal problems I heard the children offer had to do with role play demands. A child in the mother role may claim she has to finish feeding her baby; a child pretending to be a lion may claim she cannot use her hands; a fireman may claim that he has to put out a fire in another part of the yard.

In one instance, when I was observing in the afternoon group, I witnessed the following sequence. Brian lay on the ground in the outside yard when clean-up time was announced. Shortly thereafter, a TA, Marie, told Brian to start cleaning up, but he did not respond and continued to lay motionless. Marie then said, "Brian, quit pretending to sleep and start helping us clean up." Brian still did not move, but Vickie, who was cleaning up, spoke for him. "He can't help. He's dead, killed by poison," Vickie told Marie.

Marie looked over to me and we both laughed. For some reason, I found the phrase "killed by poison" to be funny, and Marie seemed to as well. However, Marie was not about to let Brian escape from work. She knelt down next to him and pretended to pour something into his mouth.

"There," said Marie, "I gave Brian the antidote to the poison. He will now come back to life."

Brian, however, still remained motionless, and Vickie said, "The antidote didn't work."

"Yes it did," responded Marie who began to tickle Brian. Brian giggled and squirmed away from Marie.

"See, he's all alive now and is going to help us clean up," said Marie. Brian got to his feet and began to help, not killed by poison after all.

A final strategy the children consistently employed to evade clean up was deceptively simple, but highly effective. I will refer to this strategy as "pretending not to hear." When employing this strategy, the children, upon hearing the clean-up time signal, would merely continue to play as if the announcement had not been made at all. The TAs would then repeat the announcement in a louder tone of voice. The children still would not respond. Then the TAs would generally repeat the signal, still louder, for from one to seven more times and receive no response. Finally, the TAs would stop their own work and insist that the children begin to help. At this point, the children would say "ok," as if hearing the announcement for the first time, and begin to work. However, the strategy was often effective because there was normally little work remaining to be done after several repetitions of the announcement. In fact, the "pretending not to hear" is often more effective than the other two strategies, because the children's failure to respond is a less noticeable tactic than the active offering of a reason for not cleaning up.

All three types of secondary adjustments to the clean-up rule are excellent examples of what Goffman calls "working the system." The children have discovered that the TAs need to get the school in order so that meeting time can begin. In short, the TAs must meet organizational demands regarding the scheduling of activities. As a result, the TAs tend to do more than their share of the work when the children delay. In fact, the TAs were often so intent on finishing clean up that they were not aware of how much of the job they—as opposed to the children—were doing. The children were working the system in that they exploited a routine of official activity—cleaning up in a certain period of time—to meet their personal ends (i.e., keeping their own clean-up work to a minimum). These secondary adjustments are impressive because "to work a system effectively, one must have an intimate knowledge of it" (Goffman, 1961:212).

But do the children actually share an awareness of these secondary adjustments to the clean-up time rules? In other words are the secondary adjustments really a shared element of peer culture? I believe they are, even though I have little direct data to substantiate my belief, since the children seldom discuss secondary adjustments. However, the following example from field notes does provide direct support for the claim that the children share an awareness of at least one of the secondary adjustments to the clean-up rules.

Example 5.20

December 4
Morning Episode 3
Scene: Outside, Swinging Tire
Participants: Barbara and Betty

FN: Barbara and Betty are playing in outside yard near climbing house. Barbara is swinging in a tire suspended from the roof of the enclosed area of the outside yard. Betty is standing in front of her, and I am sitting nearby on the ground. As Barbara swings, Betty bends over and looks down at her and says: "It's clean-up time!" Barbara smiles, ignores Betty, and keeps swinging. Betty repeats in a louder tone of voice, "It's clean-up time!" Barbara ignores Betty and keeps swinging. Betty then repeats "It's clean-up time!" seven times and keeps raising her voice. She is practically shouting right into Barbara's face during the last repetition. But Barbara continues to smile and to swing and to ignore Betty. Suddenly, Barbara stops swinging, jumps from the tire and says, "Now it's my turn." "Ok," says Betty and she quickly replaces Barbara in the swing. The girls then repeated the routine.

PN: Although I was not sure at first, it became clear with the role switch that the children were "playing teacher." In a sense, they were mildly mocking the TAs, who seem unaware of the delaying nature of the children's strategy of pretending not to hear the clean-up time signal.

Conclusion

It is clear that the children's secondary adjustments can be seen as makeshift means to obtain ends or needs that are restricted or denied by adult rules. But as Goffman maintained in his work with adults, I feel that such an explanation "fails to do justice to these undercover adaptations for the structure of self" (1961:319). As I noted in the introduction to this section, Goffman sees secondary adjustments as essential elements for the maintenance of self and *individual identity*. It is my thesis that, for the nursery children, secondary adjustments are best seen as a way of developing and maintaining *group identity*. In collectively resisting adult rules, children develop a sense of community and "we-ness," which is extremely important in their acquisition of a sense of social structure (Cicourel, 1974). For, by sharing a communal spirit as a member of peer culture, children come to experience how being a member of a group affects both themselves as individuals and how they are to relate to others. Through secondary adjustments, children come to see themselves as part of a group (in the nursery school, a peer culture) which is in some instances aligned with, while in others opposed to, other groups (in the nursery school, adult rules and culture). In resisting adult rules through cooperative secondary adjustments, children not only develop a sense of group identity, they also acquire more detailed knowledge of adult norms and organizations. The acquisition of such knowledge is essential for children's movement through a succession of peer cultures and their eventual entry into the adult world.

Conclusion

Childhood socialization involves children's acquisition and use of social interactive and communicative skills and social knowledge in their everyday life worlds. In this chapter, I have identified and described stable elements of peer culture in the nursery school. I also discussed the significance of features of peer culture for understanding children's social development, and, more generally, the significance of the concept of peer culture for socialization theory.

Regarding children's social development, there is a need for the integration of information on children's lifeworlds—discovered in microethnographies of the type employed in this study—into interactionist or constructivist theories of human development. According to constructivist theories like those of Piaget, Mead, and Vygotsky, children acquire skills and knowledge through interaction with the environment. If children construct social knowledge and acquire interactive skills by acting on the environment, there is then a need to examine these actions within their social context (i.e., within the lifeworlds of children).

In this chapter, I have addressed how specific experiences resulting from participation in peer culture may affect the children's acquisition of interactive skills and social knowledge. The main features of the analysis are summarized in Table 10.1, where I have linked the various features of peer culture to specific types of learning.

Although actual developmental processes can not be fully substantiated without longitudinal data, the findings summarized in Table 10.1 identify potential sources of the development of a wide range of communicative skills and types of social knowledge. More importantly, these findings identify what is often missing in clinical interviewing studies of children's social development. In these studies (see, for example, Damon, 1978; Piaget, 1965; Selman, 1980; Turiel, 1978; Youniss, 1980), researchers identify levels or stages of skills and knowledge—an important contribution to socialization theory—but they often gloss over *how* skills and knowledge are acquired with general references to disequilibrium and the child's activity on the environment. The findings summarized in Table 10.1 can be seen as some of the sources of disequilibrium that are intricately interwoven in the peer culture of the nursery school.

Table 10.1.
Peer Culture and Children's Development
of Social Knowledge and Interactive Skills

Features of Peer Culture	Types of Social Knowledge	Interactive Skills
Values and concerns		
Social participation and the protection of interactive space	Friendship; social norms and conventions	Access rituals; cooperative sharing
Concern for the physical welfare of playmates	Personal attributes and emotions	Empathy; social perspective-taking
Concern with physical size	Status, power, and group identity	Independence; communal support
Themes in spontaneous fantasy	Story schema; morality; death or mortality; role expectations	Turn-taking; feedback cues; cooperative sharing; empathy
Behavioral routines		
Children's humor	Joke and riddle structure and routines; humor	Humor as an interactive skill; performance skills
Insult routines	Insult structures; status and power	Competitive skills; tact
Approach-avoidance	Story schema; personal attributes; sex-role concepts; role expectations;	Cooperative sharing; discourse skills; indirect action plans; sex-typed skills
Garbage man	Social time; ritual structure; occupational roles	Cooperative sharings; communal support
Secondary adjustments to adult rules	Social norms and conventions; status and power; role expectations; group identity	Independence; adaptive behavior; communal support

The identification of features of peer culture is important for reasons beyond their implications for the children's social development. These findings help us to better understand children, how they construct and participate in their peer world, and how they view the adult world. Childhood socialization theory must go beyond an identification of the steps or stages children move through to become adults. Socialization theory should also involve an understanding of the lifeworlds of children.

Socialization is not merely a process by which children become adults. It is, rather, a process in which children participate in and successively move through a series of peer cultures. Full understanding of childhood socialization depends upon the documentation of elements of peer cultures and the continual points of contact between peer cultures and the adult world.

References

Cicourel, Aaron, *Cognitive Sociology* (New York: Free Press, 1974).

Damon, William (ed.), *Social Cognition* (San Francisco, Jossey-Bass, 1978).

Goffman, Erving, *Asylums* (Garden City, NY, 1961).

Piaget, Jean, *The Moral Judgment of the Child* (New York: Free Press, 1965).

Selman, R., *The Growth of Interpersonal Understanding* (New York: Academic Press, 1980).

Turiel, E., "Social regulations and domains of social concepts." In W. Damon (ed.), *Social Cognition* (San Francisco, Jossey-Bass, 1978).

Youniss, J., *Parents and Peers in Social Development* (Chicago: University of Chicago Press, 1980).

11

The Carpool: A Socializing Adjunct to the Educational Experience*,†

Patricia A. Adler and Peter Adler

Families, schools, peer groups, and the mass media are commonly recognized agents of socialization, which shape children's developing selves as they guide them through the learning experience. Numerous childhood activities and relationships have been studied within the context of socialization, but one experience remains uninvestigated by social researchers: the carpool. In this inquiry, we examine the transport of children back and forth from school—the most prominent form of carpooling. Our sample is made up of children attending private preschools and elementary schools; Public transportation is either unavailable or unsuitable for these youngsters. Carpooling can be identified, then, as an urban and suburban practice of the middle and upper classes. Further, carpooling signifies the importance of the automobile in American life. Many people prefer the privacy and door-to-door convenience of driving their own car to utilizing public transportation, even when that option is available. Sociologically, however, carpooling represents more than just a mode of transport; its unique combination of features transforms it from a mundane backdrop into a socializing arena.

Carpooled children are thrust into the close company of several peers[1] and a parent on a regular basis, as often as 10 times weekly for as long as 45 minutes per trip. For many, it is one of the first contacts with children and adults from outside the family, neighborhood, and friendship primary groups, since, as Rubin (1980:22) notes, children younger than the age of 3 interact primarily

*Reprinted by permission of the authors and the American Sociological Association from *Sociology of Education*, 1984, 57:200–210.

†A version of this article was presented at the Annual Meetings of the American Sociological Association, San Francisco, 1982.

with objects, parents, and siblings. Carpool children's ages, then, and their lack
of social experience make them highly impressionable, receptive to a variety of
socializing influences.

Empirical studies and conceptual explorations of the socialization process can
be grouped into two camps: the normative school and the interpretive school.
The former perspective emphasizes the way children internalize society's norms
and values and learn roles for future use (Bandura, 1971; Brim, 1960; Inkeles,
1966; Merton, 1957; Parsons and Bales, 1955; Watson, 1970). In contrast, interpretive sociologists focus on the active interpersonal processes by which children develop interactional competence (Cicourel, 1970; Garfinkel, 1967; Mead,
1934; Rose, 1962; Shibutani, 1962; Speier, 1970). These forms of socialization
are usually treated as mutually exclusive, but we will show how carpool interaction encompasses bimodal forms of socialization.

Carpooling falls within a critical overlap of three predominant socializing
agents: the peer group, the family, and the school. First, children who carpool
together form a peer primary group because of their closeness in age and the regularity of their contact. The encapsulated (Zurcher, 1979) nature of the automobile setting intensifies their relationships and reciprocal influence on each
other. Thus, although carpool peer associations are involuntary, members come
to know each other well and serve as both a social base and a reference group for
each other. Second, because there is an adult in the car, parents retain a socializing influence over their children either through their own presence or through
the presence of one of the other adult drivers acting *in loco parentis*. Third, carpooling frames educational socialization. Temporally and physically surrounding the school day, the carpool provides an arena in which the school experience
can be assessed and evaluated and in which school norms and rules still affect
children's behavior. The carpool thus serves as a symbolic transition between
home and school, providing children with a special time and place where they
experience a complex intermingling of these combined socializing agents.

In this chapter, we investigate the types of interaction that take place within
the carpool setting both between children and adults and among peer group
members. We discuss the behavioral patterns and roles that commonly emerge
in this setting and analyze their impact on the developing child. We identify
and describe three carpool-generated relationships: intimate, combatant, and
obligatory. We conclude by extracting the features of carpool interaction that
correspond to both the normative and interpretive models of socialization and
show how the two can coexist rather than compete.

Methods

It was not until our third experience with carpooling that it caught our interest as being worthy of sociological consideration. Previously, we had con-

sidered it another rite of passage into a middle-class suburban subculture, often annoying, occasionally helpful, rigidly norm-bound, and populated by an assortment of mundane and odd characters. But this time things were different: Our child was commuting with an older child who had a dominant personality. As our daughter began to change, we wondered if her new attitudes and behavioral traits could have arisen through her contact in the carpool. We began talking to other parents, who concurred with our suspicions that carpooling could have a significant socializing influence on participating children.

We therefore decided to gather data more systematically. We conducted 40 intensive, taped interviews with carpool parents and 23 focused, untaped interviews with carpooling children. Children interviewed ranged in age from 4 to 10 years and came from middle-, upper middle-, and upper class households.[2] In addition, we talked informally with 15 teachers and administrators at several of the private schools that our sample population attended. Throughout the remainder of the school year (7 months), we also continued to observe our child's carpool, as well as the carpool experiences of friends' and neighbors' children.

As the data began to accumulate, we perceived a variation in the participation and reactions of different-aged children. Two groups emerged, and we began to compare the independence, peer connectedness, and socializing effects of preschool children (ages 3–6) and elementary school children (ages 7–10). Thus, at appropriate points throughout this chapter we will note how, where, and why the two groups contrast.

The Setting

Pervading and unifying all of the behavior that we will present here was one element: the automobile. The overwhelming significance of the automobile as a setting lay in its *privacy* from the outside world. As Lofland (1973:136) notes, it is a "cocoon of private space," isolating its occupants from contact with strangers. With barriers both symbolic and real, it separates children from the sounds, smells, and, for the youngest children, even the sights of the outside world, turning them inward toward each other. This restrictiveness intensifies the physical and emotional intimacy of their contact.

Another feature of the automobile is its *encapsulation*.[3] All parents we interviewed required children either to be locked into place by seat belts or to sit without undue squirming in their seats. Drivers varied in their permissiveness toward seating arrangements; some assigned children to particular locations and others allowed them to self-select, but once the trip began, the order was set and could be changed only through direct parental intervention.

Carpooling further offered children *regularity*,[4] which bred security and discontent. The trip almost always followed the same route, picked up or discharged passengers in a logical geographic sequence, and lasted for a nearly constant, predictable interval. Children were concerned with who got picked up and dropped off first because this affected their spatial location and exposure to the group and thereby influenced both their status in the group and their ability to have intimate time with particular others.

Finally, children's participation in the carpool was *involuntary*. Carpool arrangements were set up for the convenience of parents, and children's peer preferences had almost no influence. For example, children preferred to ride in less crowded vehicles, but for parents, the optimal number of participants was five drivers; children may have wanted to avoid carpooling with a disliked individual, but most parents were more concerned with geographic propinquity than with children's personalities (except in extreme cases); and depending on their ages, most children preferred to have their own parents drive them to and from school, yet they ended up in carpools. This forced companionship meant that children were unable to establish a natural peer group of people whom they liked. They interacted with (or withdrew from) a group whose composition was beyond their control, often finding themselves locked into a carpool with the same person(s) for several years.

Carpool Interaction

Within the carpool, two distinct forms of interaction were isolated, each providing different kinds of socializing experiences. The interaction between the adult driver and his or her child passengers represents normative socialization; interaction among the children represents interpretive socialization. Let us examine the form, tone, and influence of these interactions separately.

Adult–Child

The amount and kind of adult–child interaction varied, depending on who was driving. All of the children we interviewed acknowledged behaving differently in their own car. One 8-year-old boy summed up this difference:

> Kids act differently in their own mother's car. It's like it's their house; they know the rules, they tell you the rules, they boss you around. They talk a lot more and they talk to their mother. Kids break more rules in their own car because they feel like they can get away with it because it's their own mother; and they behave better in someone else's car. They're shy and they don't know what to say in someone else's car, and they can't ask for a drink or anything, so sometimes they'll ask the one whose car it is to ask his mother for them.

Thus, children derived status and authority in the group from the presence of their own parent and the use of their family's automobile.

Parents, in turn, interacted more with their offspring than with other passengers because they were unable, it seemed, to ignore their youngsters' questions, comments, and observations. This reflected the middle-class parent's emphasis on quality childrearing. As Denzin (1979:39) points out, "parents are continually reminded that the way their child turns out is a direct reflection of their competence as socializing agents." This setting, then, offered parents another opportunity to engage in normative socialization, to inculate their offspring with the norms and values they espouse, especially those pertaining to school—a highly esteemed institution among members of the middle class.

Adult–child interaction also included communication between children and others' parents. Interchange between the driver and the passengers always occurred to some degree, whether it was verbal or nonverbal, continuous or rare, directed toward parent or nonparent, child-initiated, or adult-led. Early in the school year each adult attempted to convey to the children his or her rules of automobile behavior. Though these may not have been as explicitly stated as those Zurcher (1979:89) describes for airline passenger socialization, basic safety regulations were usually repeated throughout the year (usually responsively when children got boisterous or carried away with fighting or play). In addition, each carpool driver had his or her own standards of the level of interaction that would be tolerated. Thus, adults communicated a set of tones and attitudes, so the children knew what to expect for the remainder of the season: They would either sit in silence and play the radio, ignoring whatever interaction happened to arise, or they would be strict in defining how children were allowed to behave.

Adults varied in their modes of interacting with a carpool full of children. From the quietest to the most boisterous, a continuum of styles will be traced. The most active and involved type of adult was the *moderator*.

Moderators interacted as regular participants in the automobile conversation. This mode was noticeable in carpools of preschool children, where parents assumed that children needed assistance in conducting their interpersonal relations. One 4-year-old girl acknowledged her interactional difficulty when discussing why she preferred drivers who took an active role in the group conversation:

> I like when Julie's mother drives or my mother drives [two moderators] because then I don't get in fights with other children, because they might stop it before it gets into a fight. They're more strict than Ben's mother.

Moderators often initiated conversation, setting examples of acceptable interactional styles by role modeling. In this way, they related to children as concerned adults who cared about the children's well-being and development, making sure that each one was treated fairly and equally. One mother described how she demonstrated thoughtful, courteous behavior:

> I always try to draw them out and I think every parent should. There's nothing worse than having to sit silently in a car while some adult plays the radio. I encourage them all to contribute to the conversation. Sometimes, I used to have to remind them to hold back from talking when Josh was trying to express himself, because he's so shy. But over the course of the year I've been so proud to see how he's come out of himself. He really wants to get his two cents in now.

Moderators also related to children as teachers and entertainers, singing songs to them, telling them facts about the world, telling them jokes, or keeping them interested in a series of amusing conversations.

When a moderator was driving, the tone of the automobile interaction was clearly adult-dominated. Children could participate, but they had to follow the behavioral guidelines established by the carpool driver.

A second group of adults were *interventionists*. Found in both preschool and elementary school carpools, interventionism was the most widespread mode of driver behavior. Interventionists did not direct the topic and tone of the children's conversation the way moderators did. They gave children more freedom to construct their own discussions. These adults answered questions, when asked, or reacted to complaints, taking a more responsive posture. Their interaction with the children was thus apt to be occasional rather than regular.

Interventionists also enforced certain standards or limitations on the behavior of their passengers. As such, they assumed responsibility for being the "guardian of the situational order" (Goffman, 1963:227), ensuring adherence to social norms and values such as safety, thoughtfulness, etiquette, and morality. Parents who took this posture constantly made spot decisions about the intensity and style of their intervention, because children were frequently inclined to test the limits of what would be allowed.[5]

Some interventionists utilized a "benign control" (Goffman, 1974), gently stopping the offensive behavior and redirecting it into more acceptable channels:

> When they get into the kind of conversation I don't like, sometimes I'll just interrupt and change the subject. I'll point to a billboard or some scenery and ask some questions about it, or I'll bring up something that they're doing in school and try to get them all talking about it.

By interrupting and recasting the tone and focus of the conversation, parents reaffirmed the dominance of their status and their power in the setting. But they also implicitly reaffirmed the children's lack of interpersonal skills by subtly asserting that their behavior was subject to inattention, open scrutiny, and blunt correction (West and Zimmerman, 1977:521).

Other interventionists took a more dictatorial role, openly utilizing disciplinary measures. Corporal punishment was rare, but many adults stopped the car until decorum was regained, or separated children who were causing problems. As one experienced carpool driver explained,

> I make it my business to pull off the main street and stop the car a few times very early in the year until they behave like I'm telling them to. They always realize that they want to get home just as badly as I do, so they knock it off; and that lets them know I mean business, so they pay attention to what I say.

A third group of drivers were *laissez-fairists*. Parents who followed this mode did not converse much with the passengers. They made sure that children were strapped into place, and then they occupied themselves with their own thoughts, often playing music to enhance the separation between the youngsters and themselves. Some did this because they did not want to hear the children's conversation, but others were merely passive, letting the children entertain and supervise themselves. Laissez-faire behavior was both habitual and occasional: Some parents regularly removed themselves, and others just did it when they were tired, distracted, or in a bad mood. One parent explained her laissez-fairism:

> I don't care what goes on back there. I'm not going to get involved. I hate carpooling and I just get in there and grit my teeth 'til it's over. I mind my own business and let them work out whatever they get into.

For others, the decision to withdraw from constant or intermittent supervising and policing of children's behavior was based less on personal reasons and more on an acknowledgment of the children's increasing interactional competence. Laissez-faire behavior was, thus, more commonly observed in carpools of older, elementary school children.

When a laissez-fairist was driving, the children's social circle became liberated from constant adult supervision. Their interaction at these times came the closest to being truly peer-dominated. Within reason, they could say and do what they wanted with minimal fear or benefit of parental intrusion. Some children welcomed this freedom and privacy, but others complained that it left them unprotected from other children's rowdy or nasty behavior. Yet, being forced to defend themselves made children acquire additional interactional skills. One 9-year-old girl described how she learned to handle a carpool situation involving an antagonistic other:

> He was kicking me and throwing spitballs and pinching me and made me real mad. I told him to stop it. I said if he didn't stop I'd tell the driver. But when I told her, she said "work it out yourselves." So then I thought about it and I asked him nicely and he stopped.

The different modes of adult carpool behavior can thus be correlated often, although not exclusively, with the age of the passengers. Preschool children noted and expected more supervision from their drivers on both a moderating and regularly interventionist basis. Parents driving them to school made rules, settled disputes, entertained them, and protected them from aggressors. Elementary school children gradually learned not to expect as much parental intervention. Their greater experience with occasional interventionists and laissez-fairists generated an atmosphere of greater privacy from adults.

These adult styles of interaction correspond to the normative and interpretive models of socialization discussed earlier. One of the most noticeable socializing influences carpooling adults had on children stemmed from their positions as role models, demonstrating and stressing the importance of certain values and behavioral norms. Those norms most endemic to the structure of the carpool setting included appropriate automobile safety; tolerance for other people and their differences; respect for people's feelings, privacy, and personal space; fairness; good citizenship and good manners; turn-taking; and sharing.

The interpretive perspective on socialization was also apparent, as adults prodded children to develop the skills necessary to interact competently with a variety of friendly and antagonistic others. They progressively withdrew, first, their moderating control and, then, their interventionist protection as the children grew older. Parents thus acknowledged children's growing capacity to socialize on an increasingly mature level by granting them greater freedom from adult dominance, slowly transforming the atmosphere of the setting into one of peer authority.

A feature of carpooling that promoted easier interaction between adults and children, facilitating their ability to get along with and learn from each other, was the basic *value and norm consensus*. Because they were drawn from the same neighborhoods and selected the same schools for their children, most families were quite homogeneous in their background, socioeconomic status, and child-rearing standards. The role models that adult drivers provided, then, through both their instructional and disciplinary forms of interaction, reinforced the behavioral norms that the children encountered at home.

However, when there was some conflict between home standards and carpool behavior, children and parents were apt to discuss this outside of the carpool setting. Minor areas of conflict or divergence included ownership of material possessions, kinds of food children were allowed to eat (e.g., candy, junk food), sharing requisites, and tolerance of rowdy behavior. One parent explained how she handled these divergences from their family standards with her children:

> My girls would often get upset over the behavior of this one boy in the carpool; and I knew what that meant because I saw how wild, disrespectful, and teasing he was

when I would drive. I've talked to his mother but it's no use, because it goes in one ear and out the other. So I just have to talk to my girls. I have to tell them that the way he acts is not right, and they have to rise above it and be bigger than he is by ignoring his teasings.

Thus, parents reacted to the occasional minor normative divergence by using violators as negative examples, framing their child's interpretation of the situation with their own evaluations.

When consensus between the norms and values of participating families was threatened by more major conflict, parents' reactions became more severe. These differences were likely to involve highly sensitive and value-laden topics, such as religion and sex. In one example we observed, two families of different religions were carpooling together. After a while, one set of parents began to notice that one of the children was proselytizing to their child. In another situation, one mother noticed that the carpool conversation frequently revolved around nudity and genitalia, casting these topics in an alluringly forbidden and "dirty" light. Upon closer examination, this last mother became convinced that one of the children in the carpool was instigating sexually perverse discussion and behavior, which was carrying over to her child's behavior at home. She became concerned and conferred with her husband, the other carpool drivers, and the children's teacher. In both of these cases, the carpools were disbanded. Thus, when one child displayed or espoused behavior that threatened the attitudes and belief systems of another family, the foundation of parent-to-parent carpool relations eroded. For parents, the threat to their value system entailed in such fundamental differences in the orientation of the other family superceded the conveniences that the carpool offered.

Child–Child

In and around periods of parental intervention, children interacted directly with each other. It was here that the differences in their ages became most apparent, since elementary school children had more peer-group experience than preschool children and interacted at different levels of sophistication. The interactional dynamics of children took varied and complex forms, shifting rapidly and leaving old topics and allegiances completely forgotten. We will examine the most commonly recurring interactional typologies.

Most of the time, children's carpool play was characterized by *friendship* and *cooperation*. This was especially true for preschoolers, who were apt to greet new children enthusiastically and without reservation. Although shy at first, they made repeated attempts to find areas of commonality to discuss. One

5-year-old boy explained that he looked on the carpool as an opportunity to make new friends:

> I like the carpool because I can get more friends. Because if I see them, I'll play with them if I know them, and I'll get more friends to know. I'll know the different kids a little better and then I can play with them and have more friends.

Special friendships frequently formed in carpools among children of the same age and sex. One 7-year-old girl described how her relationship with a girl in her class changed after they began to carpool together:

> We're better friends now. I saw her before, but now that she's in my carpool, I like her better.

These relationships were carried over to home and school, where the children had additional time to spend together.

Because these children were thrust together, friendships formed across the boundaries of age and sex (which, as Rubin [1980:192] notes, is somewhat unusual for children of these ages). One 9-year-old girl described her reactions when she and her sisters had to start carpooling with two younger boys:

> At first I was really upset and I said to my mother, "Oh, do we have to?" But being in the carpool with them made me understand them better. I know how they feel about things; and so I guess I got to like them.

When friendships and cooperation broke down, they were sometimes replaced by *antagonism* and *hostility*. Such behavior either surfaced on an occasional basis or came to pervade the carpool atmosphere, resuming each day when children entered the car. As a temporary phenomenon, antagonism was somewhat influenced by the time of day. Children were more cooperative on the way to school, when they were rested and well fed, than on the way home, when they were apt to be worn out, cranky, and more irritable.[6]

Children placed in carpools with disliked others displayed regular patterns of hostility, which increased in intensity because of their forced contact. One 6-year-old boy described the effects of carpooling with someone he did not like: "It made me hate them worse." Children displayed antagonism toward each other in the most raw, unsocialized forms. Most commonly, we saw teasing, taunting, and chanting, often communicated in a sing-song tone that intensified its abrasiveness. One 5-year-old girl illustrated the tone of some carpool conversations:

> Kids talk about what they're going to do. If it's something good to do they say, ha ha ha or na na na na na, and that's being mean to the other person; that really hurts their feelings.

Invidious comparisons and competitiveness also sprang up, pitting the children against each other. The foci of this competition varied, but most often it involved accomplishments at school, toys, clothes, and outdoor play experiences.

Sometimes antagonisms between children became learned behavior, carrying over from one situation to the next. Recurrent taunting and hostility had a lasting effect that was noticeable beyond the carpool frameworks. One child who was constantly exposed to malicious behavior came home in tears and reported, "She hurt my feelings Mommy. Why does she do that?" Wounding jabs seemed to penetrate more deeply among elementary school children than among their younger counterparts, affecting their image and sense of self-worth. Preschool children, however, were more likely to imitate such behavior indiscriminately, as one father of a 3-year-old girl described:

> Our child used to be such a sweet and innocent young thing until she started into carpooling with this horrible kid. Everything out of the kid's mouth was mean, and it really confused Heidi. But after awhile Heidi started learning how to be mean from this child and she would dish it right back. She even started being mean to her other friends when they would come over to play, so much so that they would ask to go home. Eventually we had to dissolve the carpool, no matter how convenient it was.

A third mode of child–child interaction was *withdrawal into privacy*. This usually occurred after communication had deteriorated and repeated instances of hostility had erupted. Schwartz (1968:741) cites the distraction and relief of privacy as a means of conflict avoidance: Rather than engage in antagonistic behavior with abrasive others, people withdraw into themselves. One 9-year-old boy explained how he arrived at this solution on his own:

> There's one girl in my carpool that bosses everybody around. She really gets on my nerves. After about a month of fighting with her I just started to ignore her when she starts to get bossy. It didn't make any difference, really, because she still bossed everybody around. But at least we didn't fight.

This type of perception, interpretation, and anticipatory behavior was occasionally observed among elementary school children, but preschoolers had a more difficult time exerting self-control and refraining from antagonistic interaction. These younger children frequently lacked the ability to anticipate the results of their behavior and to recognize the developing spiral of bickering. Some forms of fighting, followed by adult intervention and discipline, usually occurred before the child realized that withdrawing into privacy offered the best solution. Tearful, tired, and sullen, they sank into their seats and sucked their thumbs, studied their laps, or, as Bell (1981:33) notes, engaged in daydreaming, often closing their eyes to further indicate their unavailability to others. For older children, who had more years of experience and maturity, the decision to utilize privatizing behavior to avoid conflicts came sooner, although not always prior to the outbreak of hostility. In these carpools, where the encapsulated situation made interaction intense, we thus saw not only affection and open hostility, as Freud's [(1921) 1960:41–42] principle of ambivalence suggests, but withdrawal behavior as well. The use of withdrawal represented a form of tolerance learning, which children utilized to help maintain their relationships with others.

Interactional dynamics within the carpool sometimes varied with the *size of the group*. The two-child situation offered the most intense experience, since participants had little diversion or escape from each other. Thrust into deep exploration of each other's personalities, they often reacted in extremes, developing either intimate companionship or hostile antagonism. When the bond was positive, children generally increased their interpersonal contact by playing together after school; but when the reaction was negative, they were still forced to stay in the situation. Large carpools, in contrast, offered the most diffuse experience, providing children with a greater range of possible friends and more sources of refuge from an unpleasant combatant. When five or six children were in the car it was difficult for any one child constantly to dominate the character of group behavior, so the overall dynamics were more varied and changing. According to parents, the most troublesome number of participants was three, for as Simmel (1950:135–36) notes, "no matter how close a triad may be, there is always the occasion on which two of the three members regard the third as an intruder." This left the third child feeling expelled and jealous of the intimacy of the other two.

In this latter situation, and in many other situations, we observed *forming* and *shifting cliques:* Children created alliances with each other that lasted for a while, only to abandon and replace them with new ones. One 10-year-old described how friendship groups shifted:

> Kids are always changing around who they're friendly with. You're best friends with one kid one day and another the next. You're always changing around because kids get into fights with each other and then gang up along people's sides. Alot of times people ask me to choose whose side I'm on, and if you take somebody's side, then they're your friend and the other one isn't.

While allied into "withs" (Goffman, 1971:19–27), children utilized a variety of techniques to demonstrate both their membership in the group and their closure toward outsiders. They established a "conversational preserve" (Goffman, 1971:40), which served as an invisible barrier, repelling unwanted intruders.

When children formed into cliques, there was usually a difference in the patterns and rationale between preschoolers and elementary school children. Older children affiliated themselves into status groupings organized around such determinants as age, level of accomplishment, height, strength, and school social status. The status hierarchy could and did exhibit flexibility, as when birthday parties drew near, but it was fairly stable. In contrast to this status structure was the affect structure (Secord, Backman, and Slavitt, 1976:189–99) displayed by preschoolers. Younger children did not create status hierarchies but clustered instead into groups according to simpler likes and dislikes. Some dimensions of friendship preference were stable and enduring, based on similarities in development levels, temperaments, and behavioral styles (Rubin, 1980:25). More often, however, preschool friendships were based on transitory attributes such as physical propinquity (who is sitting next to whom), material possessions brought into the car (such as "show and tell" items), and the favoritism of power and information held by the child whose parent was driving. At these times, preschool children displayed "momentary playmateship" (Selman and Selman, 1979:71), shifting pairs and groups of friendships much more frequently and unpredictably than their older counterparts.

Another interpersonal dynamic displayed in the carpool was *dominance* and *submission*. At these young ages, children were enmeshed in the roles of teaching and being taught by parents, teachers, and siblings. Thus, they naturally fell into such leading and following behaviors; older or more aggressive children dictated the perceptions, interpretations, and attitudes formed by younger or more docile children. They also enforced behavioral norms (such as elementary social etiquette) onto each other, practiced role modeling, and engaged in the "anticipatory socialization" (Mead, 1934) of role playing. This was often a positive experience for youngsters as they gained skill at forming peer relations and got a chance to try out new roles, but several parents expressed dismay at what was being communicated through this interaction. One mother of a 4-year-old girl articulated her reservations:

> At first I was pleased at the way Rebecca was interacting with this older girl in her carpool: she's so bossy to me around the house that I was happy to see her engaged in a follower role. But then I started noticing the content of the ideas and attitudes she was picking up from this kid and I stopped being so pleased. She was picking up sexist and religious stereotypes and expressing negative attitudes about things that are important to us and our family, like "Melanie says she hates school and so do I" or "Melanie hates her new baby and so do I."

Some early carpool experiences were thus frightening to parents who witnessed the first signs of peer-group influence on children who had been relatively sheltered. Carpool interaction often produced the most noticeable socializing influences on first and only children who had little previous exposure to older peers, partly because parents of first and only children tended to be more overprotective, more sensitive to their children's experiences, and more aware of subtle changes in their character. Subsequent children were not usually reared with the same degree of scrutiny, because the carpool offered parents the rare opportunity to view peer interaction closely in a relatively informal setting. Perhaps, then, they were more sensitized to the effects of carpool socialization because they had observed the behavior and were anticipating its results.

A final dimension of carpool interaction was the one most heavily influenced by the physical setting: *territoriality*.[7] Children staked out, claimed, and defended their "posessional territories" (Goffman, 1971:38) with a fierce, but intensely vulnerable, rawness. Their obvious degree of caring left them open to all kinds of encroachment as soon as petty bickering arose. Carpool territoriality usually took two forms: sitting in a favorite place and guarding the "ecological boundary" (Cavan, 1970:561–2) immediately surrounding one's position.

Seating preferences were most easily handled by parents, and once a decision was made, the issue did not arise again for the remainder of the trip. Most children preferred to sit in the front seat next to their parent on days when it was their family's turn to drive. Sitting next to favorite others (such as babies) or sitting in special seats (such as the third row of a station wagon or the extra front seat) could be negotiated with the adult driver and was usually arranged either on an evenly rotating basis or by the system that most successfully discouraged in-fighting.

Defending against intrusions into one's personal enclave was not so easily managed, however, and often caused interpersonal friction. Especially on the ride home, when interaction started to degenerate due to hunger and fatigue, children typically followed an escalating pattern of baiting each other, which began with taunting and jesting and lead rapidly into poking, intruding their arms and legs into the other's domain, and eventually striking each other. One 7-year-old girl offered an example of this behavior:

> There's a boy in my carpool that I don't like. He's in the third grade and he's loud and he's mean. One time he kept turning around and yelling at us. So we kept on touching him, and he kept on saying "yecch." Then he started pushing us, which he's not supposed to do, so we told the driver and she told him to cut it out.

This form of territorial violation was especially affected by the carpool setting, as the compounding elements of time and interactional behavior affected children's perceptions of their spatial boundaries. These boundaries were not fixed, but fluctuated as children were added to and discharged from the car and as the tone of communication ranged from cooperative to antagonistic. Thus, within the carpool, as Scheflen and Ashcraft (1976:4–5) note, the study of human territory goes beyond the mere notion of space to incorporate dimensions of motion, behavior time, and context.

Discussion

Throughout this presentation, we have attempted to shed some light on the structural and dynamic features of carpooling, an uninvestigated social phenomenon. We have shown that carpooling is not treated by most parents as simply a mode of transportation; rather, it takes on the dimensions of a socializing arena. Serving as a daily experience for preschool and elementary school children, the carpool is unique because it falls under the combined formative influence of three socializing agents: the school, the family, and the peer group. It is therefore a place governed by three overlapping sets of rules and expectations. The way these behavioral prescriptions, roles, and values are presented to children and the way children perceive, evaluate, and integrate them into their developing selves constitutes their socialization experience.

Carpool interaction can be seen to involve concurrently both of the socialization models depicted by sociologists. Children become socialized, according to the *normative* theorists' perspective, as they acquire the culture's norms, values, and roles. In the carpool setting, this internalization of norms and values occurs primarily through children's interaction with the adult driver. This formal socialization process is characterized by an asymmetrical power relationship in which the agents of socialization have physical and social power over the children. Parents transmit roles, norms, and values in two ways: (1) by explicitly instructing children in the importance of these qualities and (2) by implicitly role modeling for them the means of expediting these values.

Carpool behavior also displays the *interpretive* model of socialization, as children's informal peer interactions offer them the opportunity to develop and refine their interactional competence. Involuntarily thrust together, children engage in a variety of role-taking activities. By observing and learning new roles from others, they begin to see the world from new sets of perspectives and to anticipate new forms of behavior. They then try out these new roles on each other via a series of exploratory dominant, submissive, and imitative relationships. These roles and relationships are then integrated into their repertoire for selective future use. As they age and develop greater interactional competence they are given more responsibility for managing their own interaction, and most drivers' behavior gradually evolves from the dominating moderator role to the withdrawn laissez-fairist role.

Framing the school experience, the carpool constitutes a symbolic transition between home and school. Superficially, it provides a time and place for children to shift their orientation from their home perspectives and roles to their school selves in the morning and back again at the end of the day. On a deeper level, the carpool serves as an intermediary, especially for younger children, buffering them from being immediately thrust into or out of the school arena. In contrast to the protected home environment and the exposed school environment, the carpool constitutes a semiprivate environment. Once out of the house and into the carpool, the children begin to acclimate themselves, making a gradual transition to school instead of an abrupt separation or shift. In this way the carpool symbolically mediates between these two childhood worlds.

Finally, the socializing influence of carpooling is heightened by its structural features: It is a regularly recurrent, encapsulated setting. This time and space intensity fosters the development of three carpool-generated relationships. Friendly peer relationships are elevated to *intimate* status through the concentration and closeness of children's repeated exposure. Abrasive relationships are raised to a *combatant* plane through children's continual reirritation by and inability to escape from antagonistic others. But perhaps unique to carpool settings and distinct from the ways students are frequently grouped in school is the introduction of *informally structured obligatory* relationships. Here, children who would otherwise avoid each other learn to get along benignly and to tolerate irritating traits in each other for the sake of expediency. Informal obligatory relationships are characterized by a superficial friendliness that gives way to avoidance after tensions begin to mount. Here, the withdrawal into privacy is utilized to stave off the intensification of unpleasant exchanges. Obligatory role learning prepares children for the many similar situationally necessitated relationships they will encounter throughout their childhood and adulthood among neighborhood groups, school groups, work groups, political groups, interest groups, and the like.

This research has shown how an often overlooked arena like the carpool can have potent socializing influences. Preschool and elementary school children are young and highly impressionable and therefore open to learning about human nature and human behavior through a variety of direct and indirect means. The present study has shown how socialization occurs concurrently through both normative and interpretive modes, suggesting cooperation rather than estrangement for proponents of these schools. Future researchers could profit from looking at the socializing effects of other non-classroom, informal school experiences.

Acknowledgments

We would like to thank Jean Blocker, Mary Haywood Metz, Louis Zurcher, and anonymous reviewers for helpful comments on an earlier draft.

Notes

1. Though many sociological definitions of peer groupings require strict age bounding, we use the term loosely here, including children who are 3–4 years apart in the same peer group. We also apply the term to a captive population, though it is used primarily with reference to voluntary associations.
2. Of the 23 children we interviewed, 10 were in the preschool grades and 13 attended elementary school. These interviews were supplemented with our own observations and others' accounts of carpools containing children down to the age of 3.
3. Other forms of public transportation share carpooling's encapsulated nature (see Zurcher, 1979), yet individuals utilizing them strive to increase rather than decrease social distance, thereby avoiding both socializing and socialization.
4. Other forms of school transportation (i.e., school bus, walking) share carpooling's regularity but lack parental supervision over children and forced closeness with unchosen others. Here, the ability to be alone or surround themselves with selected friends offers children some protection against the socializing experiences found in carpools.
5. Coser (1961) suggests that the reactive interventionist pose, in which adults act as mediators or discipline children to ensure that their behavior complies with behavioral norms, is characteristic of the role relationship between role-partners (here, the parents) and status-occupants (here, the children) in which the subordinates' activities are directly observable by their superiors.
6. One general exception was found among siblings who shared the same carpool and carried an argument that had begun at home into the car.
7. Joffe (1973:107) has observed, in her analysis of a preschool setting, the way children engage in territoriality. Mandell (1984) refers to children's invasions of each others' personal space as "crowding."

References

Bandura, A. *Social Learning Theory* (New York: McCaleb-Seiler, 1971).

Bell, R. *Worlds of Friendship* (Beverly Hills, CA: Sage, 1981).

Brim, O. G. Jr. "Personality Development as Role Learning." In I. Iscoe and H. W. Stevenson, eds., *Personality Development in Children* (Austin: University of Texas Press, 1960).

Cavan, S. "The Etiquette of Youth." In G. Stone and H. Farberman, eds., *Social Psychology through Symbolic Interaction* (Waltham, MA: Xerox, 1970).

Cicourel, A. V. "The Acquisition of Social Structure." In J. D. Douglas, ed., *Understanding Everyday Life* (Chicago: Aldine, 1970).

Coser, R. L. "Insulation from Observability and Types of Social Conformity." *American Sociological Review*, 1961, 26:28–39.

Denzin, N. "Children and Their Caretakers." In P. Rose, ed., *Socialization and the Life Cycle* (New York: St. Martin, 1979).

Freud, S. *Group Psychology and the Analysis of the Ego* (New York: Bantam, 1960. First published in 1921).

Garfinkel, H. *Studies in Ethnomethodology* (Englewood Cliffs, NJ: Prentice-Hall,

1967).

Goffman, E. *Behavior in Public Places* (New York: Free Press, 1963).

Goffman, E. *Relations in Public* (New York: Harper Colophon, 1971).

Goffman, E. *Frame Analysis* (New York: Harper Colophon, 1974).

Inkeles, A. "Social Structure and the Socialization of Competence." *Harvard Educational Review*, 1966, 36:265–83.

Joffe, C. "Taking Young Children Seriously." In N. Denzin, ed., *Children and their Caretakers* (New Brunswick, NJ: Transaction, 1973).

Lofland, L. *A World of Strangers* (New York: Basic, 1973).

Mandell, N. "Children's Negotiation of Meaning." *Symbolic Interaction*, 1984, 7.

Mead, G. H. *Mind, Self and Society* (Chicago: University of Chicago Press, 1934).

Merton, R. "The Role Set." *British Journal of Sociology*, 1957, 8: 106–120.

Parsons, T., and Bales, R. *Family, Socialization and Interaction Process* (Glencoe, IL: Free Press, 1955).

Rose, A. M. "A Systematic Summary of Symbolic Interaction Theory." In A. M. Rose, ed., *Human Behavior and Social Processes* (Boston: Houghton Mifflin, 1962, pp. 3–19.

Rubin, Z. *Children's Friendships* (Cambridge, MA: Harvard University Press, 1980).

Scheflen, A. E., and Ashcraft, N. *Human Territories* (Englewood Cliffs, NJ: Prentice-Hall, 1976).

Schwartz, B. "The Social Psychology of Privacy." *American Journal of Sociology*, 1968, 73: 741–52.

Secord, P., Backman, C., and Slavitt, D. *Understanding Social Life* (New York: McGraw-Hill, 1976).

Selman, R. L., and Selman, A. P. "Children's Ideas about Friendship: A New Theory." *Psychology Today*, 1979, 13:71–72, 74, 79–80, 114.

Shibutani, T. "Reference Groups and Social Control." In A. M. Rose, ed., *Human Behavior and Social Processes* (Boston: Houghton Mifflin, 1962).

Simmel, G. *The Sociology of Georg Simmel* (ed. and trans. K. H. Wolff) (New York: Free Press, 1950).

Speier, M. "The Everyday World of the Child." In J. D. Douglas, ed., *Understanding Everyday Life* (Chicago: Aldine, 1970).

Watson, J. B. *Behaviorism* (New York: Norton, 1970. First published in 1925).

West, C., and Zimmerman, D. "Women's Place in Everyday Talk: Reflections on Parent–Child Interaction." *Social Problems*, 1977, 24: 521–529.

Zurcher, L. A. "The Airplane Passenger: Protection of Self in an Encapsulated Group." *Qualitative Sociology*, 1979, 1:77–99.

12

Friends, Impression Management, and Preadolescent Behavior*

Gary Alan Fine

Introduction

Coexisting with adult society in contemporary America is a subsociety whose members are classified not by race, ethnicity, or religion, but by age. This is the social world of childhood—that stratum of social structure that Glassner (1976) termed "Kid Society." Children's society has a robust culture significantly different from that of parents and guardians. Increasingly, folklorists, anthropologists, and sociologists have become interested in exploring the social world of children. Their exploration seems to be an extension of research in youth culture and "adolescent society" (Coleman, 1961). The underlying contention is that children (and adolescents) maintain a social system relatively autonomous from adults. The goal of this chapter is to describe this social system, the abilities necessary to interact in it successfully, and the means by which members come to acquire these abilities; that is, how children become socialized to a "peer culture." In pursuit of this goal, we shall examine in some detail one particular social world—that of Little League baseball. Observations of Little League baseball players—both in the game and in their free time—suggest that boys by preadolescence have acquired skills in impression management and that their acquisition is, in part, a consequence of their friendships.

*Reprinted by permission of the author and Cambridge University Press from Steven R. Asher and John M. Gottman (eds.), *The Development of Children's Friendships*, pp. 29–52. Copyright © 1981, Cambridge University Press.

Research Perspective: Symbolic Interactionism

My research perspective is symbolic interactionism, an approach to under-standing social life developed by Charles Horton Cooley, George Herbert Mead, Herbert Blumer, and Erving Goffman, among others. Blumer (1969) argued that three premises are crucial to this perspective. First, human beings act toward things on the basis of the meanings that these objects have for them. Thus, actions or objects are said to have no a priori stimulus value. Second, the meanings of these stimuli emerge through social interaction. Third, and per-haps most important, these meanings are not static, but can be modified through an interpretive process. Meanings, therefore, are not reified, but are poten-tially subject to interpersonal negotiation. Through this assumption the sym-bolic interactionist perspective orients itself to change and development. A fur-ther assumption is that social meanings are shaped through communication and therefore that causes of action are not primarily biological and subconscious, but social and conscious.

The symbolic interactionist approach can be differentiated on two dimen-sions from the three major approaches to social development, psychoanalysis, learning theory, and cognitive stage theory. It differs from psychoanalysis and learning theory in rejecting the concept of the child as a relatively passive organism whose actions are largely predetermined by environment or biology (or in sophisticated analyses by their interaction); it construes the child as an active interpreter of situations (Faris, 1937/1971, p. 233). Further, it differs from psychoanalysis and cognitive stage theory in rejecting the existence of an invariable sequence of universal stages of development.

Socialization has been conceived of as process by which the child becomes acculturated into adult standards; deviation from this ideal is thought to repre-sent a failure of the acculturation process. This process is seen as deriving from the child's identification with the adult. For example, Parsons *et al.* (1951) claim that "there is approximate agreement that the development of identification with adult objects is an essential mechanism of the socialization process. . . . The child becomes oriented to the wishes which embody for him the values of the adult, and his viscerogenic needs become culturally organized needs, which are shaped so that their gratification is sought in directions compatible with his integration into this system of interaction" (pp. 17–18).

Such a view is clearly "adultist." The concept of a single class of objects of identification is inadequate for the segmentation between adults and peers begins early, and the self is segmented according to situational needs. Fre-quently, several groups or individuals may be identified with (Fine and Klein-man, 1979). The conception of the child as having a single adult source of iden-tification (role model or ego ideal) leads to children being seen as incomplete adults, lacking, but steadily learning, the norms that will incorporate them as full members of their society. Furthermore, identifications tend not to be total but are situationally bounded, a function of the activation of latent cultures or systems of behaviors characteristic of sets of social relationships (Becker and Geer, 1960).

The distinctions between symbolic interactionism and other approaches should not be drawn too firmly. For example, the interactionist approach is congruent with Zigler and Child's (1969) definition of socialization as "the whole process by which an individual develops through transaction with other people, his specific patterns of socially relevant behavior and experiences" (p. 474). The interactionist perspective attempts to give the child (or any actor) more credit for his or her actions than deterministic theories allow, and this has led to criticism that symbolic interactionism is astructural and indeterminate (Zeitlin, 1973), although most interactionists admit there are biological and social constraints on behavior. No theory can reveal the whole truth of development, and symbolic interactionism is no exception; however, by exploring some of the implications of this approach for social development, childhood behavior can be better understood and traditional developmental approaches can be better informed about children's roles in shaping their own social worlds.

Issues Underlying the Symbolic–Interactionist Approach

Three important issues underlie the symbolic–interactionist approach to development, all of which represent processes that occur early in childhood and are well developed by preadolescence. These issues are: the development of the self through the perception of others, the importance of communication and the use of symbols, and the development of the ability to behave appropriately as a function of the expectations of others.

The relationship between self and other is seen by symbolic interactionists as crucial to the development of behavior (Wiley, 1980). The other is the mirror by which individuals learn of their selves (Mead, 1934, p. 158), and it is the other with whom the self must negotiate lines of collective action. Cooley (1902/1964) argues that the child's conception of the self is a product of interaction and that, when acquiring vocabulary, the child learns to know others before learning to be self-reflective (Cooley, 1908; Bain, 1936). Thus, the self-concept develops through social interaction and emerges from the child's ability to take the role of the other. This role taking is also seen as crucial by Piaget for the development of the concrete operations stage. However, contrary to the implications of cognitive approaches, symbolic interactionists argue that the child does not develop a conception of self (or "I") until after a conception of others has been acquired. Thus, the concept of an egocentric stage is not accurate according to the symbolic interactionist perspective. For the young child, the most important others typically are the child's parents or adult guardians, and these individuals are particularly significant in channeling the content of the child's self-concept. The shaping of the child's self by others is expanded with the onset of schooling, at which time the child must learn to deal with multiple others—what Mead (1925) termed the "game stage." This diverse social world shapes the child's self through exposure to a variety of behavioral options.

Simultaneous with the development of self (and a component of this development) is the growth of communication skills. Mastery of language and gestures is crucial for the preschool child in that it permits an understanding of and participation in interaction. The extent of symbolic universes of discourse varies depending on social factors; for example, the extent to which linguistic codes are elaborated or restricted (Bernstein, 1975). By the time the child is ready for formal schooling, this symbolizing process is well advanced (Denzin, 1977).

The third feature of development emphasized by interactionists is the acquisition of competence in behaving properly in a variety of social settings. The young child increasingly acquires the ability to interact with peers and near peers and spends more time in settings in which adults are not present to enforce their views of mannered interaction (Speier, 1973; MacKay, 1973). Situations in which dominance is not a direct result of age become common, and children must refine their techniques for constructing social meanings consensually; they mutually fit together lines of action, rather than have their situational definitions and courses of action constrained by adults (Elkin and Handel, 1978). Further, children learn, through the response of others, that their behaviors have consequences. While children may define situations as they feel proper and act according to these definitions in the presence of adults, if these definitions and actions are not congruent with adult prescriptions, children discover that their behaviors may have real (and painful) consequences. Among peers, contrary situational definitions may have negative outcomes as well, but in such situations there is no shared assumption that one party's definition is necessarily legitimate, although sociometric status influences the usage of social power.

Once the child recognizes that different sets of individuals have different expectations and that different situations may require different behaviors, the attempt to master a single, consistent set of core behavior patterns is no longer relevant. Symbolic interactionists emphasize the importance of the child's ability to see himself or herself as an object of appropriation (Mead, 1934). By this Mead means that the individual can place himself or herself in relation to an other or set of others (a process Blumer [1969] terms "self-indication") and can shape his or her behavior in light of others' expectations. Stone (1970, p. 399) conceived of identity as a "coincidence of placements and announcements" whereby the evaluation of one's self by others is similar to the desired evaluation of the self. By later childhood the key interactional task is to refine one's social identity and to acquire the skills necessary for the successful positioning of the self in multiple social worlds.

Preadolescent Social Development

Our focus in this chapter will be on the preadolescent period. During this period, the three features of development have become established. In particular, this chapter focuses on peer relations during preadolescence and examines, from the interactionist perspective, how they influence socialization.

Preadolescence (broadly, ages 7–12) represents a particularly significant period because in it children are expected to develop social lives that are not merely extensions of situations dominated by adults (parents and teachers). While this may occur somewhat earlier or later, in most locales preadolescents are not expected to be under the watchful eye of an adult chaperone and can thus develop their own private relationships. Researchers have noted the importance of friends—either the single chum or the gang—in preadolescent peer relations (see Fine, 1980a; Hartup, 1978 for a summary of this literature). These patterns of chumship and ganging are found in many areas of the globe, although not in every society, according to anthropological reports. It is believed that these relationships have considerable impact in shaping the child's social behavior and attitudes. For example, Sullivan (1953) writes: "In the company of one's chum, one finds oneself more and more able to talk about things which one had learned, during the juvenile era, not to talk about . . . about the last chance [troubled children] have of favorable change is based on their need for getting along with a chum in preadolescence" (pp. 227, 252). Whatever the validity of Sullivan's explicit connection between friendship and psychiatric therapy, friendships produce moments of shared fantasy that Cottle (1971) has argued allow children to escape the boundaries of their troubled existence. Groups also allow children to learn about themselves and society: "The school-age child spends as much of his time as possible in the company of his peers, from whom he learns at first hand about social structures, about in-groups and out-groups, about leadership and followership, about justice and injustice, about loyalties and heroes and ideals" (Stone and Church, 1968, p. 364).

These groups are arenas for social action: They are social locations in which the preadolescent is able to explore available role options and to master methods of impression management in a supportive social environment. Having a set of close friends or a single chum is important to the child, because preadolescent interaction is generally not placid (Opie and Opie, 1959) but is filled with the possibilities of sudden denigration. As Stone and Church suggest, "the feeling of inclusion seems to necessitate someone's exclusion" (1957, p. 221). Thus, in this socially tempestuous time, having a friend with whom one can feel secure provides a solid base from which interpersonal confidence can be built, even given the notoriously fickle affections of children.

Preadolescent Social Relations and Little League Baseball

This chapter is intended to be a theoretical analysis of the socializing effects of preadolescent friendship, not a description of a world of childhood activities. However, the theoretical assessment is grounded in a set of research experiences, some of which will be described in the following pages. The research consisted of a 3-year participant-observation study of preadolescent males. During these 3 years, Little League baseball leagues in four American communities were examined by the author: (1) Beanville,[1] an upper middle-class professional suburb of Boston, Massachusetts; (2) Hopewell, an exurban township outside of the Providence, Rhode Island metropolitan area consisting of a string of small towns, beachfront land, farms, and a campus of the state university; (3) Bolton Park, an upper middle-class professional suburb of St. Paul, Minnesota, similar to Beanville except for geographical location; and (4) Sanford Heights, a middle to lower middleclass suburb of Minneapolis, Minnesota, composed of a large number of modern mass-produced homes. A research assistant, Harold Pontiff, conducted a parallel investigation of a Little League baseball program in Maple Bluff, an urban, upper middle-class area of St. Paul.

The Little League baseball organization was founded in Williamsport, Pennsylvania, in 1939 for the purpose of allowing boys (ages 9–12) to play organized baseball under adult supervision. (For an evaluation of this program see Fine and West [1979].) The organization has grown enormously. It is now international and comprises over 600,000 players in about 5,000 leagues. The program was designed for boys and for a long time excluded girls. As a result of court suits, Little League now admits both boys and girls, although only 10 girls played in the five leagues in the period under examination. Because of the small number of girls observed, I will limit my discussion to preadolescent boys. There is evidence that males and females differ in their play patterns (Lever, 1976) and relationships (Waldrop and Halverson, 1975), and thus we must be cautious in generalizing our analysis to girls without confirming evidence.

The primary methodology employed to collect data about Little Leaguers and their friends was participant observation (see Bogdan and Taylor, 1975). In order to focus the observations, two teams in each league were chosen for intensive study. Detailed records were kept of the players on 10 teams (12–15 players per team), less detailed records were kept on 32 other teams, and information was collected on scores of preadolescents who were not involved in the league. At first the intention was to examine the Little League teams, but it soon became apparent that the only way in which preadolescent social behavior could be understood was through observing the larger context of their spring and summer leisure-time patterns. Thus, considerable time was spent with the players and their friends outside of the baseball context. [For a detailed treatment of this research see Fine and Glassner (1979); Fine (1980b)]. While it would be misleading to claim that the research settings are representative of the environments of American children, they do cover a substantial range. Like the Little League organization itself, the primarily middle-class sample has fewer rural children, urban children, and poor children than would be expected by chance. While I will speak in generalities, one should remember the sample from which this analysis derives.

Children and Presentation of Self

Central to the process of growing up is learning ways of displaying one's social self in public. Adults fear that children will say the wrong thing in public. For example, they may tell Aunt Millie about what they really think of her homemade apple pie, or they may tell rich Uncle Joe the private conversations their parents have had about him. Such images provide an endless source of jokes and indicate the anxiety that adults feel about the potential so-called indiscretions of their offspring. Somewhat facetiously, we might suggest that the danger is that the child has not mastered the art of being hypocritical. Less facetiously, one can note that the issue is one of learning situational proprieties—behavior that is deemed proper in one situation is considered grossly improper in another. While etiquette books for children emphasize rules for behavior appropriate in all situations (Cavan, 1970), these rules must be negotiated in their social contexts. Preadolescents do not behave toward their peers in the same way they behave toward their parents, a point that most parents recognize. While parents may not get upset if their children curse or tell dirty jokes with their friends, this does not mean that the children are given license to behave this way in front of their parents. Conversely, the fact that a child may be willing to admit affection to relatives does not imply that the same child will admit this to peers. Stone and Church comment that "no ten-year-old boy would be caught dead saying that he 'loved' anything" (1957, p. 220). This evaluation is confirmed by my observation that children who too readily admit to affection become the objects of teasing or scorn.

By preadolescence a boy normally finds himself in several distinct social worlds, and he discovers that appropriate behavior is dependent upon his interpretation of the nature of these worlds. The popular and socially integrated preadolescent is the one who has mastered techniques of impression management in order to present himself through flexible role performances (see Elkins, 1958) and to altercast others (Weinstein and Deutschberger, 1963; Weinstein, 1969) into roles that support his role position. In other words, through his actions the child is able to control the behavioral roles of his interaction partners in ways that complement his social position.

In his discussion of presentation of self, Goffman (1959) does not consider the development of impression–management skills, because his interest is primarily in knowledgeable adults. Goffman's model of a human being is of a schemer or actor who must manipulate a world of complex and deceptive meanings (see Goffman, 1974). The acquisition of this competence seems not to be confined to the preadolescent period but develops from birth. However, my research indicates that by puberty the child has acquired the basic techniques of impression management, although interactional subtlety is still to be mastered.

Cooley (1902/1964) notes the importance of the early development of the social self and suggests that very young children attempt to manipulate the impressions that others have of them: "The young performer soon learns to be different things to different people, showing that he begins to apprehend personality and to foresee its operation. If the mother or nurse is more tender than just she will almost certainly be 'worked' by systematic weeping" (p. 197). However, it is unlikely that prior to schooling children attempt to present different identities or even to shape the impressions that others have of them. More likely, children manipulate others to achieve some end, and their impressions are shaped indirectly. Cooley notes that "a child obviously and simply, at first, does things for effect. Later there is an endeavor to suppress the appearance of doing so; affection, indifference, contempt, etc., *are simulated* to hide the real wish to affect the self-image. It is perceived that an obvious seeking after good opinion is weak and disagreeable" (p. 199; emphasis added). This later concern involves constructing one's behavior so as to manipulate and constrain others. Corsaro's research with nursery school children indicates that some rather young children have considerable ability and finesse in structuring situations to their own advantage, particularly in terms of controlling the access of peers to ongoing play groups. However, it is during preadolescence, with its concern with peer status, that this ability and desire to position oneself in situations consciously to affect one's presentation of self becomes critical to long-term popularity. In order to manage the impressions of others, the preadolescent must expand his or her facility at taking the role of the other

(Mead, 1934), and through this must role play to create the desired impression.[2] By preadolescence the child must deal with a wide range of others who may expect the child to behave according to several distinct standards of behavior. A 4-year-old can use a single behavioral repertoire, but the preteen must learn that several repertoires need to be mastered for different settings. The development of presentation-of-self ability is exemplified in the child's increasing sophistication in getting along with others and in developing moral and philosophical systems (Selman's stages 3 and 4) in which flexibility of interaction as a function of the needs of one's friend becomes recognized as a part of friendship.

Rules and Negotiation

The growth of social competency can be observed in the child's increasing sophistication in the practice of game rules. Piaget suggests in his analysis of marble playing (1932/1962) that until the age of 3 the child has rules only in that there are ritual repetitions that he or she performs with play objects. At this stage rules are not grounded in social interaction, and what regularities exist appear to be idiosyncratic. Piaget suggests that until games are played collectively, rules in a meaningful sense do not exist.

The second stage is termed the stage of egocentrism and lasts until approximately the age of 6, although Piaget admits that these ages are not invariant in all cultures and social classes (p. 46). Marble playing at this age becomes social, but according to Piaget, children's rules are egocentric: "When they play together they do not watch each other and do not unify their respective rules even for the duration of one game" (p. 40). Piaget's data on two marble players suggest that although different sets of rules seem to be operating, the children construct a social interaction sequence that is satisfying to both parties and is dependent on the presence of each other (as indicated by the existence of different rules when the child plays alone). While these interactants are not playing a "game" (an adult-defined category of activity), they are interacting in a fashion that is meaningful for them.

The two later stages of the development of the practice of rules represent the growth of the preadolescent's ability to deal with peers. During early preadolescence (ages 7–10) the child recognizes the importance of rules as a regulator of others' behavior. Rules are claimed to ensure reciprocity in the game world. However, this notion of rules as a model for play does not imply that rules are not used to strategic advantage. For example, Piaget points out that in this stage knowledge of rule content may vary widely. Thus children construct their game reality (the rule structure) in the course of play: "It is only when they [the marble players] are at play that these same children succeed in understanding each other, either by copying the boy who seems to know most about it or, more frequently, by omitting any usage that might be disputed" (p. 42).

Although children claim that rules are absolute, in practice they are negotiated. Further, the rules may be used by the knowledgeable player to limit the options of the less familiar (or deliberately naive) player. In this case, Piaget says of himself, "When I play carelessly, and let the shooter drop out of my hand, Ben exclaims *"Fan-coup"* to prevent me from saying *'coup-passe'* and having another shot" (p. 44). Rules are conditional, and their use becomes something of a game. A player may get another shot if he says *"coup-passe," unless* the opponent first says *"fan-coup."* This requires the ability to place oneself in the opponent's position in order to recognize the appropriate moment for such a challenge. This decision may be based upon the importance of the game and the relationship between player and challenger. While challenges are legitimate, they may create hard feelings and indicate that the game is "serious" and not "merely" play (Riezler, 1941). Rule-governed games carry with them the potential to be played according to several perspectives. These perspectives imply different social meanings, and when game meanings are disputed, inferences about the character of the disputants may be drawn by their fellow players.

By late preadolescence the negotiation of game rules provides almost as much interest as the game itself (Knapp and Knapp, 1976). Boys acquire techniques for "getting along"—they learn when to use threats of force, when to trade favors, when to use reason, when to back off gracefully, and when to leave the field angrily. Piaget notes that this is a period of "juridical discussions" (p. 43) in which "the dominating interest seems to be interest in the rules themselves." This observation of late preadolescence as a period in which a quasi-legal system operates has been confirmed by Glassner (1976), who notes that children are able to settle interpersonal disputes with a minimum of violence through informal processes of childhood jurisprudence. This process is evident when preadolescents must determine ordering. On one occasion I brought several empty beer cans from Colorado for preadolescent beer-can collectors in Minnesota. Because the cans had different values, it was necessary for the children to determine an order for choosing. After discussion, players were able to order themselves in such a way that no player felt publicly humiliated. For example, the high-status boy who chose first claimed that the next time I brought beer cans he would pick sixth. Opie and Opie (1959) speak of children as having a "Code of Oral Legislation" that binds them to allow social relations to take particular forms (e.g., possession typically being 100% of the law) if ritual declarations, such as those asserting ownership ("finders keepers, losers weepers"), are followed.

The rules as a code of conduct are not crucial during late preadolescence. More important is the social experience that derives from learning to manipulate the social order (the use of rules)—the issue is rights and privileges. Despite the supposed inflexibility of the rules (as explained to an interested adult), they are not enforced uniformly; some children are allowed leeway, and others are not. Both the legitimacy of rules and the legitimacy of preferential treatment are being acquired in this process. Knapp and Knapp (1976) note: "As they [children] argue about rules, add new ones, agree to exceptions, and censure a playmate who is cheating, they are exploring how necessary rules are, how they are made, and what degree of consensus is needed to make them effective. They are also learning something about the relationship of personality to power, and of fairness to order" (p. 17). Rules provide guidelines for interaction but do not control the interaction itself; they are topics for negotiation. The sometimes bewildering complex of rules exists not because preadolescents wish every contingency to be considered so that fights are impossible, but because a set of rules provides a store of information that boys can use in their arguments with each other in defining ambiguous situations in the game. It is the process of negotiation that is central to interaction, rather than the formal rules themselves.

An example of this negotiation process is depicted by Dennison (1969) in a description of a fight among five troubled boys with severe learning and behavior problems. These preadolescents are supposedly "out of control" and unable to cope with social interaction; they attend a school for delinquent children. In the course of the school year a hostile rivalry developed between three Puerto Rican friends (Jose, Julio, and Vicente) and two non-Hispanic buddies (Stanley, white, and Willard, black). These preadolescents engaged in a series of violent altercations, and finally the boys decided to fight it out, with Dennison, their teacher, only insisting that they not use weapons. I will quote from his account at some length, because it indicates the subtlety of preadolescent impression management and the development of standards for behavior as a result of interaction:

A great shout went up, a roar, and all five piled into each other . . . and stopped abruptly to let Jose take off his shirt. Stanley and Willard took their shirts off, too. They were about to clash again when Stanley paused and took off his shoes, and so Willard and Jose took their shoes off, too. The roar went up again and they tangled, Stanley and Willard against Jose, Julio, and Vicente. . . . There was much cursing, many shouts of pain—strange shouts, really for each one had in it a tinge of protest and flattery. It was in these overtones that one could sense the fine changes in their relations. They were saying things for which they had not words, and the refinement of this communication was extraordinary and beautiful. It was apparent immediately that the boys had set some kind of limit to their violence, though they had not spoken of limits. Rules, codes, acknowledgements popped up spontaneously and changed swiftly. When anyone got hurt, he stepped off the mats . . . and the rule was accepted by all, without having been announced that no one could be attacked when he stepped off the mat. . . . Occasionally as the boys rolled and squirmed, they also punched each other in the ribs. These blows, however, were almost formal and were very subtly adjusted. The loser must prove that he is really struggling, and so in order to ensure himself against the contempt of the victor, he punches him in the ribs. Delivered with just the right force, these punches remain compliments. . . . They are tributes, too, to the reality of the fight. Delivered a bit harder, they are "unfair." Delivered still harder, they precipitate a bloodletting. And so they are very nicely attuned. . . .

Willard is grinning and trying different holds, but in between the grins he exerts himself to the utmost and still can't pin Jose. And so he shouts again and again, "Give up?" and Jose cries, "You have to kill me!" The decision is in Willard's hands. Soon he lets Jose up, but punches him on the arm so Jose won't think he has been let up. Willard shows great tact in his awareness of victory. He smiles openly at Jose, not a triumphant smile, but a friendly one. [Dennison, 1969, pp. 133–137]

These "maladjusted" preadolescents are highly sophisticated in techniques of impression management and in the staging of social encounters. Even an emotional fight is not a random sequencing of aggressive actions but is socially ordered, and this structuring occurs not before the event but during it. While there are certain characteristics that these boys could report about "fighting norms" or rules, the application of these procedures occurs during the fight and is responsive to immediate considerations. This structuring of interaction is equally relevant to games that have rules as part of the oral tradition, but these rules may not be followed or may be altered in the course of the game.

Individuals in these social situations have the power to altercast their fellow interactants. Thus, Willard had the opportunity to defeat his enemy Jose, with a presumable explicit loss of status to Jose; however, he refrained from doing this, possibly as an attempt to drain the encounter of emotional intensity. This process of constructing social meanings is characteristic of social interaction, even among children.

Friendship and Socialization

By preadolescence, peer relationships have become central to the child's social world. Their centrality reveals itself in children's self-consciousness about the impressions that others have of them and in the importance they give to their friendships. By incorporating the needs for impression management and friendship, I argue that the friendship bond creates a setting in which impression–management skills are mastered and in which inadequate displays will typically be ignored or corrected without severe loss of face. Outside of friendship bonds, preadolescents have a critical eye for children's behaviors that are managed inadequately.

Typically, preadolescents name many children as friends. For example, in Sanford Heights, 48 of the 50 12-year-olds in the Little League were asked to evaluate their relationships to the other 12-year-olds in the league. In our sample, 18% of all possible relationships are said to be close friends, 31% are friends, 2% are disliked, and 49% are neither friends nor disliked. It is the boys' rather large network of "friends" that comprises the bulk of the society in which they spend their social leisure time.

Friendship has generally been conceptualized as an affective bond, a relationship charged with positive feeling, in some cases approaching "love." Other features should be emphasized as well. Friendship is also a staging area for interaction, a cultural institution for the transmission of knowledge and performance techniques, and a crucible for the shaping of selves. Each of these aspects of the friendship relationship has implications for interaction within and outside of the friendship bond.

Friendship as a Staging Area

Friendship is a social relationship, a bond between two individuals. As such it is not a physical entity but a spiritual or ideational one. However, friendships are not continuously salient, and when they are not, their effects on social interaction are slight. One's position as a friend can be conceived of as akin to a partial identity that is activated when relevant, with the understanding that multiple friendship identities can be activated simultaneously. Obviously, a friendship identity is likely to be activated when the friend is physically present. Thus, the analysis can be expanded from an emphasis on the ideational aspect of the relationship to include an emphasis on the friendship context. A friendship bond, therefore, can be described as a staging area for action.

The presence of friends produces a social context that allows for the performance of actions that would otherwise be improper. For example, in an earlier paper (Fine, 1980a) I described the social ecology of preadolescent pranks among 12-year-olds in Sanford Heights. Of the 70 prank partners named for four different types of pranks, 89% were close friends of the namer, 9% more were friends, and the remaining 2% were former friends. Close friendships thus can provide a staging area for pranks, which some scholars (Dresser, 1973; Knapp and Knapp, 1976) claim socialize children by allowing them to explore the boundaries of allowable behavior and to gain social poise in stressful situations.

The friendship bond, in allowing for a wide latitude of behavior, creates a setting in which the child is able to explore modes of expressing sexual attitudes, aggression, and attitudes toward school and work. Even if negatively sanctioned behavior occurs, the sanctioning typically does not imply a derogation of the actor, and the disapproved action is not seen as part of the actor's identity.

Friends typically have sufficient "idiosyncracy credits" (Hollander, 1958) to allow for a wide range of technically inappropriate actions. The actions of a friend are much less likely to be defined as inappropriate than are the identical behaviors of others.

The friendship group seems of particular importance as a context for action in terms of the developing relationship between boys and girls. Broderick (1966) notes that at ages 12 and 13, 56% of the boys and 76% of the girls in his sample prefer double- or group-dating to single-dating. One group of 12-year-old boys in Hopewell even formalized this to the extent that they formed a club whose major function was the support of members in their dealings with girls. This form of social activity is also evident in private parties of preadolescents (Martinson, 1973). These parties, in which the boys are supported by their male friends and the girls are in the company of their friends, are staging areas for quasi-sexual and quasi-aggressive behavior. Boys in Sanford Heights informed me that "making out" occurred at these events, and this "making out" apparently consisted of kissing and above-the-waist petting ("getting to second base"). However, roughhousing may also occur, because boys are ignorant of adolescent social norms of chivalrous behavior to girls or ashamed of showing tenderness to girls. One young adult male recalled the way in which male peers are used for social support in situations where social norms are ambiguous and self-presentation becomes a considerable challenge: "As I remember there weren't many fellows who were on the dance floor. They were all in a group in the corner, and that is where I ended up too. We told jokes, tested our strength on the bars that stood along the walls, and teased any fellow who dared to ask a girl to dance" (Martinson, 1973, pp. 84–85).

On one occasion I went with three preadolescent friends from Sanford Heights to a large amusement park in the Minneapolis–St. Paul area:

The boys seem very interested in the girls that they see, and there is considerable whispering and teasing about them. Tom had received a small coin bank as a prize which he decides that he no longer wishes to keep. At this time we are standing in line for a roller coaster directly behind three girls—apparently a year or two older than these twelve-year-olds—one of whom is wearing a hooded jacket. Frank tells Tom to take the bank and "stuff it in her hood," which Tom does to the annoyance of his victim. When she turns around, Tom and Hardy tell her that Frank did it, and of course Frank denies this, blaming Tom. The girls tell the boys to shut up and leave them alone. As things work out, Hardy has to sit with one of these girls on the ride and he clearly appears embarrassed, while Tom and Frank are vastly amused. After the ride Tom and Frank claim that they saw Hardy holding her. Frank said that he saw them holding hands, and Tom said: "He was trying to go up her shirt." Hardy vehemently denies these claims. A short while later we meet these girls again, and Frank turns to Hardy, saying "Here's your honey." The girl retorts as she walks away, "Oh, stifle it." [Field notes]

The male friendship group provides a supportive staging area for these boys to practice their impression–management skills on each other and on their female contacts as they develop sexualized selves. It is attention rather than tenderness that orients the staging of boy–girl encounters in this period:

> A group of boys come across a preadolescent girls' softball team from a different area of town, sitting around a park picnic table. The boys begin teasing them with sexual taunts: "Hey, suck me where the sun never shines," "Pluck my hairs," or "You're innocent like my butthole." The girls are not visibly outraged at this and actually seem to enjoy the attention that the boys are giving them— at one point singing to attract their attention. After whispering discussion about what they should do to their victims, the boys steal the girls' thermos and pour out the water in it—at which the girls squeal but don't get seriously upset. Later the boys return to the picnic table and throw beer cans at the girls, who giggle and scream. [Field notes]

The presence of one's friends seems to provide a legitimation for this type of activity, which has important consequences for the sexual socialization of preadolescents. It provides them with a range of experience in dealing with the opposite sex and a testing of their social poise (Stone, 1965). Players are socialized to respond to the demands of a variety of social situations, and their friendships serve to provide access to these situations.

Friendship as a Cultural Institution

Suttles (1970) has described friendship as a social institution, and this description certainly applies to the didactic function of friendship. Information transmitted through friendship ties varies in the extent of its diffusion. Some information is highly localized, perhaps shared only by members of a dyad, while other information is widely known among preadolescents or Americans in general. These dyads and groups not only create a private culture (Suttles, 1970; Fine, 1980a), but also transmit cultural information relevant to the problems of growing up. This is of particular significance to socialization, in that it provides the child with a stock of knowledge and repertoire of behavior useful for encounters with other peers. Children acquire information from many sources—the media, schools, religious organizations, and their families—all adult-dominated institutions. In contemporary American society, adults typically share an ideology that prescribes what children should and should not know. There are several topic areas in which children are interested but that they cannot learn about from adults: the practice of sex, informal rules of institutions (how *really* to succeed in school), the art of making negative evaluations (insults), and how to have excitement and adventure (pranks, mischief, and illegal behavior).

For example, one 12-year-old boy explained to his friends in clinical detail how to "french" a girl. The first part of the account outlines the basic behaviors in "frenching," but of perhaps greater importance is the latter section of the transcript, which transmits signals about the structure of sexual relations in contemporary America:

Tom:　　First of all, you gotta make sure you don't get no more "Ahhhk!" burps in your mouth (Hardy and Frank both laugh). It would be very crude to burp. I mean you make sure you don't have a cold, cause greenies [mucus] going through there (Tom laughs), going through her mouth would taste awful horseshit (all laugh).

Frank:　　And one thing, don't spit while frenching.

Tom:　　And make sure . . . make sure you don't breathe out of your mouth (all laugh) unless you're doing mouth-to-mouth resuscitation. After all that frenching, you just gotta do mouth-to-mouth to keep your air up. OK, now you take a squirt of your favorite after-shave. You rub it on your hair, and you rub it all around you. And you (Tom giggles "hysterically") and you rub it all around. It sure feels good (more giggling). Frank's choking under pressure. Listen (more "hysterical" laughter), he's got a boner (more laughter). He's got a boner. He's got a boner and he'd like to suck it off.

Hardy:　　Listen, listen, his lips are on it.

Tom:　　He's sucking (all laugh).

Frank:　　Nuhhh. Nuhhh. Nuhhh (joking, making almost mooing sounds, apparently designed to simulate a sexually excited woman) . . .

Tom:　　Hardy, do you like to put anything in my act?

Hardy:　　No.

Tom:　　Only that he's got a, Ahhh!, stiff boner (Hardy giggles). Frank. Frank ain't got stiff, uh-uh. Since we're talking about Hardy's girl friend, he's sorta, you know what I mean, doncha?

Hardy:　　No! (Frank laughs).

Tom:　　He sorta hit the jack, uh, hit the jack. Hit the jack-off, you know.

Hardy:　　No, I don't know.

Tom:　　I do (Tom and Hardy both laugh). Well, anyway, I get to my second lesson. First you walk in, you see a sexy girl in the telephone booth. You don't know who she is, just see the back of her. Gotta make sure she doesn't have a big butt, you know. . . . You just walk into the telephone booth, put your arm around her and say "Hi." And she goes "Uhhh! Ohhh, hi" (tone sounds surprised at first, then "feminine" and "willing"). With her tongue around, wrapped around, wrapped around the microphone, her teeth, her teeth are chattering from so much shock. You just take your pants . . . no . . . well.

Hardy: You take her pants.

Tom: Well, you just stick out your tongue, and you say (Tom sings in a mocking romantic fashion): "Want to, oh baby, you mean it, you let me under your skin." [Taped transcript]

This is a fragment of a longer conversation that is one of numerous conversations among one set of close friends. This conversation is not much different from those of other precocious preadolescents. Taken together, these conversations allow for an examination of the dynamics of the acquisition of the male sex role. Through the content of these conversations boys learn what is expected of them by their peers. The importance of this talk does not derive from the acquisition of sophisticated techniques of french kissing (although specific content learning does occur); rather, boys learn how to present themselves to male peers as "males." This conversation suggests that males are expected by each other to be sexually aggressive and that females wait for their attempts with undisguised arousal. This short dialogue offers a world view that is consistent with male dominance and female submission. By this talk, preadolescents are learning skills that will allow them to handle themselves within the context of similar lines of talk and prepare them to act as "males."

The same process is evident in other areas as well. Preadolescents, in discussing how to evade schoolwork or cut classes (e.g. claim that you have a church confirmation, since teachers never check), acquire rhetoric about schooling. Again, it is less important to learn specific facts and procedures than to learn ways to talk. These tools for interactional negotiation allow the child to deal competently with peers.

Through the support of friends, the child also learns techniques of evaluation, when to use insults and when to avoid them, and the social implications of this process of evaluation. The case of one 10-year-old boy in Sanford Heights who was criticized by several older boys is instructive. The 10-year-old, Tommy, is the son of a Little League manager. In one postseason practice in preparation for a state-wide tournament, Tommy and Harmon, a 12-year-old teammate, angrily traded insults. Harmon's temper had caused problems all season, and this episode was the final straw. Tommy's father announced that he was quitting as manager of the team. After the anger subsided he returned, but Harmon's father felt that it was in everyone's best interest if Harmon left the team. The following week some of Harmon's friends met Tommy on a school bus:

Hardy sees Tommy get on the bus and announces loudly, "Tommy sucks." Rod adds: "Tommy's a wuss." In unison Jerry and Rod tell Tommy as he approaches, "You suck." Rod particularly is angry at Tommy, "Harmon can't play because of you. What a fag!" Tommy doesn't respond to the abuse from his older tormentors, but looks dejected and perhaps near tears (which is what Rod and Hardy later tell

Harmon). The insults build in stridency and anger as Hardy calls Tommy a "woman," Jerry knocks off his hat, and Rod says, "Give him the faggot award." Finally Jerry takes the baseball cap of Tommy's friend and seatmate and tosses it out the window of the moving bus. [Field notes]

It is a frequent observation that preadolescents can be distressingly cruel to each other, but the social context of this cruelty is not sufficiently emphasized. The cruelty is almost always expressed in the presence of friends. Insults seem to be expressed as much for reasons of self-presentation to one's peers as to attack the target. This point has also been made about sounding or playing the dozens by black adolescents (e.g., Kochman, 1972; Abrahams, 1970). The case cited here is representative in that there was an attempt by the insulters to test the boundaries of proper insults and the insult crescendo continued until the target either became upset and withdrew, or until one of the perpetrators did something that was outside the range of legitimate behavior in that situation. Thus, in this case, tossing the baseball cap out of the bus window ended the insults. Jerry's action was outside the realm of legitimate behavior, and he sullied his social self. Although he was not sanctioned by his friends, he apologized to the victim, claiming that he didn't really intend to get rid of the hat.

To summarize, socialization does not consist of rote learning of behaviors or of an encyclopedia of practical knowledge. Socialization can best be considered instruction in dealing with situations, or, as Denzin (1977) suggests, learning to fit together lines of action. The child needs to learn the process by which social meanings are constructed, ways of knowing the expectations of others, and methods of determining their likely actions (Mead's notion of the Generalized Other). The friendship group, by placing the child in such situations in a supportive environment, provides the opportunity to acquire and refine skills that are necessary for interaction with others.

Friendship as a Shaper of the Social Self

The third way in which friendship contributes to the socialization of the preadolescent is through its effects on self-image. Friendship is a crucial factor in the development of the social self, both for popular boys and for boys with few close friends.

The literature on the correlates of popularity reveals a wide array of explanations of children's interpersonal success. The factors associated with interpersonal success include acceptance of school ideology (Gold, 1962), attractiveness of the first name (McDavid and Harari, 1966), role-playing skills (Mouton, Bell, and Blake, 1956), intelligence (Barbe, 1954; Gallagher, 1958), adjustment to parents and teachers (Feinberg, 1953), physical attractiveness

(Dion and Berscheid, 1974), and attitude to school (Davis, 1957). I shall not review this extensively researched problem, but shall only agree with Hartup (1970) that acceptance or rejection is clearly a multidimensional phenomenon. One might be tempted to suggest that this area has been overstudied, because these correlations do not successfully convey the dynamics of making and breaking friends as they occur in children's societies.

There is some quantitative evidence that suggests that social interpretations are related to friendship choices. Davitz (1955), examining friendship patterns of male and female summer campers, found that those who are chosen as best friends are perceived as more similar to the chooser in activity preferences than are children who are not liked. Individuals perceive their best friends as more similar to themselves than they actually are; in this study these best friends were not more similar to the chooser than were children who were not liked. Elkins (1958) found in interviews with a sample of early adolescents that children who were the most chosen were more flexible in role performances and had the ability to meet the needs of others.

The friendship relation provides the nexus in which this development of self and role flexibility can occur. The child who has best acquired the ability to take the role of the other will be most flexible in role performance. Consequently, as Elkin's research suggests, this individual will be popular, perhaps because he or she is socially rewarding. Such individuals, through their flexibility of role performances, will likely be perceived as more similar to each of those with whom they interact than their self-ratings or average ratings might suggest. Thus, peer leaders are those who are most skilled at impression–management techniques.

Gottman and his colleagues (Gottman, Gonso, and Rasmussen, 1975) have argued that popular children have more knowledge and ability of how to make friends than do their unpopular companions. Style of interaction seems central to friendship (Asher and Renshaw, this volume). Research indicates that social training may help isolated children learn techniques of making friends and thus improve their social standing (Gottman, Gonso and Schuler, 1976; Oden and Asher, 1977; Walker and Hops, 1973), lending support to the theory of the existence of presentational aspects of popularity. This process operates in both directions, for the support of friends provides a mechanism for the development of self-presentational ability.

From the symbolic interactionist perspective, individuals can be conceived of as having multiple selves, which are functions of setting and audience. From this standpoint, the developmental issue is not the traditional psychiatric one of the unitary development of the self, but the interactional issue of acquiring behavioral flexibility to cope with situations and of seeing the behaviors involved in this coping as part of one's repertoire of behavior.

In friendship there is less likelihood that any action will produce a negative evaluation and a dramatic change in the status of the relationship, because friendships tend to be relatively stable over time, even during preadolescence. Each action has a small incremental effect upon the person's image because of the larger base of previous experiences with that person. It follows that the actor will be freer of self-conscious constraints placed on his behavior in the presence of friends than of nonfriends. Further, friends tend to perceive themselves as relatively similar to each other in their preferred activities and thus believe that they share patterns of behavior. One of the frequent responses received when I inquired why a boy was friends with another dealt with common interests and activities: "He likes to do the things I like to do."

In childhood friendships, the child's self (the perceived unitary composite of his multiple selves) develops in situations in which serious threats to the self are not likely to be present. This argument returns us to the social psychiatric model of friendship proposed by Sullivan (1953). The affective ties between preadolescent chums consist of an interest in and acceptance of the other, and accompanying this interest is a close attention to role taking and assuming the perspective of the other. Sullivan (1953) argues that "your child [at preadolescence when he finds a chum] begins to develop a real sensitivity to what matters to another person. And this is not in the sense of 'what should I do to get what I want,' but instead, 'what should I do to contribute to the happiness or to support the prestige and feeling of worthwhileness of my chum'" (p. 245).

Because the chum has the same orientation, Sullivan suggests that this is the last, best chance for dramatic changes in the child's "self-system". It is a time for the individual's self (the "I" in Mead's terms) to be validated through social interaction. Whether Sullivan is correct about the relative importance of this period is not of concern; more important is the existence of this validation of the self through friendship.

Conclusion

In this chapter I have argued that children's friendships should be analyzed in terms of their contribution to the development of the child's interactional competence. As in all interaction, participants are able to generate social meanings through peer relations, and these meanings affect behavior and self-indication. I have argued that preadolescents develop considerable competence at mastering self-presentational skills and that regular interaction partners are of particular importance in this social learning. These social skills differ from many that the child is acquiring in that they do not consist of a core of knowledge, behavior patterns, or social norms; rather, they consist of techniques for negotiating social reality. This negotiation is a process that requires an understanding of the social dynamics of peer interaction.

In particular, preadolescent friendships serve three functions that contribute to the development of interactional skills—functions that are generally not considered in developmental literature on friendship. First, friendships provide a staging area for behavior. Friendships are situated in social environments that have implications for the acquisition of interactional competencies. Second, friendships are cultural institutions, and as such they provide didactic training. Third, friendships provide, a context for the growth of the child's social self, a context within which he or she can learn the appropriate self-image to project in social situations. While these functions of friendship are not limited to preadolescence, they seem characteristic of this period because at this age the child is simultaneously particularly influenced by peers and is striving to acquire information and behavior necessary for social competence in adult society.

Acknowledgments

The author wishes to thank David Crist, Jeylan Mortimer, and Zick Rubin for helpful comments on a draft of this chapter.

Notes

1.   All personal and place names used in conjunction with the discussion of the Little League baseball research are pseudonyms.
2.   For the distinction between role-taking and role-playing, see Coutu (1951).

References

Abrahams, R. *Deep Down in the Jungle* (Chicago: Aldine, 1970. Rev. ed.).
Bain, R. "The Self-and-Other Words of a Child. *American Journal of Sociology*, 1936, 41:767–775.
Barbe, W. B. "Peer relationships of Children of Different Intelligence Levels." *School and Society*, 1954, 80:60–62.
Becker, H. S., and Geer, B. "Latent Culture: A Note on the Theory of Latent Social Roles." *Administrative Science Quarterly*, 1960, 5:304–313.
Bernstein, B. *Class, Codes and Control* (New York: Schocken, 1975).
Blumer, H. *Symbolic Interactionism: Perspective and Method* (Englewood Cliffs, N.J.: Prentice-Hall, 1969).
Bogden, R., and Taylor, S. J. *Introduction to Qualitative Research Methods* (New York: Wiley-Interscience, 1975).
Broderick, C. B. "Socio-Sexual Development in a Suburban Community." *Journal of Sex Research*, 1966, 2:1–24.
Cavan, S. The Etiquette of Youth." In G. P. Stone and H. A. Farberman, eds., *Social Psychology through Symbolic Interaction* (Waltham, Mass.: Xerox, 1970).

Coleman, J. *The Adolescent Society* (New York: Free Press, 1961).

Cooley, C. H. "A Study of the Early Use of Self-Words by a Child." *Psychological Review*, 1908, 15:339–357.

Cooley, C. H., *Human Nature and the Social Order* (New York: Schocken, 1964. First published, 1902).

Cottle, T. J. "Prospect Street Moon." In T. J. Cottle, *Time's Children* (Boston: Little, Brown, 1971).

Coutu, W. "Role Playing versus Role Taking: An Appeal for Clarification." *American Sociological Review*, 1951, 16:180–187.

Davis, J. A. Correlates of Sociometric Status among Peers." *Journal of Educational Research*, 1957, 50:561–569.

Davitz, J. R. "Social Perception and Sociometric Choice of Children." *Journal of Abnormal and Social Psychology*, 1955, 50:173–176.

Dennison, G. *The Lives of Children* (New York: Vintage, 1969).

Denzin, N. K. *Childhood Socialization* (San Francisco: Jossey-Bass, 1977).

Dion, K., and Berscheid, E. "Physical Attractiveness and Peer Acceptance." *Sociometry*, 1974, 37:1–12.

Dresser, N. "Telephone Pranks." *New York Folklore Quarterly*, 1973, *29:* 121–130.

Elkin, F., and Handel, G. *The Child and Society: The Process of Socialization* (New York: Random House, 1978. Third ed.).

Elkins, D. "Some Factors Related to the Choice Status of Ninety Eighth-Grade Children in a Social Setting." *Genetic Psychology Monographs*, 1958, 58:207–272.

Faris, E. *The Nature of Human Nature* (New York: McGraw-Hill, 1971. First published, 1937).

Feinberg, M. R. "Relation of Background Experiences to Social Acceptance." *Journal of Social Psychology*, 1953, 48:206–214.

Fine, G. A. "The Natural History of Preadolescent Male Friendship Groups." In H. Foot, A. H. Chapman, and J. Smith, eds., *Childhood and Friendship Relations (Chichester: Wiley, 1980). (a)*

Fine, G. A. Cracking Diamonds: The Relationship between Observer Role and Observed Content in Little League Baseball Settings." In W. Shaffir, A. Turowetz, and R. Stebbins, eds., *The Social Experience of Fieldwork* (New York: St. Martin's Press, 1980). (b)

Fine, G. A., and Glassner, B. "The Promise and Problems of Participant Observation with Children." *Urban Life*, 1979, 8:153–174.

Fine, G. A., and Kleinman, S. "Rethinking Subculture: An Interactionist Analysis." *American Journal of Sociology*, 1979, 85:1–20.

Fine, G. A., and West, C. S. "Do Little Leagues Work: Player Satisfaction with Organized Preadolescent Baseball Programs." *Minnesota Journal of Health, Physical Education and Recreation*, 1979, 7:4–6.

Gallagher, J. J. "Social Status of Children Related to Intelligence, Propinquity, and Social Perception." *Elementary School Journal*, 1958, 58:225–231.

Glassner, B. "Kid Society." *Urban Education*, 1976, 11:5–22.

Goffman, E. *Presentation of Self in Everyday Life.* (Garden City, New York: Anchor, 1959).

Goffman, E. *Frame Analysis* (Cambridge, Mass.: Harvard University Press, 1974).

Gold, H. A. "The Importance of Ideology in Sociometric Evaluation of Leadership." *Group Psychotherapy*, 1962, 15:224–230.

Gottman, J., Gonso, J., and Rasmussen, B. "Social Interaction, Social Competence and Friendship in Children." *Child Development*, 1975, 46:709–718.

Gottman, J., Gonso, J., and Schuler, P. "Teaching social skills to isolated children." *Journal of Abnormal Child Psychology*, 1976, 4:179–197.

Hartup, W. W. "Peer Interaction and Social Organization." In P. Mussen, ed., *Carmichael's Manual of Child Psychology* (vol. 2) (New York: Wiley, 1970).

Hartup, W. W. "Children and Their Friends." In H. McGurk, ed., *Issues in Childhood Social Development* (London: Methuen, 1978).

Hollander, E. P. "Conformity, Status, and Idiosyncrasy Credit." *Psychological Review*, 1958, 65:117–127.

Knapp, M., and Knapp, H. *One Potato, Two Potato . . . : The Secret Education of American Children* (New York: Norton, 1976).

Kochman, T. "Toward an Ethnography of Black American Speech Behavior." In T. Kochman ed., *Rappin' and Stylin' Out: Communication in Urban Black America* (Urbana: University of Illinois Press, 1972).

Lever, J. "Sex Differences in the Games Children Play." *Social Problems*, 1976, 23:478–487.

McDavid, J. W., and Harari, H. "Stereotyping of Names and Popularity in Grade School." *Child Development*, 1966, 37:453–459.

MacKay, R. "Conceptions of Children and Models of Socialization." In H. P. Dreitzel, ed., *Childhood and Socialization* (New York: Macmillan, 1973).

Martinson, F. M. *Infant and Child Sexuality: A Sociological Perspective* (St. Peter, Minn.: Book Mart, 1973).

Mead, G. H. "The Genesis of the Self and Social Control." *International Journal of Ethics*, 1925, 35:251–277.

Mead, G. H. *Mind, Self and Society* (Chicago, Ill.: University of Chicago Press, 1934).

Mouton, J. S., Bell, R. L. Jr., and Blake, R. R. "Role Playing Skill and Sociometric Peer Status." *Group Psychotherapy*, 1956, 9:7–17.

Oden, S., and Asher, S. R. "Coaching Children in Social Skills for Friendship Making." *Child Development*, 1977, 48:495–506.

Opie, I., and Opie, P. *The Lore and Language of School Children* (Oxford: Oxford University Press, 1959).

Parsons, T., Shils, E. A., Allport, G. W., Kluckhohn, C., Murray, H. A., Sears, R. R., Sheldon, R. C., Stouffer, S. A., and Tolman, E. C. "Some Fundamental Categories of the Theory of Action: A General Statement." In T. Parsons and E. A. Shils, eds., *Toward a General Theory of Action* (Cambridge, Mass.: Harvard University Press, 1951).

Piaget, J. *The Moral Judgment of the Child* (New York: Collier, 1962. First published, 1932).

Riezler, K. "Play and Seriousness." *Journal of Philosophy*, 1941, 38:505–517.

Speier, M. *How to Observe Face-to-Face Communication* (Pacific Palisades, Cal.: Goodyear, 1973).

Stone, G. P. "The Play of Little Children." *Quest*, 1965, 4:23–31.

Stone, G. P. "Appearance and the Self." In G. P. Stone and H. A. Farberman, eds., *Social Psychology through Symbolic Interaction* (Waltham, Mass.: Ginn-Blaisdell, 1970).

Stone, L. J., and Church, J. *Childhood and Adolescence* (New York: Random House, 1957).

Stone, L. J., and Church, J. *Childhood and Adolescence* (New York: Random House, 1968. Second ed.).

Sullivan, H. S. *The Interpersonal Theory of Psychiatry* (New York: Norton, 1953).

Suttles, G. D. "Friendship as a Social Institution." In G. J. McCall, M. McCall, N. K. Denzin, G. D. Suttles, and S. B. Kurth, eds., *Social Relationships* (Chicago: Aldine, 1970).

Waldrop, M. F., and Halverson, C. F. Jr. "Intensive and Extensive Peer Behavior: Longitudinal and Cross-Sectional Analysis." *Child Development*, 1975, 46:19–26.

Walker, H. M., and Hops, H. "The Use of Group and Individual Reinforcement Contingencies in the Modification of Social Withdrawal." In L.A. Hamerlynck, L. C. Handy, and E. J. Mash, eds., *Behavior Change: Methodology, Concepts, and Practice* (Champaign, Ill.: Research Press, 1973).

Weinstein, E. A. "The Development of Interpersonal Competence." In D. A. Goslin, ed., *Handbook of Socialization Theory and Research* (Chicago: Rand McNally, 1969).

Weinstein, E. A., and Deutschberger, P. "Some Dimensions of Altercasting." *Sociometry*, 1963, 4:454–466.

Wiley, N. "The Genesis of Self: From Me to We to I." In N. K. Denzin, ed. *Studies in Symbolic Interaction* (vol. 2) (Greenwich, Conn.: JAI Press, 1980).

Zeitlin, I. *Rethinking Sociology* (Englewood Cliffs, N.J.: Prentice-Hall, 1973).

Zigler, E., and Child, I. L. "Socialization." In G. Lindzey and E. Aronson, eds., *The Handbook of Social Psychology* (vol. 3) (Reading, Mass.: Addison-Wesley, 1969. Second ed.).

PART VII

Television and Its Influence

Television was invented in the 1930s and was exhibited at the New York World's Fair in 1939, but its introduction was delayed by the buildup to (1940–41) and the fighting (1941–45) of World War II. During the 1950s ownership of a TV set became fairly common and eventually almost universal, with many families owning more than one set. One of the earliest studies of audience responses to television found that people could be classified in three broad groups: those who *embraced* television, those who *protested* it, and those who *accommodated* to it (Glick and Levy 1962). The author of the Preface to that study notes that "From its beginning, television in America has been a fighting word, a battleground, a stormy topic filled with many conflicts" (Warner 1962).

While the intensity of conflicts may not be quite as great today as earlier, some of them continue to this day. Most prominent, probably, is the conflict over depictions of violence and their presumed impact on children. The greatest concern has been that watching such scenes is likely to make children indifferent to violence and possibly to stimulate them to commit violent acts. There is some research that supports this view and some that refutes it. Part of the reason for such conflicting results is that there is disagreement about exactly what goes on when people watch television. What is the nature of the relationship between the viewer and the program? The question is more complex than it seems, and there is no simple answer. From Judith Van Evra's (1998) book, *Television and Child Development*, Second Edition, I have selected her chapter on Theoretical Perspectives to provide readers with an introduction to the variety of ways that television viewing can be understood.

Another main area of conflict is the role of television in consumer culture. American society has become one in which shopping has become a major activity, as manufacturers and advertisers endlessly promote products. Children watch a lot of television and see a great many commercials, which stimulate them to ask their parents to buy the advertised product. This can lead to parent-child hassles when annoyed parents say "no" to tearfully imploring children. Who is to blame for these unhappy moments? Demanding children? Greedy advertisers? Mean but sensible parents?

Perhaps a bit of perspective can be gained by referring to the early days of the automobile industry a hundred years ago. When Henry Ford devised the assembly line that enabled him to mass produce cars, they were all painted black. Associates advised him to offer cars in other colors, and he is reported to have said something like "People can have any color car they want as long as it's black." He held to that opinion for several years until Louis Chevrolet started producing cars in several colors, and then Ford found himself in a battle to hold on to his customers. People wanted new and different products—before there was television. But together Ford, and Chevrolet and others created a new world in which cars became cultural objects—something to pay attention to and compare and talk about. Cars became an important part of consumer culture. Ellen Seiter presents a view of children and television and consumer culture that is rather similar to this example. Indeed, she states that "Toys and children's television programs are cultural products that mimic adult culture . . ." So we have this paradox: the world of children's television programs with commercials for toys, candy, cereals, and other products for children's consumption has been created by adults and introduces children to the consumer role that they will likely fill when they become adults. Along the way they will poke fun at some commercials and be persuaded by others. Not all commercials (or products) succeed with children. In addition to the fact that this aspect of children's culture mimics adult culture, Seiter makes a point that is often overlooked. The advertised toys and other products that children do acquire become a basis for establishing relationships with other children and thus a means of helping them integrate into a social world of peers.

References

Glick, Ira O. and Sidney J. Levy. *Living with Television* (Chicago: Aldine, 1962).
Van Evra, Judith. *Television and Child Development*. Second Edition (Mahwah, NJ: Lawrence Erlbaum Associates, 1998).
Warner, W. Lloyd. Preface to *Living with Television* (Chicago: Aldine, 1962).

13

Theoretical Perspectives*

Judith Van Evra

A thorough study of television's influence on children's development requires a close look both at the communication side and at developmental characteristics of the child viewers that influence their experience. Integration of these two major fields of research is essential; emphasizing only one leaves out a whole side of the equation. The wealth of research data on all aspects of children's television experiences has led to the development of various theoretical interpretations and explanations within both the communication literature and the psychological and child development literature. Three theoretical perspectives are discussed in this chapter, and an integrative approach is proposed.

Social Learning Theory

Basic Assumptions

Social learning theory was one of the first theories to be used to explain television's impact on children. Much of the early work in this area, spearheaded by Bandura's (1967) work in the 1960s, pointed to observational learning and imitation of modeled behavior as the critical components of television's impact. In the classic studies by Bandura, children who viewed violence directed against a Bobo doll were observed in later play sessions. Those who had seen the aggressor punished did not engage in aggressive behavior following the viewing, whereas the others did. In other words, the children imitated the model unless they were deterred through the effects of vicarious learning. Both groups "learned" the aggressive behaviors, but only one group

*From Judith Van Evra, *Television and Child Development*, 2nd edition, 1998. Reprinted by permission of Lawrence Erlbaum Associates.

actually imitated them in the later play sessions. The other group inhibited them until the post viewing conditions were changed; then they, too, engaged in more aggressive behavior, thus demonstrating their latent learning of the aggressive response.

Bandura (1967) himself related one of the most graphic and entertaining accounts of modeling:

> I remember reading a story reported by Professor Mowrer about a lonesome farmer who decided to get a parrot for company. After acquiring the bird, the farmer spent many long evenings teaching the parrot the phrase, "Say Uncle." Despite the devoted tutorial attention, the parrot proved totally unresponsive and finally, the frustrated farmer got a stick and struck the parrot on the head after each refusal to produce the desired phrase.
>
> But the visceral method proved no more effective than the cerebral one, so the farmer grabbed his feathered friend and tossed him in the chicken house. A short time later the farmer heard a loud commotion in the chicken house and upon investigation found that the parrot was pummeling the startled chickens on the head with a stick and shouting, "Say Uncle! Say Uncle!" (p. 42)

A considerable amount of research done since then on the relation between viewing violent television and increased aggressive behavior has replicated and extended Bandura's findings. Concern about gender-role stereotyping on television stems from our knowledge of imitative behavior and the effects of modeling on children's attitudes and behavior. Similarly, studies that have been done on prosocial behavior have attributed the appearance of desirable behavior to the child's observation and imitation of models who have demonstrated those behaviors and who were reinforced for them.

On the other hand, not all children imitate all of the behavior they see in their many hours of television viewing and the variables affecting their learning and imitation are discussed in the following paragraphs.

Variables Affecting Modeling

Similarities between viewer and model, the credibility of the model, the context of the viewing, and similarities and differences between the televised models and real-life models in the child's environment are important determinants of which behaviors are actually imitated. A child's motivational state, the perceived reality of what is being observed, and the number of other experiences that provide competing models and information are additional significant influences on the imitation of television models that social learning theory predicts.

According to script theory, children do not simply imitate behavior that they view. Rather, they acquire behavioral scripts through observational learning that can then be activated by cues in the environment or activation of memory (Huesmann, 1988). Thus TV viewing affects behavior by activating certain scripts in the viewer, such that the behaviors seen on television are associated in the viewers' minds with other thoughts, events, or conditions.

The determinants of imitation, then, are complex and involve significant cognitive activity, learning, and semantic associations.

Evaluation

Despite the consistency of many findings, there are limitation and problems with using only social learning theory to explain the data. First, not all children imitate what they see. Moreover, as the relation reported often is based on correlational data, causation cannot be demonstrated definitively. For example, although viewing violence on television may lead to imitation of that content and increased aggression, it also is possible that aggressive children may choose to watch more violent programs, and independent factors that lead both to viewing high levels of violence and to increased aggressive behavior need to be investigated further.

It is also important to look at the viewer's perception in the viewing situation. What some individuals find to be very violent may be seen as harmless by others (Gunter, 1985). Young children's greater reliance on perceptually salient cues, for example, and their more concrete approach to material (e.g., reacting to things that look violent), may result in very different perceptions than those of older children. Thus, age and gender differences, as well as personality, experiential, and contextual ones, interact with the television content to affect what is perceived as violent and what the viewer response will be.

Social learning theory has been used most effectively to interpret the short-term effects that have been demonstrated in the many laboratory experiments that have been conducted, rather than the long-term socialization influences that are examined in naturalistic studies (Milavsky et al., 1982; Wackman et al., 1977). The long-term effects of viewing, and the relative influence of many other factors that contribute to the appearance of specific behaviors are not as obvious, however. Clearly the elements of observational learning, modeling, vicarious reinforcement, and imitation are essential components of a child's viewing experience, but they are mediated by a host of other variables.

Cultivation Theory

The cultivation hypothesis as espoused by Gerbner, Gross, Morgan, and Signorielli (1980, 1982, 1986) asserts that for heavy viewers, television cultivates reality perceptions of the world that are consistent with television's portrayals and that lead to homogeneity of perceptions (Cook et al., 1983). The more time spent viewing television, the more likely the viewer is to accept television's version of things, especially in areas where the viewer has little direct experience, such as in the expectation of violence or in getting information about other groups with whom the person does not interact.

Cultivation analysis is "the investigation of the consequences of this ongoing and pervasive system of cultural messages" (Gerbner et al., 1980, p. 14), and of television's contribution to viewer conceptions (Gerbner et al., 1982). Cultivation theory predicts or expects frequent viewers to give more answers consistent with television's portrayal of the world as shown in content analyses, than of the real world as shown by actual statistics (Wright, 1986).

According to a cultivation perspective, the amount of viewing or exposure is a very important variable in television's impact on thought and behavior. According to Gerbner et al. (1982), heavy viewers differ systematically from light viewers in beliefs, values, and assumptions that may relate in consistent ways to the groups' life situations and views. Cultivation theory assumes that heavy viewers are also less selective in their viewing, engage in habitual viewing, and experience a good deal of sameness of content. Moreover, television's impact is greatest when it functions as the only information source and when it is relevant to the person. Light viewers are more likely to have many other sources of information (whether social interaction, reading, or vocational experience) that take up much of their time and displace TV viewing time. They have more diverse sources of information and a greater number of behavioral models; they are also, perhaps, less likely to take television content seriously. Heavy viewers have few other sources of ideas and thus are more likely to report reality perceptions that are consistent with television portrayals (Gerbner et al., 1980).

However, television does not act in a vacuum; nor does it act on everyone in the same way. Not only do heavy viewers at one developmental level have a different experience than heavy viewers at another level; those of a different gender, socioeconomic level, or family background also experience television differently. Any potential cultivation effect must be evaluated against the significance and impact of these other factors on a child's development and experience.

Television also dramatically changes children's access to information about the world. Because of their more limited experience and knowledge base and in the absence of competing information, television may have a particularly potent effect on them. Huston and her colleagues (1992) reported that children who are heavy viewers of television show a high level of concern about getting sick and have higher perceptions of medical relief and over-the-counter remedies. We must look, then, at the developmental differences, over the long run, between children who have been brought up on television—those for whom television has portrayed and defined "reality" to a larger extent—and those whose television experience has been more limited, either to a certain period of their lives, in terms of total amount of viewing, or as an informational source.

Perceived Reality

An important variable in any cultivation effect is perceived reality. If the television content is seen as real, it is more involving and relevant, which should enhance its effect (Hawkins & Pingree, 1980). Moreover, viewers who perceive and believe in television as a source of useful information that can help them to solve problems vicariously and to cope likely also perceive television as fairly realistic (Potter, 1986).

Even the concept of perceived reality itself appears to be more complex than has usually been thought. Potter (1986, 1988), for example, discussed the importance of identity, or "the degree of similarity the viewer perceives between television characters and situations and the people and situations experienced in real life" (Potter, 1986, p. 163). Individuals high on this dimension feel close to television characters, have a strong sense of reality about them, and feel about them the way they feel about real friends. They believe that television characters are similar to individuals they meet in real life, and they are likely to be more susceptible to television's influence.

Finally, Kubey and Csikszentmihalyi (1990) pointed out, however, that television and film are likely to have more of a homogenizing effect than print because people's perception of content on television is more likely similar to others' than is true of print. Viewers know exactly what a character looks like, for example, and do not have to construct an image in their mind.

Mainstreaming and Resonance

According to Gerbner, Gross, Morgan, and Signorielli (1980), there are varying patterns of associations between amounts of viewing and conceptions of reality for different social groups that can be explained in relation to two systematic processes, mainstreaming and resonance.

Mainstreaming refers to an overall effect of television portrayals and it is related more to general norms and images and social reality (Gerbner et al., 1980). In mainstreaming, the viewing may override differences in behavior or perspective that arise from other cultural, social, and demographic influences in "a homogenization of divergent views and a convergence of disparate views" (Gerbner et al., 1986, p. 31), or the cultivation of common outlooks in heavy viewers. That is, heavy viewers, even in high-educational and high-income groups, share a commonality that light viewers do not (Gerbner et al., 1980).

According to cultivation theory, then, television has the power to cultivate mainstreamed perceptions or outlooks (such as fear or mistrust) and to assimilate groups that ordinarily diverge into a mainstream. There is more interpersonal distrust among heavy viewers, an idea that people cannot be trusted or that they will take advantage of others (Signorielli, 1987), "a heightened and unequal sense of danger and risk in a mean and selfish world" (p. 267). Heavy viewers in one study (Shrum, 1996) gave significantly higher estimates of the frequency of real-world crime, particular occupations, and marital discord than light viewers did.

Others have found very different reactions and perceptions among viewers. For example, Rubin and his colleagues (1988) found that respondents felt safe and connected to others regardless of exposure levels, and in fact higher exposure was associated with perceived safety. Moreover, in contrast to what cultivation theory would predict, heavy and ritualistic viewing was not associated with negative effects, which instead depended on specific content (Rubin et al., 1988).

Television interacts with real world and demographic factors as well. Signorielli (1990) noted that the unequal sense of danger and vulnerability or general malaise from "entertainment" evokes aggression, but also repression and exploitation as people who are fearful are more easily controlled and manipulated and are more likely to yield to tough, hard-line positions that are "deceptively simple." (p. 102).

Resonance on the other hand, refers to situations in which television information about specific issues has particular salience, and what is seen is congruent with a person's actual experiences, with reality, or with the individual's perceived reality (Gerbner et al., 1980). That combination then may give added weight to the television message and lead to an increased effect. The "congruence of the television world and real-life circumstances may 'resonate' and lead to markedly amplified cultivation patterns" (Gerbner et al., 1980, p. 15). Thus, resonance occurs when a topic in the television world has special salience or personal relevance for a group (e.g., overvictimization of the elderly) and it is in that situation that correlations with heavy viewing are clearest.

As research cited earlier indicates, young children find television content more realistic and have greater difficulty distinguishing realistic material from unrealistic material, so its impact on them should be stronger. This impact is enhanced even more by the fact that they have fewer alternative or competing sources of information with which to compare television's messages, so in situations in which parents or peers have minimal input or influence, television is more likely to have an effect. Thus, personal interaction and affiliation reduce cultivation, presumably by providing alternate sources of information (Gerbner et al., 1986).

New Technologies and the Cultivation Effect

According to Perse and her colleagues (Perse, Ferguson, & McLeod, 1994), new technology may change how television viewing could cultivate beliefs about social reality because of the diversity of programming and increased viewer control and selectivity. Perse et al. (1994) found more interpersonal distrust with higher exposure to broadcast-type channels, but less mistrust and less fear of crime with greater exposure to more specialized cable channels. Cable had the greatest impact on television's mainstreaming effect, but these researchers also found an inverse relation between fear of crime and ownership of VCRs.

Perse et al. (1994) suggested that cable may pull away from dominant themes of networks, or may offer other themes that are reassuring or that increase perceptions of self-efficacy. Cable may weaken a mainstreaming impact over time; that is, new technologies change the homogenization of heavy viewing, but heavy viewers are less likely to own a VCR and may use cable for "more of the same." These researchers urged more study of the impact of new technology on traditional ideas about media effects.

Evaluation

Not everyone agrees with the validity of this conceptualization, however, and cultivation analysis has been criticized on methodological grounds. Rubin and his colleagues (1988) concluded that factors such as response bias may explain cultivation effects that had previously been seen as a function of levels of exposure to television. Moreover, cultivation studies also have omitted attention to antecedent and intervening variables, and factors like program choice or perceived reality may override television content in structuring one's perceptions (Rubin et al., 1988). In addition, as it is basically a correlational analysis, causal direction is not easily established. Although heavy viewers may develop a certain perception of the world, their perception of the world also may determine their viewing habits and program choices. Moreover, heavy and light viewers also differ in other ways and some subgroups seem to show an effect, whereas others do not (Dominick, 1987).

Other variables such as age, socioeconomic level, gender, and perceived realism predicted faith in others better than television exposure, and there is a need for further study of the impact of viewer choice and individual differences on perception, especially with the greater diversity of communication alternatives (Rubin et al., 1988).

Other serious criticisms have been leveled against Gerbner's cultivation theories (Wober, 1978; Wober & Gunter, 1988). Wober and Gunter (1988), for example, claimed that those theories have not been verified empirically, that other research has shown the conclusions to rest on small correlations without other related variables being partialed out, and the hypothesis did not hold for Blacks. In a survey commissioned by the Independent Broadcasting Authority in Great Britain involving over 1,000 adults, Wober (Wober & Gunter, 1988) asked questions based on items from Gerbner's work. She found no systematic tendency toward feelings of less security among heavy viewers than among light viewers, which should have occurred if the claimed effects were robust.

After reviewing studies that questioned Gerbner's findings, Wober and Gunter (1988) offered the following possible explanations for the discrepancies between U.S. and British findings:

1. Cultivation effects may be specific to U.S. audiences.
2. The nature of the questions in Gerbner's work.
3. Levels of real violence in viewers' worlds were not taken into account but could affect perceived threat and amount of viewing (e.g., staying in to watch television).
4. Regarding giving "TV answers" for opinions about various events, "substantially different patterns of association between viewing and social beliefs can emerge for different social groups" (p. 39).
5. Not everyone watches the same programs, so the content that is viewed and the information obtained vary depending on a viewer's choice of what to watch.

Shrum (1995) applied social cognitive theory to cultivation research and found that heuristic processing strategies are more likely to be used when involvement in a judgment task is low or when one feels pressure to make a judgment quickly. This, according to Shrum, has implications for cultivation effects because both of those conditions exist in the usual survey research used in much of the cultivation research that has been published. Shrum suggested that passive viewers are more likely to show a cultivation effect (when measured by first-order judgments such as prevalence estimates of people or behaviors or objects) because of heuristic processing, so viewer involvement is important. Virtually all people overestimate such things as violent crime and prevalence of certain occupations, such as police. This may not have anything to do with television viewing, however; the important difference is the one between the estimates of heavy and light viewers (Shrum, 1995).

Amount of viewing alone, however, does not appear to be the most important cause of a cultivation effect, according to Potter (1986). More recent research suggests that any cultivation effect that is observed is a function of more complex variables than simple level of viewing. For example, Potter found a cultivation effect only in the high school students who were high on the Magic Window dimension; and, in fact, a reverse effect was observed on some measures in the group that was low on that dimension. Levels of identification with television characters and levels of perceived reality also need to be taken into account (Potter, 1986), as do developmental factors. Four-year-old heavy viewers do not receive and respond to the same information as 14-year-old viewers or 40-year-old viewers. Their needs and their motivations for viewing differ widely, their ability to comprehend and retain television information is very different, and their experience and the scripts by which they interpret television material are widely disparate.

Cultivation results cannot be explained away via situational or attitudinal variables, however, and perhaps they could be accounted for by some third variable, or a competing information source (Hawkins & Pingree, 1980). Interactions among such variables as cognitive maturity, attention, experience with television, viewing context, family attitudes, and other social and emotional variables need to be addressed in any effort to understand whether and how a phenomenon, such as a cultivation effect, occurs in children's television viewing experience. Other possible explanations and interpretations are discussed later in this chapter.

Uses and Gratifications Theory

Whereas cultivation theory emphasizes the impact of television content on heavy viewers, other theoretical perspectives place more emphasis on viewer characteristics and motivations and on the processes and interactions involved in the viewing experience. For example, social learning theory focuses on both the content and the viewer and on the modeling, vicarious reinforcement, and other processes that determine viewers' imitation of observed behavior. A uses and gratifications model deals with the actual motivations of viewers, the uses they make of television, and the actual needs they have that are satisfied by the media. It looks at what people do with the media rather than what the media do to them (Wright, 1986).

Further, a uses and gratifications model addresses the functional alternatives to one's use of the media, the social and psychological environments of viewers, and their communication behavior and its consequences (Rubin, 1986b).

Basic Assumptions

The various uses and gratifications that can be derived from the television experience fall into four major categories, summarized by Dominick (1987):

1. Cognition, to obtain information or knowledge.
2. Diversion, for stimulation, relaxation, or emotional release.
3. Social integration, utility, to strengthen contact with others, to overcome loneliness, to allow parasocial relationships with TV characters and so on.
4. Withdrawal, for example, to provide a barrier or avoid chores.

Television also can help in the resolution of developmental tasks or life-stage issues, such as adolescent crises, by providing direct learning and information, stimulating fantasies, or stimulating interpersonal discussion of options (Faber, Brown, & McLeod, 1986).

Motivation for Viewing

A uses and gratifications approach assumes that individuals interact actively with the media based on their needs and motivations, and that the media compete with other sources of satisfaction. The motives for viewing may vary with television content and among viewers (Rubin, 1984), but children and adolescents, as well as adults, use media content to satisfy personal needs or wants (Rubin, 1985). It is further assumed that the audience selects and uses content that will best meet their needs and that the same program may gratify different needs in different audience members (Fiske, 1982).

Personality differences among viewers affect not only what they watch and why they watch but also how they react emotionally to the content. A large segment of the television audience may seek out viewing as a simple, effortless, and mildly involving activity that is rewarding in itself, regardless of content (Tannenbaum, 1985; Winn, 1985).

Johnston (1995), for example, used a uses and gratifications model to study adolescents' motivations for viewing graphic horror. She found that their motivations for viewing slasher films differed and mediated the relation between violent content and affective and cognitive responses to it. She also found that the motivations were related to different preferences, ideas about positive attributes of those movies, patterns of affect before and after viewing, character identification, and different personality profiles. The four motivations she discussed reflected very different affective and cognitive experiences in the viewers' response to violence. The motives (gore watching, thrill watching, independent watching, and problem watching) were each associated with vary-ing levels of empathy, positive and negative affect, adventure seeking, sub-stance abuse, and identification with victim or killer. It seems clear that such distinctions among viewers of violence would shed considerable light on the differential effects of television violence on child and adolescent viewers.

Important differences also exist between heavy viewers and nonviewers in motivation toward or away from television. Foss and Alexander (1996) found that heavy viewers generally attribute their reason for viewing to external cir-cumstances (e.g. being ill, having time, having nothing better to do). Both groups felt that television viewing could have negative consequences, such as addiction, but heavy viewers felt immune because they viewed television just for escape and relaxation. Nonviewers chose not to watch so that they would not succumb to addictive effects or become passive or noncritical thinkers. Heavy viewers saw television as unimportant and simply a means to relax; non-viewers also saw television as unimportant, but chose to spend their time doing other things. Therefore, even agreement on these basic themes of motivation, consequences, and importance, and on the addiction metaphor, still led to very different behavior in the two groups.

Selective Exposure

Zillmann and Bryant (1985b) suggested that viewers are sensitive to the effects of various program characteristics and that they use that knowledge to choose messages that are most capable of achieving desirable results. That is, they emphasize and focus on exposure to content involving comforting mes-sages and tend to minimize exposure to programs with disquieting information; they use or select messages for their therapeutic value (Zillmann & Bryant, 1985a). Individuals who are in a bad mood or want to extend a good one are more likely to choose humor and comedy, for example (Zillmann, 1985). Such selective exposure occurs under, or as a function of, all kinds of conditions and moods, including fear, stress, and boredom (Zillmann & Bryant, 1985a).

The therapeutic value of television entertainment lies in its power to improve one's mood, to calm one down, to reduce boredom, or in other ways to provide psychological benefits from viewing it (Zillmann & Bryant, 1986). Even chil-dren as young as 4 or 5 years old were found to use television to improve their moods, although results were clearer for boys than for girls (Zillmann, 1985).

Kubey (1986) stressed the importance of examining the actual experience of individuals in a wide range of activities—of which television viewing is one—to try to discern correlates and causal directions. Studying moods should help establish when and why individuals view television. The Experience-Sampling Method (ESM) can be used to get data, in naturalistic settings, on the frequency and patterns of various daily activities and interactions, on psychological states and on thought patterns; and evidence for its validity exists in the correlations with physiological measures, psychological tests, and behavioral indices (Csikszentmihalyi & Larson, 1987). ESM data are based on self-reports of individuals at random points through their waking hours, measuring variability within people over time (Kubey & Csikszentmihalyi, 1990).

Kubey and Csikszentmihalyi (1990) employed three dimensions: location (where participants were when they were beeped), activity (what they were doing when they were beeped), and companionship (whether they were alone or with someone and, if so, with whom when they were beeped). They found a relation between amount of viewing and discomfort during solitary and unstructured time, especially for those with marital disruption or breakup and for less affluent and less educated viewers. Such viewers are more likely to continue viewing to avoid time alone with feelings and thoughts and turn to TV when they feel bad and others are not around (Kubey, 1986).

Anderson, Collins, Schmitt, and Jacobvitz (1996) also suggested that viewers use media to displace thoughts that might lead to dysphoric moods and choose content that will lead to positive moods. However, they warned that if TV is used chronically to avoid thinking about problems and how to solve them, it will interfere with the development of more effective coping strategies. Nonetheless, television viewing may be a good way to reduce stress and anxiety temporarily, especially when the viewer has little control over the stress, and perhaps viewers who feel especially stressed use TV for this purpose (Anderson et al., 1996). Children also use television viewing to reduce stress, especially because they have even less control over many stressful events in their lives.

Finally, some cultural differences have been reported as well. Zohoori (1988), for example, reported that foreign children, compared with U.S. children, were more likely to use television to learn about themselves and others, although they all used television for escape in equal numbers.

Instrumental and Ritualistic Viewing

In a further analysis of audience motives, Rubin (1984, 1986b, Rubin & Perse, 1987) distinguished between an active audience that selects specific programs and views purposefully, and one in which viewers watch nonselectively and ritualistically. Such a distinction between instrumental and ritualized types of viewing also provides information about amount of viewing and content preferences.

Instrumental viewing, for example, refers to a goal-directed use of the media, such as for information. It is selective, purposeful, and infrequent, and it does not show high regard for television as a medium (Rubin, 1984). Viewing is more selective and intentional or purposeful, and there is greater involvement. Ritualized viewing, on the other hand, is a more habitualized, frequent, and nonselective use of television such as for diversion, or to relax or pass time, and television is valued as a medium (Rubin, 1984). Thus, the activity of the audience may vary by degree and kind.

All audiences are not active for the same reason or in the same way. Audience activity is a variable concept and individuals might view television instrumentally or ritualistically depending on time, background, and situation (Rubin, 1984). Finally, with new technological developments, viewers have many more alternatives and paths by which they can gratify their needs (Williams, Phillips, & Lum, 1985).

Developmental Variables

Developmental level is an important variable in a uses and gratifications approach, and developmental changes in the use of television as a medium have emerged in many studies. Filling time was the most common one across ages, and there was a general decline in all motivations with age (Rubin, 1977). Moreover, the use of television for excitement decreases between age 9 and 17 (Rubin, 1985). Rubin's (1977) findings suggest that motivation for purposeful viewing changes with age, whereas for nonpurposeful viewing it does not. One would expect less reliance on television with increasing age because of the greater likelihood of other sources of information. Young children watch more both because they lack other information and experience and because they more often see it as realistic and therefore more relevant. Age is also important because an age cohort is an indicator of what role individual and social factors play at different developmental levels (Rubin, 1985).

Evaluation

Uses and gratifications theory also has come under serious criticism in more recent work, however. Kubey and Csikszentmihalyi (1990), for example, noted that the assumptions underlying a uses and gratifications approach assume voluntary use of the media to satisfy needs and do not take into account that users do not always have choice about what is viewed. Family members may view a program because that is what other family members are watching. In addition, insufficient consideration is given to the fact that viewers have many needs at the same time, and they might be satisfied by a wide range of programs. However, the strongest concern is that uses and gratifications thought sees gratifications and effects as separate, when, according to Kubey and Csikszentmihalyi, gratifications *are* effects. They also claimed that uses and gratifications theory ignores the fact that many people are affected in similar ways and there are general media effects that hold the greatest potential for studies of mass communication.

An Overview and Integration

Each of the various theoretical perspectives discussed in the previous sections has a very different focus or emphasis. Cultivation approaches stress the media content and its power to cultivate attitudes among heavy viewers. Discussions about information-processing abilities, perceived reality, and social learning processes focus on the viewer's cognitive processes as intervening variables between the medium and behavioral effects. Studies of family influence and mediation point to the environment in which children watch television and place television within a socialization context. Finally, a uses and gratifications approach emphasizes the interaction between the television message and viewer characteristics, needs, and motives. Looking at the television viewing experience from only one of these perspectives leads to an incomplete understanding and, perhaps, misinterpretation of many research data. What is needed is a means by which these various theoretical perspectives and emphases can be integrated into a consistent and coherent conceptualization of what actually happens during and as a result of a child's television viewing, and how those events are caused, mediated, facilitated, or impeded.

If one takes into account the diverse theoretical views and empirical data described throughout this book, two rather distinct viewing patterns emerge that help to integrate many of the research findings. These patterns consist of viewing variables that tend to cluster together and reflect very different viewing experiences.

In the first one, television is viewed seriously in an effort to derive information and knowledge from what is being viewed. A considerable amount of mental effort is invested, and logical and critical skills are brought to bear in goal-directed viewing. Such viewers have more intense and focused attention and stronger motivation to extract relevant information from the television content. Under those conditions, television would be expected to have maximum impact *in that content area*; it is being taken seriously. Whether that influence was positive or negative would depend on the content being viewed. Moreover, if they engage in heavy viewing, and hence displace opportunities for comparing television information with that from other sources, one would expect those viewers to be particularly vulnerable to television's influence and to the cultivation of attitudes and outlooks by the television portrayals.

This interpretation is entirely consistent with script theory in that individuals with little information in an area would have only a limited script (little alternate information) and would depend more heavily on the television experience for information to develop a script for a given area or topic. If the television portrayal is the only, or the major model for a child (or for viewers who are disadvantaged, in minority groups, poorly educated, or lower functioning), or if it is the only or major source of information for a script, that viewer will be more likely to take it seriously, to emulate the television model, or to internalize the television script.

On the other hand, if viewers already have a rich variety of informational sources and are viewing television simply for diversion or entertainment, not for information, they are more likely to experience the television content in a more emotional and less critical way, to exert less mental effort, and to take it less seriously. They would seem to be less susceptible to television's influence or to cultivation of attitudes by its content. Even if they engage in heavy viewing, its impact might be less than if they were using television as a serious and primary source of information, although subtle messages are still conveyed.

The considerable significance of developmental level must be taken into account, however. In the absence of other informational sources, and without extensive experience, as is the case with young children, viewing large amounts of television for entertainment might also serve an important informational function. Young children may use entertainment to gain information they need. If they have few other avenues to learn about a content area, heavy viewing, even for entertainment, would likely provide them with information and would increase television's impact on them.

One way to interpret the data, then, is to underscore the complex interaction that appears to exist between cultivation and uses and gratifications approaches, an interaction that is made more complex by developmental differences among viewers. When television is used differently—to satisfy specific needs—other aspects of the viewing experience also differ significantly. In addition, perceived reality mediates whether the portrayals viewed actually have an impact, particularly if there are few competing views from other informational sources. Even in the case of light viewers, then, when television is being used for information, and when the content is perceived to be very realistic, one would expect it to have more effect than if it is being used for diversion and/or if it is perceived as less realistic. These complex interactions are illustrated in Fig. 13.1.

Thus, the use made of television and the seriousness of one's involvement in it may be more important than sheer level of exposure. Cultivation theory suggests that heavy viewers are most influenced by television's messages. Perhaps the amount of viewing is secondary to the motivation for viewing, at least for older children who have other experiences and sources of information to counter television's messages. Viewers who demonstrate a cultivation effect

Figure 13.1. Interactions among use and amount of viewing with perceived reality and information alternatives. Developmental level, socioeconomic level, race, gender, and other factors determine use made of television, reality perceived, amount viewed, and informational alternatives.

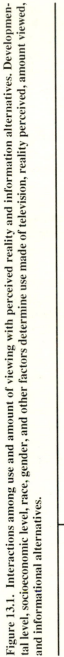
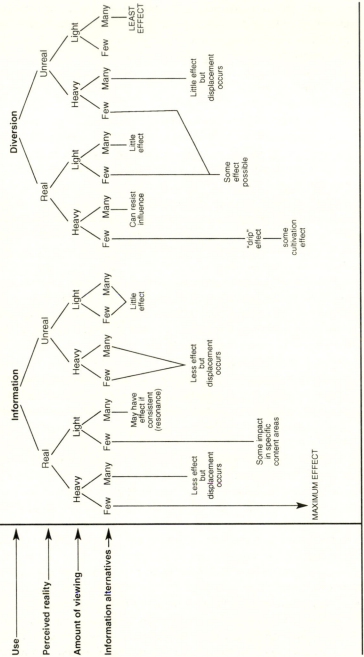

are likely the ones who take television seriously and who rely on it for information. Indeed, recent data have confirmed this expectation. Perse (1986), for example, contrary to cultivation hypothesis assumptions, found that the limited cultivation effect that she found was related to instrumental viewing motives, as well as to higher levels of perceived reality and affinity. The instrumental motives, however, included a search for exciting entertainment as well as for information. The key component, then, in the limited cultivation effect observed appeared to be the goal-directedness of the viewing.

The cultivation effect often associated with heavy viewing, then, may be greater in some viewer groups, not only because they watch more television, but also because they are members of groups (e.g., ethnic minorities, disadvantaged individuals, young children, elderly, poorly educated) who use television very differently. They more often rely on television as a source of information, and they have fewer, or less diverse alternative sources. Even if those heavy viewers use television primarily for entertainment, if they perceive it to be realistic, and if they have little competing information, they are still likely more vulnerable to its influence.

Because individuals view specific programs for various reasons and at different times, they may use television for one purpose on one occasion, or for a given program or time period, and use it for another reason at another time.

With increasing maturity, then, and the greater likelihood of having alternative sources of information, television may have less impact. One would expect television to be taken less seriously with age, to be perceived as less realistic, and to be used more often for diversion, entertainment, and escape, although SES, gender, content, and format variables also affect its influence. For children who have reasonable educational and interpersonal opportunities, television should play a less central role in their lives and socialization as they mature, and as their range of experiences expands.

For those older children and adults who do not have other sources of information, however, or who have not developed skills to obtain it, television would be expected to continue to be a primary source of information and to exert a stronger influence. For children from disadvantaged homes, children with reading problems, or children whose parents are not involved in their viewing and are not thereby providing alternative information (i.e., for children who watch a considerable amount of television in order to get the information that they need), the potential for influence and cultivation of attitudes is much greater.

Such a distinction also helps to clarify seemingly conflicting views among researchers who claim that children do not take television seriously, such as Cullingsford (1984), and those who claim that children are very much affected by it, such as those who explain its effect through social learning and modeling (e.g., Bandura, 1967; Winett & Kramer, 1989) or script theories (e.g., Berkowitz & Rogers, 1986; Durkin, 1985; Eron, 1982; Huesmann, 1988).

When one studies viewers who are using television as a serious source of information, all of the characteristics, intervening variables, and processes discussed in earlier chapters on information processing of television material are very relevant and important and they further complicate the issue. The effects of formal features on attention, for example, the varying levels of comprehension, the factors that influence retention, the importance of verbal encoding and rehearsal, the effects of age and previous experience on a child's interpretation of television content, and many other variables interact to determine the level and accuracy of the information that the child derives from the viewing experience. Therefore, even when a child is using television seriously to obtain information, many developmental and experiential factors influence the actual quality of the information obtained. Two children viewing the same program for the same purpose (e.g., for information) still might well get very different input from the experience, depending on their age, gender, socioeconomic level, cognitive maturity, general experience, and family background. The study of television's impact on children, then, is clearly an extraordinarily complex and challenging task.

Cultivation theory has been criticized as relying too heavily on correlational findings in its claim that heavy viewers are more likely to develop attitudes consistent with television portrayals, when in fact it is perhaps those attitudes that lead to heavy television viewing. An emphasis on the purpose of the viewing, however, provides an intervening variable to help explain the relation between amount of viewing and attitudes. Whether heavy viewing leads to the development of a cultivated perception of the world or whether one's perception leads to heavy viewing, why one views television, the use made of television, and the seriousness with which it is taken, as well as other sources of competing information, are important considerations in predicting the extent of its influence.

Viewing preferences are also important, because if one is seeking information, the content selected may be rather different than if one is watching for entertainment or diversion, although individual viewers vary in their judgments about which content is informational and which is entertaining. Hence patterns of viewer preference also affect the influence that television has, not necessarily directly through the content perhaps, as much as through the purpose for which the viewer watches that content.

Television content itself can be seen as varying along informational and entertainment dimensions, but its interpretation and the use made of it also can vary depending on the motivation of the viewer. On the surface, one might assume, for example, that shows such as news shows and documentaries would appeal primarily to individuals seeking information and shows such as situation comedies would appeal primarily to those looking for diversion. However, young and inexperienced children, socially inhibited children, or shy adults (i.e., those with limited alternative information and strategies) might rely on situation comedies for information as well, as a model for social interaction, or as a source of strategies in their own interpersonal relationships.

Such television portrayals, then, in the face of less competing information, and especially if viewed alone without input from others about the relative effectiveness of those interactions, should exert a far greater impact than is ordinarily associated with them. Conversely, some viewers are likely to watch documentaries solely for diversion or entertainment rather than to obtain information. There may also be a kind of blending of the two as "infotainment" (Morgenstern, 1989), in which information is presented entertainingly. Morgenstern (1989) pointed out that most Americans connect with reality through television rather than through newspapers, and that the television medium is "where relentless sensationalism is now blurring the line between information and entertainment" (p. 28).

The fact that empirical data do not consistently support cultivation theory (Berkowitz & Rogers, 1986) may be because the purpose of viewing or the use made of television and developmental differences among viewers were not taken into account at the same time. Identical content viewed for different reasons by viewers with very different levels of information and experience should have quite different effects. Moreover, the importance of other variables that have been found in a considerable amount of research, such as age, viewing context, SES, and minority status, may well lie, at least in part, in their impact or influence on the use that is made of specific television content at any given point in time. Conceptualizing the research data in this way allows for integration of many seemingly contradictory findings into a more consistent explanatory picture of television's impact.

Summary

Various theoretical perspectives and models for explaining and interpreting the complex interaction of variables and events that influence children's television experience have been put forward over the years. The earliest of these in the psychological literature was a social learning perspective, which emphasized observational learning and modeling of behaviors viewed on television.

Research in the communication field has emphasized television's potential for the cultivation of attitudes and behavior change in viewers. It also has stressed the needs of viewers, the context of viewing, the use that is made of television viewing, and the gratifications that viewers obtain from their television experiences. Perceived reality of the content and the availability of and access to alternative and competing sources of information, as well as the purpose for viewing, are critically important variables in the assessment of television's impact. Knowledge of the interactions among media components and content; viewer variables, perceptions, and motivations; and characteristics of the viewing context are essential factors in our efforts to understand children's television experiences.

References

Anderson, D. R., Collins, P. A., Schmitt, K. L., and Jacobvitz, R. S. 1996. "Stressful Life Events and Television Viewing." *Communication Research*, 23 (3):243–60.

Bandura, A. 1967. "The Role of Modeling Processes in Personality Development." pp. 42–58 in W. W. Hartup and N. L. Smothergill (eds.) *The Young Child: Reviews of Research*. Washington, DC: National Association for the Education of Young Children.

Berkowitz, L. and Rogers, K. H. 1986. "A Priming Effect Analysis of Media Influences." pp. 57–81 in J. Bryant and D. Zillman (eds.), *Perspectives on Media Effects*. Hillsdale, NJ: Lawence Erlbaum Associates.

Cook, T. D., Kendzierski, D. A., and Thomas, S. V. 1983. "The Implicit Assumptions of Television Research: An Analysis of the 1982 NIMH Report on Television and Behavior." *Public Opinion Quarterly*, 47:161–201.

Csikszentmihalyi, M. and Larson, R. 1987. "Validity and Reliability of the Experience-Sampling Method." *Journal of Nervous and Mental Disease*, 175(9):526–36.

Cullingsford, C. 1984. *Children and Television*. Aldershot, England: Gower.

Dominick, J. R. 1987. *The Dynamics of Mass Communication*. New York: Random House.

Durkin, K. 1985. *Television, Sex Roles, and Children: A Developmental Social Psychological Account*. Philadelphia: Open University Press.

Eron, L. 1982," Parent-Child Interaction, Television Violence, and Aggression of Children." *American Psychologist*, 37(2):197–211.

Faber, R. J., Brown, J. D., and McLeod, J. M. 1986. "Coming of Age in the Global Village: Television and Adolescence." pp. 550–72 in G. Gumpert and R. Cathcart (eds.) *Inter/Media: Interpersonal Communication in a Media World*. New York: Oxford University Press.

Fiske, J. 1982. *Introduction to Communication Studies*. London: Methuen.

Gerbner, G., Gross, L., Morgan, M., and Signorelli, N. 1980. "The 'Mainstreaming' of America: Violence Profile No. 11." *Journal of Communication*, 30(3):10–29.

Gerbner, G., Gross, L., Morgan, M., and Signorielli, N. 1982. "Charting the Mainstream: Television's Contribution to Political Orientation." *Journal of Communication*, 32(2):100–27.

Gerbner, G., Gross, L., Morgan, M., and Signorielli, N. 1986. "Living with Television: The Dynamics of the Cultivation Process." pp. 17–40 in J. Bryant and D. Zillman (eds.) *Perspectives on Media Effects*. Hillsdale, NJ: Lawrence Erlbaum Associates.

Gunter, B. 1985. *Dimensions of Television Violence*. Aldershot, England: Gower.

Hawkins, R. P. and Pingree, S. 1980. "Some Processes in the Cultivation Effect." *Communication Research*, 7(2):193–226.

Huesman, L. R. 1988. "An Information Processing Model for the Development of Aggression." *Aggressive Behavior*, 14:13–24.

Johnson, D. D. 1995. "Adolescents' Motivations for Viewing Graphic Horror." *Human Communication Research*, 21(4):522–52.

Kubey, R. W. 1986. "Television Use in Everyday Life: Coping with Unstructured Time." *Journal of Communication*, 36:108–23.

Kubey, R. and Csikszentmihalyi, M. 1990. *Television and the Quality of life: How Viewing Shapes Everyday Experience*. Hillsdale, NJ: Lawrence Erlbaum Associates.

Milavsky, J. R., Kessler, R. C., Stipp, H. H., and Rubena, W. S. 1982. *Television and Aggression: A Panel Study*. New York: Academic Press.

Morgenstern, J. 1989, "TV's Big Turnoff: Can USA Today Be Saved?" *The New York Times Magazine*, Section 6, pp. 13–15, 26–68. January 1, 1989.

Perse, E. M. 1986. "Soap Opera Viewing Patterns of College Students and Cultivation." *Journal of Broadcasting and Electronic Media*, 30(2):175–193.

Perse, E. M., Ferguson, D. A., and McLeod, D. M. 1994. "Cultivation in the Newer Newer Media Environment." *Communication Research*, 21(1):79–104.

Potter, W. J. 1986. "Perceived Reality and the Cultivation Hypothesis." *Journal of Broadcasting and Electronic Media*, 30(2):159–74.

Rubin, A. M. 1984. "Ritualized and Instrumental Television Viewing." *Journal of Communication*, 34(3):67–77.

Rubin, A. M. 1985. "Media Gratifications through the life Cycle." pp. 195–208 in K. E. Rosengren, L. A. Wenner, and P. Palmgreen (eds.) *Media Gratifications Research: Current Perspectives*. Beverly Hills, CA: Sage.

Rubin, A. M. 1986. "Uses, Gratifications, and Media Effects Research." pp. 281–301 in J. Bryant and D. Zillman (eds.) *Perspectives on Media Effects*. Hillsdale, NJ: Lawrence Erlbaum Associates.

Rubin, A. M. and Perse, E. M. 1987. "Audience Activity and Television News Gratifications." *Communication Research*, 14(1):58–84.

Rubin, A, M., Perse, E. M., and Taylor, D. S. 1988. "A Methodological Examination of Cultivation." *Communication Research*, 15(2):107–34.

Shrum, L. J. 1995. "Assessing the Social Influence of Television: A Social Cognition Perspective on Cultivation Effects." *Communication Research*, 22(4):402–29.

Shrum, L. J. 1996. "Psychological Processes Underlying Cultivation Effects. Further Tests of Construct Accessibility." *Human Communication Research*, 22(4):428–509.

Signorielli, N. 1987. "Children and Adolescents on Television: A Consistent Pattern Of Devaluation." *Journal of Early Adolescence*, 7(3):255–68. Signorelli, N. 1990.

Signorielli, N. 1990. "Television's Mean and Dangerous World: A Continuation of the Cultural Indicators Perspective." pp. 85–106 in N. Signorielli and M. Morgan (eds.) *Cultivation Analysis: New Directions in Media Effects*. Newbury Park, CA: Sage.

Tannenbaum, P. H. 1985. " 'Play it Again, Sam.' Repeated Exposure to Television Programs." pp. 225–41 in D. Zillman and J. Bryant (eds.) *Selective Exposure to Communication*. Hillsdale, NJ: Lawrence Erlbaum Associates.

Wackman, D. B., Wartella, E., and Ward, S. 1977. Learning to be Consumers: The Role Of the Family." *Journal of Communication*, 27(1):138–51.

Wartella, E. 1986. "Getting to Know you: How Children Make Sense of Television." pp. 537–49 in G. Gumpert and R. Cathcart (eds.) *Inter/Media: Interpersonal Communication in a Media World*, 3rd ed. New York: Oxford University Press.

Williams, F., Phillips, A. F., and Lum, P. 1985. "Gratifications Associated with New Consumer Technologies." pp. 241–52 in K. E. Rosengran, L. A. Wenner, and P. Palmgreen (eds.) *Media Gratifications Research: Current Perspectives.* Beverly Hills, CA: Sage.

Winett, R. A., and Kramer, K. D. 1989. "A Behavioral Systems Framework for Information Design and Behavior Change." pp. 237–57 in J. L. Salvaggio and J. Bryant (eds.) *Media use in the Information Age: Emerging Patterns of Adoption and Consumer Use.* Hillsdale, NJ: Lawrence Erlbaum Associates.

Winn, M. 1985. *The Plug-In Drug.* New York: Penguin.

Wober, M. 1978. "Televised Violence and Paranoid Perception: The View from Great Britain." *Public Opinion Quarterly,* 42:315–21.

Wober, M. and Guner, B. 1988. *Television and Social Control.* New York: St. Martin's.

Wright, C. R. 1986. *Mass Communication: A Sociological Perspective,* 3rd ed. New York; Random House.

Zillman, D. 1985. "The Experimental Exploration of Gratifications from Media Entertainment." pp. 225–39 in K. E. Rosengren, L. A. Wenner, and P. Palmgreen (eds.) *Media Gratifications Research: Current Perspectives.* Beverly Hills, CA: Sage.

Zillman, D. and Bryant, J. 1985a. "Affect, Mood, and Emotion as Determinants of Selective Exposure." pp. 157–90 in D. Zillman and J. Bryant (eds.) *Selective Exposure to Communication.* Hillsdalle, NJ: Lawrence Erlbaum Associates.

Zillman, D., and Bryant, J. 1985b. "Selective-Exposure Phenomena." pp. 1–10 in D. Zillman and J. Bryant (eds.) *Selective Exposure to Communication.* Hillsdale, NJ: Lawrence Erlbaum Associates.

Zohoori, A. R. 1988. "A Cross-Cultural Analysis of Children's Television Use." *Journal of Broadcasting and Electronic Media,* 33(1):105–13.

14

Children's Desires/Mothers' Dilemmas: The Social Contexts of Consumption*

Ellen Seiter

> *Goods are for mobilizing other people.*
> —Mary Douglas

Toys, commercials, and animated programs are the lingua franca of young children at babysitters' and grandmothers' houses, day-care centers, and pre-schools across the United States. Most children leave home long before they enter the public school system, to spend their day away from parents and with other children their own age. At the snack table they admire one another's T-shirts and lunchboxes emblazoned with film and television characters. At show-and-tell or "sharing" time they proudly present the Ninja Turtles, Barbies, Batmen, and My Little Ponies purchased at Toys "R" Us and given them at birthday parties. Most children know the same commercials, television programs, movies, and music. By wearing their media preferences on their sleeves and carrying their most prized possessions everywhere they go, children make visible their identifications with those more ephemeral objects of consumer culture—namely, films, videos, and television programs.

Consumer culture provides children with a shared repository of images, characters, plots, and themes: it provides the basis for small talk and play, and it does this on a national, even global scale. Outside the house, children can bank on finding that nearly every other child they meet will know some of the same things—and probably *have* many of the same things—that they do. Thus very young children are now sufficiently immersed in a consumer culture to be able to strike up a conversation with one another about a character imprinted on a T-shirt or a toy in hand, to spot one of their kind—a fan of My Little Ponies or Ninja Turtles—across the aisles of Safeway or Toys "R" Us. Mass-market commodities are woven into the social fabric of children's lives: they are seen on sleepovers, at show-and-tell in school, on the block or in the apartment building, on the T-shirt. Young children's consumption holds an ambiguous position between domestic space and public space. Young children are only in the process of learning the distinctions between public and private and the activities appropriate to each. In a sense, this is why their consumption activities are so interesting compared with the more restrained and compartmentalized behaviors of adults.

Within the family, children's taste for certain television shows and certain toys can set them apart from their elders. Sometimes young children feel their knowledge and mastery of consumer culture to be a kind of power: something they know, but of which adults are ridiculously ignorant. Young children cannot make purchases or watch television without adult assistance, however, so parents—usually mothers—are implicated in their consumption and often disapprove of their desires. Thus the battle lines between parents and children over toys and media are drawn when the child is very young. Many mothers, and nearly all middle-class intellectuals, view popular toys and children's television as an alien culture with which they are uncomfortable to varying degrees. Adults often perceive TV and toys as dumb and sexist, or depraved and violent. Many parents find the television shows hard to watch, the commercials offensive, and the toys kitschy. Among the upper middle class the conflict between parents and children over toys and television is not based on affordability but on ideological and aesthetic objections. Upper middleclass parents want their children to like things that are "better to like";[1] they struggle to teach them the tastes for classic toys, the aesthetics of natural materials, and the interest in self-improving "educational" materials favored by their class—and to spurn children's consumer culture as mass, TV based, commercial, and plastic.

Mothers may object to children's consumer culture, but they usually give in to it as well, largely because of the usefulness of television programs and toys as convenience goods for caretakers of children. While giving in, adults often harbor profound doubts about the effects of children's consumer culture today and worry that their own children are learning from the mass media an ethic of greed and a proclivity for hedonism.

I believe it is a mistake to judge children's desires for toys and television programs exclusively in terms of greed and individual hedonism. Children's desires are not depraved. In wanting to have toys and see television programs, children are also expressing a desire for a shared culture with their schoolmates and friends and a strong imagination of community. Moreover, observing children's use of consumer goods and popular media can remind adults of the importance of material culture in their own lives. Adults as well as children invest intense feeling in objects and attribute a wealth of personal and idiosyncratic meanings in mass-produced goods.

It is true that young children do not originate any of the symbols of this subculture; rather, a group of professional adults designs toys and TV shows for children that—when their market research tells them it will be appealing to children—deliberately violate the norms and aesthetics of middle-class culture. Market researchers seek children on whom to test their ideas on colors, cuteness, humor, and heroism, but children participate passively in the design process. Girls may love ponies, but they did not make them a cultural symbol on their own. Toys are made in certain ways using certain materials dictated by the availability of cheap labor, usually in China. Similarly, children's television shows are appropriated into young children's culture on a large scale, but adult scriptwriters devise the stories. What children get is limited by the professional ideologies of advertising and entertainment industry workers, the capabilities of industrial production and design of children's goods and media, and the influence of manufacturers and television producers on governmental regulation and broadcasting policy.

It is a mistake, however, to see marketers as evil brainwashers and children as naive innocents, as they are so often depicted in journalists' accounts of the toy industry. The toy and television industries defense against their critics is that children are the ones who make or break the toys and television programs offered to them, that they vote with their remote controls and their dollars. This belief must be treated as more than cynical apologism. Children's desire for toys and media is more than the direct fulfillment of the designs of manufacturers and marketers, however attractive this notion may be in its simplicity. The industry's characterization of the children's audience as fickle and discriminating must be taken seriously. We know that children make meanings out of toys that are unanticipated by—perhaps indecipherable to—their adult designers, who are often baffled by the success of toys like Teenage Mutant Ninja Turtles. Children are creative in their appropriation of consumer goods and media, and the meanings they make with these materials are not necessarily and not completely in line with a materialist ethos. Children create their own meanings from the stories and symbols of consumer culture.

By emphasizing the creative processes of consumption, I am also suggesting that a more useful approach to toys and children's television programs is to insist that they *are* culture. As the British anthropologist Daniel Miller argues:

Mass goods represent culture, not because they are merely there as the environment in which we operate, but because they are an integral part of that process of objectification by which we create ourselves as an industrial society: our identities, our social affiliations, our lived everyday practices. The authenticity of artifacts as culture derives not from their relationship to some historical style or manufacturing process—in other words, there is no truth or falsity immanent in them—but rather from their active participation in a process of social self-creation in which they are directly constitutive of our understanding of ourselves and others.[2]

As cultural objects, toys and children's television deserve much more careful analysis and attention than they are usually granted. They deserve to be studied as complex, hybrid manifestations of adult culture, which are engaged with in various and contradictory ways by different children under different circumstances. To study children's toys in this way demands the suspension of adult judgment for a time. I believe that we need a break from the blanket condemnation of children's consumer culture in order to understand it; we need to identify clearly the resemblances as well as the differences between children's and adults' culture; and we need to clarify the elitist aspects of many critical disparagements of children's mass culture.

Toys and children's television programs are cultural products that mimic adult culture by imitating popular entertainment genres and borrowing from them characters, plots, locales, and costumes. Action-adventure stories, science fiction, musicals, soap operas, and melodramas contribute a store of themes and symbols to children's television. In some cases, children's toys and television characters copy themes of the adult culture but present them in exaggerated versions unacceptable to adults. Gender roles are a notorious example of this. Female characters are marked by exaggerated aesthetic codes: high-pitched voices, pastel colors, frills, endless quantities of hair, and an innate capacity for sympathy. Male characters appear as superheroes with enormous muscles, deep voices, and an earnest and unrelenting capacity for action and bravery. Children's commercial television is also what we may call utopian, universally appealing to children in its subversion of parental values of discipline, seriousness, intellectual achievement, respect for authority, and complexity by celebrating rebellion, disruption, simplicity, freedom, and energy.

Attention to the utopian aspects of popular culture—a type of analysis originated by the Marxist philosopher Ernst Bloch—has been advocated by literary theorist Fredric Jameson as a useful antidote to manipulation theories of the mass media and the tendency to see television as nothing but false consciousness. Film critic Richard Dyer has also identified an element of utopianism in a wide variety of entertainment forms from musicals to comedy to television news: "the image of 'something better' to escape into, or something we want deeply that our day-to-day lives don't provide. Alternatives, hopes, wishes—these are the stuff of utopia, the sense that things could be better, that something other than what is can be imagined and may be realized."[3] In this tradition, certain aspects of mass culture are seen to relate to "specific inadequacies in society": abundance replaces scarcity and the unequal distribution of wealth; boundless energy replaces exhaustion. Dreariness is countered by intensity—"the capacity of entertainment to present either complex or unpleasant feelings in a way that makes them seem uncomplicated, direct and vivid, not 'qualified' or 'ambiguous' as day-to-day life makes them."[4] Transparency replaces manipulation; community replaces fragmentation.

The kind of utopianism found in entertainment is severely restricted, however. Although they see positive sides to utopianism, Jameson notes a "profound identity" between "utopian gratification and ideological manipulation," and Dyer warns that the consideration of problems is typically limited to those for which capitalism itself offers remedies—through consumption. Too often, entertainment "provides alternatives *to* capitalism which will be provided *by* capitalism."[5] Still, the concept of utopian sensibility can help to explain much of the appeal of children's cartoons and commercials. They portray an abundance of the things most prized by children—food and toys; their musical themes and fast action are breathtakingly energetic; they enact a rebellion against adult restriction; they present a version of the world in which good and evil, male and female, are unmistakably coded in ways easily comprehended by a young child; and they celebrate a community of peers. Children's mass culture rejects the instrumental uses of toys and television for teaching and self-improvement preferred by parents.

The contemporary mass culture of childhood can be found in magazine ads and television commercials, toys and toy stores, and television programs aimed at children. How do these reflect differing and conflicting viewpoints between adults and children? How do contemporary advertising, toy sales, and commercial television programming create and reflect the gap between adults and children? How are race, gender, and class differences highlighted or submerged in children's consumer culture? How do children's media borrow and transform popular genres in adult entertainment? How has the market of affluent parents been targeted by "alternative" toy and video makers? The differences as well as the resemblances between children's and parents' consumer cultures form the topic of this book.

With a clear understanding of the limitations of utopianism in mind, I want to consider how children's consumer culture and the promises it makes grew as big as they are today. The history is complex, involving changes in parents' workloads, the dominance of developmental psychology and the way it has formed our attitudes toward toys, and the impact of television on the nuclear family. I believe it is necessary to place children's popular culture in the contexts of historical changes in households and in the work mothers and fathers do, attitudes toward child rearing encouraged by experts and marketers, and the widespread present perception that television is bad for children. I also wish to examine hedonism and emulation, explanations for consumerism from sociological theory, in light of their special relevance to the predicament of parents' and young children's differing perceptions of children's consumer culture.

Television

Given the extraordinary amount of unpaid work required of women maintaining households with children, it is unsurprising that television sets—with their potential use as a babysitting machine—were purchased so fast by so many families in the 1950s and that families with children were the first to want them.[30] Television offered mothers a break. Television historian Lynn Spigel has documented the ways that television was at first hailed as a medium of family togetherness, a source of increased domestic harmony and intimacy in the dream home, an alternative to the mother as a source of learning for children at home. But watching television also increased the potential conflicts with children over wanting more than mothers were able or willing to buy for them, and it offered idealized images of the happy housewife and mother fulfilling her job with ease. Worries over television's effects on children—ranging from facial tics to passivity—soon came to the fore, and experts assigned to mothers the job of censoring, monitoring, and accompanying the child's viewing. If a mother heeded the experts' advice, she lost the free time television provided; if she did not, she used television as a babysitter only at the cost of feeling guilty about it.

In social discourse, various portrayals of television compete with one another, each informed by and representing a specific set of interests. In writing about children's television, competing and contradictory positions are advanced by industry producers, consumer protection groups such as Action for Children's Television; academic "childhood professionals," such as educators, pediatricians, psychologists, and social workers; and academic media researchers. Each of these groups contributes to a discourse that allows certain things to be said and rules out other things—or makes them unimaginable. The discourse of child experts usually assumes a certain normative view of what children are like (naive, impressionable, uncritical), of what television should do (help children learn to read and to understand math and science), of what is an appropriate way to spend leisure time (being physically and mentally active, *doing* things), and of what television viewing is (passive and mindless). These ideas derive from larger medical, religious, and social science bodies of thought.

When parents and teachers read about children, toys, and television, they normally rely on journalists' accounts published in newspapers and women's magazines. The tone of such articles has been frequently alarmist, fueling mothers' fears about commercial television's long-term effects on children and inspiring guilt over taking advantage of television's convenience. Warnings from child psychologists about television's effects have been curiously out of step with much mass communications research, which has stressed a view of media consumption as active rather than passive and enumerated the variety of "uses and gratifications" to be gained from the media. Nonetheless, blaming television for everything that's wrong with children is a rhetorical strategy for which the print media seem to have a special attraction. The most quotable and attractive sources for journalists—the story makers—are people who will say in the simplest possible terms that children are unwitting victims of the devil television. It is a satisfying notion: to find a single source with direct, casually observable effects to blame for all that is wrong with children today.

The most widely held belief about television among parents and educators is that television viewing is passive. This notion circulates regularly in media targeted to parents: pediatricians' pamphlets, magazines, agony columns, advice literature. "There is a powerful, idealised image of childhood as a time of activity and doing that reinforces some of my misgivings about television," explains one parent.[31] Complaints about children's TV viewing—such as those voiced by media critics Marie Winn and Neil Postman—are backed by a nostalgic mourning for an idealized vision of a "lost" childhood: a childhood that was a time of doing, of direct experience.[32]

Why is passivity the attribute so often used to condemn children's television viewing? In sharp contrast to eighteenth- and nineteenth-century Anglo-American notions about children, in which submission, obedience, and docility were prized, today passive is about the worst thing a child can be. As I have noted, developmental psychology is now the dominant model of childhood in teaching, psychology, social work, and medicine. Passivity is especially problematic, even pathological, according to this model.[33] The notion of children watching television offends the widely held belief in the importance of the child *actively* achieving developmental tasks. Child experts, television critics, and protectionists are convinced that television deters children from achieving normative agendas of child development: direct interaction with peers and parents, "large motor" skills, socialization, cognitive and physical development. Television is excluded from the list of activities that can "stimulate" growth—and stimulation is something that parents are supposed to provide in endless supply from infancy onward.

Experts regularly advise that the less television viewing, the better; videotapes are preferable to broadcast television because they have no commercials; if you must let your child watch, make it PBS; no viewing is best of all. As one media researcher pointed out: "The amount of television children watch is still quoted in a way which presupposes adult amazement and disapproval. We speak of 'heavy' or 'light' viewers as if there is indeed a measurable 'amount' of the thing called TV viewing which has entered into the child's system and stays there like a dead weight."[34] Child experts can be exacting taskmasters when they advise parents to monitor children's viewing: "Establish ground rules, prevent TV from becoming an addiction," say Dorothy and Jerome Singer in *Parents* magazine: no TV before school, during meals, during daytime hours, or before homework is done. "And don't suggest that the child 'go watch TV' whenever you are feeling overwhelmed or need privacy."[35] Obesity, violence, and poor school performance are continually held up as the threatened results of television viewing.

The first major North American study of children and television, based on data collected between 1958 and 1960, was adamantly neutral about television viewing.[36] Among preschool children, those who watched television started school with larger vocabularies and more knowledge about the world than children who had not watched television. For older children, television was found to be neither particularly beneficial nor harmful. The physical effects of television viewing were negligible, and any correlation between viewing and passivity depended on other factors in the home life of the child. The researchers, Wilbur Schramm, Jack Lyle, and Edwin Parker, noted different attitudes among parents toward television: blue-collar parents were more grateful for television's convenience and less critical of its programs; whereas middle-class parents held stronger reservations about television. In every aspect of the relationship between television viewing and a child's worldview, IQ, social class, and social relations were powerful determinants.

What filtered down to advice literature from this and other early studies was a tendency to urge mothers to work harder at their children's television viewing: by censoring, accompanying viewing, and discussing programming with the child, thus losing the free time that television might offer. Certainly television has changed children's lives. But it has done so in complex—and not necessarily negative ways—demonstrated in a wealth of sophisticated research in the 1970s and 1980s by scholars such as Jennings Bryant, Suzanne Pingree, Ellen Wartella, James Anderson, Daniel Anderson, and Elizabeth Lorch.[37] Recently, a number of mass communications researchers employing qualitative methods to study children's viewing habits have again challenged the notion that children are passive in relation to television. Unfortunately this work has gathered little attention outside academic circles.

Two recent studies based on parents' reports of their children's viewing have sketched a more active—and interactive—picture of children's viewing. Patricia Palmer, in an observational study of Australian children watching TV at home, has charted the great variety of ways children behave when watching television—from intent viewing of a few favorite programs to distracted viewing combined with other activities, such as playing with toys or pets, chatting, drawing. Palmer found that children had a propensity for performing, reenacting, and reinterpreting the material—especially television commercials—often as an affectionate interaction with parents, siblings, and friends. Children spend a lot of time discussing television, arguing about it, and criticizing it, both on the playground with friends and at home with parents and siblings. Palmer's work is important for simply listing the enormous range of children's response to television. Television goes on in the lives of children long after it is seen, and it is constantly subject to discussion and reinterpretation. Palmer reminds us how rich a source of material for social interaction television is, something denied by the persistent image (and I mean this literally, as in magazine and newspaper illustrations) of the child alone before the television set.[38] Far from passive, children, Palmer argues, are a lively audience for television.

The best research on children and television conceives of children's cognitive skills as embedded in a social world and developing at an early age. Dafna Lemish's study of children under two indicates how very early television viewing skills develop, and how babies' experience of television is tied to the everyday world of the family. Lemish's U.S. study, based on parents' recording of their children's behavior, chronicles the rapid changes in babies' attention to and selective perception of television material. Well before the age of two, children were able to monitor television at a glance for interesting material and had mastered a host of audiovisual signs that they used to distinguish among programs and genres. As reported in so many studies of children and television, the toddlers in Lemish's study found television commercials (which *Sesame Street*'s short, dynamic sequences deliberately resemble) especially appealing. Their appreciation of television material progressed rapidly from recognizing familiar objects (children, animals), to selecting favorite animated musical sequences, to attending live-action "story" segments. Young children could distinguish at a glance adult material, such as the news, from children's programming. The children seemed to enjoy teasing parents about their control of the set, manipulating the television as a toy (volume and channel controls) while parents tried to watch adult programs. A study by Paul Messaris found, as did Lemish, that mothers were fascinated by their children's rapid development in relation to television and enjoyed discussing it—but the specter of expert advice hung over them: they wished not to be badly thought of for expressing an interested enthusiasm over their children's viewing.[39] Most adults watch television and most parents let their children watch television, but many mothers feel compelled to apologize for it and see regulating children's consumption of television as part of their job.

The most theoretically sophisticated work on children's television is that of Robert Hodge and David Tripp, who analyze a single episode of an unexceptional 1978 cartoon called *Fangface*.[40] Their project benefits from the contributions of semiotics, structuralism, ideological analysis and post-structuralism; it is a good example of the kind of work currently identified by the term "cultural studies." Cartoons have only occasionally been subject to any kind of literary analysis—and never to the kind of painstaking attention Hodge and Tripp expend on *Fangface*. Instead, child psychologists and media sociologists have tended to use the methods of quantitative content analysis to "measure" the children's cartoon during a fixed block of hours during the broadcasting schedule. Content analysts count how many acts of violence occur, how many males and females there are, how many minority characters appear, how often villains speak with a foreign accent, and so on. The virtue of a structuralist/semiotic analysis is that it focuses on the combinations and structures of meaning. This level of understanding tends to be lost in content analysis, in which the meanings of discrete units of information in a television program are not related to the context in which they appear.

Hodge and Tripp argue that cartoons—widely considered one of the lowest forms of television—are surprisingly complex. Children are fascinated by them not because they have been turned into television zombies but because they are understandably engaged by the complex blend of aesthetic, narrative, visual, verbal, and ideological codes at work in them. Although cartoons are characterized by a great deal of repetition and redundancy, Hodge and Tripp argue that their subject matter, as well as their way of conveying it, is complicated stuff. Children use these cartoons to decipher the most important structures in their culture.

In their analysis, Hodge and Tripp demonstrate "the enormous complexity of what is often taken to be a very simple and straightforward message structure": *Fangface* negotiates the categories of nature and culture, the central myth of society in Lévi-Strauss's terms.[41] Hodge and Tripp grant that the meanings they find in *Fangface* may not be thought of as "residing" in the text at all, but are a product of their own interaction with the text. They allow for the options of chaotic or idiosyncratic meanings in the children's decoding of *Fangface*, as well as the possibility that children will ignore many elements in the cartoon simply because they are irrelevant to them.[42] Hodge and Tripp stop short of relativizing all "decoding" or arguing that "anything goes" in interpreting cartoons. Yet they emphasize the limited and partial nature of the responses that children (and adults) will make about television: how these will be created by the context—the classroom, the home, the laboratory—in which children are speaking; how gender, race and age differences within the group will influence the discussion.[43] Researchers such as Hodge and Tripp, Palmer, and Lemish share my position that children are not passive in their use of television, and their work enumerates the diversity of children's viewing as it is practiced in the living room. The actual behaviors of TV watching can be construed as more active than advice literature normally allows, and I would argue that children's television—even the most banal cartoons—adequately challenges children on a cognitive level.

Despite heavy reliance by mothers on the medium, the middle-class belief in the badness of television content is very firmly entrenched. Complaints and fears often involve its moral reductionism, its lack of reality, its racism and sexism, and its violence. One kind of complaint is based on the types of stories children's television presents, as Peggy Charren of Action for Children's Television put it: "It's all cartoon characters—no real people, no character development. The story is always a simple good-versus-evil, with no complexity and no human emotions: this battle, that crash, this one triumphs, that one fails, and it's all over. History, science, mystery, the arts—these are scarce because they haven't been presold to the 32.5 million children in America's TV households."[44] I agree with critics that the content of children's television warrants serious attention, and I focus on these issues in my discussion of commercials and toy-based programs—the most despised of children's TV genres. The charges directed at children's shows, however, are based on adult attention that is casual and erratic. When adults look more closely at children's television, they will seldom find that it delivers a single, unambiguous message to children. Instead, children's television, borrowing and adapting long-standing adult genres of U.S. popular culture, tends to reproduce familiar stereotypes, settings, and plots.

A more valid basis for faulting children's television is its store of words and images that are loaded with histories of oppression—based on class, gender, race and ethnicity. Children's television—like much of children's literature—places white boys at the center of the action. Children of color and girls of all races are dispersed to the sidelines as mascots, companions, victims. A child's identification with television is at best problematic when that child is Asian American or Black or Latino, or working-class or female—to name just a few examples. What needs to be untangled in the discussion of children's television are the aesthetic norms of high culture from the political critique of race, gender, and class stereotypes.

Hedonism and Emulation

As any mother can tell you, television is good at inspiring one form of activity: requesting toys, drinks, cereals, candy—and more television programs. Thus television provides mothers with a break but hardly a free lunch, as they must grant or fend off requests in the grocery store for cereals and candy as well as demands for toys. *Working Mother* magazine quoted one mother on the subject: "Commercials tend to put ideas in children's head of what they must have, and our lives become unbearable when we refuse." The popularity of video over broadcast television stems in part from the desire to shelter children from television commercials. A thornier complaint about commercial television, then, is that it makes kids want toys and foods. One dimension of this

complaint is the painful experience of working-class parents who must repeatedly deny their own children the goodies that surround them in stores and that
other children seem to have so many of. But the growth of children's consumer
culture has made some things cheap enough that poor parents can provide
them, at least occasionally: the two-dollar McDonald's Happy Meal with its
Barbie or Hot Wheels toy, the four-dollar Ninja Turtle.

The other dimension arises from parents who have the money to grant a
child's product request but feel a profound discomfort with the very intensity
of children's wanting. Children's consumption is now the focus of a protective,
paternalistic concern that previously focused on women and the working class.
Children's desires for consumer goods trigger fears of a decline in morals and
the emergence of a narcissistic personality type. Adults condemn children as
hedonistic and believe that television and liberal child-rearing practices have
produced children gravely lacking in self restraint. Parents are baffled or
revolted by their children's taste for mass-market goods, while they fail to recognize their own use of consumption for status purposes.

Young children have good reasons for liking television and wanting toys,
and mothers have good reasons for providing them. Children's interest in consumer culture involves much more than greed, hedonism, or passivity: it
involves the desire for community and for a utopian freedom from adult authority, seriousness, and goal directedness. As a mass culture, toys and television
give children a medium of communication—this is why I have described it as
a lingua franca. Consumer culture does, however, limit children's utopian
impulses. When engaged with consumer culture, children promote some identifications—those of a same-sex peer group—while demoting others. Peer
groups offer a limited basis for social alliances when considered apart from
other aspects of social identity—race, ethnicity, gender, class, region. But consumer culture changes through use, and it is inflected by children with surprising originality in everyday life. The basis of my approach is that toys and
television must be placed in the larger culture of childhood, the relations
between parents and children, the links between consumption and social identity, and the intersections of media reception and material consumption.

Notes

1. The line is Judy Holliday's from the film *Born Yesterday*. Charlotte Brunsdon
   quotes Holliday and discusses the low status of television viewing in her article
   "Television: Aesthetics and Audiences," in *Logics of Television: Essays in Cultural Criticism*, ed. Patricia Mellencamp (Bloomington: Indiana University
   Press, 1990), 62.
2. Daniel Miller, *Material Culture and Mass Consumption* (Oxford: Basil Blackwell, 1987), 215.

3. Richard Dyer, "Entertainment and Utopia," in *Movies and Methods*, vol. 2, ed. Bill Nichols (Berkeley and Los Angeles: University of California Press, 1985), 222.

4. Ibid., 224–225.

5. Fredric Jameson, *The Political Unconscious: Narrative as a Socially Symbolic Act* (Ithaca, N.Y.: Cornell University Press, 1981), 69. Dyer's argument is familiar from Hans Magnus Enzensberger and Herbert Marcuse; Dyer, "Entertainment," 229.

6. Some useful reviews of this research can be found in Ellen Carol Dubois et al., *Feminist Scholarship: Kindling in the Groves of Academe* (Urbana and Chicago, University of Illinois Press, 1987), 113–125; Stephanie Coontz, *The Social Origins of Private Life: A History of American Families* (London: Verso, 1988), 349–354; and Dolores Hayden, *Redesigning the American Dream: The Future of Housing, Work, and Family Life* (New York: Norton, 1984), 65–95.

7. Ruth Schwartz Cowan, *More Work for Mother* (New York: Basic Books, 1986).

8. Hayden, *Redesigning*, 55–56.

9. Arlie Hochschild, *The Second Shift* (New York: Avon, 1989), 2.

10. Hayden, *Redesigning*, 64–65.

11. Sarah Fenstermaker Berk, *The Gender Factory: The Apportionment of Work in American Households* (New York: Plenum Press, 1985), 197.

12. Cowan, *More Work*, 213; Arlie Hochschild's book *The Second Shift* paints a vivid picture of the fatigue created by what she calls the "leisure gap."

13. Hochschild, *Second Shift*, 3. The summary of the research is included in Hochschild's appendix, "Research on Who Does the Housework and Childcare," 277–279.

14. Ibid., 9.

15. Cited in ibid., 250.

16. Coontz, *Social Origins*, 337.

17. Phyllis Palmer, *Domesticity and Dirt: Housewives and Domestic Servants in the United States, 1920–1945* (Philadelphia: Temple University Press, 1989), 13.

18. Hochschild, *Second Shift*, 246.

19. Ibid., 232.

20. Cited in Nona Glazer-Malbin, "Housework," *Signs* 1, no. 4 (1976): 913.

21. Bert Leiman, associate director of children's research, Leo Burnett Co., interview with author, Chicago, August 1989.

22. Ann Oakley, *Woman's Work: The Housewife, Past and Present* (New York: Vintage Books, 1974), 210.

23. Christina Hardyment, *Dream Babies: Three Centuries of Good Advice on Child Care* (New York: Harper & Row, 1983), 242.

24. Ibid., 226.

25. Roland Marchand, *Advertising the American Dream: Making Way for Modernity, 1920–1940* (Berkeley and Los Angeles: University of California Press, 1985), 230.

26. Ibid., 228–232.

27. Ibid., 232.

28. Nancy Chodorow, *The Reproduction of Mothering: Psychoanalysis and the Sociology of Gender* (Berkeley and Los Angeles: University of California Press, 1978), 232.

29. Marchand, *Advertising*, 232.

30. See Lynn Spigel, "Television and the Family Circle: The Popular Reception of a New Medium," in Mellencamp, *Logics of Television*.
31. Philip Simpson, ed., *Parents Talking Television* (London: Comedia, 1987), 65.
32. Marie Winn, *The Plug-in Drug* (New York: Viking Press, 1977). Neil Postman, *The Disappearance of Childhood* (New York: Delacorte Press, 1982).
33. For an extensive critique of developmental psychology, see Julian Henriques et al., *Changing the Subject: Psychology, Social Regulation, and Subjectivity* (London: Methuen, 1984).
34. Palmer, *Lively Audience*, 135.
35. Quoted in Julius and Zelda Segal, "The Two Sides of Television," *Parents*, March 1990, 186.
36. Wilbur Schramm, Jack Lyle, and Edwin Parker, *Television in the Lives of Our Children* (Palo Alto, Calif.: Stanford University Press, 1961); I have relied on the summary of this research in Shearon Lowery and Melvin L. De Fleur, *Milestones in Mass Communication Research* (New York and London: Longman, 1983), 267–295.
37. Much of this work is summarized in Jennings Bryant and Daniel R. Anderson, eds., *Children's Understanding of Television: Research on Attention and Comprehension* (New York: Academic Press, 1983).
38. Palmer, *Lively Audience*. Television meanings as inextricable from family interactions and the domestic space has been a focus of attention in research by David Morley, James Lull, Jan-Uwe Rogge, and Hermann Bausinger.
39. Dafna Lemish, "Viewers in Diapers: The Early Development of Television Viewing," in *Natural Audiences: Qualitative Research of Media Uses and Effects*, ed. Thomas Lindlof (Norwood, N.J.: Ablex, 1987), 33–57. See also Paul Messaris, "Mothers' Comments to Their Children about the Relationship between Television and Reality," in Lindlof, *Natural Audiences*, 95–108.
40. *Fangface* was an animated series about the adventures of the werewolf Sherman Fangsworth and his teenage companions Kim, Biff, and Pugsie. Generically, the series was based primarily on a comedy-mystery type of story (sometimes called the "Let's get out of here" adventure formula) found in many examples of cartoons, from *Scooby Doo* (1969–1980) to *Slimer and the Real Ghostbusters* (1986–).
41. Robert Hodge and David Tripp, *Children and Television: A Semiotic Approach* (Stanford, Calif.: Stanford University Press, 1986), 26.
42. Ibid., 71.
43. David Morley makes this point, which has been increasingly taken up by cultural studies, in *Family Television: Cultural Power and Domestic Leisure* (London: Comedia, 1986), 30.
44. Peggy Charren quoted in Margaret B. Carlson, "Babes in Toyland," *American Film*, January–February 1986, 56.
45. T. J. Jackson Lears, "From Salvation to Self-realization: Advertising and the Therapeutic Roots of Consumer Culture, 1880–1930," in *The Culture of Consumption*, ed. Richard Wightman Fox and T. J. Jackson Lears (New York: Pantheon, 1983), 3.
46. Miller, *Material Culture*, 166.
47. Daniel Horowitz, *The Morality of Spending: Attitudes toward the Consumer Society in America, 1875–1940* (Baltimore: Johns Hopkins University Press, 1985), 166.

48. Daniel Miller comments dryly that "the argument that there is a thing called cap-italist society which renders its population entirely pathological and dehuman-ized, with the exception of certain theorists who, although inevitably living their private lives in accordance with the tenets of this delusion, are able in their abstracted social theory to rise above, criticize and provide the only alternative model for society, is somewhat suspicious." (*Material Culture*, 167).

49. For theoretical discussions of Marx's concept of use value that adapt it to contemporary consumer culture see Susan Willis, *A Primer for Daily Life* (London: Routledge, 1991); Wolfgang Haug, *Critique of Commodity Aesthetics* (Minneapolis: University of Minnesota Press, 1986); Jean Baudrillard, *The Mirror of Production* (St. Louis: Telos Press, 1975) and *For a Critique of the Political Economy of the Sign* (St. Louis: Telos Press, 1981).

50. A fascinating pedagogical exercise that demonstrates the inescapability of the significance of clothing has been developed by Professor Chuck Kleinhans at Northwestern University, Evanston, Illinois, who devotes one day of his class to photographing students' attire, pronouncing that each student will be assumed to be making a fashion statement based on what he or she is wearing that day.

51. The bread-baking phenomenon was sufficiently widespread to be attacked by marketers who now offer a range of gadgetry (flour mills, convection ovens, dough risers) and supplies (whole grains, health foods) to aid in the process.

52. Thorstein Veblen, *The Theory of the Leisure Class: An Economic Study of Institutions* (1899; reprint, New York: Modern Library, 1934), 101.

53. Stuart Ewen, *All Consuming Images: The Politics of Style in Contemporary Culture* (New York: Basic Books, 1988), 62; the concept of "consumption com-munities" is Daniel Boorstin's.

54. Miller, *Material Culture*, 206.

55. Mary Douglas, "Goods as a System of Communication," in *In the Active Voice* (London: Routledge & Kegan Paul, 1988), 24.

56. Ibid., 24.

57. Sut Jhally, *The Codes of Advertising: Fetishism and the Political Economy of Meaning in the Consumer Society* (New York: St. Martin's Press, 1987), 50.

58. Ibid., 51.

59. Colin Campbell, *The Romantic Ethic and the Spirit of Modern Consumerism* (Oxford: Basil Blackwell, 1987), 203.

60. Daniel Miller points out that Veblen's analysis focused on a newly emerging social group in the late nineteenth century, the nouveaux riches, and the strate-gies of conspicuous consumption and conspicuous leisure that they adopted in imitation of those with "old money," the aristocratic class.

61. Veblen, *Leisure Class*, 103.

62. Grant McCracken, *Culture and Consumption: New Approaches to the Sym-bolic Character of Consumer Goods and Activities* (Bloomington: Indiana Uni-versity Press, 1988), xiv. Georg Simmel, "Fashion," in *On Individuality and Social Forms: Selected Writings*, ed. Donald N. Levine (Chicago: University of Chicago Press, 1971), 302.

63. N. McKendrick, "Commercialization and the Economy," in N. McKendrick, J. Brewer, and J. Plumb, *The Birth of a Consumer Society: The Commercializa-tion of Eighteenth-Century England* (Bloomington: Indiana University Press, 1982), 20.

64. Pierre Bourdieu, *Distinction: A Social Critique of the Judgment of Taste*, trans. Richard Nice (Cambridge: Harvard University Press, 1984), 6.
65. Ibid., 56, 57.
66. Michele Lamont and Annette Lareau, "Cultural Capital: Allusions and Glissandos in Recent Theoretical Developments," *Sociological Theory* 6 (1988): 163.
67. Ibid., 163.

PART VIII

Gender Socialization

Human beings are differentiated into two biological categories, male and female. They play complementary parts in sexual reproduction. Most societies have created ways to add on to this biological difference behavioral expectations *that have no connection to biology, but that members of the society believe are biologically appropriate.* Certain types of work have been considered men's work and others women's work. For example, not many women are automobile mechanics; not many men are elementary school teachers. Men have more leeway than women in using curse words. Women are more likely than men to receive disapproval for openly showing strong anger, while men are more likely to receive disapproval for crying in public. These are but a few quick illustrations of behaviors that are socially defined as masculine (appropriate for a male) or feminine (appropriate for a female).

Occupation, language use, style of emotional expression, and many other aspects of behavior have long been socially defined in these ways. Sociologists and psychologists long referred to them as sex roles. However, beginning in the 1970s sociologists, largely influenced by the women's movement, focused on the fact that since these expected behaviors had nothing to do with sexual biology but were the products of social construction, it was misleading to refer to them as sex roles. Further, using this term contributed also to misleading people into believing that these behaviors and expectations were somehow vaguely based on biology and therefore unchangeable. To emphasize the distinction between what is biologically sexual and what is socially added on (and therefore potentially changeable) sociologists now use the term *gender roles* to refer to what is socially expected. In the last forty years there have been many dramatic changes in gender roles. Consider that forty years ago women were widely believed not fit for high political office. At this writing, 10 out of the 100 United States Senators are women, and women have been state governors, mayors, and held many other important political offices. In other countries, women have held even higher offices. Gender roles changed to make this kind of work and such high statuses available to women. Many societies reinterpreted gender and recognized that it was not dictated by biological sex.

Sociologists now recognize that gender is socially constructed. Ideas, beliefs, values, and emotions about gender are promulgated in a variety of institutions— through images in movies and television, practices and preachings in churches, synagogues, and mosques, practices and teachings in school classrooms and playgrounds. For any individual child, gender begins to be constructed in the family. Sociologist Scott Coltrane reviews the major theories that seek to understand the part parents play in children's development. He then discusses many different kinds of studies that illuminate parental practices in shaping their children's gender.

As a result of a review of various studies, psychologist David Lisak develops a thoughtful but provocative argument that gender socialization of males is a major factor in the perpetration of sexual abuse. The path is not a direct one, and he recognizes that not all males are gender socialized in the same way. But he identifies a socialization pattern that he considers widespread and that he calls "warrior masculinity" which is based on denial of fear and any form of vulnerability. This leads, in turn, to emotional deficits, including, importantly, a reduced ability to have empathy for the feelings of others. His chapter may not be the last word on this subject, but his discussion of the emotional socialization of males rings true as a common pattern, if not the only one. Chapter 5 in Part III also deals with gender socialization.

15

Engendering Children*

Scott Coltrane

The vast majority of American parents in the 1950s earnestly believed that the world was naturally, inevitably, and beneficially divided into two mutually exclusive categories—male and female. Because the notion of complementary sex difference was so taken for granted, most parents did not stop to question that there might be negative impacts associated with turning their sons into manly men and their daughters into girlish women. This was the way things were supposed to be.

Because they loved their children and wanted them to fit in, parents dressed their boys in pants and their girls in dresses. They gave their boys trucks and balls to play with and gave their daughters dolls and tea sets. If, as often happened, a boy played with dolls, he could be chastised and called a "sissy" or, alternately, steered away from such activities under some pretense. Pretty soon, he would get the message. If a girl wanted to wear pants, climb trees, and play ball, she was often tolerated—up to a point. It was OK to be a tomboy as long as she still dressed up in her fancy dress for church on Sunday. But if she tried to carry such activities beyond her childhood years and into her teens, she was likely to get a good talking to. The advice she got was often about the difficulties of getting a boy to notice her unless she made herself pretty and started acting "like a lady."

But, you might protest, that was many decades ago, and we are way past the days of telling girls to act dumb so that boys will feel smart. The women's movement changed all that, . . . didn't it? In this chapter, I will begin to address that question by exploring how children are raised today. Does gender just naturally develop in children, or do they acquire it in interaction with their parents? It will probably come as no surprise that parents' actions make a big difference, and you already know that gender is socially constructed. But you might be surprised to learn that even people who believe strongly that women and men are equal often end up paying more attention to their sons than to their daughters. For all their good intentions, parents are still part of the larger culture, and they often unwittingly pass on ideas about gender inequality via subtle and indirect actions. Children develop ideas about gender through observation and imitation, by doing the little things children do in their daily lives, and by noticing, parents' and others' reactions to them. In this chapter, I explore how these processes work and ask what might happen if we changed the way we raised children.

Images of Childhood Gender Difference

Differences between boys and girls are assumed to be natural, but most of these differences must be taught. Later in the chapter, I review studies that describe what parents are doing today to teach children about gender. First, however, I focus on some old messages about gender from the popular culture and outline psychological and sociological theories of gender acquisition.

Fairy tales are stories that are told to young people for their enjoyment and education. All cultures have different versions of such stories, and similar tales have appeared in different countries of Europe, Asia, and North America dating back several centuries. Most fairy tales work with polarities of good and bad, beautiful and ugly, and tell of the adventures of a hero or heroine who overcomes supernatural forces to reach a lofty goal. In the modern, sanitized versions of such tales (most produced by Walt Disney Studios), the hero also wins the girl and they live happily ever after. Most children know about *Cinderella, Snow White, Beauty and the Beast, the Little Mermaid,* and so on through animated movies, whereas tales such as *Jack and the Beanstalk, Little Red Riding Hood,* and *The Three Little Pigs* are more often read aloud to children or recited from memory as in past times. These morality tales teach about good and evil, but they also carry implicit messages about gender. By paying attention to who gets to be the hero and who needs rescuing, we can see that men and women are rarely interchangeable in such tales and that the boys generally get the good parts. Although these tales are not presented as true, children take them much more literally than do adults, primarily because young children are less able to distinguish between what is real and what is fantasy.

Nursery rhymes are an even older form of oral tradition containing implicit messages about gender. These short poems are recited or sung to entertain young children (in repeated, ritual fashion). They often contain a single verse, sometimes more, and are usually anonymous. Some of the earliest published nursery rhymes in the English language appeared in a collection called *Mother Goose's*

Melody in 1760. Many other versions of Mother Goose have appeared since then in Europe and America. Often, the original intent or specific social meaning of the rhyme have been lost, but they live on through repetition. Like fairy tales, however, they provide a template for seeing and thinking about gender.

The World According to Mother Goose

<u>Boys</u>

What are little boys made of, made of?
What are little boys made of?
Frogs and snails
And puppy-dog tails,
That's what little boys are made of.

Little Jack Horner
Sat in the corner;
Eating a Christmas Pie;
He put in his thumb;
And pulled out a plum;
And said, What a good boy am I!

Georgie Porgie, pudding and pie;
Kissed the girls and made them cry;
When the boys came out to play;
Georgie Porgie ran away.

Ding, dong, bell;
Pussy's in the well.
Who put her in?
Little Johnny Green.
Who pulled her out?
Little Tommy Stout.
What a naughty boy was that
To try to drown poor pussy cat;
Who never did him any harm;
And killed the mice in his father's barn.

When I was a little boy
My mama kept me in;
Now I am a great big boy
I'm fit to serve the king;

<u>Girls</u>

What are little girls made of, made of?
What are little girls made of?
Sugar and spice
And all things nice,
That's what little girls are made of.

Little Miss Muffet
Sat on a tuffet,
Eating her curds and whey;
There came a big spider,
Who sat down beside her
And frightened Miss Muffet away.

There was a little girl,
and she had a little curl,
Right in the middle of her forehead;
When she was good,
she was very, very good,
But when she was bad she was horrid.

Mary, Mary, quite contrary,
How does your garden grow?
With silver bells and cockle shells,
And pretty maids all in a row.

Little Polly Flinders
Sat among the cinders,
Warming her pretty little toes;
Her mother came and caught her
And spanked her little daughter
For spoiling her nice new clothes.

Polly, Dolly, Kate, and Molly,
All are filled with pride and folly.
Polly tattles, Dolly wriggles,
Katy rattles, Molly giggles;

I can handle a musket;
And I can smoke a bonny girl
And I can kiss a bonny girl
At twelve o'clock at night.

Whoever knew such constant rattling,
Wriggling, giggling, noise, and tattling.

<u>Men</u>
Peter, Peter, pumpkin eater;
Had a wife and couldn't keep her;
He put her in a pumpkin shell
And there he kept her very well.

<u>Women</u>
There was an old woman
who lived in a shoe,
She had so many children
she didn't know what to do;
She gave them some broth
without any bread;
She whipped them all soundly
and put them to bed.

Excerpted from *The Real Mother Goose*, 1916, pp. 13, 20, 26, 32, 39, 84, 90, 98, 108.

What messages do children get about gender from these ritualized rhymes? Girls are sweet, cute, and prone to wriggle, giggle, and tattle. They need to remember to keep their clothes clean, are easily frightened, and although generally good, can be very bad. Boys, on the other hand, are rough, tough, and mischievous. They are proud of themselves, take risks, want to be grown up, and like to kiss girls (sometimes against their will). As for grown men, besides smoking a pipe, handling a musket, and serving the king, like Peter, they need to keep their wives, even if they have to lock them up in a pumpkin to do it. Mothers, if the old woman in the shoe is any guide, are too busy worrying about their many children to do much else.

Like the characters in fairy tales (or even those in modern cartoons, movies, and comic books), these nursery rhyme personalities are more stereotyped by gender than most real people. But that is intentional. These stories teach young people the cultural standards for masculinity and femininity. Many are cautionary tales about what happens when one violates those cultural standards. Most portray conventional heterosexual relations, but there are a few exceptions. Consider, for example, the following *Mother Goose* rhyme about two young men:

> *Robin and Richard were two pretty men,*
> *They lay in bed till the clock struck ten;*
> *Then up starts Robin and looks at the sky,*
> *"Oh, brother Richard, the sun's very high!*
> *You go before, with the bottle and bag,*
> *And I will come after on little Jack Nag."*

Excerpted from *The Real Mother Goose*, 1916, p. 20.

Although these "brothers" get to lounge in bed together until midmorning, there is a cautionary element to their gay tale. After they realize that it is late, they devise a plan to depart separately—presumably so they will not be seen together and identified as lovers. This example reminds us that popular culture, like real life, does not necessarily conform to conventional standards for gender relations, sexuality, or other social practices. Literature, songs, and theater, from Shakespeare and Mother Goose to modern rock music and performance art, frequently expose and exploit the contradictions between social norms and human lives. For ironic art forms to work, however, the audience needs to be aware of the conventional taken-for-granted social expectations. Instilling conventional expectations in boys and girls is what gender socialization is all about.

Theories of Gender Socialization

Social scientists have long been concerned with how children grow and develop and how they become fully functioning adult members of society. This process of socialization happens in many ways and in many different contexts, but it is generally assumed that the most important processes begin in the family. Children also develop and learn about life through other means, but most theories assume that parents, or other regular adult caregivers, are the major socializing agents for developing children. This reflects the idea that although people continue to change and learn throughout life, it is during childhood that they acquire enduring personality characteristics, interpersonal skills, and social values (Maccoby, 1992).

In the early part of the century, little attention was spent on documenting how and why children developed specific gender-linked traits, but during the 1950s and 1960s, social scientists began to pay more attention to the role of parents in shaping childhood gender (Maccoby, 1992). As noted in the previous chapter, researchers were primarily interested in figuring out how parents could make sure that boys would turn out masculine and girls feminine. In other words, the social theories and psychological studies of the day were concerned with helping children occupy their "proper" or "natural" place in the family and in society. These theories and studies about gender, like all forms of knowledge, were products of cultural understandings prevalent at the time. Not surprisingly, the 1950s suburban ideal of separate spheres shaped how researchers, doctors, social workers, religious leaders, and parents thought about children's needs. In general, there was a consensus among the experts that boys and girls should be treated differently, that this differential treatment was normal, and that it would benefit the entire society.

Since the 1970s, a new set of ideas about gender have entered into popular and scientific debates about how children should be raised. As a result of social movements focusing on equal rights for minorities and women, people began to question how child-rearing techniques might promote prejudice and perpetuate inequality. The new ideas about gender that emerged focused on how rigid and polarized stereotypes prohibited boys and girls from developing their full human potential. This was a switch from the earlier idea that boys needed manly role models and girls needed stay-at-home moms, or else they would be misfits in society. It also reflects a shift toward valuing individualism and emotional expression in children as well as in adults. The movement toward more gender-neutral child rearing continued to gain popularity throughout the 1980s and 1990s, although some conservative countermovements advocated the continuation of corporal punishment and sex segregation in schools.

Because the old ideal of separate spheres has not disappeared, debates about the proper way to raise children continue to be heard within individual families, in churches, and in political campaigns. Hoping to gain support for the political agendas they support, some social scientists focus on a "decline in family values" to argue that boys and girls should be raised differently and that only married heterosexual couples should raise children. The underlying assumption of such arguments is that boys and girls need different things, that women are better at raising children than are men, that women need husbands, and that all children need to be raised by their biological parents. These separate spheres arguments are predicated on the false assumption that anatomical sex is the same thing as gender (e.g., Blankenhorn, 1995; Popenoe, 1996; but compare with Stacey, 1996).

In contrast, a general consensus has developed among social scientists that sex and gender are not the same thing and that both men and women are capable of performing almost any task. Sexual identity and the choice of sex partners may be somewhat shaped by biological factors, but they are also influenced by the cultural categories available for describing, experiencing, and understanding such things. Gender, on the other hand, is almost wholly a social and cultural creation and is therefore subject to change. The most recent research on sex and gender suggests that the relationship between the two is far more complicated and malleable than was previously assumed by more biologically based models of human behavior (for reviews, see Bleier, 1984; Butler, 1990; Epstein, 1988).

Despite any biological predispositions that males and females might have, and despite the religious convictions or political beliefs that people hold, everyone is subject to the larger cultural and economic shifts that have been occurring throughout this century. The changes that have moved U.S. society toward more equality between men and women have also moved us toward more gender-neutral styles of child rearing. Experts continue to argue about whether true shared parenting is possible, and how much difference it would make if parents began to treat sons and daughters similarly, but most agree that families are slowly moving in that direction (Coltrane, 1996; Ehrensaft, 1987; Segal, 1990).

Child Socialization

To evaluate conflicting arguments about gender acquisition in the family, one needs to understand how parents and others influence their children's development. Older individualized models of childhood socialization provided by Freud, Piaget, and their followers from the earlier part of the 20th century were both social and biological, and although they differed from each other, most included the basic idea that individual children passed through a set of predetermined stages of increasing competence and self-regulation. More social theories, such as those of Durkheim and Mead, focused on how the structure and functioning of society were maintained because children eventually internalized common norms governing thought, emotion, and action. Whether socialization theories were focused on the individual or on the social structural level of analysis, they described how young people gradually become competent members of a specific culture (see Bem, 1993; Goodman, 1985; Peterson & Rollins, 1987).

Virtually all theories of socialization have agreed that the major experiences shaping children's identity occur within families, although most recognize that children are also socialized by schools, churches, the media, peer groups, and other social institutions. As a microcosm of society, families locate children within a social structure and provide a first exposure to culture. The simple fact of being born into a family provides a particular set of socialization experiences for children. These experiences include where they live, what they eat, whom they see, what they wear, how they talk, what type of medical care they get, what type of work they do, and a host of other small and large things. These experiences are important because to a large extent, they determine children's living conditions and life chances as they grow up. Sociologists summarize these types of influences on socialization by talking about the social class, ethnicity, or composition of the families into which children are born (Collins & Coltrane, 1995; Peterson & Rollins, 1987).

Families are also important because they provide the children's first exposure to interaction with other humans. Compared with other animals, all humans are born premature, insofar as they are born with awkwardly functioning bodies and only partly developed brains. Consequently, human newborns need significant amounts of care and attention to survive. Many other animals have the ability to learn how to live in the world in a matter of days or months, but human babies need to grow and develop for many years before they can be self-sufficient and assume their place in society. Although different cultures expect children to do different things at different ages, human children cannot survive without the care of their parents or other adults for the first few years of their lives. Children's extreme dependence on others makes the socialization that occurs in families particularly salient and is one of the major reasons that adult-child relationships remain emotionally charged well into adult life (Maccoby, 1992).

Not all families look alike, of course, and most societies have had families that are larger and less isolated than the American version (mostly contained in smaller and more collective dwellings). This means that children have typically grown up interacting with more people and observing more adults than contemporary American children do. Regardless of how living arrangements differ, however, babies have usually developed the capacity to roll over, sit up, crawl, walk, and run in family settings. Similarly, children learn how to recognize faces, make gestures, and eventually to talk by interacting with family members and other people in the immediate household. Not only do most developmental processes unfold in such contexts, but children also first learn the meaning of authority and gain awareness of what is acceptable and unacceptable behavior within the family and in other daily caregiving situations. As children grow, the importance of the family decreases somewhat, and the importance of the peer group, schools, and other socializing agents increases. Most researchers agree, however, that the family (or more precisely the household in which the children spend the most time) remains the primary socializing agent for children at least until the teenage years (Maccoby, 1992; Peterson & Rollins, 1987).

Socialization can be seen as a holistic process of turning children into "cultural natives" (Bem, 1993, p. 139). Children (and adults) end up feeling as if they belong in their culture because their daily lives are organized in similar ways and because they use the same frameworks for seeing the world. Becoming a cultural native is a subtle process that happens with little effort. As individuals grow and develop and participate in similar types of social rituals, they adopt culturally approved cognitive lenses and emotional capacities that allow them to "see" and "feel" the same social reality (see also Berger, 1963; Geertz, 1973; Shweder & LeVine, 1984).

Children are not socialized primarily through direct and explicit instruction. Rather, ways of understanding and thinking are transmitted in a continuing and unconscious way, so that preferred cultural understandings are the only ones that seem possible. The culture does not get transferred directly into the heads of passive children as if they were empty vessels waiting to be filled with knowledge. Instead, they learn culturally appropriate ways of thinking and being as they follow routine rituals and respond to the everyday demands of the world in which they live. Because they are active, pattern-seeking beings, children both create and assimilate the culture around them as they grow and develop. They do not learn how to be cultural natives all at once but gradually decipher the meanings embedded in social practices a little at a time, eventually establishing a set of behaviors and an identity that allow them to fit into their social surroundings (Bem, 1993).

Socialization is thus a delicate interplay between how daily life is structured, how people perceive it, and how they react to their circumstances. The same can be said for gender socialization. Because everyday practices are based, to a large extent, on a gendered division of labor and on culturally accepted notions of appropriate gender behavior, children assimilate and shape the meaning of gender as they go through normal steps in their development. What they do, how they feel about themselves, and what they become are influenced in important ways by the organization of gender in the family and in the larger society.

Separating Boys and Girls

There is not room in this chapter to cover all that researchers know about how baby boys are turned into men and baby girls into women (for more complete reviews, see Bem, 1993; Huston, 1983). Nevertheless, a few of the most influential ideas about how children acquire gender deserve attention. The most important insight from research on gender socialization is that because boys and girls are treated differently and put into different learning environments, they develop different needs, wants, desires, skills, and temperaments; in short, they become different types of people—men and women—who hardly question why they are different or how they ended up that way.

Although the specific social and psychological processes through which gender socialization occurs are the subject of much debate, the basic underlying model is that of the self-fulfilling prophecy (Bem, 1993; Merton, 1948; Rosenthal & Jacobson, 1968). Because people think boys and girls are supposed to be different, they treat them differently and give them different opportunities for development. This differential treatment promotes certain behaviors and self-images that recreate the preconceived cultural stereotypes about gender. The process repeats itself over and over in an unending spiral across the generations, so that although gender stereotypes are being constantly re-created and modified, they seem natural and impervious to change.

The self-fulfilling prophecy is more complicated than this simple summary suggests, but the basic idea remains the same: Treat boys and girls differently, and they become different. This fits nicely with the social constructionist idea of doing gender introduced earlier in this book. It is not just that boys and girls are naturally and fundamentally different in some unchanging way. Rather, to be considered competent members of society, they must learn how to fit in as appropriately gendered individuals. This is not an optional process. Because gender is so important to the adults in our society, children are called on to conform to the gender standards currently in force. For children to develop identities, they must also develop gender identities, and they must work to make their actions and thoughts conform to what the people around them expect. Children literally "claim" gender identities as they interact with adults and other children (Cahill, 1986; Thorne, 1993). This concept of doing gender, which is something that both children and adults are required to do, helps us see that gender is not something innate but rather something that must continually be re-created (West & Fenstermaker, 1993; West & Zimmerman, 1987).

The doing gender concept alerts us to the idea that gender is not a single fixed thing. There are now, and have always been, multiple forms of masculinity and multiple forms of femininity (Connell, 1995; Lorber, 1994). What it means to be a man will be different in various types of families, depending on the family members' needs, desires, and experiences. Masculinity in a two-parent house-hold with a Marine drill sergeant father will look different from masculinity in a fundamentalist minister's home, a gay couple's home, or a single mother's home. It will look different in an inner-city African American household from what it is in an affluent African American household in the suburbs. Masculin-ity will not mean the same thing in a Mexican immigrant family as it does in a fifth-generation middle-class Chicano family. The dominant popular cultural ideal of a "real" man, whether from action movies or fairy tales, will undoubt-edly be at odds with actual men's experiences. As a consequence, boys (and men) end up constructing a private and personal manhood from their own expe-riences and the images, ideals, and expectations of their social surroundings.

To describe gender as socially constructed in this way does not mean that most people believe they have choices about it, or even that they give it much thought at all. We rarely question how our identities are tied up with the mean-ing of gender, and most of us are unaware of how gender shapes our expecta-tions for children. But in countless little ways, beginning before babies are even born, we make gender so important that it is impossible for children to ignore. I recently asked a newly pregnant woman I had just met if she was going to have her doctor perform a test (amniocentesis) to determine the sex of her baby. She replied that she always thought she would want to be surprised at the birth, but for practical reasons, she was going to have the test done. I asked what was practical about it, and she said, "If I know the sex, then I can get all the right kinds of clothes and work on setting up the nursery, and all of that." She reasoned that she could not get started acquiring physical things for the baby until she knew the baby's sex. To her, girl babies had to be dressed in pink frilly outfits right from the start, and everything from her crib, to her toys, to the paint on the wall had to be for a girl. She explained that this would save money and time because people could give the "right" baby gifts, she could buy the "right" items, and she would not be bothered with returning the "wrong" stuff.

Although the needs of newborn girls and newborn boys are identical, this mother-to-be took for granted that they *must* be treated differently. Her belief in gender difference was so central to her thinking that she was willing to undergo a painful medical procedure—one that significantly increases the chances of a miscarriage—all for decorating purposes!

Our gender prescriptions (what boys should do and what girls should do) and our gender proscriptions (what boys shouldn't do and what girls shouldn't do) become so habitual that we rarely concern ourselves with them. So, although doing gender is a constant and continuing process, it does not seem that way. Our sense of gender is so built in to our everyday activities that it takes on a life of its own. In a basic sense, it becomes a lens through which we see the world. This gender lens gets transmitted to children without parents even noticing.

Although I am focusing on babies and young children in this chapter, socialization is not limited to childhood. Socialization never stops because adults continue to be faced with social pressures to adopt appropriate behaviors and thoughts. Still, the dependence of children on adults and their need to develop a sense of self in interaction with others make them especially likely to internalize messages about gender from the larger culture. How does this internalization come about?

In the following discussion, I focus on two social psychological theories that attempt to explain how gender understandings structure feeling and thinking: one psychoanalytic and one cognitive. These two explanations focus attention on different aspects of the process of acquiring gender lenses and maintaining gender differences. They show how gender can be simultaneously socially constructed and deeply embedded in personalities. The theories also remind us that the internalized psychic structures that make gender seem so fixed can change as the social, economic, and family conditions that shape them undergo their own transformations.

Psychoanalytic Gender Theory

In the late 1800s and early 1900s, Dr. Sigmund Freud treated his patients' physical and emotional ailments through a radical new talking therapy called psychoanalysis, which used free association and the interpretation of patients' dreams. According to Freud, it was necessary to look below the surface of normal everyday talk and activity to uncover unconscious mental processes. For example, most people have heard the term *Freudian slip*, referring to times when persons embarrass themselves by mistakenly using the wrong word (usually one with a sexual meaning). For instance, a person might be making small talk, trying to ask whether the attractive waiter or waitress was making much money in tips that evening, but instead blurt out, "How are your *lips* tonight?"

According to psychoanalytic theory, the lips slip reveals a desire that the conscious mind did not want to reveal or maybe did not even realize it had. Freud focused on these sorts of hidden thoughts, emotions, and sexual urges that people usually try to keep submerged below the surface of consciousness. According to Freud, we must understand these deep psychological workings if we want to understand how children develop into adults with a normal sexual identity.

Many of Freud's (1905/1938, 1924) theories about child development and the unconscious originated during the prudish Victorian era when sex was a taboo subject. His early ideas focus on the importance of repressed sexual feelings in the developing child. According to Freud, every child has unconscious emotional needs and erotic feelings that emerge in relation to the mother and develop in interaction with others. Because many of these thoughts and feelings threaten to overwhelm the child, Freud said that the child represses them into the unconscious during normal stages of development. Infant sexuality, in Freud's terms, was *polymorphously perverse*, meaning that it took many forms, was not focused on one body part, and was not necessarily directed toward a heterosexual partner. The theory did not assume that just because a boy infant has a penis, he would automatically develop a male sexual identity and be sexually attracted to females. According to Freud, such things are formed in the interplay of sexual attractions between child and mother and go through various stages or complexes that must be successfully resolved. In the oral stage, for example, the child's sexual urges are focused on the act of sucking, whereas in the anal stage, they are focused on the withholding and expelling of feces. During the phallic stage, the normal child is supposed to recognize genital differences and develop feelings of attraction toward the mother (or father). In the so-called Oedipus complex, boys renounce their erotic love for the mother because they come to fear the father's jealousy. According to Freud, this process helps boys develop a superego (a sort of moral conscience) and allows them to transfer their sexual urges toward adult women. Freud had much more trouble explaining the psychosexual development of girls, who were supposed to transfer their early sexual urges toward the mother to the father and men.

Many of the specifics of Freud's developmental framework have been challenged and discredited through the years. For example, both psychoanalysts and feminists have pointed out not only that things such as "penis envy" and the "castration complex" are relatively rare among girls but that Freud's whole analytic scheme treated boys and men as normal and girls and women as deficient. Nevertheless, Freud's basic insights about the unconscious mind and sexual or erotic impulses have become part of our cultural stock of knowledge, and many psychologists and even feminist theorists have used them to try to understand the psychology of sex and gender (Chodorow, 1978; Erikson, 1950; Mitchell, 1974).

Psychoanalytic ideas are now so integrated into modern ways of thinking that many people do not even realize that Freud popularized them. For example, terms such as *unconscious, subconscious, repressed, neurotic, hysterical, id, ego, superego*, and *Oedipus complex* are commonly used throughout the Western world. Although it was not necessarily true during Freud's day, the medical profession now even acknowledges that the mind can cause a range of emotional and physical symptoms—called psychosomatic illnesses. In addition, modern versions of talking therapies that originated with psychoanalysis are now common treatments for many family problems and psychological disorders. Freud's ideas are not necessarily popular with psychologists who work in university settings today, however; most research-oriented psychologists reject psychoanalysis in favor of more rational models of human behavior and scientific experiments that isolate specific causal variables.

Freud's ideas are too complex and debates about them too numerous to cover in detail here, but one offshoot of Freudian theory can help us think about how modern children learn about gender. Newer versions of psychoanalytic theory are especially helpful in figuring out why gender identity seems so fixed and stable. Freud said that children had innate sexual urges and that they learned to direct these urges toward appropriate others in the context of family interactions. Freud's theories assumed that the important interactions happened early in the child's life, that these early childhood experiences shaped the gender identity of the child, and that they set the emotional tone and shaped the psychological dilemmas faced after the child becomes an adult. Most of this happens at an unconscious level.

According to Freud, infants do not have a firm sense of individual self. At first, their sense of self is merged with the mother, and only later do they develop an autonomous self by separating from her. Because infants are usually cared for by the mother, she is symbolically and unconsciously incorporated into both boys' and girls' psyches. Because she provides suckling and care, the mother is also the first erotic love object for children of both sexes. For the child to mature and develop in sexually appropriate ways, Freud speculated that this early erotic attachment to the mother must be broken and directed outward.

Nancy Chodorow (1976, 1978, 1985) extended this part of Freudian theory, as did some other women psychoanalysts (e.g., Deutsch, 1944; Horney, 1967) and feminist theorists (Dinnerstein, 1976; Johnson, 1988; Mitchell, 1974), by placing more emphasis on early infancy and correcting for Freud's relative neglect of girls' psychological development. According to Chodorow, because girls are the same sex as their mothers, they do not need to sever the deep primary attachment to mothers in the same way that boys do. Girls are given more permission to be close and affectionate with mothers for a much longer time than are boys, and because their identity is not dependent on being different from them, they stay much closer to mothers both physically and emotionally. This means that girls can form a self without severely separating from mothers and from the internalized unconscious image of mothers that develops within them. Consequently, girls tend to develop a personality that allows them to intuitively experience the world in connection with others. According to Chodorow, girls thus retain more of the sense of merging with the world that all infants experience in the original love relationship with mothers. The "feminine" personality that subsequently develops in girls tends to direct their attention toward other people and instills in young women the desire and emotional capacities to mother in later life.

Boys, on the other hand, end up with "masculine" personalities that are more separated and independent than those of girls. This is because they are also raised by mothers but must reject them in the normal course of establishing a sense of self. Because boy babies realize that they are not like their mothers, and because they are treated differently by mothers, they establish an identity based on being different from mothers. According to the theory, because boys have internalized mothers in early infancy and experienced them as the first erotic love object, they must distance themselves from a deep part of their own psyches as well as from the actual mothers. This results in boys and men who experience the world as fundamentally separate from others. They develop more rigid ego boundaries, tend to be more distant from others, are less focused on their own and others' emotions, and are therefore more prone than are women to be instrumental and domineering. Finally, Chodorow (1976) believes that for boys to separate from mothers, they must devalue both women and what is feminine. According to other social theorists, this routinely produces men who fear their own sensitivities and makes them likely to engage in warfare and aggression (Balbus, 1983; Easlea, 1981). It also encourages men to fear anything feminine and leads directly to sexual exploitation and the rape and abuse of women because men can so easily objectify others (Benjamin, 1988; Dinnerstein, 1976; Lisak, 1991).

Chodorow's (1978) Freudian psychoanalytic theory gives a social explanation, on the basis of who does the parenting, of why men and women seem so different in a deep psychological sense. They seem to have quite different personalities and to have different emotional perceptions of the world. Men (at least stereotypically) seem to focus on things instead of people, preferring the world of action, competition, sports, machinery, work, science, and power. This preference seems deeply ingrained in their very being. Women, on the other hand, seem to focus on people and emotions, and especially on romance, family, and babies. Stereotypical women are more "relational" with more fluid ego boundaries and a greater ability and desire to merge with those around them. They prefer intimacy and warmth in personal relationships, and their identity comes more from how others receive them than from solitary pursuits or accomplishments. As with the men, this temperamental difference feels deep-seated and is resistant to change. According to Chodorow, it also provides the best explanation for why women continue to be the ones who take primary responsibility for raising children.

Chodorow's (1978) theory is a general view of how mothering is reproduced from generation to generation and how parenting practices perpetuate personality differences based on gender. The theory also suggests how current patterns might change. If men began to take on more of the parenting duties while children were still young, boy and girl babies would both start out by psychologically merging with both the mother and the father. Hypothetically, boys' and girls' paths toward independence would be more similar, and both would develop more balanced ego structures. According to the theory, the average girl would end up more assertive and independent than today, and the average boy would end up more sensitive and emotionally connected (for more on this, see also Coltrane, 1996).

Actual gender development is influenced by much more than psychological object relations, and some social scientists reject the premises of Chodorow's neo-Freudian theory. Most scholars agree that parenting practices play an important role in the development of children's gender identities, but social psychological research shows that gender-linked personality traits are less fixed and more influenced by events later in childhood or adulthood than psychoanalytic models imply (Huston, 1983; Risman, 1986; Ruddick, 1989; Spence et al., 1985). Gender theorists argue about whether personality traits should be considered the cause or the consequence of parenting practices, and some question whether the heavy emphasis on deep psychology is appropriate (Collins, Chafetz, Blumberg, Coltrane, & Turner, 1993; Lorber, Coser, Rossi, & Chodorow, 1981). Others agree with parts of the theory but place more emphasis on biological constraints (Mead, 1949; Rossi, 1977), cross-cultural variations (e.g., Mead, 1935/1963; Whiting, 1965), or economic and social structural elements (Chafetz, 1990; Hartsock, 1983; Johnson, 1988; Lorber, 1994). Nevertheless, psychoanalytic accounts provide a provocative explanation for how deep-seated personalities and emotional lives of boys and girls come to be different and, coincidentally, how they might be changed.

Cognitive Gender Theory

Whereas psychoanalytic theories have focused on sexuality, emotions, and the unconscious mind, cognitive theories have focused on how the developing child perceives the world, processes information, and develops the capacity for rational thought. Theories in this general area of psychology are so widespread and studies so plentiful that it is impossible to summarize them here, but I can review one important variant of the cognitive approach to gender, called *gender schema theory* (Bem, 1983).

Like psychoanalysis, many cognitive theories have assumed that children will naturally and automatically become sex-typed as the result of the unfolding of internal psychological processes. Piaget (1932), Kohlberg (1966), and other cognitive theorists argued against the assumption that children learned by passively absorbing knowledge from parents and other adults around them. Instead, they assumed that children sought information from their environment and organized it in predictable ways as they aggressively tried to make sense of the world and their place within it. In other words, children were not simply passive recipients of knowledge. They were active cognitive beings who were constantly engaged in seeking patterns and figuring out categories even if their minds could grasp only certain concepts at specified ages. According to these theories, children actively develop cognitive capacities as they spontaneously construct a sense of self and learn about social rules. For Kohlberg, the nature of children's cognitive processing and the natural perceptual salience of the male-female dichotomy lead children to choose gender as a major organizing principle for social rules. For Piaget, Kohlberg, and others (Bem, 1983; Maccoby, 1992; Martin, 1993), the childhood preoperational stage leads them to think that same-sex behavior is morally required and rigidly fixed.

More recently, cognitive psychologists have found that gender development is more variable than Kohlberg and others first thought and that it must be understood in a cultural context. Although children do seem to be active participants in the process of gender acquisition, psychologist Sandra Bem (1993) notes that they are motivated to match their behavior to gender stereotypes only to the extent that society demands it. Her research shows that gender is not something that is naturally prominent in the minds of children but that it reflects the gender polarization in the larger culture. Her theory about this rejects the narrow ages and stages view of Piaget or Kohlberg but retains an emphasis on how children process information about the world as they develop increasingly complex cognitive and reasoning skills.

Bem (1983) focuses on the development of a cognitive structure called a *schema*. A schema is a way of organizing information in the mind—a type of human computer program for collecting, sorting, processing, and storing information according to predetermined categories. A schema allows individuals to impose structure and meaning onto a vast array of incoming stimuli, but it is also highly selective. Bem (1993) suggests that gender *schematicity*

> is the imposition of a gender-based classification on social reality, the sorting of persons, attributes, behaviors, and other things on the basis of the polarized definitions of masculinity and femininity that prevail in the culture, rather than on the basis of other dimensions that could serve equally well. (p. 125)

It is a perceptual lens that predisposes individuals to see the world in two neatly defined opposites—male and female, masculinity and femininity.

According to gender schema theory, when the culture (language, art, customs, economy, polity, etc.) is stereotyped according to gender, children become gender schematic without even realizing it. They develop networks of associations that guide their perceptions, so that they come to see the world in gender-polarized ways. Bem (1983) notes that a gender schema is anticipatory, promoting a readiness to search for and assimilate information if it fits with the schema. Gender categories or "equivalence classes" can incorporate a variety of information and implicitly force individuals to ignore other ways of categorizing people or things. For example, terms such as *tender* and *nightingale* might spontaneously be placed in a feminine category, whereas terms such as *assertive* and *eagle* might be placed in a masculine category (p. 604).

Bem's theory forges important links between gender polarization in the larger culture, the organization of everyday life, and the child's developing view of the world. Gender polarization organizes the daily lives of children from the moment they are born: from pink versus blue to dolls versus trucks. The overriding importance of the male-female distinction is communicated to children in the different ways adults talk to boys and girls, the different social experiences adults provide children, and the different expectations adults have for them. Children learn that virtually everything in their world can and should be classified according to gender. A gender schema is not just something that people can use if they want to, according to Bem, but a culturally mandated way of viewing the world. By being programmed into the very ways of perceiving and thinking, gender becomes unavoidable (see also Kessler & McKenna, 1985; West & Zimmerman, 1987).

Gender polarization means more than just different toys or clothes for boys and girls because, ultimately, every child learns to apply gender schematicity to the self. Children evaluate their own thoughts, feelings, and actions according to the gender polarization they observe in the culture and come to see themselves according to its rigid either/or dichotomy. They tend to favor those traits and behaviors that seem to fit the gender schema and avoid those that do not. They learn that it is inappropriate for girls to desire autonomy and power and for boys to desire intimacy or have feelings of vulnerability, and they enact these stereotypical scripts in their daily lives. Thus, according to Bem's (1983) cognitive approach, children's self-concepts become gender stereotyped and "the two sexes become, in their own eyes, not only different in degree, but different in kind" (p. 604).

The idea of a gender schema organizing our perceptions and our social world is a persuasive one. Most research supports the idea that children develop cognitive frameworks and gender scripts that reflect cultural values and shape future behavior (Martin, 1993; Signorella, Bigler, & Liben, 1993). A person with a polarized gender schema is more likely than others to notice and pay attention to things that fit the schema and to quickly store that information in memory according to its link with gender. As Bem (1983) notes, "sex-typed individuals" (those with polarized gender schemata) "have a greater readiness than do non-sex-typed individuals to encode information in terms of the sex-linked associations that constitute the gender schema" (p. 607). People with polarized gender schemas are also significantly faster at endorsing gender-appropriate attributes and rejecting gender-inappropriate attributes than are others (p. 608). Bem also found that individuals who describe themselves as more gender stereotyped sort information into categories on the basis of gender, even when other categories would work better for sorting the information. This leads people to exaggerate gender differences and to ignore those things that are similar between men and women.

Other researchers have confirmed and extended Bem's work on gender schema by considering how children form gender "scripts" (Levy & Fivush, 1993). Even young children organize their knowledge of the world in scripts—time-ordered routines that they regularly see and in which they participate. For example, there are scripts for changing a diaper, going to bed, eating dinner, going to a birthday party, and so on. Scripts provide children with sets of expectations about what to expect from different people in particular situations. Scripts are like schemas because they organize perceptions and allow children to comprehend, process, and predict events and event-related information. Children use scripts to help them acquire language, develop cognitive categories, and learn logical reasoning (Nelson, 1986).

Gender scripts are particularly important to the thought processes of developing children. For younger children, an occurrence that is inconsistent with a gender script is likely to be ignored, not remembered, or distorted in memory to conform to the script (Levy & Fivush, 1993). Like a gender schema, a gender script teaches children that boys and girls are different and provides prescriptions and proscriptions for their respective behaviors. Early research shows that preschool children pay more attention to scripts for their own sex, and some researchers find that boys have more elaborate scripts and are more concerned with following them than are girls (Fagot, 1985; Levy & Fivush, 1993).

Other theories of childhood gender acquisition combine the insights of the cognitive approach with those of interactionist theories (e.g., Mead, 1934/1967), granting children even more agency. For example, Spencer Cahill (1986) suggests that children regulate their gender performance relative to the participation of parents and others. As acquiescent participants, they accept the gender investiture made by parents and other significant adults on the basis of their biological sex class. With continued exposure to gender-differential treatment and social bestowal of "gender-appropriate" traits, children begin, unwittingly, to respond behaviorally in gender-differentiated ways. Acquiring the use of language and more agency with age and maturity, children then begin to explore various gender identity options. At this stage, however, the children find, through both direct and indirect approbation and censure, that the alternatives are limited to either the derogatory category of "baby" or the alternate positive category of "big girl" or "big boy." Beginning to comprehend the boundaries of appropriate gender behavior that will lead to a favorable categorization, children typically start to incorporate a commitment to socially correct gender behavior that corresponds to their assigned sex class. Thus, "by the end of the preschool age years . . . children are self-regulating participants in the interactional achievement of their own normally sexed identities" (Cahill, 1986, p. 177; see also Coltrane & Adams, forthcoming; Thorne, 1993).

Patterns of Gender Socialization

Although the psychoanalytic, cognitive, and interactionist theories summarized above focus on different ways that children learn about gender, they all suggest that what adults do with children influences their outlook on gender. Not only do children learn at a conscious level that the world is divided into boys and girls, men and women, but they also learn this in a subconscious way. At the level of unconscious emotions and in automatic perception and memory, children develop ways of seeing the world that are deeply gendered. These ways of seeing become incorporated into developing selves as children test out gender categories in interaction with people around them. All this contributes to the sense that gender is something that is natural, fixed, and unalterable (although gender means different things in different cultures, and different forms of masculinity and femininity coexist in any particular society).

Not surprisingly, the vast majority of American children conform to the expectations of the larger culture regarding gender. Following gender schemas and gender scripts, children consider most objects and activities as exclusively appropriate for only boys or girls. Responding to deeply gendered ways of relating emotionally, boys and girls feel that they are fundamentally different. Boys and girls also prefer and enforce same-sex play for themselves and for their peers, which further reinforces gender differences (Huston, 1983). As theories and research show, this is primarily because parents insist on treating boys and girls as categorically different. In the remainder of the chapter, I review the many studies showing how boys and girls are treated differently. Keep in mind, however, that these patterns are changing as societal attitudes toward gender change and as parenting practices change. According to theories discussed above, as child socialization practices change, there should also be less rigid personality differences and less polarized gender schemas.

Gender Differences in Treatment of Infants

Male and female infants are similar to one another, but most adults go to great lengths to make them appear dissimilar. As noted above, differential treatment by gender begins as soon as parents and other adults know the infant's sex. The newborn nursery typically provides color-coded blankets and identification bracelets, with pink for girls and blue for boys. People select gifts for newborns depending on their sex, with girls receiving pastel outfits, often with ruffles, and boys receiving tiny jeans and boldly colored outfits (Fagot & Leinbach, 1993). Parents routinely dress their tiny infants in sex-appropriate clothes and attempt to style their hair in stereotyped ways so that others can quickly categorize them according to sex (Shakin, Shakin, & Sternglanz, 1985). Even the bedrooms of infants are arranged according to gender, with girls' rooms typically painted pink and populated with dolls, whereas boys' rooms tend to be blue, red, or white and contain plenty of vehicles and sports gear (Pomerleau, Bolduc, Malcuit, & Cossette, 1990).

To assess how important knowing the sex of babies is to adults, researchers have devised some ingenious tests. In one study, parents were asked to rate and describe their own babies shortly after they were born. Because they had spent little time with their newborns, one of the only pieces of information they could rely on was the child's sex. Although the boy and girl infants in the study showed no differences on any objective measures, girls were rated as littler, softer, finer featured, and more inattentive than boys (Rubin, Provenzano, & Luria, 1974).

When some of my students read about the results of this study, they told me that things had changed since the "dark ages" of the 1970s. Much to their surprise, studies from the 1980s and 1990s show the same propensity to label boys and girls differently, although some of the stereotypes are starting to weaken (Fagot & Leinbach, 1993; Stern & Karraker, 1989). In one type of labeling study, people are exposed to a baby and asked questions about the baby's personality traits or behaviors. Often, the same baby is dressed in gender-neutral clothes but labeled *male* for some people and *female* for others. People are typically given little, if any, information about the infant other than the sex. Because the baby's sex is always the same, these studies can isolate the impact of calling the baby a boy or girl.

Although specific results from two dozen such studies vary, in general they show that the actual sex of the babies makes little difference because people use gender stereotypes in rating the babies. This is especially true when the people doing the rating are children (Cowan & Hoffman, 1986; Stern & Karraker, 1989). For example, in studies using child raters, boy babies were routinely perceived as bigger, stronger, and noisier; often seen as faster, meaner, and harder; and sometimes seen as madder and smarter than girl babies (Stern & Karraker, 1989).

Studies also looked at how adults interacted with the infants. In several studies, labeled girls received more verbalization, interpersonal stimulation, and nurturance play. Similarly, labeled boys received more encouragement of activity and more whole-body stimulation. This pattern has also been observed for parents with their own children, especially for fathers (Cherry & Lewis, 1976; Fagot, 1974, 1978; Fagot & Leinbach, 1993; Stern & Karraker, 1989).

Some of the infant-labeling studies looked at toy choice as a way of measuring whether adults were using gender stereotypes in interacting with infants. No differences were found in about half of the studies, probably because most of the toys were inappropriate for infants. Nevertheless, dolls were more often given to girl babies, and a football or hammer more often given to boy babies, supporting the idea that adults encourage gender-specific toys, even in infants under a year old (Stern & Karraker, 1989).

The conclusion from these laboratory experiments with infants is that people tend to treat boy and girl babies differently, although not always. Knowledge of an infant's sex is most likely to influence adults' evaluation of an infant if they have little other information or if the infant's behavior is ambiguous. Most of these studies have been conducted on college campuses with well-educated subjects who were probably trying to avoid acting in rigidly gender-stereotyped ways (Stern & Karraker, 1989). Although it is harder to draw statistical conclusions from studies on parents in their own homes interacting with their own infants, it is here that most gender stereotyping occurs. The research suggests that even with infants under a year old, parents expect different things from girls and boys, set up their environments in different ways, treat them differently, and in many subtle ways direct them toward gender-appropriate behavior (Deaux, 1984; Fagot, Leinbach, & O'Boyle, 1992; Huston, 1983).

Because infants and toddlers develop gender schemas and gender scripts on the basis of what they are exposed to in their immediate environment, parents' and other adult caretakers' attitudes and behaviors tend to have a substantial impact on their gender development. Infants enter the world much more prepared to extract information from their environment than social scientists once thought. Indeed, infants are actively engaged in processing information from their earliest days, and they are exposed to gender-relevant messages from the beginning. By the age of seven months, infants can discriminate between men's and women's voices and generalize this to strangers. Infants less than a year old can also discriminate individual male and female faces. Even before they are verbal, young children are developing gender categories and making general-izations about people and objects in their environments, although they have not yet developed gender schemas (Fagot & Leinbach, 1993).

Gender Differences in Treatment of Children

Preschool-age children are more adept at differentiating between genders than infants. Between the ages of two and four, most children master gender labels as applied to themselves and other children, but they cannot always link gender to anatomical sex (Fagot & Leinbach, 1993). To illustrate, Bem (1993) tells a story about her son who went to nursery school one day wearing bar-rettes and was told by another boy that he was a girl because "only girls wear barrettes." After repeatedly insisting that he was a boy because he had a penis, he became exasperated and pulled down his pants. To this, the second boy remarked, "everybody has a penis; only girls wear barrettes" (p. 149). By the time they are two years old, 80% of American children can distinguish males from females on the basis of social cues such as hairstyle and clothing. But only half of three- and four-year-olds can distinguish males from females if all they have to go on are biologically natural cues such as genitalia and body physique (Bem, 1989, 1993, p. 114). In other words, preschool children in the United States learn that the cultural trappings of gender are more important than the underlying physical differences between boys and girls.

Children quickly incorporate new information into their developing gender schemas. Before the age of five, American children assign *bears, fire*, and *something rough* to boys and men, whereas *butterflies, hearts*, and *flowers* are associated with girls and women (Leinbach & Hort, 1989). These children are not taught directly to put bears and men together, but by this age they are able to categorize using a gender schema that associates qualities such as strength or dangerousness with males. Similarly, flowers and butterflies become associated with females through a metaphorical cognitive process that associates women with gentle qualities (Fagot & Leinbach, 1993, p. 220).

During the preschool and kindergarten years, parents provide even more gender-stereotyped toys and furnishings than they did for infants. Boys' rooms contain more vehicles, sports equipment, animals, machines, and military toys. Girls' rooms, in contrast, contain more dolls, dollhouses, and domestic toys (Bradbard, 1985; Etaugh & Liss, 1992; Pomerleau et al., 1990; Rheingold & Cook, 1975). Many children do not have all the toys and interior decorating that the upper-middle-class children in these studies enjoyed. But even when homeless children are given toys, the packages are specially marked to make sure that boys get "boy toys" and girls get "girl toys." When preschool children of all social classes ask for toys, parents are much more willing to provide them if they are the "right" type according to gender stereotype (Robinson & Morris, 1986). Different toys and furnishings promote different activities, which, in turn, reinforce rigid gender schemas and scripts. "Masculine" toys such as trucks and balls promote independent or competitive activities that require little verbal interaction. "Feminine" toys such as dolls encourage quiet, nurturing interaction with another, physical closeness, and verbal communication (Wood, 1994a).

Not only do parents provide gender-stereotyped environments, but they also interact with preschool and school-age children in different ways depending on their gender. Parents often reward gender-typical play and punish gender-atypical play (Huston, 1983; Jacklin, DiPietro, & Maccoby, 1984; Lytton & Romney, 1991). Boys are often discouraged from playing house, and girls are sometimes discouraged from engaging in vigorous competitive games. (This is changing somewhat as more girls are getting involved in organized sports such as soccer, baseball, and swimming.) Virtually all studies using preschool and school-age children find that parents engage boys in physical play more than they do girls (Lytton & Romney, 1991; Maccoby & Jacklin, 1974; Parke, 1996).

Another consistent finding is that parents assign boys and girls gender-segregated household tasks, although this is less common in all-girl or all-boy households, in single-parent households, and in African American households. In the majority of houses, however, chores such as cooking and cleaning are usually given to girls, whereas more active chores such as mowing the lawn are typically assigned to boys (Goodnow, 1988; McHale, Bartko, Crouter, & Perry-Jenkins, 1990). As with toys, different chores encourage specific ways of experiencing and understanding the world. Girls' chores usually take place inside and emphasize taking care of other people, whereas boys' chores usually take place outside and emphasize the maintenance of things.

Studies of gender socialization in other areas report more mixed results. Some studies find that parents show more emotional warmth toward girls and encourage more emotional dependence in them. Others report little difference in parents' tolerance of boys' and girls' proximity and comfort seeking (Fagot, 1978; Lytton & Romney, 1991; Maccoby & Jacklin, 1974). Although differences are typically small, research shows that parents more frequently encourage achievement in boys, discourage aggression in girls, and use more physical discipline with boys (Lytton & Romney, 1991). Researchers report that these patterns can vary by ethnic or cultural group, with African American boys and girls socialized more equally toward both autonomy and nurturing than white children and more likely to participate in household chores than other children (Albert & Porter, 1988; Bardewell, Cochran, & Walker, 1986; Hale-Benson, 1986). Research on children's task sharing in Latino families is just beginning, but anecdotal evidence suggests that children in Mexican American households, especially daughters, are called on to do more housework than are children in Anglo households (Coltrane & Valdez, 1993).

Boys and Masculinity

Bem (1993) reports that boys are more rigidly socialized to gender norms and allowed less crossover behavior than girls: She finds that it is easier for girls to be tomboys than for boys to be "sissies." In her study of children's play on elementary school playgrounds, sociologist Barrie Thorne (1993) reports similar findings. High-status girls were most able to cross gender boundaries and play in boys' games, but boys who tried this were usually ridiculed. Thorne finds that the labels of "tomboy" and "sissy" were largely replaced by labels of "fag" or "faggot." Being labeled a tomboy (i.e., like a boy) was seen as praise, whereas being labeled a sissy or fag (i.e., like a girl) was a put-down. Thorne finds considerable crossover between girls' culture and boys' culture, with girls much more likely to try to get into boys' games than the reverse. Nevertheless, gender "borderwork" on the playground—rituals such as "cooties" and chasing games—serve to reinforce the boundaries between the boys and girls.

On the playground and at home, both girls and boys learn that they should conform to gender-appropriate behaviors, but studies find that boys are encouraged to conform to masculine ideals more than girls are encouraged to conform to feminine ideals. In addition, boys tend to receive more rewards for gender conformity than girls (Wood, 1994a). In part, this is because boys tend to get more attention than girls. Children, as well as adults, generate more restrictive gender rules for young boys than for young girls (Bem, 1989). Another consistent finding across studies is that fathers enforce gender stereotypes more than mothers do, especially in sons. This is generally true across types of activities, including toy preferences, play styles, chores, discipline, interaction, and personality assessments (Caldera, Huston, & O'Brien, 1989; Fagot & Leinbach, 1993; Lytton & Romney, 1991).

The receipt of more gender restrictions by boys than by girls seems a bit contradictory because men, as a group, have more social power than do women. Men are more likely to hold positions of authority, occupy a wider range of professional roles, earn more money, and have greater freedom of movement than women. This is also true in the comparison of adolescent boys with adolescent girls. It is also true that school-age boys tend to be given more freedom of movement and are given fewer chores than school-age girls. So why do we allow young girls more gender freedom than boys? Because we have a male-dominated or androcentric cultural bias that values masculine traits over feminine traits, we are more likely to approve of those traits whether they are exhibited by boys or girls (Broverman, Broverman, Clarkson, Rosenkrantz, &

Vogel, 1970). But boys are more forcefully encouraged to adopt culturally valued masculine traits and more often discouraged from adopting the lower-status feminine traits (Bem, 1993; Kimmel & Messner, 1992; Lorber, 1994). According to the psychoanalytic and cognitive theories noted earlier, masculine gender identity is also more fragile than feminine gender identity and must be continually re-created (Bem, 1993; Chodorow, 1978; Dinnerstein, 1976; Mead, 1949). Because it requires the suppression of human feelings of vulnerability and denial of emotional connection, the maintenance of a stereotypically masculine identity requires more psychic effort than the maintenance of feminine identity (Chodorow, 1978; Maccoby & Jacklin, 1974). Because masculinity is inherently fragile and defined in opposition to femininity, researchers note that men spend considerable time and energy maintaining gender boundaries and denigrating women and gays (Connell, 1995; Kimmel & Messner, 1992). For these reasons, boys are given less gender latitude than girls, and fathers are more preoccupied than are mothers with making sure that their sons are not sissies.

Although adult men are more concerned than are women with instilling masculinity in boys, a father's role in perpetuating gender difference is neither fixed nor inevitable. The finding that mothers are less apt to enforce gender stereotypes is related to the amount of time they spend with children. Because they are doing most of the child care, mothers are more realistic about both similarities and differences between children and less likely to let preconceived notions of gender stereotypes shape their perceptions of an individual child's abilities or needs. Similarly, researchers find that when men coparent or take care of children as single parents, they act more like conventional mothers than like conventional fathers (Coltrane, 1996; Risman, 1986). Like mothers, involved fathers encourage sons and daughters equally and use similar interaction and play styles for both. They avoid rigid gender stereotypes and avoid the single-minded emphasis on rough-and-tumble play common among traditional fathers (Coltrane, 1989; Parke, 1996). When fathers exhibit a close, nurturing, continuing relationship with their preschool or school-age children, boys hold less stereotyped gender attitudes as teenagers and young adults (Hardesty, Wenk, & Morgan, 1995; Williams, Radin, & Allegro, 1992).

Parenting and Gender Inequality

Perhaps the most consistent and important finding from the childhood gender socialization research of the past few decades is that parents and other adults create different learning environments for boys and girls and ask them to do different things. Girls are given dolls and stoves to play with and are encouraged to cuddle, clean house, and care for others. Boys are given balls and trucks to play with, are engaged in rough-and-tumble play, and are asked to take out the trash. In general, girls are expected to be kind and caring, whereas boys are expected to be independent and aggressive.

Differences in the ways that adults treat boys and girls have perpetuated separate spheres for men and women. By setting up different social and interpersonal environments for them, parents encourage girls to develop nurturing behaviors and boys to develop autonomy. By shaping different environments and holding different expectations for boys and girls, parents promote the formation of gender schemas, gendered personalities, and taken-for-granted gender scripts that make gender differences seem natural and inevitable (Crouter, McHale, & Bartko, 1993; Eccles, Jacobs, & Harold, 1990; Etaugh & Liss, 1992; Thompson & Walker, 1989). For example, most girls grow up more interested in babies, are more responsive to them, and take more responsibility for them than boys (Ullian, 1984). Because girls experience more contact with young children, they also have more opportunities to develop nurturing capacities, and by the time they reach child-bearing age, they are predisposed to want to bear children and to take primary responsibility for their care (Bem, 1993; Chodorow, 1978).

Not all girls are subjected to these socialization pressures in the same way, however, and lately, most girls have also been strongly encouraged to do well in school and to pursue careers. Even in the past, some women have excelled at conventionally masculine pursuits, and an individual girl's disposition or personal desires have motivated her to deviate from a narrow path of conventional femininity. Because different ways of life have produced different styles of femininity, women have always had some choice in the matter. Some models of femininity have emphasized helplessness or physical beauty, but others have emphasized emotional strength and creativity. Not all feminine ideals include domestic or maternal traits. For example, compare the stereotyped images of the stoic Midwestern farmwife, the strong-willed inner-city mother, the cheery suburban housewife, the shapely Hollywood starlet, the prompt and efficient secretary, the athletic gym teacher, the serious and weathered naturalist, and the elegant lady of high society. All are images of femininity, and all have been available for girls and women to emulate during the past few decades. Not only has there been enormous variability in feminine stereotypes, but the gender stereotyping that parents do to children is never so uniform or controlling that girls have not had some choices. And the choices that women have are expanding rapidly.

Boys, in contrast to girls, have been socialized to occupy a privileged status in families and in society. There is wide variation in this, as minority men have often been granted privileges within their families but denied them in the larger society (Taylor, 1994). In all racial/ethnic groups, however, when compared with women, men have been encouraged to be competitive, individualistic, and often unemotional. If men have access to jobs and wealth, they tend to enact masculinity through being breadwinners and providers. If they are denied access to decent jobs and earnings, they tend to enact masculinity through "cool pose," hard living, and violence (Majors, 1992; Rubin, 1976, 1994). Most boys develop into young adult men who are relatively uninterested in babies and unprepared to care for the emotional needs of others. In addition, our child-rearing practices and social ideals tend to produce young men who feel entitled to the domestic or sexual services of women, are preoccupied with reaffirming their masculinity, and are prone to use violence when they feel threatened (Connell, 1995; Kaufman, 1993; Kimmel & Messner, 1992).

As is the case for girls, however, not all boys grow up to fit this narrow masculine mold. Many men turn out to be kind, sensitive, and loving, and most men share their deepest feelings with others (although usually still with women). As with femininity, there have always been various models of masculinity. Compare the physical toughness of a construction worker with the intelligence of a rocket scientist or the arrogant authority of a rich banker—all representing a specific acceptable form of masculinity. There have always been multiple forms of masculinity whose definitions have been played off against the others and against stereotyped notions of femininity. Some have been subordinated, but still visible, as evidenced by the Mother Goose nursery rhyme about Robin and Richard. Although dominant forms of masculinity have reflected the norm among men with more power and authority, oppositional forms of masculinity have always coexisted. The suburban middle-class European American masculinity ideal of rationality and unemotionality is not the same as that found, for example, among suburban middle-class African Americans, inner-city ghetto dwellers, recent Mexican immigrants, or urban gay youth (Connell, 1995).

The choices that are open to men and boys are expanding. More emphasis is placed on being kind and loving fathers, both in the media and in real men's lives. The movement toward more active fathering is not limited to just one segment of the population, as evidenced by a rapid increase in the number of single fathers and the prevalence of pro-father groups, from the African American Million Man March to the fundamentalist Christian Promise Keepers. There are more two-job families and more two-career professional couples, a development that is turning husbands into equal partners rather than benevolent bosses. In contrast, many men, especially those who are chronically unemployed, are more likely to stay single or get divorced. As male baby boomers age, increasing numbers of men are seniors and retirees. Older men, especially those who are not in positions of authority, have always been allowed more latitude in expressing emotions and caring for other people. As the number and proportion of men of color expand in the coming decades, their unique styles of masculinity will also flourish and become more visible. Younger men, in particular, have a greater willingness to accept women as equals and to engage in more mixed-gender social activities. More men are admitting that they are gay, and despite a continuing backlash against them, it is more possible to be openly gay in this country than ever before. Popular images of men and masculinity in the media also provide a much wider range of hypothetical options than in the past (although shoot-'em-up action heroes still predominate). Even nursery rhymes—at least most of the new ones—have become less sexist. The choices of how to be a man are considerably more varied than before, and so the narrow gender stereotyping of children described above is not necessarily a blueprint for the future.

I summarized the conventionality of past socialization practices to highlight the real, and sometimes quite large, differences in the ways that parents treat children according to gender. By raising children to be "proper" boys and girls, parents and other family members have re-created broad gender differences and prepared the next generation to occupy unequal positions in a system of gender hierarchy. But things are changing. Most families now look different from the typical family of the 1950s. Indications are that children who experienced a divorce, those raised in single-mother families, those in stepfamilies, and those excluded from material prosperity are developing new ideas about how boys and girls should be treated. Even those from stereotypical traditional families are reevaluating their past experiences and asking new questions about how children should be raised to meet the gender expectations of a new century.

You will need to refer to your own experiences to see how many of the gender socialization patterns I described apply to you or your family. You should also remember that even when you are socialized in a particular way, you always have many opportunities for changing your own actions, so that your personal gender traits, gender schemas, and gender scripts can also change. The same theories that show how gender differences have been socially constructed provide a glimpse into how they might change in the future. As I discuss in the next chapter, strong institutional forces are operating in society that limit how much things might change. But also, other institutional, cultural, and economic forces are propelling the United States toward even more possibilities for change. These conflicting tendencies will put crosscutting pressures on parents and families of the future. My prediction is that gender socialization practices will continue their movement toward equality. We may not train the next generation of boys and girls to be equally assertive and sensitive, but even small changes in that direction will have ripple effects on the rest of society. Just as inequality in the social and economic structures governing our lives produces contrasting gender cultures, so too will similarities in children's gender schemas help lessen inequalities in the society at large.

References

Alber, A. A., and Porter, J. R. 1988. "Children's Gender-Role Stereotypes: A Sociological Investigation of Psychological Models." *Sociological Forum*, 3:184–210.

Bardewell, J. R., Cochran, S. W., and Walker, S. 1986. "Relationships of Parental Education, Race, and Gender to Sex Role Stereotyping in 5-Year-Old Kindergarteners. *Sex Roles*, 15:275–81.

Bem, S. L. 1983. "Gender Schema theory and its Implications for Child Development: Raising Gender-Aschematic Children in a Gender-Schematic Society." *Signs*, 8:598–616.

Bem, S. L. 1989. "Genital Knowledge and Constancy in Preschool Children." *Child Development*, 60:649–62.

Bem, S. L. 1993. *The Lenses of Gender*. New Haven, CT: Yale University Press.

Berger, P. 1963. *Invitation to Sociology*. New York: Doubleday.

Blankenhorn, D. 1995. *Fatherless America: Confronting Our Most Urgent Social Problem*. New York: Basic Books.

Bleier, R. 1984. *Science and Gender*. New York: Pergamon.

Bradbard, M. R. 1985. "Sex Differences in Adults' Gifts and Children's Toy Requests At Christmas." *Psychological Reports*, 56:969–70.

Broverman, I., Broverman, D., Clarkson, R., Rosenkrants, P. and Vogel, S. 1970. "Sex Role Stereotypes and Cllinical Judgments of Mental Health." *Journal of Consulting and Clinical Psychology*, 34:1–7.

Butler, J. 1990. *Gender Trouble: Feminism and the Subversion of Identity*. New York: Routledge.

Cahill, S. 1986. "Childhood Socialization as a Recruitment Process: Some Lessons From the Study of Gender Development." *Sociological Studies of Child Development*, 1:163–86.

Caldera, Y. M., Huston, A. C., and O'Brien, M. 1989. "Social Interactions and Play Patterns of Parents and Toddlers with Feminine, Masculine, and Neutral Toys." *Child Development*, 60:70–6.

Chafetz, J. S., 1990. *Gender Equity: An Integrated Theory of Stability and Change*. Newbury Park, CA: Sage.

Cherry, L. and Lewis, M. 1976. "Mothers and Two-Year-Olds: A Study of Sex-Differentiated Aspects of Verbal Interaction." *Developmental Psychology*, 12: 278–82.

Chodorow, N. 1976. "Oedipal Asymmetries and Heterosexual Knots." *Social Problems*, 23:454–67.

Chodorow, N. 1978. *The Reproduction of Mothering: Psychoanalysis and the Sociology of Gender*. Berkeley: University of California Press.

Chodorow, N. 1985. "Beyond Drive Theory: Object Relations and the Limits of Radical Individualism." *Theory and Society*, 14:271–319.

Collins, R., Chafetz, J., Blumberg, R., Coltrane, S., amd Turner, J. 1993. "Toward an Integrated Theory of Gender Stratification." *Sociological Perspectives*, 36:185–216.

Collins, R. and Coltrane, S. 1995. *Sociology of Marriage and the Family*, 4th ed. Chicago: Nelson-Hall.

Coltrane, S. 1989. "Household Labor and the Routine Production of Gender." *Social Problems*, 36:473–90.

Coltrane, S. 1996. *Family Man: Fatherhood, Housework, and Gender Equity*. New York: Oxford University Press.

Coltrane, S. and Adams, M. 1998. "Children and Gender." In T. Arendell (ed.) *Parenting: Contemporary Issues and Challenges. Thousand Oaks*, CA: Sage.

Coltrane, S. and Valdez, E. 1993. "Reluctant Compliance: Work-Family Role Allocation In Dual-Earner Chicano Families.

Connell, R. W. 1995. *Masculinities*. Berkeley: University of California Press.

Crouter, A. C., McHale, S. M., and Bartko, W. T. 1993. "Gender as an Organizing Feature in Parent-Child Relationships." *Journal of Social Issues*, 49:161–74.

Deaux, K. 1984. "From Individual Differences to Social Categories: Analysis of a Decade's Research on Gender." *American Psychologist*, 39:105–16.

Deutsch, H. 1944. *The Psychology of Women: A Psychoanalytic Approach* New York: Bantam.

Dinnerstein, D. 1976. *The Mermaid and the Minotaur: Sexual Arrangements and Sexual Malaise*. New York: Harper & Row.

Eccles, J. S., Jacods, J. E., and Harold, R. D. 1990. "Gender Role Stereotypes, And Parents' Socialization of Gender Differences." *Journal of Social Issues*, 46:183–201.

Ehrensaft, D. 1987. *Parenting Together*. New York: Free Press.

Epstein, C. F. 1988. *Deceptive Distinction.: Sex, Gender, and the Social Order*. New Haven, CT: Yale University Press.

Erikson, E. H. 1950. *Childhood and Society*. New York: Norton.

Etaugh, C. and Liss, M. 1992. "Home, School, and Playroom: Training Grounds for Adult Gender Roles." *Sex Roles*, 26:129–47.

Fagot, B. I. 1974. "Sex Differences in Toddlers' Behavior and Parental Reaction." *Developmental Psychology*, 10:554–8.

Fagot, B. I. 1978. "The Influence of Sex of Child on Parental Reactions to Toddler Children." *Child Development*, 49:459–65.

Fagot, B. I. 1985. "Changes in Thinking about Early Gender-Role Development." *Developmental Review*, 5:83–96.

Fagpt, B. I. and Leinbach, M. D. 1993. "Gender-Role Development in Young Childfren: From Discrimination to Labeling." *Developmental Review*, 205–24.

Fagot, B. I., Leinbach, M. D., and O'Boyle, C. 1992. "Gender Labeling, Gender Stereotyping, and Parenting Behaviors." *Developmental Psychology*, 28:225–30.

Freud, S. 1924. *A General Introduction to Psychoanalysis*. New York: Boni and Liveright.

Freud, S. 1938. "Three Contributions to the Theory of Sex." In A. A. Brill (ed.) *The Basic Writings of Sigmund Freud*. New York: Random House. (Original work published 1905.)

Geertz, C. 1973. *The Interpretation of Cultures*. New York: Basic Books.

Goodman, N. 1985. "Socialization I: A Sociological Overview." pp. 73–94 in H. A. Farberman and R. Perinbanayagam (eds.) *Foundations of Interpretive Sociology: Studies in Symbolic Interaction*. Greenwich, CT: JAI Press.

Goodnow, J. 1988. "Children's Housework: Its Nature and Functions." *Psychological Bulletin*, 103:5–26.

Hale-Benson, J. E. *Black Children: Their Roots, Culture, and Learning Style*. Provo, UT: Brigham Young University Press.

Hardesty, C., Wenk, D., and Morgan, C. S. 1995. "Paternal Involvement and the Development of Gender Expectations in Sons and Daughters." *Youth and Society*, 26: 283–97.

Hartsock, N. 1983. *Money, Sex, and Power*. New York: Longman.

Horney, K. 1967. *Feminine Psychology*. New York: Norton.

Huston, A. H. 1983. "Sex Typing." In E. M. Hetherington and P. H. Mussen (eds.) *Handbook of Child Psychology*, Vol. 4. New York: John Wiley.

Jacklin, C. N., DiPietro, J. A., and Maccoby, E. E. 1984. "Sex-Typing Behavior and Sex Typing Pressure in Child/Parent Interaction." *Archives of Sexual Behavior*, 13:413–25.

Johnson, M. M. 1988. *Strong Mothers, Weak Wives*. Berkeley: University of California Press.

Kaufman, M. 1993. *Cracking the Armour: Power, Pain, and the Lives of Men*. Toronto, Ontario, Canada: Viking.

Kessler, S. J. and McKenna, W. 1985. *Gender: An Ethnomethodological Approach* (2nd ed.). Chicago: University of Chicago Press.

Kimmel, M. and Messner, M. 1992. *Men's Lives*. New York: Macmillan.

Kohlberg, L. 1966. "A Cognitive-Developmental Analysis of Children's Sex-Role Concepts and Attitudes." pp. 82–173 in E. E. Maccoby (ed.) *The Development of Sex Differences*. Stanford, CA: Stanford University Press.

Leinbach, M. S., and Hort, B. 1989 (April). "Bears are for Boys: 'Metaphorical' Associations in the Young Child's Gender Schema." Paper presented at the Biennial Conference of the Society for Research in Child Development, Kansas City, MO.

Levy, G. D. and Fivush, R. 1993. "Scripts and Gender: A New Approach for Examining Gender-Role Development." *Developmental Review*, 13:126–46.

Lorber, J. 1994. *Paradoxes of Gender*. New Haven, CT: Yale University Press.

Lorber, J. Coser, R. L., Rossi, A. S., and Chodorow, N. 1981. "On the Reproduction of Mothering: A Methodological Debate." *Signs*, 6:482–514.

Lytton, H. and Romney, D. M. 1991. "Parents' Differential Socialization of Boys and Girls: A Meta-Analysis." *Psychological Bulletin*, 109:267–96.

Maccoby, E. E. 1992. "The Role of Parents in the Socialization of Children: An Historical Overview." *Developmental Psychology*, 28:1006–17.

Maccoby, E. E. and Jacklin, C. N. 1964. *The Psychology of Sex Differences*. Stanford, CA: Stanford University Press.

Martin, C. L. 1993. "New Directions for Investigating Children's Gender Knowledge." *Developmental Review*, 13:184–204.

McHale, S. M., Bartko, W. T., Crouter, A. C., and Perry-Jenkins, M. 1990. "Children's Housework and Psychosocial Functioning: The Mediating Effects of Parents' Sex-Role Behaviors and Attitudes." *Child Development*, 61:1413–26.

Mead, G. H. 1967 [1934]. *Mind, Self, and Society*. Chicago: University of Chicago Press.

Mead, M. 1949. *Male and Female*. New ork: William Morrow.

Merton, R. K. 1948. "The Self-Fulfilling Prophecy." *Antioch Review*, 8:193–210.

Mitchell, J. 1974. *Psychoanalysis and Feminism*. New York: Random House.

Nelson, K. 1986. *Event Knowledge: Structure and Function in Development*. Hillsdale, NJ: Lawrence Erlbaum Associates.

Parke, R. D. 1996. *Fatherhood*. Cambridge, MA: Harvard University Press.

Peterson, G. W. and Rollins, B. C. 1987. "Parent-Child Socialization." pp. 471–507. In M. Sussman and S. Steinmetz (eds.) *Handbook of Marriage and Family*. New York: Plenum.

Piaget, J. 1932. *The Moral Judgment of the Child*. London: Kegan Paul.

Pomerleau, A., Bolduc, D., Malcuit, G. and Cossette, L. 1990. "Pink or Blue: Environmental Stereotypes in the First Two Years of life." *Sex Roles*, 22:359–67.

Popenoe, D. 1996. *Life Without Father*. New York: Martin Kessler/Free Press.

Rheingold, H. L. and Cook, K. V. 1975. "The Contents of Boys' and Girls' Rooms As an Index of Parents' Behavior." *Child Development*, 46:459–63.

Risman, B. 1986. "Can Men Mother? Life as a Single Father." *Family Relations*, 5: 95–102.

Rosenthal, R. and Jacobson, L. 1968. *Pygmalion in the Classroom.: Teacher Expectations and Pupil's Intellectual Development*. New York: Holt.

Rossi, A. 1977. "A Biosocial Perspective on Parenting." *Daedalus*, 106:1–31.

Rubin, J., Provenzano, R., and Luria, Z. 1974. "The Eye of the Beholder: Parents' Views On Sex of Newborns." *American Journal of Orthopsychiatry*, 44:512–19.

Rubin, L. 1976. *Worlds of Pain: Life in the Working-Class Family*. New York: Basic Books.

Rubin, L. 1994. *Families on the Fault Line: America's Working-Class Speaks about The Family, Economy, and Ethnicity*. New York: HarperCollins.

Ruddick, S. 1989. *Maternal Thinking; Toward a Poliics of Peace*. Boston: Beacon.

Segal, L. 1990. *Slow Motion: Changing Masculinities, Changing Men.*. New Brunswick, NJ: Rutgers University Press.

Shakin, M., Shakin, S., and Sternglanz, S. H. 1985. "Infant Clothing: Sex Labeling for Strangers." *Sex Roles*, 12:955–63.

Shweder, R. and LeVine, R. A. (eds.) *Culture Theory: Essays in Mind, Self, and Emotion*. Cambridge, UK: Cambridge University Press.

Signorella, M. L., Bigler, R. S., and Liben, L. S. 1993. "Developmental Differences in Children's Gender Schemata about Others: A Meta-Analytic Review." *Developmental Review*, 13:147–83.

Spence, J. T., Deaux, K., and Helmreich, R. L. 1985. "Sex Roles in Contemporary American Society." pp. 149–78 in G. Lindzey and E. Aronson (eds.) *Handbook of Social Psychology*. New York: Random House.

Stern, M. and Karraker, K. H. 1989. "Sex Sterotyping of Infants; A Review of Gender Labeling Studies." *Sex Roles*, 20:501–22.

Thompson, L and Walker, A. J. 1989. "Gender in Families: Women and Men in Marriage, Work, and Parenthood." *Journal of Marriage and the Family*, 51:845–71.

Thorne, B. 1993. *Gender Play: Girls and Boys in School*. New Brunswick, NJ: Rutgers University Press.

Ullian, D. 1984. "'Why Girls are Good': A Constructivist View." *Sex Roles*, 11:241–56.

West, C. and Fenstermaker, S. 1993. "Power and Accomplishment of Gender: An Ethnomethodological Perspective." pp. 151–74 in P. England (ed.) *Theory On Gender/ Feminism on Theory*. New York: Aldine de Gruyter.

West, C. and Zimmerman, D. 1987. "Doing Gender." *Gender and Society*, 1:125–51.

Williams,, E., Radin, N., and Allegro, T. 1992. "Sex Role Attitudes of Adolescents Reared Primarily by their Fathers: An 11-Year Follow-Up." *Merrill-Palmer Quarterly*, 38:457–76.

Wood, J. T. 1994. *Gendered Lives: Communication, Gender, and Culture*. Belmont, CA: Wadsworth.

16

Male Gender Socialization and the Perpetration of Sexual Abuse*

David Lisak

Few people would consider male gender socialization to be a public health issue. Certainly, the Centers for Disease Control have not made such a pronouncement. Yet there is considerable evidence to support such a pronouncement, evidence that links sexual abuse and a vast array of interpersonally abusive and violent behavior to the process by which male children, male adolescents, and young men are socialized into masculinity.

Consider the prima facie evidence. U.S. prisons are overflowing with a shocking percentage of our population, and prisons are bastions of masculinity. Interpersonal violence, including sexual abuse, similarly remains a stronghold of male domination (FBI, 1992). The past two decades have seen an explosion of research on child abuse and other violations of trust and, with only a few exceptions, these forms of violence are found to be disproportionately perpetrated by men (e.g., Berliner & Elliot, 1996; Kilmartin, 1994).

Some argue that biology plays an important role in the male propensity for sexual abuse and violence (e.g., Barash, 1979). However, as yet, there is little direct evidence. Indeed, it has been argued that even relatively strong genetic influences are so mediated by environmental (e.g., socialization) conditions, that it is mistaken to conceive of biology and environment as separable influences (Fausto-Sterling, 1985). Recent research demonstrating the profound impact of psychological trauma on neurophysiology and even neuroanatomy underscores how inextricably intertwined are biology and environment (e.g., McEwan & Mendelson, 1993).

Different forms of sexual victimization—for example, child sexual abuse and sexual exploitation of patients—each have unique motivational components. Further, individual perpetrators of sexual victimization vary in their motivational make-up. However, the disproportionate role of males in perpetrating these offenses suggests that, despite these variations, there is something about being male—or growing up male—that predisposes some men to sexually victimize others.

There is actually considerable evidence indicating a link between various forms of sexual and interpersonal violence and male gender socialization. This link has been established by numerous researchers who have investigated a diverse sampling of male populations. While the evidence thus far obtained pertains disproportionately to sexual violence against women, there is both theoretical and empirical evidence indicating that the link between male gender socialization and various forms of sexual abuse and exploitation is equally salient. The evidence implicates particular behavioral and attitudinal legacies of the masculine gender socialization process—stereotyped sex role beliefs, particular attitudes toward women, hostility toward women, and hypermasculine beliefs—as part of the motivational substructure of violence against women and also of sexual abuse of children (Briere & Runtz, 1988; Crossman, Stith, & Bender, 1990; Fromuth, Burkhart, & Jones, 1991; Gold, Fultz, Burke, Prisco, & Willett, 1992; Koss, Leonard, Beezley, & Oros, 1985; Lisak & Ivan, 1995; Lisak & Roth, 1988; Lisak & Roth, 1990; Malamuth, 1986; Malamuth, Sockloskie, Koss, & Tanaka, 1991; Mosher & Anderson, 1986; Muehlenhard & Falcon, 1990; Rapaport & Burkhart, 1984; Stith & Farley, 1993).

The most rigorous test of the hypothesis that masculine socialization is implicated causally in the genesis of sexual victimization was reported by Malamuth et al. (1991). Through structural equation modeling, they tested a causal model in which masculine socialization was implicated both distally and proximally to the perpetration of sexual victimization. Distally, the factor "involvement in delinquency" consisted in part of an assessment of the subject's involvement with other delinquent youths. Delinquent peer groups have long been identified as intensive training grounds for hypermasculine behavior and attitudes (Kanin, 1984; McCord, McCord, & Thurber, 1962; Munroe, Munroe, & Whiting, 1981). Proximally, the factor "hostile masculinity" was associated with both sexual and nonsexual coerciveness.

The preponderance of this evidence relates to attitudes and beliefs because such more-or-less conscious attributes are relatively accessible to the methodologies currently in use in the social sciences, particularly psychology. However, a substantial body of work, primarily theoretical but which includes some empirical findings, has examined other, less conscious legacies of the male gender socialization process (Chodorow, 1978; Pollack, 1995). This work has focused much more on the emotional legacies of being socialized into masculinity, and it is here that this chapter will focus: pathways by which the emotional socialization of males potentiates the perpetration of sexual abuse and violence.

Theoretical Framework

An examination of any aspect of the male gender socialization process requires some clarification about language and underlying assumptions. If there *is* a "male gender socialization process"—and here the evidence from decades of social science research is overwhelming—then its endpoint, masculinity, must be a created entity; what is often now called a "cultural construction." Indeed, the evidence from recent cross-disciplinary scholarship suggests that it would be more accurate to refer to *masculinities*, because it would appear that cultures and cultures-within-cultures construct numerous forms of masculinity (Brod, 1994; Gilmore, 1990). If masculinities are constructed, then it is important to distinguish them from the biological sex category—male—with which they are typically associated. That is, while a human being may be identified at birth as male by virtue of his genitalia, this identification does not tell us anything about the nature and form of his masculinity. This will be determined by a myriad of factors, ranging from personal choice and unique psychodynamic influences, to the shaping influences of his culture, the economic constraints of his environment, and the historical epoch in which he is raised (e.g., Kimmel, 1996).

Thus, in the ensuing discussion, it is presumed that "male" is not synonymous with "masculine," and that when we speak of the legacies of masculine socialization we are not speaking of intrinsic male attributes, or of the natural unfolding of a "natural" or "normal" male personality. Rather, we are speaking of the legacies of socialization processes that are generally applied to male children, legacies that produce roughly predictable outcomes.

One of the most salient features of masculinity, a commonality that seems to characterize many of its different instantiations around the world, is its precariousness. It appears not only to be a culturally created entity, but one that is not easily created or sustained. Anthropologists have provided numerous examples of the great lengths to which many cultures go to transform male children into masculine beings; and the great lengths that these newly created masculine beings then go to preserve this state of masculinity (Gilmore, 1990; Webster, 1908). Thus, in some cultures, dramatic and even traumatic initiations are deemed necessary to create new masculine beings. In other cultures, constant proving is necessary—displays of courage, demonstrations of honor—to sustain the masculine state. In still others, the focus may be on preventing dishonor, the dreaded state of shame.

The very presence of these cultural codes and institutions further underscores the cultural origins of masculinities. One would have to wonder why, if masculinity were an innate unfolding of inherent male attributes, cultures would have evolved such dramatic and pervasive means for its creation and maintenance.

"Warrior Masculinity"

One attempt to explain the transcultural ubiquity of relatively severe forms of masculinity focuses on the survival advantages that accrue to cultures that create rigid masculine norms to which males must aspire. According to this theory (e.g., Gilmore, 1990), the underlying purpose of this type of masculine socialization is the creation of a class (gender) of people within the society who are well-conditioned to perform certain tasks for the preservation of that society. Although the most dramatic of these tasks is warfare, they also include other forms of work that require similar psychological conditioning, such as hunting.

What is the nature of the necessary psychological conditioning? Perhaps the clearest insight into this is provided by military training practices. These practices have often been compared to male initiation rituals, and the commonalities are numerous. In basic training, the new recruit is subjected to intense physical hardship and is frequently terrorized both physically and emotionally. Simultaneously, the recruit's normal, human emotional responses to such treatment—terror, vulnerability, for example—are vigorously, sometimes violently, suppressed. This process, reinforced by intense group pressure and physical isolation from family, tends to deintegrate the recruit's pretraining identity. The recruit is offered a single path toward reintegration: the identity offered by the military, that of a soldier. This "warrior identity" becomes internalized in the intense conditions of basic training just like any other identity. To the extent that the process is successful, the new recruit will now autonomously suppress those "vulnerable" emotions and convert them into anger and aggression.

The cauldron of basic training offers a clear view into the process of creating "warrior masculinity," a process that can be applied to either men or women (remember: sex does not equal gender). The clarity stems from the very focused purpose of this training—the creation of soldiers who will suppress their fears in the face of danger and function effectively within a military unit. However, the process of basic training is simply a crystalline form of the less focused process of masculine gender socialization that is generally applied to almost every male in the United States, with variations attributable to varying cultural and economic conditions.

Further, it would be mistaken to presume that the process of gender socialization that most men are subjected to is necessarily a "kinder and gentler" version of military training. If the methods appear less extreme, remember that the "men" are typically preschoolers when they first enter "masculine socialization training"; it doesn't take as much to terrorize a 4-year-old.

That masculine socialization is often, if not typically, a traumatic process was underscored in the course of an interview study conducted by the author several years ago (Lisak, 1994). The interviews were completely unstructured and autobiographical. In the course of these interviews, nearly every man described at least one—often several—intensely traumatic experiences having to do with their gender socialization. They described incidents in which they were so traumatically humiliated for displaying gender inappropriate emotions that the experiences were forever etched into memory, in just the way that traumatic experiences are.

One need not conduct an interview study to see the traumatic nature of the masculine socialization process. Witness the following scene, observed by the author in a community playground—a living laboratory in which the process of gender socialization is vividly on display:

> A 3-year-old boy and his father are standing before a spiral slide. The boy is looking up at the slide with a mixture of fear and excitement, but it is clear that the fear is winning out. The father also sees this and begins to urge, then nudge, then goad, then taunt the boy: "Come on Eric, don't be scared. It's just a slide." In response, Eric shies away more visibly. This incites the father. "Don't be a sissy, Eric. Just get on up there and do it." Now Eric is truly frightened and the corners of his mouth begin to curl downward as his face moves to the threshold of tears. At the sight of this, the father becomes angry. "Don't be such a crybaby. If you're going to cry I'm not going to hang around with you." And with that the father walks off. And of course as the father walks off, Eric begins to weep, and then to sob, because his fear is now compounded by this abandonment, and on top of it he feels the intense humiliation of being shunned by his father, and the shame of his fear. The scene ends with Eric slumping to the ground and sobbing.

Such scenes are played out millions of times every day across the country. Scenes of little boys learning to conform their behavior, and most importantly their emotions and their emotional experience, to the dictates of masculinity. Long before they have the slightest inkling of the meaning of that word—masculinity—they are well on their way to shaping themselves according to its dictates. Eric will learn very quickly that to avoid the humiliation, the terror of abandonment, and the scorn of his father, he must suppress the very human fears that he innocently expressed.

Masculinity as Regulator of Emotional Experience

Although there are many aspects to any particular form of masculinity, including attitudes and beliefs, styles of dress, physical mannerisms, and so on, it is arguable that the core—particularly of "warrior masculinity"—is the regulation of emotional experience (see e.g., Levant, 1995). Warrior masculinity is predicated on denial, suppression, and repression. Fear and other emotional states associated with vulnerability are suppressed, then their very presence is denied, and ultimately they are repressed; there remains no conscious awareness of them. Although men vary greatly in the degree to which they reach this endpoint, there is considerable evidence that this endpoint is indeed the goal of masculine socialization. To be disconnected from one's own fears and vulnerabilities, and disconnected from those of others, renders one a formidable soldier in any theater of combat, be it on the battlefield or in the "corporate jungle."

The differential emotional socialization of male and female children has by now been well-documented. It is a process carried out by virtually all of the major categories of caretakers commonly found in children's lives, from parents to daycare workers to teachers (e.g., Brody, 1985; Fivush, 1989; Kuebli & Fivush, 1992; Malatesta & Haviland, 1985). Relative to female children, male children receive far less training and reinforcement for the process of learning about their emotional experience, and are often subject to punishing humiliation for expressing "counter-gender" emotions. The product of this differential emotional socialization has also been well-documented: men experience emotions less intensely; they are less capable than women of identifying and expressing their emotions; and they are less capable of empathically responding to the emotions expressed by others (Diener, Sandvik, & Larsen, 1985; Eisenberg & Lennon, 1983; Kilmartin, 1994).

The Masculinization of Sexuality

Sexuality, like almost every facet of human experience, is almost defined by its plasticity. Sexuality is experienced both intrapersonally and interpersonally. It can be experienced as a preponderantly physical act, or its physicality can be secondary to the intense emotions to which it is so easily connected. It can be experienced as the ultimate form of human connection, or as the most painful condition of alienation and disconnection. Thus, even a behavior and experience so clearly rooted in the biological imperatives of species survival is subject to enormous cultural channeling and modification. It is little wonder then that sexuality, too, is subject to the powerful forces of gender socialization; all the more because sexuality and gender are so culturally interwoven.

While there are many ways in which masculine socialization can and does influence the development and experience of men's sexuality, and while there are many individual and cultural differences, there are also certain basic directional biases. The process of emotional socialization that so commonly accompanies men's indoctrination into masculinity has certain predictable consequences. To the extent that intense emotions—other than anger—are experienced as threatening to masculine identity, and to the extent that vulnerability, dependency, and the helplessness of being out-of-control are also so experienced, to that extent will a man's capacity to experience sexuality as an intensely emotional connection be dramatically curtailed. Normative masculine socialization, by its constrictive influence on emotional experience, inhibits the relatively natural confluence of sexuality and intense emotionality. The very intensity of sexual experience, which by its nature at least potentially can evoke intense emotions, is likely to thereby evoke the constrictive influences that most men have internalized through the process of their masculinization.

The consequences of this masculinization of sexual experience are varied. For many men, it is simply another aspect of the human condition which they experience in a somewhat disconnected form; a flattening or deadening of a potentially enlivening human experience. However, there are other, potentially more dangerous consequences. Sexuality is, by its very nature, an experience of great potential intensity. It consists of intense physical sensations; it is typically associated with enormous social meanings and taboos and is therefore easily connected to shame; it often includes the penetration of actual physical boundaries. For all of these reasons, a sexual encounter is likely to be experienced intensely. These inherent qualities of sexuality make it uniquely vulnerable to exploitation and abuse. When two people enter a sexual encounter, if one is disconnected from his capacity to experience the intense emotional component of the encounter, while the other is not disconnected, then the potential for harm and exploitation is enormously heightened. This is dramatically heightened further when the encounter itself is not mutual, but rather the result of manipulation, control, coercion, or actual physical force.

Indeed, it can be argued that the very fact of being disconnected from emotional experience dramatically increases the likelihood that someone would be able and willing to exploit and abuse the sexuality of another person. Separated from its emotional associations, unlinked from its relationship to human connection, sexuality is more likely to be experienced as simply another physical sensation; a physical need to be gratified. With the thread of human (emotional) connectedness severed, the "other" can be experienced as pure object; as a source of sexual gratification whose experience of the encounter has no reality. What this describes is a profound disruption of the human capacity for empathy.

The evidence suggests that the normative process of male gender socialization, in which males develop relatively constricted emotional lives, leads to impaired empathic capacity. Simultaneously, this normative socialization process tends to accentuate males' experience of, and access to anger, the emotion that is most sanctioned by male gender norms. Indeed, it has been argued that men who rigidly adhere to gender norms for emotional expression are likely to convert a variety of "nonmasculine" emotional states into anger (Mosher & Tomkins, 1988). This combination of impaired empathy and anger accentuation may well have something to do with the disproportionate male involvement in sexual abuse.

Pathways from Emotional Socialization to Perpetration

Empathy Deficits

Empathy has often been thought of as a critical inhibitor of interpersonal aggression, and this view is supported by considerable empirical evidence that deficits in empathy are associated with aggressive behavior (Miller & Eisenberg, 1988). Unfortunately, the concept of empathy has proven to be somewhat illusive, particularly when attempts have been made to operationalize it. However, research and theorizing during the past decade has led to significant refinements in the concept. Empathy is now thought to have a cognitive component—perspective-taking—and an emotional component—vicarious emotional responding. Further, vicarious emotional responding has itself been analyzed into at least two distinct components: "sympathy" and "personal distress."

Batson, Fultz, and Schoenrade (1987) contended that witnessing another person's distress—a situation that typically evokes some form of vicarious emotional response—can induce either a sympathetic emotional response, such as compassion and tenderness, or it can induce distressful emotions, such as alarm and "upset." They argued, citing supportive experimental evidence, that a sympathetic response may lead to helpful behavior, whereas a distressed response is more likely to lead to behavior aimed at terminating the negative internal state generated by witnessing the other person's distress. This formulation has been supported by research by Eisenberg, Fabes, Schaller, Carlo, and Miller (1991a) that has linked differential physiological responses to these alternative vicarious emotional reactions. Individuals who react sympathetically tend to manifest a decrease in heart rate, while individuals who react with distress tend to manifest an increase in heart rate.

If we extrapolate these findings to the domain of male gender socialization, we might well predict that, in general, males might be more prone to experiencing distress in reaction to witnessing another person's distress. The other person's distress, be it fear or emotional pain or some other expression of vulnerability, is likely to evoke the male's own reservoir of such vulnerable emotional states. Once evoked, these states are in turn likely to create distress, since they are precisely the emotions that the male has had to suppress in the service of achieving and maintaining his masculine identity. To the "masculinized" male, the evocation of these emotional states is a direct assault on a cornerstone of his identity. To the extent that the male begins to vicariously experience the other person's vulnerable emotions, he will begin to feel anxious ("distress" in empathy terminology), with, presumably, a concomitant increase in his heart rate.

A state of heightened anxiety tends to decrease the likelihood of prosocial behavior, and increase the likelihood of a variety of unhelpful behaviors. Anxious, "distressed" individuals tend to focus their attention on their own aversive internal state not on the originally distressed person who evoked their anxiety. They tend to seek ways to relieve their anxiety. This can be accomplished in several ways. They may disconnect their conscious awareness of their emotional reactions. That is, they disconnect their ability to resonate with the other person's distress, thereby also disconnecting themselves from their anxiety reactions. They may also attempt to relieve their anxiety through the emotional conversion process described by Mosher and Tomkins (1988). The sequence of this process would be as follows: (a) they experience some resonance with the emotional state of the distressed person; (b) these resonant emotions quickly induce an anxiety state; (c) their anxiety is quickly transformed into anger, and/or aggressive action; (d) the expression of anger and/or aggressive action relieves the anxiety state.

The conversion of "personal distress" reactions to anger and aggression may be responsible for the observed tendency among abused children to respond aggressively toward peers who display overt distress (Klimes-Dougan & Kistner, 1990; Main & George, 1985). Such aggressive reactions in a context that would ordinarily evoke sympathy are almost never seen in children who have not been maltreated. These reactions are consistent with the hypothesis that the maltreated children experience intense anxiety when confronted with other children's distress, and need to relieve the anxiety by turning it into aggressive action.

A similar process may have been responsible for the finding in the Gold et al. study (1992), in which the high "macho" males responded to a crying baby not only with less empathy, but also with more anger. The baby's cries may have evoked resonant emotions in these "hypermasculine" men, emotions that conflict markedly with the gender norms that these men try to adhere to. By converting the emotions quickly into anger, the men are relieved of the conflict.

The link between such anxiety or "personal distress" reactions and empathy deficits is also supported by the observation that the abuse of infants and children is often triggered by the child's expression of distress (Zeskind & Shingler, 1991). Frodi and Lamb (1980) have demonstrated experimentally that child abusers are more physiologically reactive (increased heart rate and skin conductance) and experience greater aversion to the sound of a crying infant. This increased aversive arousal can be interpreted as a physiological manifestation of the evocation of distress in the abuser. The heightened distress experienced by abusers would motivate them to seek to terminate this aversive state rather than to sympathize with the distressed child.

The Relationship between Empathy for the Self
and Empathy for Others

In dramatically—and traumatically—constricting the male's capacity to experience the full range of his emotions, masculine socialization does more than obstruct the male's ability to respond sympathetically to other people's distress. It also obstructs his ability to respond sympathetically to his own distress. As he learns that vulnerable emotional states are "unmasculine," and that they must be expunged from his experience lest he be forced to label himself "unmasculine," the male is forced to respond as aggressively to his own internal displays of vulnerability as he would to those of others. The harsh and denigrating words inflicted on him in the course of his socialization into masculinity are internalized. If he shows himself his fear or his hurt, he is likely to respond spontaneously with the vocabulary of masculine epithets: "you're a girl," "a sissy," "weak," "a crybaby."

Thus, the normative socialization process for males is likely to leave them quite intolerant of their own innate, human tendency to experience vulnerable emotional states in response to the inevitable stresses of life. This intolerance is then very likely to transfer to other people's vulnerable emotions. Barnett and McCoy (1989) demonstrated this relationship in a study that has since been replicated by Ivan (1996). College students were asked to identify a range of distressing experiences they had experienced during childhood, and to then rate how distressing each of those experiences was for them. They were also given a measure of empathy for others. There was no relationship between the number of distressing experiences a person had and their current empathy level. However, their rating of how distressing their experiences were for them was related to current empathy. Those who rated their experiences as relatively *more* distressing displayed higher levels of current empathy. In other words, if they were able to acknowledge their own distress, they were more able to resonate with distress felt by others.

A number of other studies lend support to the link between people's capacity to tolerate their own distressful emotions and their capacity to empathize with distress in others. Lenrow (1965) demonstrated experimentally that children who openly expressed their own distress in stressful situations were more responsive to the expression of distress in others. A study reported by Bryant (1987) provides a clue to the origins of these differences among children. He found that children whose mothers were more positively responsive to them when they experienced stress at age 10 were significantly more empathic at age 14 than children whose mothers had been less responsive. By responding in such positive ways, these mothers may have been teaching their children to be tolerant of their distressful emotional states, a tolerance that later transferred to a tolerance and sympathy for distress in others. In a similar finding, Eisenberg et al. (1991b) reported a significant correlation between the sympathy levels of fathers and their male children. Further, parents who strongly discouraged their male children from expressing sadness and anxiety had sons who were low in sympathy. The authors concluded that "children who receive negative reactions when they respond emotionally may learn to deny or suppress their emotional reactions and to experience anxiety internally" (Eisenberg et al., 1991a, p. 1405). They further noted that this process was more evident in boys than in girls, a finding that is consistent with "cultural norms regarding the importance of males' inhibition of emotion."

These findings suggest that there is a relationship between a person's capacity to experience and express their own painful emotions and the capacity to respond sympathetically to the emotional pain of another person. To the extent that the masculine-socialized male has internalized stereotypical gender norms that dictate a suppressive attitude to those painful emotions, he will be less likely to respond sympathetically to his own distress, and therefore to the emotional distress of another person.

The Interaction of Childhood Abuse, Masculine Socialization, and Perpetration

In the search for the causes of sexual victimization, one of the most consistent findings is a history of childhood abuse among its perpetrators. These findings have led to the "cycle of violence" hypothesis, which posits that childhood abuse is a predisposing factor for the later perpetration of violence. It is clear that the relationship between early abuse and later perpetration is far from direct (Widom, 1989). In a series of studies from our own laboratory at the University of Massachusetts-Boston, in which more than 1,000 men were assessed, two-thirds of abused men never perpetrated either sexual or non-sexual forms of interpersonal violence (Lisak, Hopper, & Song, 1996; Lisak,

Miller, & Conklin, 1996). However, a strong majority of the men who perpetrated had themselves been victimized as children; the data suggest that the proportion is at least two-thirds. The strongest relationship holds for men who perpetrate sexual violence against children. Of these men, more than 80 percent had themselves been abused as children.

There are good reasons to suspect that masculine gender socialization may be partly responsible for this link between early abuse and later perpetration; and once again, emotional experience may play an important role. The interaction between early abuse and the process of masculine socialization can create an intense conflict for male victims. To be abused as a child is to experience fear, helplessness, powerlessness, shame, and humiliation, and at an intensity that is overwhelming. Herein lies the core of the conflict that will plague the male abuse victim. He is plunged by the abuse into a sea of emotions that have already been identified as inherently non-masculine; emotions that in fact define nonmasculinity. Yet he is experiencing them and they become indelible parts of him, because they are traumatically etched into his memory and therefore his experience of himself; of who he is.

As intense as this conflict is, it is based on an illusion, the illusion of masculinity. In reality, the male victim is simply a human being who is responding to traumatic injury precisely the way humans are endowed to respond. But his gender socialization prevents him from ever seeing the utter normalcy and simplicity of his response; the humanness of his fear, his pain, and his vulnerability. His gender socialization ensures that he will war against these basic human responses. He will try to excise them; he will beg them to go away; he will pretend they don't exist; he will seal up vast chambers of his humanity in a futile effort to believe they have disappeared. All because he has already internalized his culture's dictates about which parts of himself are appropriate and acceptable, and which are emblems of nonmasculinity.

How does the male victim live with such a conflict? Our research and clinical findings suggest that it is not easy. It appears that the majority of men who struggle with the interacting legacies of abuse and gender socialization suffer the predictable consequences of the conflict. Many feel inadequate. They feel like failures; they feel alienated from other men; they feel they must hide the telltale signs of that inner brand that marks them forever as nonmen. They struggle and suffer with intrapersonal and interpersonal consequences of the conflict (Lisak, 1994).

Faced with such an unrelenting conflict, and an unrelenting assault on their deep-felt need for a masculine identity, some men "choose" to psychologically banish one side of the conflict—the abuse, and/or the psychological legacies of the abuse. For these men, this "choice" actually becomes more of a drive; a driven need to expunge the evidence of their vulnerability, of their nonmasculinity. To accomplish this, they must banish their fear, their helplessness, their powerlessness, and their shame, because now they are all dangerous nodal points that can draw them back into that expunged nonmasculine state.

These men monitor their world, both inside and out, for any sign or gesture that might link back to that repressed but vibrating core of pain and vulnerability that they have entombed within themselves. These are the men whom you learn not to tease about certain things; the men you are careful not to shame. These are the fathers in the playground who cannot tolerate to see the childlike fear in their sons' eyes because that fear has the power to resonate through the circuits of their memory and open the door to their own fear that they are desperate to hold shut.

The role of masculine socialization, and in particular gender rigidity and emotional constriction, in mediating the link between childhood abuse and the perpetration of sexual abuse has received some empirical support (Lisak, Hopper, & Song, 1996). In this sample of nearly 600 men, abused men who perpetrated scored higher on measures of gender rigidity and of emotional constriction than abused men who did not perpetrate. Interestingly, the abused men who did not perpetrate actually scored *lower* on these measures than the non-abused "control" subjects. Together, these results point to divergent adaptations to the conflict created by the interacting legacies of abuse and of masculine socialization. One group—the nonperpetrators—appear to have evolved a less rigid gender identity than is the norm, perhaps in response to their abuse experiences. The other group—the perpetrators—appear to have evolved a rigid, hypergendered masculine identity.

Two recent follow-up studies have added credence to this interpretation. In one sample, abused perpetrators scored significantly lower on measures of psychological distress than did abused non-perpetrators, including a measure of Posttraumatic Stress Disorder (Lisak, Miller, & Conklin, 1996). These results are consistent with the hypothesized hypergendered adaptation of abused perpetrators—men who deny and suppress their emotional distress, but who are more likely to act out violently against other people. In the second study, abused perpetrators scored significantly lower than abused non-perpetrators on a measure of empathy (Hopper, 1996).

Together, these results paint the picture of an identifiable adaptation to the conflict between abuse and masculine socialization. It is an adaptation in which the abused male is driven to suppress the emotional legacy of his abuse in the service of adhering to male gender norms, norms that prohibit the experience or expression of such intense and vulnerable emotional states. The fact that those emotional states are nevertheless indelible parts of his experience necessitates a rigid, hypergendered masculinity, with a concomitant increase in emotional constriction, a denial or suppression of emotional distress, and a decrease in the capacity for empathy.

These findings are consistent with the research cited earlier that points to a relationship between a person's capacity to experience and express their own painful emotions, and their capacity to respond sympathetically to the emotional pain of another person. To the extent that the abused male has internalized stereotypical gender norms that dictate a suppressive attitude to those painful emotions, he will be less likely respond sympathetically to his own distress, and therefore to the emotional distress of another person.

Two studies that compared the consequences of alternative responses to childhood abuse experiences provide support for this relationship. Hunter and Kilstrom (1979) compared abused mothers who did and did not abuse their own children. They found the non-abusing mothers were able to describe in more detail their own abuse experiences and were more expressive of their anger. In contrast, the abusing mothers were more vague in their recollections, less willing to talk, and less expressive of anger.

Very similar differences were noted by Burgess, Hartman, McCausland, and Powers (1984) in their study of children and adolescents abused in sex and pornography rings. Those victims who had integrated the event were more able to talk openly about their experiences and manifested less anxiety when doing so. Other victims manifested an avoidant strategy, in which their anxiety lingered but was "sealed off." These children were considerably more symptomatic and were more likely to have engaged in antisocial acts. Another group of children appeared to have identified with their perpetrators. These children minimized the negative nature of their experiences and were also more likely to be engaging in antisocial acts.

Support for the relationship between suppression of abuse-related emotions and increased propensities for aggression can also be found in the literature on clinical interventions with abused males. Friedrich, Berliner, Urquiza, and Beilke (1988) reported that the abused boys they treated were generally unable to verbalize their feelings about their abuse, typically denied their existence, and instead manifested them in various forms of acting out, including sexualized aggressiveness. They noted that in treatment groups for abused girls there was typically far less denial and sexual aggressiveness, a finding that suggests the importance of gender socialization in channeling children's response to abuse.

Freeman-Longo (1986) concluded that most incarcerated sex offenders have never dealt with the emotional legacies of their own abuse experiences and do not consider that their victims must experience the same emotions. Schact, Kerlinsky, and Carlson (1990) argued, on the basis of their experience leading groups for abused boys, that the boys were unable to consciously experience their feelings of fear and vulnerability and so they induced them in other people, where they could experience them vicariously and therefore more safely.

The evidence cited above suggests that there may be two, perhaps interrelated, ways in which intolerance of distressful emotions leads to inhibited empathy. To the extent that such intolerance leads to a constriction of the experience of such distressful emotions, the constricted individual will be less likely to be able to vicariously experience the distressful emotions experienced by others. They may in fact recognize that the other person is experiencing distressing emotions, but there will be no emotional resonance within them; their disconnection from their own distressful emotions impairs their capacity to vicariously experience those emotions in others.

The second apparent pathway to inhibited empathy is through the evocation of a "personal distress" reaction in response to witnessing distress in another person. Such a reaction has been shown to decrease the individual's tendency to respond sympathetically, and increase their need to find a way to terminate their aversive state. This may be accomplished by active avoidance of the stimulus, or possibly by converting the distressful emotions that have been evoked into one that may be experienced as less distressful, such as anger. Once evoked, this anger may well be channeled as aggression against the "other" who is perceived to be in distress. The aggression may be purely instrumental, designed to terminate the state of inner distress by "getting rid" of the perceived external source of it (the other person). Or, the aggression may be rooted in a similar, but somewhat more complex dynamic. In this case, the distress and vulnerability expressed by the other person triggers resonant, unconscious emotions in the perpetrator. The perpetrator then turns on these despised emblems of his vulnerability by crushing them in the other person through an act of aggression. In such a case, what the perpetrator actually perceives in the other person is largely irrelevant, since the dynamic is essentially one of projection, followed by an unconscious reaction to the projection.

Case Study: From Abuse to Perpetration to the Recovery of Empathy on Death Row

Death row is hardly what most people would think of as a therapeutic environment. Condemned prisoners spend most of their days alone in tiny cells, waiting out the legal process that for many of them ends in execution. Yet for some of these men (there are only a handful of women on the nation's death rows), death row represents the first environment in which they are free of the unrelenting violence, poverty, and degradation of their lives. In this environment, some prisoners embark on a reevaluation of their lives, a process that for some leads to significant psychological transformation.

Don G. was sentenced to death for the murder of a woman with whom he had had a brief, stormy relationship mostly centered on the consumption of drugs and alcohol. While this murder was the only crime for which Don had been convicted, during the course of the evaluation he disclosed other offenses he had committed, including sexually exploitative and abusive acts. As a young adolescent, Don had sexually abused slightly younger children on two occasions. These acts, it became evident, mirrored the abuses he had himself suffered as child.

After 10 years on death row, Don was undergoing the first comprehensive psychological evaluation organized by his attorneys, an evaluation intended to provide mitigating evidence to support an appeal of his death sentence. The evaluation involved many hours of interviews covering Don's entire developmental history; it also included the examination of virtually every school, medical, and psychiatric record that could be recovered; and it included interviews with numerous family members, friends of the family, former teachers, and treating professionals. Such an evaluation, rarely even attempted in the routine of normal psychological assessments, can provide a remarkably thorough delineation of the developmental factors that lead a man to death row.

Don was born into a chaotic, poverty-stricken family. His parents, both alcoholics and drug abusers, beat each of the five children and subjected them to an array of sadistic punishments. When Don was not being beaten—with fists, shoes, telephones, and whatever was within reach—he was neglected to the point of hunger and malnutrition. His teachers recalled him as emaciated, skittish, forlorn, and depressed. Although Don was at first loath to acknowledge it, interviews with his brothers and others who knew the family revealed that he had also been sexually abused. Eventually, Don began to disclose these victimizations: an uncle and an older cousin orally raped him before he was 10; a middle-aged woman friend of his father seduced him into intercourse when he was 11; between the ages of 12 and 15, he was anally raped on three separate occasions by men who picked him up off the streets where he had sought refuge from the violence and neglect of his home.

As Don matured into adolescence, the terror, humiliation, and degradations of his childhood were sealed away as memories that were unreachable but yet tormented him and drove his behavior. He became what he called a "survivor," which to him also meant a perpetrator. In his world, there were only predators and prey; to him, growing into manhood meant the opportunity to finally turn predator. Which he did, committing numerous assaults and at least several rapes before he was arrested and convicted of the murder of his girlfriend.

As the years on death row tolled onward, the seals that secured the bottomless pain of his childhood became frayed. By the time the evaluation began, 10 years into his incarceration, they were ready to be broken. As the interviews progressed, Don began having nightmares that were repetitive reexperiences of the rapes he had suffered. Soon he was tormented both day and night by the sounds, the smells, and the physical sensations of being orally and anally raped. He stopped sleeping entirely, could not eat, had constant headaches, and his muscles were tensed like drawstrings. Finally, midway through one of the interviews, he broke down, sobbing uncontrollably for 45 minutes, until an alarmed prison guard had him escorted back to his cell.

Don's breakdown initiated a whole new series of disclosures. There were other abuses he had suffered, but most importantly, he disclosed and reexperienced the details, the actual pain of the multiple traumas of his childhood and adolescence. Then, at the conclusion of one of the final interviews, as he collected himself and prepared for the strip search that followed each meeting, he suddenly began sobbing again. After 15 minutes, he pulled himself together enough to say that he could now not bear the pain of knowing what he had done to the women he had raped. He forced out those words through shame and guilt and physical pain that were literally contorting his body. His last statement at the end of the final interview was, "My lawyers may save my life, but I don't know if I can live with myself." In the ensuing months, Don experienced similar levels of excruciating remorse over the sexual abuses he had committed when he was a young teenager, and over the rapes he had committed later during his adolescence and young adulthood.

The transformation that Don underwent was essentially the recovery of his humanity; a reconnection to his human capacity to feel. It began with a reconnection to the pain of his childhood, and resulted in a restoration of his ability to connect to the pain of other human beings—his capacity to empathize. The transformation represented an unraveling of Don's lifelong adaptation to his traumatic childhood, an adaptation that was organized and facilitated by a masculine ideology that was provided to him by his culture.

The extremity of the abuse that Don had suffered, and the environment in which he grew up, foreclosed most positive outcomes for him. Adolescence produced an option for Don that could not be turned down: a masculine identity that validated his rage, validated his repression of his enormous reservoir of pain and vulnerability, and offered him "valid" targets for his vengeance—children, women, anyone more vulnerable than he was. As social science research has demonstrated, Don's adaptation to the pain of his childhood exemplified a masculine ideology that is endorsed by a large proportion of males. For some men, those whose endorsement is driven by such profound levels of pain and rage, such a masculine ideology clears the path to the sexual exploitation of others, and to the perpetration of interpersonal violence.

Conclusion

Sexual abuse and sexually exploitative behavior are interpersonally violent and damaging acts committed disproportionately by men. Among the many factors contributing to this violence, male gender socialization is one of the most prominent. Stereotyped masculine attitudes and behaviors have been linked to the perpetration of sexually exploitative acts by both clinical and experimental research.

At the core of the male gender socialization process is the often traumatic constricting of the male's capacity to experience and express his emotions. In particular, emotions associated with vulnerability—such as fear and shame—are excised and often supplanted by the acceptably male emotion of anger. The result often is a relatively disconnected experience of sexuality, in which intense emotions are suppressed, and an impaired capacity for empathy. Both of these impairments increase the male's capacity for sexually exploitative or sexually violent behavior.

References

Barash, D. (1979). *The whisperings within*. New York: Harper & Row.

Barnett, M. A., and McCoy, S. J. (1989). The relation of distressful childhood experiences and empathy in college undergraduates. *Journal of Genetic Psychology*, 150:417–426.

Batson, C. D., Fultz, J., & Schoenrade, P. A. (1987). Distress and empathy: Two qualitatively distinct vicarious emotions with different motivational consequences. *Journal of Personality*, 55:19–39.

Berliner, L., and Elliot, D. M. (1996). Sexual abuse of children. In L. Briere, L. Berliner, J. A. Bulkley, C. Jenny, and T. Reid (Eds.), *The APSAC handbook on child maltreatment* (pp. 51–71). Thousand Oaks, CA: Sage.

Briere, J., and Runtz, M. (1988). Symptomology associated with childhood sexual victimization in a nonclinical adult sample. *Child Abuse and Neglect, 12*, 51–59.

Brod, H. (1994). Some thoughts on some histories of some masculinities. In H. Brod and M. Kaufman (Eds.), *Theorizing masculinities* (pp. 82–96). Thousand Oaks, CA: Sage.

Brody, L. R. (1985). Gender differences in emotional development: A review of theories and research. *Journal of Personality*, 53:102–149.

Bryant, B. K. (1987). Critique of comparable questionnaire methods in use to assess empathy in children and adults. In N. Eisenberg and J. Strayer (Eds.), *Empathy and its development* (pp. 361–373). Cambridge, England: Cambridge University Press.

Burgess, A. W., Hartman, C. R., McCausland, M. P., and Powers, C. (1984). Response patterns in children and adolescents exploited through sex rings and pornography. *American Journal of Psychiatry*, 141:656–662.

Chodorow, N. (1978). *The reproduction of mothering*, Berkeley: University of California Press.

Crossman, R. K., Stith, S. M., and Bender, M. M. (1990). Sex role egalitarianism and marital violence. *Sex Roles*, 22:293–304.

Diener, E., Sandvik, E., and Larsen, J. (1985). Age and sex effects for affect intensity. *Developmental Psychology*, 21:542–546.

Eisenberg, N., Fabes, R. A., Schaller, M., Carlo, G., and Miller, P. A. (1991). The relations of parental characteristics and practices to children's vicarious emotional responding. *Child Development*, 62:1393–1408.

Eisenberg, N., Fabes, R. A., Schaller, M., Miller, P., Carlo, G., Poulin, R., Shea, C., and Shell, R. (1991). Personality and socialization correlates of vicarious emotional responding. *Journal of Personality and Social Psychology*, 61:459–470.

Eisenberg, N., and Lennon, R. (1983). Sex differences in empathy and related capacities. *Psychological Bulletin*, 94:100–131.

Fausto-Sterling, A. (1985). *Myths of gender*. New York: Basic Books.

Federal Bureau of Investigation. (1992). *Uniform crime reports of the United States*. Washington, DC: U.S. Government Printing Office.

Fivush, R. (1989). Exploring sex differences in the emotional content of mother-child conversations about the past. *Sex Roles*, 20:675–691.

Freeman-Longo, R. E. (1986). The impact of sexual victimization on males. *Child Abuse and Neglect, 10*:411–414.

Friedrich, W. N., Berliner, L., Urquiza, A. J., and Beilke, R. L. (1988). Brief diagnostic group treatment of sexually abused boys. *Journal of Interpersonal Violence*, 3:331–343.

Frodi, A. M., and Lamb, M. E. (1980). Child abusers' responses to infant smiles and cries. *Child Development*, 51:238–241.

Fromuth, M. E., Burkhart, B., and Jones, C. W. (1991). Hidden child molestation. *Journal of Interpersonal Violence*, 6:376–384.

Gilmore, D. D. (1990). *Manhood in the making*. New Haven, CT: Yale University Press.

Gold, S. R., Fultz, J., Burke, C. H., Prisco, A. G., and Willett, J. A. (1992). Vicarious emotional responses of macho college males. *Journal of Interpersonal Violence*, 7:165–174.

Hopper, J. (1996). *The relationship between childhood abuse, male gender socialization, and perpetration*. Doctoral dissertation, University of Massachusetts, Boston.

Hunter, R. S., and Kilstrom, N. (1979). Breaking the cycle in abusive families. *American Journal of Psychiatry*, 136:1320–1322.

Ivan, C. (1996). *Big boys don't cry: Socialization of emotional displays and emotional empathy in males*. Doctoral dissertation, University of Massachusetts, Boston.

Kanin, E. (1984). Date rape: Unofficial criminals and victims. *Victimology*, 9:95–108.

Kilmartin, C. T. (1994). *The masculine self*. New York: Macmillan.

Kimmel, M. (1996). *Manhood in America*. New York: Free Press.

Klimes-Dougan, B., and Kistner, J. (1990). Physically abused preschoolers' responses to peers' distress. *Developmental Psychology*, 26:599–602.

Koss, M. P., Leonard, K. E., Beezley, D. A., and Oros, C. J. (1985). Nonstranger sexual aggression: A discriminant analysis of the psychological characteristics of undetected offenders. *Sex Roles*, 12:981–992.

Kuebli, J., and Fivush, R. (1992). Gender differences in parent-child conversations about past events. *Sex Roles*, 27:683–698.

Lenrow, P. B. (1965). Studies of sympathy. In S. L. Tomkins and C. E. Izard (Eds.), *Affect, cognition, and personality* (pp. 264–294). New York: Springer.

Levant, R. F. (1995). Toward the reconstruction of masculinity. In R. F. Levant and W. S. Pollack (Eds.), *A new psychology of men* (pp. 229–251). New York: Basic Books.

Lisak, D. (1994). The psychological consequences of childhood abuse: Content analysis of interviews with male survivors. *Journal of Traumatic Stress*, 7:525–548.

Lisak, D., Hopper, J., and Song, P. (1996). Factors in the cycle of violence: Gender rigidity and emotional constriction. *Journal of Traumatic Stress*, 9:721–743.

Lisak, D., and Ivan, C. (1995). Deficits in intimacy and empathy in sexually aggressive men. *Journal of Interpersonal Violence*, 10:296–308.

Lisak, D., Miller, P., and Conklin, A., (1996). *The relationship between abuse, perpetration, and the experience of emotional distress*. Manuscript submitted for publication.

Lisak, D., and Roth, S. (1988). Motivational factors in nonincarcerated sexually aggressive men. *Journal of Personality and Social Psychology*, 55:795–802.

Lisak, D., and Roth, S. (1990). Motives and psychodynamics of self-reported, unincarcerated rapists. *American Journal of Orthopsychiatry*, 60:268–280.

Main, M., and George, C. (1985). Responses of abused and disadvantaged toddlers to distress in agemates: The day care setting. *Developmental Psychology*, 21, 407–412.

Malamuth, N. M. (1986). Predictors of naturalistic sexual aggression. *Journal of Personality and Social Psychology*, 50:953–962.

Malamuth, N. M., Sockloskie, R. J., Koss, M. P., and Tanaka, J. S. (1991). Characteristics of aggressors against women: Testing a model using a national sample of college students. *Journal of Consulting and Clinical Psychology*, 59:670–681.

Malatesta, C., and Haviland, J. M. (1985). Signals, symbols and socialization: The modification of emotional expression in human development. In M. Lewis and C. Saarni (Eds.), *The socialization of emotions* (pp. 89–115). New York: Plenum Press.

McCord, J., McCord, W., and Thurber, E. (1962). Some effects of paternal absence on male children. *Journal of Abnormal and Social Psychology*, 64:361–369.

McEwan, B. S., and Mendelson, S. (1993). Effects of stress on the neurochemistry and morphology of the brain: Counterregulation versus damage. In L. Goldberger and S. Breznitz (Eds.), *Handbook of stress: Theoretical and clinical aspects* (pp. 101–126). New York: Free Press.

Miller, P. A., and Eisenberg, N. (1988). The relation of empathy to aggressive and externalizing/antisocial behavior. *Psychological Bulletin*, 103:324–344.

Mosher, D. L., and Anderson, R. (1986). Macho personality, sexual aggression, and reactions to guided imagery of realistic rape. *Journal of Research in Personality*, 20:77–94.

Mosher, D. L., and Tomkins, S. S. (1988). Scripting the macho man: Hypermasculine socialization and enculturation. *Journal of Sex Research*, 25:60–84.

Muehlenhard, C. L., and Falcon, P. L. (1990). Men's heterosocial skill and attitudes toward women as predictors of verbal sexual coercion and forceful rape. *Sex Roles*, 23:241–259.

Munroe, R., Munroe, R., and Whiting, J. (1981). Male sex-role resolutions. In R. Munroe, R. Munroe, and B. Whiting (Eds.), *Handbook of cross-cultural human development* (pp. 611–632). New York: STM Press.

Pollack, W. S. (1995). No man is an island: Toward a new psychoanalytic psychology of men. In R. F. Levant and W. S. Pollack (Eds.), *A new psychology of men* (pp. 33–67). New York: Basic Books.

Rapaport, K., and Burkhart, B. (1984). Personality and attitudinal characteristics of sexually coercive college males. *Journal of Abnormal Psychology*, 93:216–221.

Schacht, A. J., Kerlinsky, D., and Carlson, C. (1990). Group therapy with sexually abused boys: Leadership, projective identification, and countertransference issues. *International Journal of Group Psychotherapy*, 40:401–417.

Stith, S. M., and Farley, S. C. (1993). A predictive model of male spousal violence. *Journal of Family Violence*, 8:183–201.

Webster, H. (1908). *Primitive secret societies*. New York: Macmillan.

Widom, C. S. (1989). Does violence beget violence? A critical examination of the literature. *Psychological Bulletin*, 106, 3–28.

Zeskind, P. S., and Shingler, E. A. (1991). Child abusers' perceptual responses to newborn infant cries varying in pitch. *Infant Behavior and Development*, 14:335–347.

PART IX

Social Stratification and Inequality in Socialization

Ever since the writings of Karl Marx in the mid-nineteenth century, social stratification has been a central focus of concern in Western industrialized societies. Inequalities of power, wealth and income, and social status have engaged Marxist and non-Marxist thinkers. The causes of these inequalities are not agreed upon, but the part played by socialization in perpetuating them is beginning to receive renewed attention. After a period of concentration on this topic in the 1940s and 1950s, significantly influenced by W. Lloyd Warner and his colleagues, interest in the topic faded somewhat, but in the late 1960s and 1970s it began to revive. A new spurt of interest came in the late 1990s. (For a review of the earlier work see Bronfenbrenner 1958).

Marx analyzed industrial society as divided into two main classes, determined by their relationship to the means of production. Capitalists (or bourgeoisie) own the means of production—land, factories, machinery. Workers (the proletariat) own nothing and must get their living by selling their labor for a wage to the bourgeoisie. Both because of social changes since the time of Marx and refinements in thinking about the question, a more complex portrait of social classes has emerged. For example, in a large-scale study carried out in Boston and Kansas City in the 1970s, Richard P. Coleman and Lee Rainwater concluded (1978) that Americans identify seven main social classes: (1) The old rich of aristocratic family name; (2) the new rich—this generation's success elite; (3) the college-educated professional and managerial class; (4) middle Americans of comfortable living standard' (5) middle Americans just getting along; (6) a lower working class of people who are poor but not on welfare; (7) the nonworking welfare class (p. 124). The college-educated professionals and managers are often referred to as the upper middle class. Some analyses (e.g. Gilbert and Kahl 1993) posit six classes by combining the top two into one. Also, the term "underclass" has come into use by some to designate those at the bottom of the social structure.

Although Americans, perhaps more than almost any other people, believe that a person can and should rise to whatever station in life his/her talents allow rather than being restricted to the station the person was born to, and although some social mobility (both upward and downward) does occur, socialization processes tend to have an impact that usually prepares the person for remaining at the same social level. Families and schools play a central part in producing this effect.

The first selection in this part consists of the opening pages of Annette Lareau's recent substantial study of socialization in upper-middle-class and working-class families (Lareau 2003). Here she presents what is perhaps the central finding of her study: upper-middle-class parents raise their children following a strategy of *concerted cultivation*, while working-class parents follow a strategy of *accomplishment of natural growth*. These different outlooks lead to different kinds of outcomes for children in the two classes.

Julia Wrigley's chapter shows social class differences in a different way. According to a 1991 survey, over 40 percent of upper-middle-class parents had hired caregivers to look after their children (Wrigley 1995: ix). In New York and Los Angeles, where she did her study, these caregivers are often poor, not well educated immigrant women. Wrigley here examines the conflicts in values and childrearing philosophy between parents, especially mothers who usually have professional or managerial jobs, and the caregivers, who often have very different ideas about how children should be brought up.

Schools have the obligation to educate every child, and they are a possible agency for mobility of children from informationally, as well as financially, impoverished backgrounds. Yet it has long been known that the schools fail to educate children from such backgrounds as successfully as those from middle class ones. Jean Anyon looks closely at educational practices in classrooms that vary by social class of their children, and she sheds some light on how schools help perpetuate existing social classes.

References

Bronfenbrenner, Urie. "Socialization and Social Class through Time and Space." pp. 400–25 in E. E. Maccoby, T. M. Newcomb, and E. L. Hartley (eds.) *Readings in Social Psychology* (New York: Holt, Rinehart, and Winston, 1958).

Coleman, Richard P. and Lee Rainwater. With Kent A. McClelland. *Social Standing in America* (New York: Basic Books, 1978).

Gilbert, Dennis and Joseph A. Kahl. *The American Class Structure*, 4th ed. (Belmont, CA: Wadsworth Publishing Company, 1993).

Lareau, Annette. *Unequal Childhoods* (Berkeley: University of California Press, 2003).

Warner, W. Lloyd, Robert J. Havighurst, and Martin B. Loeb. *Who Shall Be Educated? The Challenge of Unequal Opportunity* (New York: Harper and Bros., 1944).

Wrigley, Julia. *Other People's Children* (New York: Basic Books, 1995).

17

Concerted Cultivation and the Accomplishment of Natural Growth*

Annette Lareau

Laughing and yelling, a white fourth-grader named Garrett Tallinger splashes around in the swimming pool in the backyard of his four-bedroom home in the suburbs on a late spring afternoon. As on most evenings, after a quick dinner his father drives him to soccer practice. This is only one of Garrett's many activities. His brother has a baseball game at a different location. There are evenings when the boys' parents relax, sipping a glass of wine. Tonight is not one of them. As they rush to change out of their work clothes and get the children ready for practice, Mr. and Mrs. Tallinger are harried.

Only ten minutes away, a Black fourth-grader, Alexander Williams, is riding home from a school open house.[1] His mother is driving their beige, leather-upholstered Lexus. It is 9:00 P.M. on a Wednesday evening. Ms. Williams is tired from work and has a long Thursday ahead of her. She will get up at 4:45 A.M. to go out of town on business and will not return before 9:00 P.M. On Saturday morning, she will chauffeur Alexander to a private piano lesson at 8:15 A.M., which will be followed by a choir rehearsal and then a soccer game. As they ride in the dark, Alexander's mother, in a quiet voice, talks with her son, asking him questions and eliciting his opinions.

Discussions between parents and children are a hallmark of middle-class child rearing. Like many middle-class parents, Ms. Williams and her husband see themselves as "developing" Alexander to cultivate his talents in a concerted fashion. Organized activities, established and controlled by mothers and fathers, dominate the lives of middle-class children such as Garrett and Alexander. By making certain their children have these and other experiences, middle-class parents engage in a process of *concerted cultivation*. From this, a robust sense of entitlement takes root in the children. This sense of entitlement plays an especially important role in institutional settings, where middle-class children learn to question adults and address them as relative equals.

Only twenty minutes away, in blue-collar neighborhoods, and slightly farther away, in public housing projects, childhood looks different. Mr. Yanelli, a white working-class father, picks up his son Little Billy, a fourth-grader, from an after-school program. They come home and Mr. Yanelli drinks a beer while Little Billy first watches television, then rides his bike and plays in the street. Other nights, he and his Dad sit on the sidewalk outside their house and play cards. At about 5:30 P.M. Billy's mother gets home from her job as a house cleaner. She fixes dinner and the entire family sits down to eat together. Extended family are a prominent part of their lives. Ms. Yanelli touches base with her "entire family every day" by phone. Many nights Little Billy's uncle stops by, sometimes bringing Little Billy's youngest cousin. In the spring, Little Billy plays baseball on a local team. Unlike for Garrett and Alexander, who have at least four activities a week, for Little Billy, baseball is his only organized activity outside of school during the entire year. Down the road, a white working-class girl, Wendy Driver, also spends the evening with her girl cousins, as they watch a video and eat popcorn, crowded together on the living room floor.

Farther away, a Black fourth-grade boy, Harold McAllister, plays outside on a summer evening in the public housing project in which he lives. His two male cousins are there that night, as they often are. After an afternoon spent unsuccessfully searching for a ball so they could play basketball, the boys had resorted to watching sports on television. Now they head outdoors for a twilight water balloon fight. Harold tries to get his neighbor, Miss Latifa, wet. People sit in white plastic lawn chairs outside the row of apartments. Music and television sounds waft through the open windows and doors.

The adults in the lives of Billy, Wendy, and Harold want the best for them. Formidable economic constraints make it a major life task for these parents to put food on the table, arrange for housing, negotiate unsafe neighborhoods, take children to the doctor (often waiting for city buses that do not come), clean children's clothes, and get children to bed and have them ready for school the next morning. But unlike middle-class parents, these adults do not consider the concerted development of children, particularly through organized leisure activities, an essential aspect of good parenting. Unlike the Tallingers and Williamses, these mothers and fathers do not focus on concerted cultivation. For them, the crucial responsibilities of parenthood do not lie in eliciting their children's feelings, opinions, and thoughts. Rather, they see a clear boundary between adults and children. Parents tend to use directives: they tell their children what to do rather than persuading them with reasoning. Unlike their middle-class counterparts, who have a steady diet of adult organized activities, the working-class and poor children have more control over the character of their leisure activities. Most children are free to go out and play with friends and relatives who typically live close by. Their parents and guardians facilitate the *accomplishment of natural growth.*[2] Yet these children and their parents interact with central institutions in the society, such as schools, which firmly and decisively promote strategies of concerted cultivation in child rearing. For working-class and poor families, the cultural logic of child rearing at home is out of synch with the standards of institutions. As a result, while children whose parents adopt strategies of concerted cultivation appear to gain a sense of entitlement, children such as Billy Yanelli, Wendy Driver, and Harold McAllister appear to gain an emerging sense of distance, distrust, and constraint in their institutional experiences.

America may be the land of opportunity, but it is also a land of inequality. This book identifies the largely invisible but powerful ways that parents' social class impacts children's life experiences. It shows, using in-depth observations and interviews with middle-class (including members of the upper-middle-class), working-class, and poor families, that inequality permeates the fabric of the culture. In the chapters that lie ahead, I report the results of intensive observational research for a total of twelve families when their children were nine and ten years old. I argue that key elements of family life cohere to form a cultural logic of child rearing.[3] In other words, the differences among families seem to cluster together in meaningful patterns. In this historical moment, middle-class parents tend to adopt a cultural logic of child rearing that stresses the concerted cultivation of children. Working-class and poor parents, by contrast, tend to undertake the accomplishment of natural growth. In the accomplishment of natural growth, children experience long stretches of leisure time, child-initiated play, clear boundaries between adults and children, and daily interactions with kin. Working-class and poor children, despite tremendous economic strain, often have more "childlike" lives, with autonomy from adults and control over their extended leisure time. Although middle-class children miss out on kin relationships and leisure time, they appear to (at least potentially) gain important institutional advantages. From the experience of concerted cultivation, they acquire skills that could be valuable in the future when they enter the world of work. Middle-class white and Black children in my study did exhibit some key differences; yet the biggest gaps were not within social classes but, as I show, across them. It is these class differences and how they are enacted in family life and child rearing that shape the ways children view themselves in relation to the rest of the world.

Cultural Repertoires

Professionals who work with children, such as teachers, doctors, and counselors, generally agree about how children should be raised. Of course, from time to time they may disagree on the ways standards should be enacted for an individual child or family. For example, teachers may disagree about whether or not parents should stop and correct a child who mispronounces a word while reading. Counselors may disagree over whether a mother is being too protective of her child. Still, there is little dispute among professionals on the broad principles for promoting educational development in children through proper parenting.[4] These standards include the importance of talking with children, developing their educational interests, and playing an active role in their schooling. Similarly, parenting guidelines typically stress the importance of reasoning with children and teaching them to solve problems through negotiation rather than with physical force. Because these guidelines are so generally accepted, and because they focus on a set of practices concerning how parents should raise children, they form a *dominant set of cultural repertoires* about how children should be raised. This widespread agreement among professionals about the broad principles for child rearing permeates our society. A small number of experts thus potentially shape the behavior of a large number of parents.

Professionals' advice regarding the best way to raise children has changed regularly over the last two centuries. From strong opinions about the merits of bottle feeding, being stern with children, and utilizing physical punishment (with dire warnings of problematic outcomes should parents indulge children), there have been shifts to equally strongly worded recommendations about the benefits of breast feeding, displaying emotional warmth toward children, and using reasoning and negotiation as mechanisms of parental control. Middle-class parents appear to shift their behaviors in a variety of spheres more rapidly and more thoroughly than do working-class or poor parents.[5] As professionals have shifted their recommendations from bottle feeding to breast feeding, from stern approaches to warmth and empathy, and from spanking to time-outs, it is middle-class parents who have responded most promptly.[6] Moreover, in recent decades, middle-class children in the United States have had to face the prospect of "declining fortunes."[7] Worried about how their children will get ahead, middle-class parents are increasingly determined to make sure that their children are not excluded from any opportunity that might eventually contribute to their advancement.

Middle-class parents who comply with current professional standards and engage in a pattern of concerted cultivation deliberately try to stimulate their children's development and foster their cognitive and social skills. The commitment among working-class and poor families to provide comfort, food,

shelter, and other basic support requires ongoing effort, given economic challenges and the formidable demands of child rearing. But it stops short of the
deliberate cultivation of children and their leisure activities that occurs in
middle-class families. For working-class and poor families, sustaining children's natural growth is viewed as an accomplishment.[8]

What is the outcome of these different philosophies and approaches to child
rearing? Quite simply, they appear to lead to the *transmission of differential
advantages* to children. In this study, there was quite a bit more talking in
middle-class homes than in working-class and poor homes, leading to the
development of greater verbal agility, larger vocabularies, more comfort with
authority figures, and more familiarity with abstract concepts. Importantly,
children also developed skill differences in interacting with authority figures in
institutions and at home. Middle-class children such as Garrett Tallinger and
Alexander Williams learn, as young boys, to shake the hands of adults and look
them in the eye. In studies of job interviews, investigators have found that
potential employees have less than one minute to make a good impression.
Researchers stress the importance of eye contact, firm handshakes, and displaying comfort with bosses during the interview. In poor families like Harold
McAllister's, however, family members usually do not look each other in the
eye when conversing. In addition, as Elijah Anderson points out, they live in
neighborhoods where it can be dangerous to look people in the eye too long.[9]
The types of social competence transmitted in the McAllister family are valuable, but they are potentially less valuable (in employment interviews, for
example) than those learned by Garrett Tallinger and Alexander Williams.

The white and Black middle-class children in this study also exhibited an
emergent version of the *sense of entitlement* characteristic of the middle-class.
They acted as though they had a right to pursue their own individual preferences and to actively manage interactions in institutional settings. They
appeared comfortable in these settings; they were open to sharing information
and asking for attention. Although some children were more outgoing than others, it was common practice among middle-class children to shift interactions
to suit *their* preferences. Alexander Williams knew how to get the doctor to listen to his concerns (about the bumps under his arm from his new deodorant).
His mother explicitly trained and encouraged him to speak up with the doctor.
Similarly, a Black middle-class girl, Stacey Marshall, was taught by her mother
to expect the gymnastics teacher to accommodate her individual learning style.
Thus, middle-class children were trained in "the rules of the game" that govern interactions with institutional representatives. They were not conversant
in other important social skills, however, such as organizing their time for
hours on end during weekends and summers, spending long periods of time
away from adults, or hanging out with adults in a nonobtrusive, subordinate

fashion. Middle-class children also learned (by imitation and by direct training) how to make the rules work in their favor. Here, the enormous stress on reasoning and negotiation in the home also has a potential advantage for future institutional negotiations. Additionally, those in authority responded positively to such interactions. Even in fourth grade, middle-class children appeared to be acting on their own behalf to gain advantages. They made special requests of teachers and doctors to adjust procedures to accommodate their desires.

The working-class and poor children, by contrast, showed an emerging *sense of constraint* in their interactions in institutional settings. They were less likely to try to customize interactions to suit their own preferences. Like their parents, the children accepted the actions of persons in authority (although at times they also covertly resisted them). Working-class and poor parents sometimes were not as aware of their children's school situation (as when their children were not doing homework). Other times, they dismissed the school rules as unreasonable. For example, Wendy Driver's mother told her to "punch" a boy who was pestering her in class; Billy Yanelli's parents were proud of him when he "beat up" another boy on the playground, even though Billy was then suspended from school. Parents also had trouble getting "the school" to respond to their concerns. When Ms. Yanelli complained that she "hates" the school, she gave her son a lesson in powerlessness and frustration in the face of an important institution. Middle-class children such as Stacey Marshall learned to make demands on professionals, and when they succeeded in making the rules work in their favor they augmented their "cultural capital" (i.e., skills individuals inherit that can then be translated into different forms of value as they move through various institutions) for the future.[10] When working-class and poor children confronted institutions, however, they generally were unable to make the rules work in their favor nor did they obtain capital for adulthood. Because of these patterns of legitimization, children raised according to the logic of concerted cultivation can gain advantages, in the form of an emerging sense of entitlement, while children raised according to the logic of natural growth tend to develop an emerging sense of constraint.[11]

Social Stratification and Individualism

Public discourse in America typically presents the life accomplishments of a person as the result of her or his individual qualities. Songs like "I Did It My Way," memoirs, television shows, and magazine articles, celebrate the individual. Typically, individual outcomes are connected to individual effort and talent, such as being a "type A" personality, being a hard worker, or showing leadership. These cultural beliefs provide a framework for Americans' views of inequality.

Indeed, Americans are much more comfortable recognizing the power of individual initiative than recognizing the power of social class. Studies show that Americans generally believe that responsibility for their accomplishments rests on their individual efforts. Less than one-fifth see "race, gender, religion, or class as very important for 'getting ahead in life.'"[12] Compared to Europeans, individuals in the United States are much more likely to believe they can improve their standard of living. Put differently, Americans believe in the American dream: "The American dream that we were all raised on is a simple but powerful one—if you work hard and play by the rules, you should be given a chance to go as far as your God-given ability will take you."[13] This American ideology that each individual is responsible for his or her life outcomes is the expressed belief of the vast majority of Americans, rich and poor.

Yet there is no question that society is stratified. As I show in the next chapter, highly valued resources such as the possession of wealth; having an interesting, well-paying, and complex job; having a good education; and owning a home, are not evenly distributed throughout the society. Moreover, these resources are transferred across generations: One of the best predictors of whether a child will one day graduate from college is whether his or her parents are college graduates. Of course, relations of this sort are not absolute: Perhaps two-thirds of the members of society ultimately reproduce their parents' level of educational attainment, while about one-third take a different path. Still, there is no question that we live in a society characterized by considerable gaps in resources or, put differently, by substantial *inequality*. As I explain in the next chapter, however, reasonable people have disagreed about how best to conceptualize such patterns. They also have disagreed about whether families in different economic positions "share distinct, life-defining experiences."[14] Many insist that there is not a clear, coherent, and sustained experiential pattern. In this book, I demonstrate the existence of a cultural logic of child rearing that tends to differ according to families' social class positions. I see these interweaving practices as coming together in a messy but still recognizable way. In contrast to many, I suggest that social class does have a powerful impact in shaping the daily rhythms of family life.

The Study

It is a lot of work to get young children through the day, especially for their parents. When I embarked on this study, I was interested in understanding that labor process. In choosing to look at families, rather than just at children *or* parents, I hoped to capture some of the reciprocal effects of children and parents on each other. My approach also meant moving beyond the walls of the home to understand how parents and children negotiate with other adults in children's lives.

This book is based on intensive "naturalistic" observations of twelve families (six white, five Black, and one interracial) with children nine and ten years old. The twelve families are part of a larger study of eighty-eight children from the middle-class, working-class, and poor.[15] (For details of how the study was done, see Appendix A, Methodology.) I met most of these children when I visited their third-grade classrooms in the urban school, Lower Richmond, and a suburban school, Swan (both of which are described in the next chapter). With the help of white and Black research assistants, I carried out interviews first with the mohers and then with many of the fathers of these children. To better understand the expectations that professionals had of parents, I also interviewed the children's classroom teachers and other school personnel.

Notes

1. Choosing words to describe social groups also becomes a source of worry, especially over the possibility of reinforcing negative stereotypes. I found the available terms to describe members of racial and ethnic groups to be problematic in one way or another. The families I visited uniformly described themselves as "Black." Recognizing that some readers have strong views that Black should be capitalized, I have followed that convention, despite the lack of symmetry with the term white. In sum, this book alternates among the terms "Black," "Black American," "African American," and "white," with the understanding that "white" here refers to the subgroup of non-Hispanic whites.

2. Some readers have expressed concern that this phrase, "the accomplishment of natural growth," underemphasizes all the labor that mothers and fathers do to take care of children. They correctly note that working-class and poor parents themselves would be unlikely to use such a term to describe the process of caring for children. These concerns are important. As I stress in the text (especially in the chapter on Katie Brindle, Chapter 5) it does take an enormous amount of work for parents, especially mothers, of all classes to take care of children. But poor and working-class mothers have fewer resources with which to negotiate these demands. Those whose lives the research assistants and I studied approached the task somewhat differently than did middle-class parents. They did not seem to view children's leisure time as their responsibility; nor did they see themselves as responsible for assertively intervening in their children's school experiences. Rather, the working-class and poor parents carried out their chores, drew boundaries and restrictions around their children, and then, within these limits, allowed their children to carry out their lives. It is in this sense that I use the term "the accomplishment of natural growth."

3. I define a child-rearing context to include the routines of daily life, the dispositions of daily life, or the "habitus" of daily life. I focus on two contexts: concerted cultivation and the accomplishment of natural growth. In this book, I primarily use the concept of child rearing, but at times I also use the term *social-*

ization. Many sociologists have vigorously criticized this concept, noting that it suggests (inaccurately) that children are passive rather than active agents and that the relationship between parents and their children is unidirectional rather than reciprocal and dynamic. See, for example, William Corsaro, *Sociology of Childhood*; Barrie Thorne, *Gender Play*; and Glen Elder, "The Life Course as Development Theory." Nonetheless, existing terms can, ideally, be revitalized to offer more sophisticated understandings of social processes. Child rearing and socialization have the virtue of being relatively succinct and less jargon laden than other alternatives. As a result, I use them.

4. For discussions of the role of professionals, see Eliot Freidson, *Professional Powers*; Magali Sarfatti Larson, *The Rise of Professionalism*; and, although quite old, the still valuable collection by Amitai Etzioni, *The Semi-Professionals and Their Organizations*. Of course, professional standards are always contested and are subject to change over time. I do not mean to suggest there are not pockets of resistance and contestation. At the most general level, however, there is virtually uniform support for the idea that parents should talk to children at length, read to children, and take a proactive, assertive role in medical care.

5. Sharon Hays, in her 1996 book *The Cultural Contradictions of Motherhood*, studies the attitudes of middle-class and working-class mothers toward child rearing. She finds a shared commitment to "intensive mothering," although there are some differences among the women in her study in their views of punishment (with middle-class mothers leaning toward reasoning and working-class women toward physical punishment). My study focused much more on behavior than attitudes. If I looked at attitudes, I saw fewer differences; for example, all exhibited the desire to be a good mother and to have their children grow and thrive. The differences I found, however, were significant in how parents *enacted* their visions of what it meant to be a good parent.

6. See Urie Bronfenbrenner's article, "Socialization and Social Class through Time and Space."

7. Katherine Newman, *Declining Fortunes*, as well as Donald Barlett and James B. Steele, *America: What Went Wrong?* See also Michael Hout and Claude Fischer, "A Century of Inequality."

8. Some readers expressed the concern that the contrast to natural would be "unnatural," but this is not the sense in which the term *natural growth* is used here. Rather, the contrast is with words such as cultivated, artificial, artifice, or manufactured. This contrast in the logic of child rearing is a heuristic device that should not be pushed too far since, as sociologists have shown, all social life is constructed in specific social contexts. Indeed, family life has varied dramatically over time. See Philippe Aries, *Centuries of Childhood*, Herbert Gutman, *The Black Family in Slavery and Freedom, 1750–1925*, and Nancy Scheper-Hughes, *Death without Weeping*.

9. Elijah Anderson, *Code of the Street*; see especially Chapter 2.

10. For a more extensive discussion of the work of Pierre Bourdieu see the theoretical appendix; see also David Swartz's excellent book *Culture and Power*.

11. I did not study the full range of families in American society, including elite families of tremendous wealth, nor, at the other end of the spectrum, homeless families. In addition, I have a purposively drawn sample. Thus, I cannot state whether there are other forms of child rearing corresponding to other cultural logics. Still, data from quantitative studies based on nationally representative

data support the patterns I observed. For differences by parents' social class position and children's time use, see especially Sandra Hofferth and John Sandberg, "Changes in American Children's Time, 1981–1997." Patterns of language use with children are harder to capture in national surveys, but the work of Melvin Kohn and Carmi Schooler, especially *Work and Personality*, shows differences in parents' child-rearing values. Duane Alwin's studies of parents' desires are generally consistent with the results reported here. See Duane Alwin, "Trends in Parental Socialization Values." For differences in interventions in institutions, there is extensive work showing social class differences in parent involvement in education. See the U.S. Department of Education, *The Condition of Education, 2001*, p. 175.

12. In this book, unless otherwise noted, the statistics reported are from 1993 to 1995, which was when the data were collected. Similarly, unless otherwise noted, all monetary amounts are given in (unadjusted) dollars from 1994 to 1995. The figure reported here is from Everett Ladd, *Thinking about America*, pp. 21–22.

13. This quote is from President Bill Clinton's 1993 speech to the Democratic Leadership Council. It is cited in Jennifer Hochschild, *Facing Up to the American Dream*, p. 18.

14. Paul Kingston, *The Classless Society*, p. 2.

15. As I explain in more detail in the methodological appendix, family structure is intertwined with class position in this sample. The Black and white middle-class children that we observed all resided with both of their biological parents. By contrast, although some of the poor children have regular contact with their fathers, none of the Black or white poor children in the intensive observations had their biological fathers at home. The working-class families were in between. This pattern raises questions such as whether, for example, the pattern of concerted cultivation depends on the presence of a two-parent marriage. The scope of the sample precludes a satisfactory answer.

16. As I explain in Appendix A, three of the twelve children came from sources outside of the schools.

17. Arlie Hochschild, *The Second Shift*.

18. My concern here is the vast diversity in views among white Americans as well as Black Americans. The phrase "a white perspective" seems inaccurate. This is not to say that whites don't experience considerable benefits from their race in our stratified society. They do. Whites benefit from racial discrimination in many ways, including their improved ability to secure housing loans and employment as well as relatively higher market values for their homes in racially segregated neighborhoods. There are also well-documented differences in street interaction, including the ability to secure a taxi on a busy street. Thus the question is not the amount of racial discrimination in our society. Instead the question is how much being a member of a dominant group, interested in studying racial

18

Clashes in Values*

Julia Wrigley

Despite frequent differences in background, caregivers and parents see each other so intimately and depend on each other so greatly that they become aware of each other's ways of thinking. This throws their own value systems into relief. They come to realize how differently people can approach child rearing, leading a few to reconsider their own values and most to reaffirm them.

Caregivers walk a fine line; if they suppress their own values too completely they can partially lose their creativity and judgment, qualities that make adults good guides for children. They also know, though, that they are not the final decision makers. All adults who look after other people's children face similar dilemmas.[1] Those who work in child care centers, however, usually have some type of training that gives them systematic exposure to child-rearing ideologies and approaches that may differ from their own. Researchers have found that this training does make a difference in how caregivers respond to children. "With more training in child development, daycare providers are more knowledgeable, and they are also more interactive, helpful, talkative, playful, positive, and affectionate with the children in their care."[2] In essence, courses in child development help socialize caregivers into a broadly "middle class" type of care, where engagement with the child is crucial. In private homes, value differences tend to emerge piecemeal, with many possibilities for misunderstanding and confusion. They also become tangled in issues of power and control.

Caregivers, not presented with an alternative ideology in any systematic or compelling way, can be mystified, as well as troubled, by what they observe in middle-class homes. For their part, most parents do not understand their caregivers' value systems in any depth. Some au pairs argue with parents about how children should be treated; most socially subordinate caregivers do not. Parents and caregivers may not talk to each other often, or may only discuss practical matters. Many parents, though, observe concrete differences in how they and their employees treat children. Ironically, as with issues of control, it is the parents with the most egalitarian ideologies who can end up the most conflicted. They have competing principles: They want to respect their caregivers' judgments and ideas, yet they want their children treated according to their own beliefs about what is developmentally sound.

Parents may think that encouraging children to know what they want and to feel free to ask for it will make them self-motivated, confident, and articulate as adults. But caregivers may see these children as intolerably demanding. One Salvadoran employee expressed wonderment and disgust that the little girl she took care of used as many as four different cups when she had tea, trying to decide which color she preferred. The father supplied her with new ones as her preferences changed. To the caregiver, this was indulgence run amok. For the father, it may have been a way of avoiding protest, but also it may have reflected a deeper feeling that the girl's tastes were legitimate (even if unstable). Middle-class American parents, used to jobs where they operate with some authority and independence, encourage young children early on to develop their own tastes and opinions.[3]

Few middle-class parents are interested in structured academic learning for preschool children.[4] They do not want flash cards, but they want their children to be in rich environments where they learn naturally and informally. Since the mid-1960s, the child-rearing ante has been raised. Parents' anxieties have been increased by experts' emphasis on the early development of cognitive skills.[5] Combined with worry that professional jobs are increasingly hard to get, parents fear that their children will not compete successfully with others. In cities such as New York and Los Angeles, parents struggle to get their children into elite preschools that can pave the way to exclusive private schools. From early on, children face cold-eyed scrutiny from school directors, who can pick and choose freely among applicants.[6] Some parents keep their children out of school for a year if they have summer or fall birthdays, wanting them to have an edge over younger classmates. Beneath a seemingly relaxed child-rearing style, middle-class parents hope to prepare children emotionally and intellectually for the decades of schooling that lie ahead of them.[7]

Immigrant caregivers—usually raised in harsher worlds than the children in their charge, where disciplined effort to help their families counted for more than academic success—may disagree with their employers' child-rearing methods as a matter of principle. Beyond this, the indulging of children has direct costs for them. It is more work to take care of children whose opinions must be consulted. In homes where parents do not try to rein in their children, caregivers can also take the brunt of children's unrestrained temper. In the worst situations, caregivers can become deeply indignant at what they experience. Not able to take a strong stand, or to express their own values, they may withdraw. In other homes, caregivers can face a more complex conflict of values; they can come to see some benefits of their employers' child-rearing styles, while not fully embracing them.

Most dual-career middle-class parents believe they themselves provide a good learning environment when they are with their children in the evenings and on weekends, but may have doubts about whether their children's caregivers provide it. This leads some to a seemingly simple solution: hiring class peers. As we have seen, though, this choice involves its own complications. Others hire class subordinates but develop a range of strategies to try to make sure their children are socialized as they wish, despite likely differences in background and values. This chapter examines value differences and parents' strategies for dealing with them.

What Immigrant Caregivers Think About American Children

With some exceptions, the Latina and Caribbean caregivers in this study came from rural and working-class backgrounds. Most came from large families. The Latina caregivers interviewed averaged six siblings; the Caribbean caregivers averaged seven. They had had limited opportunity for education. Most commonly, the caregivers' schooling stopped at the elementary level. These women typically have major economic burdens, supporting not only themselves but elderly parents and their own children, or sometimes younger brothers and sisters. They begin work early in life and most expect to continue until they are old, as they do not have pensions or Social Security.

When they first start working in American households, Third World caregivers are often surprised by the way their employers raise their children. Of course, caregivers talk among themselves and try to prepare newcomers for what they will find. They describe American child-rearing patterns and warn women new to the work that in America parents treat their children very delicately. Despite advance preparation, some caregivers can still can be startled by what they see as a faulty balance of power. The children strike them as unduly indulged. Caregiver after caregiver mentioned this phenomenon, most contrasting it unfavorably with the adult-run homes they came from. A thirty-year-old Mexican caregiver in Los Angeles said that in the United States, "parents spoil their children. That is why they are stubborn and bad-mannered. Their parents don't teach them to be respectful. They say horrible things. Sometimes the bigger boy tells me that I'm an idiot. What can I do? If he were my boy I'd slap him so that he could respect me." The mother, she says, does not object when the boy insults her. "She always tells them that they can express whatever they feel, that she knows they're angry and that's why they're saying those things."

Some caregivers described the children they deal with as stubborn and rude. A twenty-year-old Mexican woman found the five-year-old girl she cared for "incredibly intolerable." The girl would ask her to get things, and then would add, "Hurry up!" The caregiver yearned for a Mexican-style household.

> In Mexico, we are raised differently. The parents will tell us "This is not right" and one has to obey. Here it is very different. The little girls will say, "I want to do this" and if the parents say, "It's not a good idea," the children will get upset and create a fuss until they can do what they want.

Others also commented that American children could usually get what they wanted. A twenty-year-old Salvadoran caregiver said, "Latino children, if they want something, they rarely get it. Even if they cry and cry they rarely get it. Whereas [North American children] get whatever they want." Caregivers think the parents themselves cannot control their children well, so as mere employees they have no chance of doing so. As one Guatemalan caregiver put it, "Imagine us, who are not even their mothers" trying to assert control.

Overall, the Latina caregivers who were interviewed were more negative about American child-rearing patterns than the Caribbeans were. This may stem from the greater powerlessness of Latina women, as many speak little or no English and cannot participate in the more subtle aspects of child rearing. The Caribbean women operated as if they had more authority and this made them less vulnerable to children's abuse. They might disagree in principle with American child-rearing attitudes, but had less reason to feel victimized.

Caregivers were often angered by seeing children sitting idle, while they themselves were hard at work. Raised to help their parents at an early stage, these women were surprised that American children, by and large, had no responsibilities except to do their schoolwork. The parents, said a Mexican caregiver, let their children be lazy, because they had servants to pick up after them. "Here the kids just play and go to school."

Differences in child-rearing style are not abstract matters for employees, but practical concerns, as they affect the caregivers' own authority. The more power children have, the more cautious caregivers have to be about crossing them. As a Guatemalan woman put it, "I have gotten used to this way because it is my job and I have to accustom myself to it." Caregivers don't want children to complain to their parents about them. Another Guatemalan woman, with a fourth-grade education (and six children of her own), said of the six-year-old boy in her charge, "I don't try to stop him from doing things, because that's the way his parents are. Whatever he wants to do is okay with me." Otherwise, "he could turn against me." Caregivers worried about having to win children over, because children's attachment to them provided their best job security.

Value Differences Between Parents and Caregivers

The caregivers note their employers' emphasis on education. They comment that North Americans spend a lot of time reading to their children, which did not usually happen in their own households. Caregivers also observe that children's main duty is to do well in school. They see parents as encouraging children to talk and to learn to express themselves. A Guatemalan caregiver noted her employers' style of conversation: "They include their children in their conversations and we don't do that. When adults [in Guatemala] are communicating, it is just with adults, not with children."

Caregivers with little formal schooling tend to emphasize children's moral rather than intellectual development. When Latina caregivers say they would like to be able to "educate" the children in their charge, they mean they would like to teach them right from wrong.

Not all class subordinates remain hostile to the parents' child-rearing style. Some take a step out of their own culture and like some of what they see. Santos, a forty-three-year-old Mexican caregiver with four children of her own, was impressed by the way her employers created a structured environment for their three children.

> We let our children watch whatever they want on TV; [the employers] don't. We let them eat candy and not take naps; they don't. They buy their children lots of instructive toys. When my kids were little, I didn't do this. I would buy them the toys that they wanted. From the moment the child can see, can think, can move, the parents buy instructive toys. If I were to become a mother all over again, I would buy these instructive toys.

Another Mexican woman went further, saying that her American employers do better by their children than most parents do in her own culture. Forty-nine years old, also with four children of her own, she likes her employers and has come to appreciate the way they raise their children. Latino parents, she said, do not allow children to

> freely be themselves. We hold them back; it is as if we tie them up with a rope. Here they let their children bloom, their will, their artistic talents or whatever. This is really good because you are forming an individual who will have broad capacities. [In Mexico] you couldn't even express yourself because your mother and father would silence you.

The woman added that it was more work bringing up children the North American way. To allow children to develop properly, adults had to see what they were trying to do and remove obstacles, so that they could manage on their own. "This is very tiring because you constantly have to keep your eyes open."

A thirty-one-year-old Guatemalan caregiver in Los Angeles, who left school when she was thirteen, was impressed by her employer's patience in dealing with her young son. "I think that they perhaps raise their children in a better way because [when the child is misbehaving] she talks to him even if he doesn't listen." Money, she thought, might make the difference: the mother did not have to demand anything of the child—any contribution to the household, or early independence—because nothing was needed from him.

The caregivers who admired their employers' style of child rearing did not always think it would be practical in their own culture. Because dealing with children who had their own ideas and who wanted to join adult conversations took work and patience, it helped if parents were not tired and did not have many competing demands. Santos thought the mother she worked for was remarkably patient; she ignored small acts of misbehavior that Santos said would have agitated her. She thought perhaps the parents could pursue their tolerant, attentive child-rearing style because they were "never tired." They did no physical work, so they did not get exhausted as did many of the men (laborers) and women (housecleaners) in Santos's world. The parents "go home to a clean house, their children are already attended to and cared for, because they have the means to pay someone else to do it." For her own part, she had to work at the employers' house, and then go home and start with her own four children, cleaning house and supervising them.

> One gets home and it's like the day is starting over again, attend the family, do the wash, shopping. This is the way it is for those who don't have money to pay [someone else]. So they [the employers] can ignore things that one can't ignore, because you expect that your own children will help you with the work. They don't demand that the children help them. They don't get home and get upset and start fighting with the children about the mess because they will pay for someone to clean it up.

Parents hope for loving warmth from caregivers. They may not understand the caregivers' attitudes may be more complex than it appears on the surface. Sometimes employers find it illuminating to see how caregivers treat their own children. One Los Angeles mother was surprised that her Guatemalan caregiver, Lydia, who was highly attentive to the employers' children, did not actually believe this was either necessary or desirable. When Lydia's alcoholic husband assaulted her, the employers invited her and her baby to live with them. The mother noticed that Lydia did not share her belief that babies should be held when fed.

I'm amazed how little she holds him to feed him. She's quite happy to just prop up a bottle and let him feed himself, and that has alarmed me. I told her that when she needs to feed him it's quite all right if she sits down and hugs him, but she tells me that this is how it's done in Guatemala. She wouldn't hold her children. She has four children back in Guatemala and she apparently would never hold them. There are too many things to do and her attitude was that "if I hold him he gets used to it, and over time he expects it, some day I may not be able to do it, so why train him that way?"

The mother realized she could not count on Lydia to share her beliefs. Lydia had come from a very different world, where to raise a "high-demand" child was to create expectations that probably could not be consistently met. Lydia's employers, however, paid her to meet *their* expectations regarding their children's care, and Lydia struggled to do this. She said that she watched the parents closely to see how they treated their children, and she then tried to treat them the same way. She retained strong reservations, even if she did not express them to the parents. She felt that because the parents let the children do as they chose, the children came to believe they ruled the roost. Lydia said Latinos raised their children differently. "I have gotten used to this way because it is my job and I have to accustom myself to it. But with my own children, I do it differently." Lydia worried that as the children got older, they would become still more demanding toward her.

Watching their caregivers, parents often observe that they play differently with the children than they themselves do. Sometimes the undercurrent running through the parents' comments is the idea that the caregivers are not very bright. Parents tend to see them as being satisfied with boring activities. Here, as in other realms, parents can quite easily slide into denigration of the women they hire. A New Jersey doctor commented with some wonderment that her caregiver was willing to draw hundreds of Barbie dolls; a real estate lawyer with a Jamaican caregiver said she was not bright, "but if you were very bright, you could not do this job without going crazy." Parents sometimes describe caregivers as participating in activities on the children's level. A mother of two daughters, who does freelance desktop publishing, noted that her caregiver, from Kenya, did not play with her three-year-old daughter as she herself did:

We've got these alphabet blocks and I told her that when Linda plays with the alphabet blocks she could point out what the letters are and what the sound is that the letter makes. She plays a lot differently with them than I do. Her style of play is a lot less as teacher than just as a playmate, just keeping them entertained. With me, I'm wanting them to get something out of every experience.

Parents take a long-range view of children's development, but they hire employees of uncertain job tenure, who almost certainly will take a shorter-range view. Employers worry that caregivers do what is easiest at the moment, whether this involves feeding the children junk-food snacks or letting them watch TV. One Los Angeles mother said that in her experience, caregivers gave the children whatever they wanted: "It's like, Well, let 'em have it; it's like they don't want to be bothered." Some employers see this attitude as intrinsic to caregivers' outlooks. There are, however, structural reasons for caregivers and parents to have different time orientations. Most caregivers do not get to see the children in their charge grow up; whatever investment they make, they are denied the experience of its fruition. Although many long-term caregivers come to love the children in their charge, caregivers who move from job to job say they learn not to let themselves get too attached the way novice workers and the unsophisticated do.

The different backgrounds and hierarchical positions of parents and caregivers make value divergence likely. Employers develop a range of strategies for dealing with this divergence. They try to directly and indirectly control caregivers' treatment of their children; they initiate educational activities with their children and enroll them in preschools run by trained professionals, and they replace class subordinates with class peers as children become verbal and, in the parents' eyes, more intellectually demanding. Caregivers represent only one part of a complex socialization strategy. They play key roles for a period, but their employers limit or change those roles as they see fit.

Direct and Indirect Efforts to Control Caregivers' Performance

Nearly all parents who employ caregivers maintain control over crucial areas of child rearing. In these areas, they simply tell caregivers how they want them to operate, although sometimes they do not do so until they become aware of problems. The four main areas where parents set rules are discipline, safety, health, and nutrition. Even the most tentative employers usually feel strongly about these matters and believe they have the right to demand that their wishes be followed. Caregivers usually understand that they will be fired if they do not implement parents' decisions in these areas. Parents do not want their children to come to harm, a goal even more central than having their children learn and enjoy themselves, but one that also has its culturally specific elements.

In the area of discipline, nearly all parents tell caregivers not to hit their children. Some caregivers complained about this restriction in interviews, but they knew what was expected of them, partly because it is a matter they discuss among themselves. One Latina caregiver said that she understood it was illegal to hit children in America. A few said in interviews that they had hit children anyway, but they generally refrained from doing so.

Some parents find out their caregivers have treated their children more harshly than they would have liked. One Los Angeles mother discovered, during a conflict between two employees, that one of them had locked her eighteen-month-old, who was afraid of dogs, in a dark garage with a dog. The mother confronted her, and she did not deny the charge.

> She said that she felt that I needed help with disciplining my children. We discussed it and I told her that I never wanted that to happen again and she said that it wouldn't. But it changed my feelings towards her because I never thought that she would do anything like that. And I die if I think about it. I had trusted this woman implicitly with my children, and having heard that and knowing that had happened, I could never really trust her again.

The mother, who had thought the caregiver shared her child-rearing values, began thinking about other cultural differences that disturbed her. The caregiver shamed the older boy, a five-year-old, when he cried, telling him that only girls cried. "It was a cultural thing, and she would never, ever change that." Because of the value differences, and challenges to her authority, the mother ultimately fired the caregiver.

Another Los Angeles mother, from Westwood, found out from her Bolivian caregiver's previous employers that she had put their son in a cold shower and had washed his mouth out with soap. The new employer thought the knowledge gave her an advantage.

> From the very beginning I explained to Miranda that it's very important that she only discipline in the particular way that I allowed, which was time out, and that nothing else was allowed. No washing the mouth out with soap, no cold showers, nothing like that. I knew she was capable of doing it.

This employer, a clinical psychologist, had enough confidence in her authority and insight that she kept the caregiver, who worked for her for seven years.

Caregivers also know that they risk being fired if safety rules are not followed. In 1989, employer anxiety soared in Los Angeles, after a Latina caregiver tried to help children get to sleep by shading a lamp with a towel, which then caught fire. The caregiver escaped, but the parents returned home to find their three children dead.[8] In the wake of this tragedy, one employer we interviewed asked her Latina caregiver how she would get the children out in the event of a fire. When the caregiver answered inadequately, the employer told her to leave. Other employers fired caregivers for letting in service workers such as a cable TV installer, without their permission. A Manhattan employer fired her caregiver for twice leaving the seven-month-old baby unattended in the bath when the mother called on the phone. (Remarkably, the caregiver told the mother both times what she had done, perhaps confirming the mother's judgment that she was not sharp.) Some employers and employees share a high level of anxiety. A Los Angeles employer was delighted that her Salvadoran caregiver chose, on her own initiative, to take different routes to the market so that she would not be followed.

Rules regarding health and nutrition tend to cause more conflict between parents and caregivers, as science-based and folk traditions mesh poorly and caregivers do not entirely accept parents' authority in these areas. Parents tolerate some caregivers' ideas as harmless eccentricities. One mother was surprised to find a cabbage leaf in her child's diaper, put there by the caregiver to ward off diaper rash. The doctors among the employers interviewed have more trouble with caregivers' theories and remedies. Those wedded to the germ theory of colds see caregivers' insistence on dressing children warmly as unnecessary. Employers usually accept procedures they do not see as actively harmful, but they decisively reject any attempts to interfere with Western medical practice.

Even some employers who initially tolerate caregivers' ideas on health can become disturbed over time. A Manhattan mother, who has taken time out from her film production job, employs a seventy-five-year-old Ukrainian caregiver to help with her two boys, aged eleven and two. The caregiver, who has been employed by the family for ten years, is deeply devoted to the children, loving them, she says, as if they were her own. As part of supplying loving care, she advises the mother on remedies for common ailments. At first the mother thought that Alice exhibited folk wisdom; now she thinks she exhibits folk ignorance. Alice urged the mother to catch a frog and apply it to a wart on the older boy's toe. Alice also recommended that a foot fungus be treated by having the child step in a cow patty, an item equally difficult to obtain in Manhattan. A third incident disturbed the mother more because it brought home to her the depth of her differences with Alice. When her two-year-old started crying, Alice told her he had been given the evil eye by a stranger on the street who was jealous of his beauty. This, she said, could be cured by spitting on the child three times. More prosaically, the mother attributed the child's tears to her having turned off the TV. The mother appreciates Alice's devotion toward her sons, but she also worries about the worldview they are being exposed to.

Not all parents try to control their children's nutrition, but many do. They do not want their children fed junk food. A thirty-three-year-old Salvadoran, Margarita, working in Los Angeles, expressed her surprise over her employers' dietary requirements for their eighteen-month-old son. "I feed my children everything, but he doesn't eat salt. I am not allowed to give him fat. No candies, no cookies, no nothing. I had never heard of this in all my life, but you must do as they say." Caregivers, for their part, are often dismayed by the food available for their employers' families and for themselves while they're at work.

Caregivers commonly spend their own money to buy food that they like, at least when they first come to the United States. The prevalence of prepared foods and canned items surprises them. They also dislike the lack of seasonings. As they become acclimated, though, some can adapt to a very unhealthy version of American food, which parents then try to keep away from their children. A mother described herself as perplexed by her Kenyan caregiver's feeding her children Cheese Nips and Froot Loops for lunch, given that the caregiver had worked for another American family for two years. The mother concluded that the woman's previous employers had given her specific instructions about what and what not to feed their children, a practice she then adopted.

Parents also try to enforce basic decisions about how to handle children's toilet training and sexuality. Here they do not always succeed. Some caregivers who come from other cultures have strong ideas on these matters. They can make it clear to parents they disapprove of children's late toilet training and blame parents for slowing the process. Parents can be dismayed by caregivers' negativism about any manifestation of children's sexuality. This issue caused conflict between several Los Angeles employers and their caregivers. In New York, a well-educated caregiver from Guyana, a former teacher with great sensitivity toward the children in her charge, maintains a traditional anxiety about children possibly engaging in any sex play. When she takes the young boys in her charge to visit friends, she insists on staying with them at all times, afraid, she says, that the friends' parents will not share her vigilance on the matter.

For the most part, parents and caregivers find ways to accommodate each other on these issues, but when each side feels strongly, it can lead to a parting of the ways. One Los Angeles mother was dismayed that her forty-eight-year-old Salvadoran caregiver, the only woman interviewed who had no formal education, told her daughters, seven and five, that if they did not wear underwear to bed, spiders would crawl into their vaginas. This was one factor that made the mother think perhaps she should switch caregivers: "I realized that it was something we could not overcome. I think she is uneducated, superstitious, and I couldn't change that." Another Salvadoran caregiver said she lost a job when she complained about a young girl's masturbating; the parents did not appreciate her complaints.

There are only a limited number of areas where parents can lay down explicit rules, because much caregiving involves spontaneous responses to children. Recognizing this, some parents try to indirectly control caregivers by controlling their schedules. They tell them to spend a certain amount of time at the park each day, hoping to limit passivity and TV watching. In sunny Los Angeles, some caregivers did spend a large part of the day at parks, up to about four hours. Parents also tell caregivers which television shows their children can watch and how often. Some parents allow their children to watch TV with them, but not with the caregiver. One mother, detailing her family's schedule, said that as soon as the caregiver arrived in the morning, the TV went off. As paid employees, caregivers are expected to maintain a steady focus on the children, and parents seek ways to ensure this.

Parents' Instruction of Caregivers

Some parents undertake the ambitious task of trying to instruct caregivers in the more subtle aspects of their child-rearing styles, where rules are not relevant. These are parents who invest in a particular caregiver and place priority on stability. Instruction can occur both formally and informally.

Informally, some parents, almost always mothers, take several weeks off work when they first hire caregivers and spend the time working alongside them. (They contrast with other parents interviewed, who sometimes left their children with caregivers a half hour after they first appeared.) They show them how they want their children cared for, and many caregivers report that they do in fact watch mothers closely and try to do as they think they would. One Mexican caregiver said of her employers, "You have to learn the way *they* think." After a near-accident with the preschool boy in her charge, the caregiver tried to speak to him calmly: "I knew what [the mother] would have done and I did what she would have done." Some employers ask their own mothers to come and train new caregivers. Of course, for parents who take much time to train caregivers, their departure can be a serious blow.

Other parents go further and try to present their child-rearing ideas to caregivers more formally. One mother prepared a several-page theory of parenting for her caregiver when she first arrived, outlining her philosophy on a wide range of issues. It covered "theoretically, this is the right way and this is the wrong way. [For example], Paula is not a bad girl if her behavior is bad." The mother felt impelled to prepare this document because "I did a lot of reading and a lot of research and a lot of talking about what's the right way to parent and what's the wrong way, and I didn't want it to all be for naught because somebody comes in here and doesn't know what the hell they're doing."

Another mother, a Colombian living in New York, also read much child-rearing literature after the birth of her first child. "I took a lot of courses in child psychology, child development and nutrition. I tried to share those experiences with my husband, but I had a very poor reception." The husband, from a traditional Mideast culture, said he was a "normal person" and did not need expert advice. The mother instead shared her ideas with her caregiver, a fellow Colombian she had found after a year's search. She told the caregiver that "even though she might have had different techniques, I would like her to cooperate with me, because I really needed her support. I gave her material for reading." The mother thought it worked out well. The caregiver came from a family with little education and began with values very different from the mother's. At first the caregiver did whatever the children wanted, but the mother gradually instructed her in how to control them. "I would tell her to tell them no in a positive way." Seventeen years later, the caregiver is still employed by this mother and has a close relationship with the children, now in their late teens.

Parents with troubled or difficult children can make special efforts to instruct caregivers. When they fail to do so, caregivers can feel adrift, left with children whose problems are disturbing but not officially acknowledged in the household.[9] This lack of acknowledgment can cause serious alienation on the part of the caregiver. One Swedish au pair dealt with a five-year-old girl who cried from the moment the au pair woke her until she got to school, during which time the parents stayed in bed. The girl could not get along with other children, showed no enjoyment in activities, and both hit and insulted the au pair. The parents did tell the au pair that the girl was in therapy, but they did not offer her advice or support in handling the child. The au pair left after a few months.

Some parents try to bring their caregivers on board in dealing with children who require special attention or awareness by instructing the caregivers in distinctive, expert-derived modes of care. Two psychologists in Los Angeles had a difficult daughter, not seriously troubled, but described by the mother as "very hard to handle. She tests every limit, she is smart and manipulative and really tries your ability." The mother concluded that it took a very skilled person to deal with her. She asked her Mexican caregiver to help her implement an elaborate behavioral modification program, wherein the girl could earn stars and presents for cooperating. "You know, I'm a psychologist and I'm behavioral, and I apply that in the rearing of my children." The caregiver tried to do as the mother outlined, but with only partial success. She did not, the mother thought, fully comprehend the system. "She didn't really truly appreciate how to deliver reinforcements, and it was hard for her, because I think she felt resentful towards [the child] because she would be mean to her." The system, far removed from the caregiver's natural responses, called for creating a kind of emotional distance that the caregiver could not manage. Ultimately the mother and caregiver agreed that the caregiver should leave, as the child was too difficult for her.

Some caregivers reported receiving more successful instruction. A thirty-year-old Mexican caregiver, who worked for a widowed Los Angeles mother of two boys, considered quitting the job because the older of the two boys, then eight, hit and abused her. Five previous caregivers had left for the same reason.

The caregiver was also depressed because the mother herself seemed overwhelmed by her situation and cried often. The mother told the caregiver that she knew the boy was difficult but that she really wanted her to stay.

> She recommended that we all go to see his psychologist. And it worked. The psychologist told me that when [the boy] is going to hit me, that I needed to grab him and hold him firmly, look him in the eyes, and tell him, "You are not going to hit me." He told me that I needed to *feel* that I was the boss.

Despite the caregiver's positive report, the mother said she did not think the caregiver was able to really follow the whole behavioral program worked out by the psychologist. The mother and caregiver had different interpretations of success; implementing the full program was beyond the caregiver's abilities or ambitions, but once she stopped the boy from hitting her she was at least willing to stay on the job.

Other parents also had mixed success trying to instruct caregivers in how to handle difficult children. A caregiver in her early twenties from a small Midwestern town worked for a New Jersey family with two adopted children, a boy of four and a girl of two. The boy was very aggressive and hostile. The caregiver felt sorry for him, because he would sometimes express intense self hatred, but she also found him almost impossible to manage. The parents gave her child-rearing books to read, but she found them useless; she felt she needed a more practical kind of help than they offered. She also thought the parents themselves considered them a limited resource and said the parents conveyed regret over having adopted the children. Caregivers can see emotional problems that go beyond the power of any technique to remedy, despite lingering parental faith in the power of expert opinion.

Parents' child-rearing theories do not always work in practice. For reasons that are sometimes unclear, some children do not develop the emotional stability their parents want. In most of these cases, other children in the family develop more or less normally. Troubled children call forth the parents' resources, including their access to psychologists, their knowledge of expert opinion, and their efforts to instruct caregivers in special techniques to manage the children. The parents try to repair the situation and rescue their children, but even a vast structure of class-related advantages cannot overwhelm all the forces of individual psychology and personality. One New Jersey mother, warm and loving toward her children, an excellent employer according to her caregiver, has a nine-year-old son who is difficult and fearful and often beyond her control. While being interviewed, she got a call from his school saying that he was once again in trouble. When asked whether she advised the caregiver on how to handle the boy, she replied sadly, "I wish someone would advise me." Instruction only works when parents believe they have the answers.

Tasks Parents Keep for Themselves

Although employees may provide many hours of daily care, many parents set aside crucial aspects of care to perform themselves. In divisions of household labor, class-subordinate caregivers do more of the routine work and the physical care, and parents specialize in talking and reading with their children. Nearly all educated parents read to their children in the evenings, an activity difficult for those caregivers who have little education or limited English skills. Parents will also help older children with homework, a task delegated to some class-peer employees but almost never to class subordinates. Many parents see caregivers as freeing them to specialize in "quality time" with their children.

One Manhattan mother, employed in the nonprofit sector, with a lawyer husband, wishes her Puerto Rican caregiver did more with her two girls, ten and seven, and watched TV less. She sees herself and her husband, though, as the primary forces in the girls' lives; in some respects, the caregiver's limitations help reinforce their role. The caregiver cannot help the older girl with her homework, and the mother comments, "As much as it's a pain, I think that if my child care person were doing it, I would feel left out of the process." By helping children themselves, parents show them that they value academic activities.

Some caregivers commented in interviews that parents pressure their children. A Midwestern caregiver working in New Jersey noted that where she grew up, her parents told her to do *her* best, but that in the family she works for, the goal is to be *the* best. The children strike her as very bright, but also as competitive and anxious. An Irish nanny reported that her employer was worried about his daughter in kindergarten. "Oh my gosh," he told her, "Denise has caught up on Jennifer; she can read and Jennifer can't."

Culturally specific aspects of care include not only intellectual tasks, but those connected with consumption. Parents very seldom delegate the purchase of goods to class subordinates, even when the goods involved are only groceries. Even if caregivers do most of the housework, parents keep shopping for themselves, except in rare instances (usually involving high-level immigrant employees). There are some practical reasons for this: many class subordinates cannot drive, for example. This is not the whole explanation, though, because even those who can hardly ever shop for their employers, except for picking up bread, milk, and other fill-in items.

As the parents talked about shopping in the interviews, it became evident that they viewed this as an area that required their specific skills. Their homes, usually large and well maintained, are arenas for the display of goods, and parents early teach their children about the importance of having and maintaining possessions. A "center of material display," the middle-class house is designed "not only for the private comfort of its inhabitants, but also to show visitors that the family [follows] certain canons of taste and culture."[10] Even young children are brought into this world of consumption and display through the decoration of their bedrooms and the purchase of toys for them. Caregivers marvel at the number of toys the children have. (Several commented that they felt they themselves were yet another toy.) The toys take up much space and, being composed of many small parts, require frequent organizing. Caregivers do most of this work; even those exempted from general housework, such as certain class peers, look after children's belongings. Parents can be quite demanding in this area. They insist that caregivers keep close track of these items. One Midwestern caregiver described herself as having been agitated because the two-year-old child in her charge had lost a toy truck, which the father asked her about several times. It turned out the truck was a three-dollar item. An Irish caregiver realized early on that she had to be vigilant about her five-year-old charge's toys. The mother kept a "Lost Toy Parts" list, and the caregiver dreaded seeing items going up on it.

Employers do not always trust class subordinates, in particular, to manage the family's possessions. They think caregivers do not always have the proper reverence for a family's carefully chosen goods; unaware of their distinctive quality and value, they treat them as they would ordinary objects. A Los Angeles lawyer said of her Filipina caregiver:

> Culturally, the difference is that we spend a lot of money on things with the thought that they will last a long time and they will be treasured possessions. And her background is, buy things and they're fungible. And you don't really take care of them. She cleaned a wood table with Ajax.

Even very young members of these families are heavily endowed with privately held possessions, selected by high-status people and maintained partly by low-status ones. They learn to consider their individual tastes and choices among goods to be important, just as their opinions are considered to count in other realms. Their intellectual skills, actively cultivated by their families, will, the parents hope, bring their children academic success, while their "taste" will mark them as members in good standing of a culturally privileged group.[11]

Children's Social Lives

Parents can try to control or instruct their class-subordinate caregivers, but they also want their children in the company of those who share their world and culture. Both informally and formally, parents work to keep their children within middle-class circles. As children more decisively enter the world of their parents, caregivers' roles shrink from being prime socializing agents to being supporting players.

Informal socialization takes place not only in the family, but in contacts with other children and parents of similar background. Most parents try to foster their children's social lives, a task sometimes complicated by class-subordinate caregivers' exclusion from the child's social class. In middle-class culture, arranged sociability plays a large role. People make plans to see their friends rather than relying on encountering them casually. In working-class circles, meetings with friends tend to occur more on the basis of happenstance.[12] The contrast can be clearly seen in the worlds of employers and class-subordinate caregivers. The employers have the means to arrange their social lives as they see fit; they usually have large and orderly houses suitable for entertaining. Caregivers commented in the interviews on the social lives of their employers; one Latina woman, for example, said that her employers were "people of extreme importance" in the business world and necessarily had a lot of parties. Caregivers, in contrast, have minimal ability to organize their social lives. They do meet other caregivers in parks, but they cannot count on doing so. Occasionally these relationships deepen into real friendships, but caregivers often do not know each other's last names, even when they have met frequently, and rarely sustain friendships when their work schedules no longer bring them together.

The parents' model of sociability has been extended downward. Even very young children now have arranged social lives. The play date has replaced neighborhood gatherings. Parents are anxious for their children to play with friends, both to develop their social skills and to certify their popularity. Once children leave infancy, they acquire their own miniature social circle, generally made up of children from families much like their own. This can cause problems for caregivers. They have little or no standing in their employers' social milieu, and they can feel this acutely when dealing with other families. Parents usually initiate contact with other families, but caregivers supervise the actual visits. Many caregivers report resentment at how other parents treat them and at how visiting children feel free to order them around.

Caregivers sometimes refuse to deal with certain families if they feel they have been ill-treated. This can be frustrating for their employers; one Los Angeles doctor said regretfully that her two-year-old son could no longer play with his best friend during the week, because her African-American caregiver had had a dispute with the friend's mother and nanny. "She said that the mother was being too controlling of her. . . . She felt that this woman was dictating to her what she should do and that she wasn't employed by this woman and she had no right to tell her what to do." The nanny felt the other family's caregiver also acted in a high-handed manner. The other child had come over every

Monday for the preceding year and a half, but the nanny refused to allow any more visits while she was on duty. The mother said she felt sad about the situation, but then added hopefully that the caregiver was nearing sixty and might soon retire. One Mexican caregiver told a visiting child that she would not take orders from her; the child complained to her mother, who called the caregiver's employer. The employer said, "Please, Maria, be more amiable with their friends." Maria refused, however, to agree to accept orders from the friends; she said that if they wanted anything, they could relay their requests through her charges.

Sympathetic employers sometimes back their caregivers in disputes with other parents and children. A Los Angeles professor stood behind her Guatemalan caregiver in a conflict with a neighbor, who had felt free to treat the caregiver as a servant. The professor said "she was right. And I told the neighbors she was right." Not all parents will do this, however, and if caregivers are perceived as too contentious, parents can consider firing them on this issue. They do not want caregivers' sensitivities to impede their children's social lives.

Preschool And Other Organized Activities

Increasingly, parents enroll even young children in structured activities. By the time the children of the parents we interviewed were three, nearly all attended preschools, mainly on a part-time basis. Even couples who employed full-time caregivers wanted their children to have the stimulation and organized activities provided by trained teachers.

When parents enrolled their children in preschools, they initiated a major shift in socialization strategy. As their children began structured forms of learning and care, their caregivers lost influence, a process that would accelerate when the children began more formal schooling.

The parents we interviewed also reported their children participated in music lessons, dance, gymnastics, karate, special math classes, all kinds of sports activities, and art classes. Slightly older children took computer classes. Taught by specialized teachers, these classes have great legitimacy in middle-class circles. Even parents who worry that their children no longer have time for themselves said that they could not be the only holdouts: their children had no friends to play with in the neighborhood, because those children were all off at classes. They also thought that if their children did not participate in these activities, they might be left behind socially and developmentally. These classes and activities provide a form of socialization on a contract basis. Even children's academic performance can now fall within the province of experts for hire. When their children had trouble learning to read, or had difficulty with math, the parents we interviewed often hired tutors. Few contemplated tackling these problems unassisted. As children get older, unskilled caregivers play ever smaller roles, while specialists play ever larger ones.

The wealthiest parents in the study did not simply enroll their children in classes; they brought specialists to their houses. Those with pools hired private swimming instructors; an employer with a tennis court gave room and board to a tennis "hitter" so that he would be available for her children. One Los Angeles mother stretched her budget to engage a first-grade teacher from her children's public school to come to the house twice a week and give art lessons to her daughters. On Fridays after school the teacher led a group of six girls, organized by the mother, on tours of the city's art museums. The mother did not go, reasoning that at $30 an hour, it was better for her children to get the teacher's attention. Instead of sending their children to Hebrew classes a New Jersey couple had a rabbi come by twice a week.

The Values Children Learn

Some wealthy parents take an extra step and hire multiple caregivers. With several employees, they can assemble various types of expertise within their homes. Although most employers we interviewed found that paying for, and coping with, one employee exhausted their resources, eight of the families interviewed employed multiple caregivers. Two of these hired only class subordinates; they used more than one because they had intensive labor demands (one employer, for example, required her baby to be carried around all day and also had two older children to look after; she hired two Salvadoran caregivers). The others, though, mixed class peers and class subordinates, creating a labor hierarchy like that of elites in previous generations. The highest-status workers do the most direct work with children. One Los Angeles lawyer hired many employees for help with her one son: at one time, before he started school, she had an English nanny, a Guatemalan immigrant full time, a UCLA student two mornings a week, and a regular Saturday-evening babysitter.

Children with teams of servants at their disposal sometimes develop a unique view of the world: They see all relationships as potential employment relationships. The eight-year-old son of the Los Angeles lawyer told his mother he liked some of his camp counselors and wanted her to hire them. "Right now he's in love with this one young woman and he wants her to work for us, too. I don't know how we'll use her; I have all these people already." As children get older, they recognize that caregivers are paid employees, yet many children have also experienced semi-maternal affection from them. This can create a complicated sense of how money can be used to buy emotional gratification. While these feelings may lie deeply submerged within relationships, caregivers sometimes interpret children's comments as indicating that they see their parents as having purchased caregivers for their enjoyment, just as other possessions are supplied for them.

Many employers who have egalitarian ideologies work hard to keep their children from treating caregivers disrespectfully, usually with some success. Some worry, though, that their own status as personal "dictators" cannot help influencing their children. And, whatever the children's level of respect, parents cannot keep them from becoming more distant from caregivers. Children gradually come to understand the caregivers' subordinate and temporary position, a process closely charted by the caregivers themselves; they notice small signs of children's changing regard for them. One Mexican caregiver said that the boy she looked after would include her in the pictures of his family that he drew in kindergarten. When he went to first grade, he stopped doing this. "The closeness he felt for me has grown cold. He sees me as an employee." This led her to withdraw in turn. "When he was very little, and I felt he cared for me, I felt much closer to him. Now I just see him as someone else with whom I have to work."

Caregivers whose employers do not enforce respect from children can have much worse situations. As children get older, they can come to see caregivers as their personal servants.[13] When caregivers ask them to pick up after themselves, some children tell them, "That's your job." Gradually caregivers can come to feel themselves under the control of the children who are nominally in their charge. Even caregivers who have been close to the children can come to dislike them when they assert their superiority. Adela, the Salvadoran caregiver whose employer complained she could not teach the children about art (chapter 2), had once loved the two girls in the family. But at five or six, they began telling her "You have to do this because this is why you get paid." Not only caregivers reported such treatment; some parents frankly admitted that their older children had hit or insulted caregivers. Even when treated abusively, subordinate caregivers do not feel they can strike back. One Latina woman overheard school-age boys arguing about who had the stupidest maid. She could do nothing but remain silent. This is an age-old problem for domestic workers. African-American women in the South addressed it with such sayings as "I never met a white child over twelve that I liked."[14]

In the eyes of some caregivers, the children in their charge are learning values, but not necessarily the ones officially espoused by the parents. These caregivers think the children are learning which work is done by which people. They observe how the children come to see them as employees and to recognize that they as children have more power than their adult caregivers. Few things are more painful for caregivers than to see children they once loved take a domineering tone toward them, not with the unthinking egoism of the young but with the knowing superiority of the privileged.

Children can learn an indelible lesson—just how indelible can be seen by comparing parents who grew up in families with domestic workers and those who did not. Even as adults, they respond differently to domestic employees. A few reacted against how they had seen their own parents treat workers. More commonly, those raised in a household that had domestic employees assume their right to service. They do not have to fight internal battles between inbred egalitarian and hierarchical notions; their consciousness was shaped in the hierarchical direction long before. They are re-creating the same feelings and expectations in their own children.[15]

Caregivers also know that no matter how well they perform their duties, their jobs have no future. One Salvadoran commented, "The instability of the job—one always feels it. From the moment I arrive at a home, I know that one day they will tell me to leave, thank you very much." Others are more bitter. They see the jobs as demanding love and commitment from them, but leaving parents free to dispose of them when they are no longer useful. "You get attached to these children, but at the end of the day you get thrown out of the house. You end up leaving in tears . . . but they [the employers] will send you to hell whenever they feel like it. You'll be able to do nothing but hang your head as you walk out."

Conclusions

Most dual-career couples believe they have cultural resources of value to their children. They have partially lost one time-tested method of transmitting these resources, the full investment of mothers' time in children's care. Wanting individual attention for their children, and the convenience of a household worker for themselves, parents have tried to incorporate caregivers into socialization strategies. This leads them to many subsidiary efforts to select, control, and instruct those workers in ways that enable them to serve their purposes. All of these efforts are complicated by frequent, and deep, value differences between many of the women available to do caregiving work and the parents who hire them.

Parents can instruct caregivers in many aspects of care, and can demand that their own values be respected. Caregivers usually accept that parents have the right to set the basic childrearing terms. Despite this, parents cannot be sure that the rules they have laid out will be followed; sometimes, it is clear, caregivers do not follow them. As they are essentially unsupervised workers, this is an issue that no system of control can easily address.

More important, there are areas of care that do not lend themselves to rules, but that involve subtle actions or judgments. Caregivers' ability to give focused attention to children can help them cross class boundaries when children are young, but it becomes an insufficient resource as children get older and cultural issues acquire more weight. The "quality" of care comes to be defined in more class-specific terms.

Caregivers are only a temporary element in most parents' socialization strategies, which increasingly involve contract-based care by specialists. As people whose emotions have been engaged, though, and whose livelihood had depended on particular families, their departures are not casual events. They have their own thoughts and insights into the meaning of their work. While parents seldom mention this, caregivers believe that the deepest lesson many children learn concerns their own entitlement.[16]

The road to high-level, well-rewarded careers passes through the educational system, and this is the road the children are being prepared to travel. Their caregivers can help them in their early years, by providing nurturance and love, but then the children transfer to the institutions and supports provided by middle-class culture. Along the way, however, they will have learned about privilege, and they will have exercised some.

Notes

1. Authors who discuss value differences between parents and child care providers, and between day care teachers and center directors, include Sally Lubeck, *Sandbox Society: Early Education in Black and White America* (London: Falmer Press, 1985); Caroline Zinsser, *Raised in East Urban: Child Care Changes in a Working-Class Community* (New York: Teachers College Press, 1991); Carole E. Joffe, *Friendly Intruders: Childcare Professionals and Family Life* (Berkeley: University of California Press, 1977); Elly Singer, *Child-Care and the Psychology of Development* (London: Routledge, 1992); Susan D. Holloway and Bruce Fuller, "The Great Child-Care Experiment: What Are the Lessons for School Improvement?" *Educational Researcher*, 21 (1992):12–19; and Deborah Stipek, Sharon Milburn, Darlene Clements, and Denise H. Daniels, "Parents' Beliefs about Appropriate Education for Young Children," *Journal of Applied Developmental Psychology*, 13 (1992):293–310. On family day care providers, see Margaret K. Nelson, *Negotiated Care: The Experience of Family Day Care Providers* (Philadelphia: Temple University Press, 1990).
2. Alison Clarke-Stewart, *Daycare*, rev. ed. (Cambridge, Mass.: Harvard University Press, 1993), p. 98.
3. Melvin L. Kohn, *Class and Conformity: A Study in Values*, 2nd ed. (Chicago: University of Chicago Press, 1977).
4. Stipek, Milburn, Clements, and Daniels, "Parents' Beliefs about Appropriate Education for Young Children."
5. Julia Wrigley, "Do Young Children Need Intellectual Stimulation? Experts' Advice to Parents, 1900–1985," *History of Education Quarterly*, 29 (1989): 41–75.
6. Ralph Gardner, Jr., "The Preschool Grovel," *New York Observer*, July 4–11, 1994, p. 13.

7. Annette Lareau, *Home Advantage: Social Class and Parental Intervention in Elementary Education* (London: Falmer Press, 1989).
8. Lois Timnick and John H. Lee, "Three Children Killed When Flames Engulf Pacific Palisades Home," *Los Angeles Times*, March 21, 1989, section 1, p. 3; Tracy Wilkinson, "Fatal Fire: Neighbors Can Only Shake Heads," *Los Angeles Times*, March 22, 1989, section 2, p. 1.
9. Child care experts warn parents that they should not conceal their children's problems. "In choosing a care situation for a difficult child, you need to inform the caregiver fully of your child's idiosyncracies. If the caregiver cannot accept most, or all, of your child's needs, then find another caregiver." Sandra Scarr, *Mother Care/Other Care* (New York: Basic Books, 1984), p. 191. Not all parents follow this advice, though, whether from closing their eyes to their child's problems or from a belief that caregivers should adjust to what they find.
10. David Popenoe, *Disturbing the Nest: Family Change and Decline in Modern Societies* (New York: Aldine de Gruyter, 1988), p. 73.
11. Pierre Bourdieu, *Distinction: A Social Critique of the Judgment of Taste*, R. Nice, trans. (Cambridge: Harvard University Press, 1984).
12. Michael Argyle, *The Psychology of Social Class* (New York: Routledge, 1994), pp. 68–70.
13. James H. S. Bossard, *The Sociology of Child Development* (New York: Harper & Brothers, 1948), p. 279, discusses how the presence of servants can lead children to expect a high level of personal service. Bossard argues this can help shape the child's sense of self by creating an early sense of superiority.
14. Susan Tucker, *Telling Memories Among Southern Women: Domestic Workers and Their Employers in the Segregated South* (Baton Rouge: Louisiana State University Press, 1988), p. 61.
15. Judith Rollins found that women were much influenced by family tradition in hiring domestics. See *Between Women: Domestics and Their Employers* (Philadelphia: Temple University Press, 1985), pp. 94–102.
16. In the more extreme case of slavery, Thomas Jefferson described how children learned tyranny by watching their slaveowning parents:

> The whole commerce between master and slave is a perpetual exercise of the most boistrous passions, the most unremitting despotism on the one part, and degrading submissions on the other. Our children see this, and learn to imitate it. . . . If a parent could find no motive either in his philanthropy or his self-love, for restraining the intemperance of passion towards his slave, it should always be a sufficient one that the child is present. But generally it is not sufficient. The parent storms, the child looks on, catches the lineaments of wrath, puts on the same airs in the circle of smaller slaves, gives a loose to his worst of passions, and thus nursed, educated, and daily exercised in tyranny, cannot but be stamped by it with odious peculiarities.

Thomas Jefferson, *Notes on the State of Virginia* (Gloucester, Mass.: Peter Smith, 1976), p. 155.

19

Social Class and the Hidden Curriculum of Work*

Jean Anyon

Scholars in political economy and the sociology of knowledge have recently argued that public schools in complex industrial societies like our own make available different types of educational experience and curriculum knowledge to students in different social classes. Bowles and Gintis (1976), for example, have argued that students from different social class backgrounds are rewarded for classroom behaviors that correspond to personality traits allegedly rewarded in the different occupational strata—the working classes for docility and obedience, the managerial classes for initiative and personal assertiveness. Basil Bernstein (1977), Pierre Bourdieu (Bourdieu and Passeron, 1977), and Michael W. Apple (1979), focusing on school knowledge, have argued that knowledge and skills leading to social power and reward (e.g., medical, legal, managerial) are made available to the advantaged social groups but are withheld from the working classes, to whom a more "practical" curriculum is offered (e.g., manual skills, clerical knowledge). While there has been considerable argumentation of these points regarding education in England, France, and North America, there has been little or no attempt to investigate these ideas empirically in elementary or secondary schools and classrooms in this country.[1]

This chapter offers tentative empirical support (and qualification) of the preceding arguments by providing illustrative examples of differences in student work in classrooms in contrasting social class communities. The examples were gathered as part of an ethnographical study of curricular, pedagogical and pupil evaluation practices in five elementary schools. The article attempts a

*From *Journal of Education*, 1980, Vol. 162, pp. 67–92. Reprinted by permission of publisher and author.

theoretical contribution as well and assesses student work in the light of a theoretical approach to social class analysis. The organization is as follows: The methodology of the ethnographical study is briefly described; a theoretical approach to the definition of social class is offered; income and other characteristics of the parents in each school are provided, and examples from the study that illustrate work tasks and interaction in each school are presented; then the concepts used to define social class are applied to the examples in order to assess the theoretical meaning of classroom events. It will be suggested that there is a "hidden curriculum" in school work that has profound implication for the theory—and consequence—of everyday activity in education.

Methodology

The methods used to gather data were classroom observation; interviews of students, teachers, principals, and district administrative staff; and assessment of curriculum and other materials in each classroom and school. All classroom events to be discussed here involve the fifth grade in each school. All schools but one departmentalize at the fifth grade level. Except for that school where only one fifth grade teacher could be observed, all the fifth grade teachers (i.e., two or three) were observed as the children moved from subject to subject. In all schools the art, music, and gym teachers were also observed and interviewed. All teachers in the study were described as "good" or "excellent" by their principals. All except one new teacher had taught for more than 4 years. The fifth grade in each school was observed by the investigator for ten 3-hour periods between September 15, 1978 and June 20, 1979.

Before providing the occupations, incomes, and other relevant social characteristics of the parents of the children in each school, I will offer a theoretical approach to defining social class.

Social Class

One's occupation and income level contribute significantly to one's social class, but they do not define it. Rather, social class is a series of relationships. A person's social class is defined here by the way that person relates to the process in society by which goods, services, and culture are produced.[2] One relates to several aspects of the production process primarily through one's work. One has a relationship to the system of ownership, to other people (at work and in society), and to the content and process of one's own productive activity. One's relationship to all three of these aspects of production determines one's social class; that is, all three relationships are necessary and none is sufficient for determining a person's relation to the process of production in society.

Ownership Relations

In a capitalist society, a person has a relation to the system of private own-ership of capital. Capital is usually thought of as being derived from physical property. In this sense capital is property that is used to produce profit, interest, or rent in sufficient quantity so that the result can be used to produce more profit, interest, or rent—that is, more capital. Physical capital may be derived from money, stocks, machines, land, or the labor of workers (whose labor, for instance, may produce products that are sold by others for profit). Capital, how-ever, can also be symbolic. It can be the socially legitimated knowledge of how the production process works, its financial, managerial, technical, or other "secrets." Symbolic capital can also be socially legitimated skills—cognitive (e.g., analytical), linguistic, or technical skills that provide the ability to, say, produce the dominant scientific, artistic, and other culture, or to manage the sys-tems of industrial and cultural production. Skillful application of symbolic cap-ital may yield social and cultural power, and perhaps physical capital as well.

The ownership relation that is definitive for social class is one's relation to physical capital. The first such relationship is that of capitalist. To be a member of the capitalist class in the present-day United States, one must participate in the ownership of the apparatus of production in society. The number of such persons is relatively small: While 1 person in 10 owns some stock, for example, a mere 1.6% of the population owns 82.2% of *all* stock, and the wealthiest one-fifth owns almost all the rest (see New York Stock Exchange, 1975; Smith and Franklin, 1974; Lampman, 1962).

At the opposite pole of this relationship is the worker. To be in the United States working class a person will not ordinarily own physical capital; to the contrary, his or her work will be wage or salaried labor that is either a *source* of profit (i.e., capital) to others, or that makes it possible for others to *realize* profit. Examples of the latter are white-collar clerical workers in industry and distribution (office and sales) as well as the wage and salaried workers in the institutions of social and economic legitimation and service (e.g., in state edu-cation and welfare institutions).[3] According to the criteria to be developed here, the number of persons who presently comprise the working class in the United States is between 50–60% of the population (see also Wright, 1978; Braver-man, 1974; Levison, 1974).

In between the defining relationship of capitalist and worker are the middle classes, whose relationship to the process of production is less clear, and whose relationship may indeed exhibit contradictory characteristics. For example, social service employees have a somewhat contradictory relationship to the process of production because, although their income may be at middle-class levels, some characteristics of their work are working-class (e.g., they may have very little control over their work). Analogously, there are persons at the upper income end of the middle class, such as upper middle-class professionals, who may own quantities of stocks and will therefore share characteristics of the capitalist class. As the next criterion to be discussed makes clear, however, to be a member of the present-day capitalist class in the United States, one must also participate in the social control of this capital.

Relationships between People

The second relationship that contributes to one's social class is the relation one has to authority and control at work and in society.[4] One characteristic of most working-class jobs is that there is no built-in mechanism by which the worker can control the content, process, or speed of work. Legitimate decision making is vested in personnel supervisors, in middle or upper management, or, as in an increasing number of white-collar working-class (and most middle-class) jobs, by bureaucratic rule and regulation. For upper middle-class professional groups there is an increased amount of autonomy regarding work. Moreover, in middle- and upper middle-class positions there is an increasing chance that one's work will also involve supervising the work of others. A capitalist is defined within these relations of control in an enterprise by having a position that participates in the direct control of the entire enterprise. Capitalists do not directly control workers in physical production and do not directly control ideas in the sphere of cultural production. However, more crucial to control, capitalists make the decisions over how resources are used (e.g., where money is invested) and how profit is allocated.

Relations between People and Their Work

The third criterion that contributes to a person's social class is the relationship between that person and his or her own productive activity—the type of activity that constitutes his or her work. A working-class job is often characterized by work that is routine and mechanical and that is a small, fragmented part of a larger process with which workers are not usually acquainted. These working-class jobs are usually blue-collar, manual labor. A few skilled jobs such as plumbing and printing are not mechanical, however, and an increasing number of working-class jobs are *white* collar. These white-collar jobs, such as clerical work, may involve work that necessitates a measure of planning and decision making, but one still has no built-in control over the content. The work of some middle- and most upper middle-class managerial and professional groups is likely to involve the need for conceptualization and creativity, with many professional jobs demanding one's full creative capacities.

Finally, the work that characterizes the capitalist position is that this work is almost entirely a matter of conceptualization (e.g., planning and laying-out) that has as its object management and control of the enterprise.

One's social class, then, is a result of the relationships one has, largely through one's work, to physical capital and its power, to other people at work and in society, and to one's own productive activity. Social class is a lived, developing process. It is not an abstract category, and it is not a fixed, inherited position (although one's family background is, of course, important). Social class is perceived as a complex of social relations that one develops as one grows up—as one acquires and develops certain bodies of knowledge, skills, abilities, and traits, and as one has contact and opportunity in the world.[5] In sum, social class describes relationships that we as adults have developed, may attempt to maintain, and in which we participate every working day. These relationships in a real sense define our material ties to the world. An important concern here is whether these relationships are developing in children in schools within particular social class contexts.

The Sample of Schools

With the preceding discussion as a theoretical backdrop, the social class designation of each of the five schools will be identified, and the income, occupation, and other relevant available social characteristics of the students and their parents will be described. The first three schools are in a medium-sized city district in northern New Jersey, and the other two are in a nearby New Jersey suburb.

The first two schools I will call *Working-Class Schools*. Most of the parents have blue-collar jobs. Less than a third of the fathers are skilled, while the majority are in unskilled or semiskilled jobs. During the period of the study (1978–1979) approximately 15% of the fathers were unemployed. The large majority (85%) of the families are white. The following occupations are typical: platform, storeroom, and stockroom workers; foundrymen, pipe welders, and boilermakers; semiskilled and unskilled assembly-line operatives; gas station attendants, auto mechanics, maintenance workers, and security guards. Less than 30% of the women work, some part-time and some full-time, on assembly lines, in storerooms and stockrooms, as waitresses, barmaids, or sales clerks. Of the fifth grade parents, none of the wives of the skilled workers had jobs. Approximately 15% of the families in each school are at or below the federal "poverty" level[6]; most of the rest of the family incomes are at or below $12,000, except some of the skilled workers whose incomes are higher. The incomes of the majority of the families in these two schools (i.e., at or below $12,000) are typical of 38.6% of the families in the United States (U.S. Bureau of the Census, 1979, p. 2, table A).

The third school is called the *Middle-Class School*, although because of neighborhood residence patterns, the population is a mixture of several social classes. The parents' occupations can be divided into three groups: a small group of blue-collar "rich," who are skilled, well-paid workers such as printers, carpenters, plumbers, and construction workers. The second group is composed of parents in working-class and middle-class white-collar jobs: women in office jobs, technicians, supervisors in industry, and parents employed by the city (such as firemen, policemen, and several of the school's teachers). The third group is composed of occupations such as personnel directors in local firms, accountants, "middle management," and a few small capitalists (owners of shops in the area). The children of several local doctors attend this school. Most family incomes are between $13,000 and $25,000 with a few higher. This income range is typical of 38.9% of the families in the United States (U.S. Bureau of the Census, 1979, p. 2, table A).

The fourth school has a parent population that is at the upper income level of the upper middle class and is predominantly professional. This school will be called the *Affluent Professional School*. Typical jobs are: cardiologist, interior designer, corporate lawyer or engineer, executive in advertising or television. There are some families who are not so affluent as the majority (e.g., the family of the superintendent of the district's schools, and the one or two families in which the fathers are skilled workers). In addition, a few of the families are more affluent than the majority, and can be classified in the capitalist class (e.g., a partner in a prestigious Wall Street stock brokerage firm). Approximately 90% of the children in this school are white. Most family incomes are between $40,000 and $80,000. This income span represents approximately 7% of the families in the United States.[7]

In the fifth school the majority of the families belong to the capitalist class. This school will be called the *Executive Elite School* because most of the fathers are top executives, (e.g., presidents and vice presidents) in major U.S.-based multinational corporations—for example, ATT, RCA, City Bank, American Express, U.S. Steel. A sizable group of fathers are top executives in financial firms on Wall Street. There are also a number of fathers who list their occupations as "general counsel" to a particular corporation, and these corporations are also among the large multinationals. Many of the mothers do volunteer work in the Junior League, Junior Fortnightly, or other service groups; some are intricately involved in town politics; and some are themselves in well-paid occupations. There are no minority children in the school. Almost all family incomes are over $100,000 with some in the $500,000 range. The incomes of this school represent less than 1% of the families in the United States (see Smith and Franklin, 1974).

Since each of the five schools is only one instance of elementary education in a particular social class context, I will not generalize beyond the sample.

However, the examples of school work that follow will suggest characteristics of education in each social setting that appear to have theoretical or social significance and to be worth investigation in a larger number of schools.

Social Class and School Work

There are obvious similarities among United States schools and classrooms. There are school and classroom rules, teachers who ask questions and attempt to exercise control and who give work and homework. There are textbooks and tests. All of these were found in the five schools. Indeed, there were other curricular similarities as well: All schools and fifth grades used the same math book and series (*Mathematics Around Us*, Scott Foresman, 1978); all fifth grades had at least one boxed set of an individualized reading program available in the room (although the variety and amounts of teaching materials in the classroom increased as the social class of the school population increased); and, all fifth grade language arts curricula included aspects of grammar, punctuation, and capitalization.[8]

This section provides examples of work and work-related activities in each school that bear on the categories used to define social class. Thus, examples will be provided concerning students' relation to capital (e.g., as manifest in any symbolic capital that might be acquired through school work); students' relation to persons and types of authority regarding school work; and students' relation to their own productive activity. The section first offers the investigator's interpretation of what school work is for children in each setting and then presents events and interactions that illustrate that assessment.

The Working-Class Schools

In the two working-class schools, work is following the steps of a procedure. The procedure is usually mechanical, involving rote behavior and very little decision making or choice. The teachers rarely explain why the work is being assigned, how it might connect to other assignments, or what the idea is that lies behind the procedure or gives it coherence and perhaps meaning or significance. Available textbooks are not always used, and the teachers often prepare their own dittoes or put work examples on the board. Most of the rules regarding work are designations of what the children are to do; the rules are steps to follow. These steps are told to the children by the teachers and often written on the board. The children are usually told to copy the steps as notes. These notes are to be studied. Work is often evaluated not according to whether it is right or wrong, but according to whether the children followed the right steps.

The following examples illustrate these points. In math, when two-digit division was introduced, the teacher in one school gave a 4-minute lecture on what the terms are called (i.e., which number is the divisor, dividend, quotient, and remainder). The children were told to copy these names in their notebooks. Then the teacher told them the steps to follow to do the problems, saying, "This is how you do them." The teacher listed the steps on the board, and they appeared several days later as a chart hung in the middle of the front wall: "Divide; Multiply; Subtract; Bring Down." The children often did examples of two-digit division. When the teacher went over the examples with them, he told them for each problem what the procedure was, rarely asking them to conceptualize or explain it themselves: "3 into 22 is 7; do your subtraction and one is left over." During the week that two-digit division was introduced (or at any other time), the investigator did not observe any discussion of the idea of grouping involved in division, any use of manipulables, or any attempt to relate two-digit division to any other mathematical process. Nor was there any attempt to relate the steps to an actual or possible thought process of the children. The observer did not hear the terms dividend, quotient, etc., used again. The math teacher in the other working-class school followed similar procedures regarding two-digit division, and at one point her class seemed confused. She said, "You're confusing yourselves. You're tensing up. Remember, when you do this, it's the same steps over and over again—and that's the way division always is." Several weeks later, after a test, a group of her children "still didn't get it," and she made no attempt to explain the concept of dividing things into groups, or to give them manipulables for their own investigation. Rather, she went over the steps with them again and told them that they "needed more practice."

In other areas of math, work is also carrying out often unexplained, fragmented procedures. For example, one of the teachers led the children through a series of steps to make a 1-inch grid on their papers *without* telling them that they were making at 1-inch grid, or that it would be used to study scale. She said, "Take your ruler. Put it across the top. Make a mark at every number. Then move your ruler down to the bottom. No, put it across the bottom. Now make a mark on top of every number. Now draw a line from . . ." At this point a girl said that she had a faster way to do it and the teacher said, "No, you don't; you don't even know what I'm making yet. Do it this way, or it's wrong." After they had made the lines up and down and across, the teacher told them she wanted them to make a figure by connecting some dots and to measure that, using the scale of 1-inch equals 1 mile. Then they were to cut it out. She said, "Don't cut until I check it."

In both working-class schools, work in language arts is mechanics of punctuation (commas, periods, question marks, exclamation points), capitalization, and the four kinds of sentences. One teacher explained to me, "Simple punctuation is all they'll ever use." Regarding punctuation, either a teacher or a ditto stated the rules for where, for example, to put commas. The investigator heard no classroom discussion of the aural context of punctuation (which, of course, is what gives each mark its meaning). Nor did the investigator hear any statement or inference that placing a punctuation mark could be a decision-making process, depending, for example, on one's intended meaning. Rather, the children were told to follow the rules. Language arts did not involve creative writing. There were several writing assignments throughout the year, but in each instance the children were given a ditto, and they wrote answers to questions on the sheet. For example, they wrote their "autobiography" by answering such questions as "Where were you born?" "What is your favorite animal?" on a sheet entitled, "All about Me."

In one of the working-class schools the class had a science period several times a week. On the three occasions observed, the children were not called upon to set up experiments or to give explanations for facts or concepts. Rather, on each occasion the teacher told them in his own words what the book said. The children copied the teacher's sentences from the board. Each day that preceded the day they were to do a science experiment, the teacher told them to copy the directions from the book for the procedure they would carry out the next day, and to study the list at home that night. The day after each experiment, the teacher went over what they had "found" (they did the experiments as a class, and each was actually a class demonstration led by the teacher). Then the teacher wrote what they "found" on the board, and the children copied that in their notebooks. Once or twice a year there are science projects. The project is chosen and assigned by the teacher from a box of 3-by-5-inch cards. On the card the teacher has written the question to be answered, the books to use, and how much to write. Explaining the cards to the observer, the teacher said, "It tells them exactly what to do, or they couldn't do it."

Social studies in the working-class schools is also largely mechanical, rote work that was given little explanation or connection to larger contexts. In one school, for example, although there was a book available, social studies work was to copy the teacher's notes from the board. Several times a week for a period of several months, the children copied these notes. The fifth grades in the district were to study U.S. history. The teacher used a booklet she had purchased called "The Fabulous Fifty States." Each day she put information from the booklet in outline form on the board and the children copied it. The type of information did not vary: the name of the state, its abbreviation, state capital, nickname of the state, its main products, main business, and a "Fabulous Fact" (e.g., "Idaho grew 27 billion potatoes in one year. That's enough potatoes for each man, woman and . . ."). As the children finished copying the sentences, the teacher erased them and wrote more. Children would occasionally go to the front to pull down the wall map in order to locate the states they were copying, and the teacher did not dissuade them. But the observer never saw her refer to the map; nor did the observer ever hear her make other than perfunctory remarks concerning the information the children were copying. Occasionally the children colored in a ditto and cut it out to make a stand-up figure (representing, for example, a man roping a cow in the Southwest). These were referred to by the teacher as their social studies "projects."

Rote behavior was often called for in classroom oral work. When going over math and language arts skills sheets, for example, as the teacher asked for the answer to each problem, he fired the questions rapidly, staccato, and the scene reminded the observer of a sergeant drilling recruits: above all, the questions demanded that you stay at attention: "The next one? What do I put here? . . . Here? Give us the next." Or "How many commas in this sentence? Where do I put them . . . The next one?"

The (four) fifth grade teachers observed in the working-class schools attempted to control classroom time and space by making decisions without consulting the children and without explaining the basis for their decisions. The teacher's control thus often seemed capricious. Teachers, for instance, very often ignored the bells to switch classes—deciding among themselves to keep the children after the period was officially over, to continue with the work, or for disciplinary reasons, or so they (the teachers) could stand in the hall and talk. There were no clocks in the rooms in either school, and the children often asked, "What period is this?" "When do we go to gym?" The children had no access to materials. These were handed out by teachers and closely guarded. Things in the room "belonged" to the teacher: "Bob, bring me my garbage can." The teachers continually gave the children orders. Only three times did the investigator hear a teacher in either working-class school preface a directive with an unsarcastic "please," or "let's" or "would you." Instead, the teachers said, "Shut up," "Shut your mouth," "Open your books," "Throw your gum away—if you want to rot your teeth, do it on your *own* time." Teachers made every effort to control the movement of the children, and often shouted, "Why are you out of your seat??!!" If the children got permission to leave the room they had to take a written pass with the date and time.

The control that the teachers have is less than they would like. It is a result of constant struggle with the children. The children continually resist the teachers' orders and the work itself. They do not directly challenge the teachers' authority or legitimacy, but they make indirect attempts to sabotage and resist the flow of assignments:

TEACHER: I will put some problems on the board. You are to divide.

CHILD: We got to divide?

TEACHER: Yes.

SEVERAL CHILDREN:	(*Groan*) Not again. Mr. B, we done this yesterday.
CHILD:	Do we put the date?
TEACHER:	Yes. I hope we remember we work in silence. You're supposed to do it on white paper. I'll explain it later.
CHILD:	Somebody broke my pencil. (*Crash*—a child falls out of his chair.)
CHILD:	(*repeats*) Mr. B., somebody broke my *pencil!*
CHILD:	Are we going to be here all morning?

(Teacher comes to the observer, shakes his head and grimaces, then smiles.)

The children are successful enough in their struggle against work that there are long periods where they are not asked to do any work, but just to sit and be quiet.[9] Very often the work that the teachers assign is "easy," that is, not demanding, and thus receives less resistance. Sometimes a compromise is reached where, although the teachers insist that the children continue to work, there is a constant murmur of talk. The children will be doing arithmetic examples, copying social studies notes, or doing punctuation or other dittoes, and all the while there is muted but spirited conversation—about somebody's broken arm, an afterschool disturbance of the day before, etc. Sometimes the teachers themselves join in the conversation because, as one teacher explained to me, "It's a relief from the routine."

Middle-Class School

In the middle-class school, work is getting the right answer. If one accumulates enough right answers one gets a good grade. One must follow the directions in order to get the right answers, but the directions often call for some figuring, some choice, some decision making. For example, the children must often figure out by themselves what the directions ask them to do, and how to get the answer: What do you do first, second, and perhaps third? Answers are usually found in books or by listening to the teacher. Answers are usually words, sentences, numbers, or facts and dates; one writes them on paper, and one should be neat. Answers must be in the right order, and one can not make them up.

The following activities are illustrative. Math involves some choice: One may do two-digit division the long way, or the short way, and there are some math problems that can be done "in your head." When the teacher explains how to do two-digit division, there is recognition that a cognitive process is involved; she gives several ways and says, "I want to make sure you understand what you're doing—so you get it right"; and, when they go over the homework, she asks the *children* to tell how they did the problem and what answer they got.

In social studies the daily work is to read the assigned pages in the textbook and to answer the teacher's questions. The questions are almost always designed to check on whether the students have read the assignment and understood it: Who did so-and-so; what happened after that; when did it happen, where, and sometimes, why did it happen? The answers are in the book and in one's understanding of the book; the teacher's hints when one doesn't know the answer are to "read it again," or to look at the picture or at the rest of the paragraph. One is to search for the answer in the "context," in what is given.

Language arts is "simple grammar, what they need for everyday life." The language arts teacher says, "They should learn to speak properly, to write business letters and thank-you letters, and to understand what nouns and verbs and simple subjects are." Here, as well, the actual work is to choose the right answers, to understand what is given. The teacher often says, "Please read the next sentence and then I'll question you about it." One teacher said in some exasperation to a boy who was fooling around in class, "If you don't know the answers to the questions I ask, then you can't stay in this *class!* (pause) You never know the answers to the questions I ask, and it's not fair to me—and certainly not to you!"

Most lessons are based on the textbook. This does not involve a critical perspective on what is given there. For example, a critical perspective in social studies is perceived as dangerous by these teachers because it may lead to controversial topics; the parents might complain. The children, however, are often curious, especially in social studies. Their questions are tolerated, and usually answered perfunctorily. But after a few minutes the teacher will say, "All right, we're not going any farther. Please open your social studies workbook." While the teachers spend a lot of time explaining and expanding on what the textbooks say, there is little attempt to analyze how or why things happen, or to give thought to how pieces of a culture, or, say, a system of numbers or elements of a language fit together or can be analyzed. What has happened in the past, and what exists now may not be equitable or fair, but (shrug) that is the way things are, and one does not confront such matters in school. For example, in social studies after a child is called on to read a passage about the pilgrims, the teacher summarizes the paragraph and then says, "So you can see how strict they were about everything." A child asks, "Why?" "Well, because they felt that if you weren't busy you'd get into trouble." Another child asks, "Is it true that they burned women at the stake?" The teacher says, "Yes, if a woman did anything strange, they hanged them. [sic] What would a woman do, do you think, to make them burn them? [sic] See if you can come up with better answers than my other [social studies] class." Several children offered suggestions, to which the teacher nods but does not comment. Then she says, "OK, good," and calls on the next child to read.

Work tasks do not usually request creativity. Serious attention is rarely given in school work to how the children develop or express their own feelings and ideas, either linguistically or in graphic form. On the occasions when creativity or self-expression is requested, it is peripheral to the main activity, or it is "enrichment," or "for fun." During a lesson on what similes are, for example, the teacher explains what they are, puts several on the board, gives some other examples herself, and then asks the children if they can "make some up." She calls on three children who give similes, two of which are actually in the book they have open before them. The teacher does not comment on this, and then asks several others to choose similes from the list of phrases in the book. Several do so correctly, and she says, "Oh *good!* You're picking them out! See how good we are?" Their homework is to pick out the rest of the similes from the list.

Creativity is not often requested in social studies and science projects, either. Social studies projects, for example, are given with directions to "find information on your topic," and write it up. The children are not supposed to copy, but to "put it in your own words." Although a number of projects subsequently went beyond the teacher's direction to find information and had quite expressive covers and inside illustrations, the teacher's evaluative comments had to do with the amount of information, whether they had "copied," and if their work was neat.

The style of control of the three fifth grade teachers observed in this school varied from somewhat easygoing to strict, but in contrast to the working-class schools, the teachers' decisions were usually based on external rules and regulations, for example, on criteria that were known or available to the children. Thus, the teachers always honor the bells for changing classes, and they usually evaluate children's work by what is in the textbooks and answer booklets.

There is little excitement in school work for the children, and the assignments are perceived as having little to do with their interests and feelings. As one child said, what you do is "store facts in your head like cold storage—until you need it later for a test, or your job." Thus, doing well is important because there are thought to be *other* likely rewards: a good job or college.[10]

Affluent Professional School

In the affluent professional school, work is creative activity carried out independently. The students are continually asked to express and apply ideas and concepts. Work involves individual thought and expressiveness, expansion and illustration of ideas, and choice of appropriate method and material. (The class is not considered an open classroom, and the principal explained that because of the large number of discipline problems in the fifth grade this year they did not departmentalize. The teacher who agreed to take part in the study said she is "more structured" this year than she usually is.) The products of work in this class are often written stories, editorials and essays, or representations of ideas in mural, graph, or craft form. The products of work should not be like everybody else's and should show individuality. They should exhibit good design, and (this is important), they must also fit empirical reality. Moreover, one's work should attempt to interpret or "make sense" of reality. The relatively few rules to be followed regarding work are usually criteria for, or limits on, individual activity. One's product is usually evaluated for the quality of its expression and for the appropriateness of its conception to the task. In many cases one's own satisfaction with the product is an important criterion for its evaluation. When right answers are called for, as in commercial materials like SRA (Science Research Associates) and math, it is important that the children decide on an answer as a result of thinking about the idea involved in what they're being asked to do. Teacher's hints are to "think about it some more."

The following activities are illustrative. The class takes home a sheet requesting each child's parents to fill in the number of cars they have, the number of television sets, refrigerators, games, or rooms in the house, etc. Each child is to figure the average number of a type of possession owned by the fifth grade. Each child must compile the "data" from all the sheets. A calculator is available in the classroom to do the mechanics of finding the average. Some children decide to send sheets to the fourth grade families for comparison. Their work should be "verified" by a classmate before it is handed in.

Each child and his or her family has made a geoboard. The teacher asks the class to get their geoboards from the side cabinet, to take a handful of rubber bands, and then to listen to what she would like them to do. She says, "I would like you to design a figure and then find the perimeter and area. When you have it, check with your neighbor. After you've done that, please transfer it to graph paper and tomorrow I'll ask you to make up a question about it for someone. When you hand it in, please let me know whose it is, and who verified it. Then I have something else for you to do that's really fun. (pause) Find the average number of chocolate chips in three cookies. I'll give you three cookies, and you'll have to *eat* your way through, I'm afraid!" Then she goes around the room and gives help, suggestions, praise, and admonitions that they are getting noisy. They work sitting, or standing up at their desks, at benches in the back, or on the floor. A child hands the teacher his paper and she comments, "I'm not accepting this paper. Do a better design." To another child she says, "That's fantastic! But you'll never find the area. Why don't you draw a figure inside [the big one] and subtract to get the area?"

The school district requires the fifth grades to study ancient civilizations (in particular, Egypt, Athens, and Sumer.) In this classroom, the emphasis is on illustrating and recreating the culture of the people of ancient times. The following are typical activities: The children made an 8 mm film on Egypt, which one of the parents edited. A girl in the class wrote the script, and the class acted it out. They put the sound on themselves. They read stories of those days. They wrote essays and stories depicting the lives of the people and the societal and occupational divisions. They chose from a list of projects, all of which involved graphic representations of ideas: for example, "Make a mural depicting the division of labor in Egyptian society."

Each child wrote and exchanged a letter in hieroglyphics with a fifth grader in another class, and they also exchanged stories they wrote in cuneiform. They made a scroll and singed the edges so it looked authentic. They each chose an occupation and made an Egyptian plaque representing that occupation, simulating the appropriate Egyptian design. They carved their design on a cylinder of wax, pressed the wax into clay, and then baked the clay. Although one girl did not choose an occupation, but carved instead a series of gods and slaves, the teacher said, "That's all right, Amber, it's beautiful." As they were working the teacher said, "Don't cut into your clay until you're satisfied with your design."

Social studies also involves almost daily presentation by the children of some event from the news. The teacher's questions ask the children to expand what they say, to give more details, and to be more specific. Occasionally she adds some remarks to help them see connections between events.

The emphasis on expressing and illustrating ideas in social studies is accompanied in language arts by an emphasis on creative writing. Each child wrote a rebus story for a first grader whom they had interviewed to see what kind of story the child liked best. They wrote editorials on pending decisions by the school board, and radio plays, some of which were read over the school intercom from the office, and one of which was performed in the auditorium. There is no language arts textbook because, the teacher said, "The principal wants us to be creative." There is not much grammar, but there is punctuation. One morning when the observer arrived the class was doing a punctuation ditto. The teacher later apologized for using the ditto. "It's just for review," she said. "I don't teach punctuation that way. We use their language." The ditto had three unambiguous rules for where to put commas in a sentence. As the teacher was going to help the children with the ditto, she repeated several times, "Where you put the commas depends on how you say the sentence; it depends on the situation and what you want to say." Several weeks later the observer saw another punctuation activity. The teacher had printed a five-paragraph story on an oak tag and then cut it into phrases. She read the whole story to the class from the book, then passed out the phrases. The group had to decide how the phrases could best be put together again. (They arranged the phrases on the floor.) The point was not to replicate the story, although that was not irrelevant, but to "decide" what you think the best way is." Punctuation marks on cardboard pieces were then handed out and the children discussed, and then decided, what mark was best at each place they thought one was needed. At the end of each paragraph the teacher asked, "Are you satisfied with the way the paragraphs are now? Read it to yourself and see how it sounds." Then she read the original story again, and they compared the two.

Describing her goals in science to the investigator, the teacher said, "We use ESS (Elementary Science Study). It's very good because it gives a hands-on experience—so they can make sense out of it. It doesn't matter whether it [what they find] is right or wrong. I bring them together and there's value in discussing their ideas."

The products of work in this class are often highly valued by the children and the teacher. In fact, this was the only school in which the investigator was not allowed to take original pieces of the children's work for her files. If the work was small enough, however, and was on paper, the investigator could duplicate it on the copying machine in the office.

The teacher's attempt to control the class involves constant negotiation. She does not give direct orders unless she is angry because the children have been too noisy. Normally, she tries to get them to foresee the consequences of their actions and to decide accordingly. For example, lining them up to go see a play written by the sixth graders, she says, "I presume you're lined up by some-one with whom you want to sit. I hope you're lined up by someone you won't get in trouble with." The following two dialogues illustrate the process of nego-tiation between student and teacher.

TEACHER: Tom, you're behind in your SRA this marking period.

TOM: So what!

TEACHER: Well, last time you had a hard time catching up.

TOM: But I have my [music] lesson at 10:00.

TEACHER: Well, that doesn't mean you're going to sit here for 20 minutes.

TOM: Twenty minutes! OK. (He goes to pick out a SRA booklet and chooses one, puts it back, then takes another, and brings it to her.)

TEACHER: OK, this is the one you want, right?

TOM: Yes.

TEACHER: OK, I'll put tomorrow's date on it so you can take it home tonight or finish it tomorrow if you want.

TEACHER: (to a child who is wandering around during reading) Kevin, why don't you do *Reading for Concepts?*

KEVIN: No, I don't like *Reading for Concepts.*

TEACHER:	Well, what are you going to do?
KEVIN:	(pause) I'm going to work on my DAR. (The DAR had sponsored an essay competition on "Life in the American Colonies.")

One of the few rules governing the children's movement is that no more than three children may be out of the room at once. There is a school rule that anyone can go to the library at any time to get a book. In the fifth grade I observed, they sign their name on the chalkboard and leave. There are no passes. Finally, the children have a fair amount of officially sanctioned say over what happens in the class. For example, they often negotiate what work is to be done. If the teacher wants to move on to the next subject, but the children say they are not ready, they want to work on their present projects some more, she very often lets them do it.

Executive Elite School

In the executive elite school, work is developing one's analytical intellectual powers. Children are continually asked to reason through a problem, to produce intellectual products that are both logically sound and of top academic quality. A primary goal of thought is to conceptualize rules by which elements may fit together in systems, and then to apply these rules in solving a problem. School work helps one to achieve, to excel, to prepare for life.

The following are illustrative. The math teacher teaches area and perimeter by having the children derive formulae for each. First she helps them, through discussion at the board, to arrive at $A = W \times L$ as a formula (not *the* formula) for area. After discussing several, she says, "Can anyone make up a formula for perimeter? Can you figure that out yourselves? (pause) Knowing what we know, can we think of a formula?" She works out three children's suggestions at the board, saying to two, "Yes, that's a good one," and then asks the class if they can think of any more. No one volunteers. To prod them, she says, "If you use rules and good reasoning, you get many ways. Chris, can you think up a formula?"

She discusses two-digit division with the children as a decision-making process. Presenting a new type of problem to them, she asks, "What's the first decision you'd make if presented with this kind of example? What is the first thing you'd *think*? Craig?" Craig says, "To find my first partial quotient." She responds, "Yes, that would be your first decision. How would you do that?" Craig explains and then the teacher says, "OK, we'll see how that works for you." The class tries his way. Subsequently, she comments on the merits and shortcomings of several other children's decisions. Later, she tells the investigator that her goals in math are to develop their reasoning and mathematical thinking and that, unfortunately, "there's no time for manipulables."

While right answers are important in math, they are not "given" by the book or by the teacher but may be challenged by the children. Going over some problems in late September the teacher says, "Raise your hand if you do not agree." A child says, "I don't agree with 64." The teacher responds, "OK, there's a question about 64. (to class) Please check it. Owen, they're disagreeing with you. Kristen, they're checking yours." The teacher emphasized this repeatedly during September and October with statements like, "Don't be afraid to say if you disagree. In the last [math] class, somebody disagreed, and they were right. Before you disagree, check yours, and if you still think we're wrong, then we'll check it out." By Thanksgiving, the children did not often speak in terms of right and wrong math problems, but of whether they agreed with the answer that had been given.

There are complicated math mimeos with many word problems. Whenever they go over the examples, they discuss how each child has set up the problem. The children must explain it precisely. On one occasion the teacher said, "I'm more—just as interested in *how* you set up the problem as in what answer you find. If you set up a problem in a good way, the answer is *easy* to find."

Social studies work is most often reading and discussion of concepts and independent research. There are only occasional artistic, expressive, or illustrative projects. Ancient Athens and Sumer are, rather, societies to analyze. The following questions are typical of those that guide the children's independent research: "What mistakes did Pericles make after the war?" "What mistakes did the citizens of Athens make?" "What are the elements of a civilization?" "How did Greece build an economic empire?" "Compare the way Athens chose its leaders with the way we choose ours." Occasionally the children are asked to make up sample questions for their social studies tests. On an occasion when the investigator was present the social studies teacher rejected a child's question by saying, "That's just fact. If I asked you that question on a test, you'd complain it was just memory! Good questions ask for concepts."

In social studies—but also in reading, science, and health—the teachers initiate classroom discussions of current social issues and problems. These discussions occurred on every one of the investigator's visits, and a teacher told me, "These children's opinions are important—it's important that they learn to reason things through." The classroom discussions always struck the observer as quite realistic and analytical, dealing with concrete social issues like the following: "Why do workers strike?" "Is that right or wrong?" "Why do we have inflation, and what can be done to stop it?" "Why do companies put chemicals in food when the natural ingredients are available?" etc. Usually the children did not have to be prodded to give their opinions. In fact, their statements and the interchanges between them struck the observer as quite sophisticated conceptually and verbally, and well-informed. Occasionally the teachers would prod with statements such as, "Even if you don't know [the answers], if you think logically about it, you can figure it out." And "I'm asking you [these] questions to help you think this through."

Language arts emphasizes language as a complex system, one that should be mastered. The children are asked to diagram sentences of complex grammatical construction, to memorize irregular verb conjugations (he lay, he has lain, etc. . . .), and to use the proper participles, conjunctions, and interjections in their speech. The teacher (the same one who teaches social studies) told them, "It is not enough to get these right on tests; you must use what you learn [in grammar classes] in your written and oral work. I will grade you on that."

Most writing assignments are either research reports and essays for social studies or experiment analyses and write-ups for science. There is only an occasional story or other "creative writing" assignment. On the occasion observed by the investigator (the writing of a Halloween story), the points the teacher stressed in preparing the children to write involved the structural aspects of a story rather than the expression of feelings or other ideas. The teacher showed them a filmstrip, "The Seven Parts of a Story," and lectured them on plot development, mood setting, character development, consistency, and the use of a logical or appropriate ending. The stories they subsequently wrote were, in fact, well-structured, but many were also personal and expressive. The teacher's evaluative comments, however, did not refer to the expressiveness or artistry but were all directed toward whether they had "developed" the story well.

Language arts work also involved a large amount of practice in presentation of the self and in managing situations where the child was expected to be in charge. For example, there was a series of assignments in which each child had to be a "student teacher." The child had to plan a lesson in grammar, outlining, punctuation, or other language arts topic and explain the concept to the class. Each child was to prepare a worksheet or game and a homework assignment as well. After each presentation, the teacher and other children gave a critical appraisal of the "student teacher's" performance. Their criteria were: whether the student spoke clearly; whether the lesson was interesting; whether the student made any mistakes; and whether he or she kept control of the class. On an occasion when a child did not maintain control, the teacher said, "When you're up here, you have authority, and you have to use it. I'll back you up."

The teacher of math and science explained to the observer that she likes the ESS program because "the children can manipulate variables. They generate hypotheses and devise experiments to solve the problem. Then they have to explain what they found."

The executive elite school is the only school where bells do not demarcate the periods of time. The two fifth grade teachers were very strict about changing classes on schedule, however, as specific plans for each session had been made. The teachers attempted to keep tight control over the children during lessons, and the children were sometimes flippant, boisterous, and occasionally rude. However, the children may be brought into line by reminding them that "it is up to you." "You must control yourself," "you are responsible for your work," you must "set your priorities." One teacher told a child, "You are the only driver of your car—and only you can regulate your speed." A new teacher complained to the observer that she had thought "these children" would have more control.

While strict attention to the lesson at hand is required, the teachers make relatively little attempt to regulate the movement of the children at other times. For example, except for the kindergartners, the children in this school do not have to wait for the bell to ring in the morning; they may go to their classroom when they arrive at school. Fifth graders often came early to read, to finish work, or to catch up. After the first two months of school the fifth grade teachers did not line the children up to change classes or to go to gym, etc., but, when the children were ready and quiet, they were told they could go—sometimes without the teachers.

In the classroom, the children could get materials when they needed them and took what they needed from closets and from the teacher's desk. They were in charge of the office at lunchtime. During class they did not have to sign out or ask permission to leave the room; they just got up and left. Because of the pressure to get work done, however, they did not leave the room very often. The teachers were very polite to the children, and the investigator heard no sarcasm, no nasty remarks, and few direct orders. The teachers never called the children "honey," or "dear," but always called them by name. The teachers were expected to be available before school, after school, and for part of their lunch time to provide extra help if needed.

Discussion and Conclusion

One could attempt to identify physical, educational, cultural, and interpersonal characteristics of the environment of each school that might contribute to an empirical explanation of the events and interactions. For example, the investigator could introduce evidence to show that the following *increased* as the social class of the community increased (with the most marked differences occurring between the two districts): increased variety and abundance of teaching materials in the classroom; increased time reported spent by the teachers on preparation; higher social class background and more prestigious educational institutions attended by teachers and administrators; more stringent board of education requirements regarding teaching methods; more frequent and demanding administrative evaluation of teachers; increased teacher support services such as in-service workshops; increased parent expenditure for school equipment over and above district or government funding; higher expectations of student ability on the part of parents, teachers, and administrators; higher expectations and demands regarding student achievement on the part of teachers, parents, and administrators; more positive attitudes on the part of the teachers as to the probable occupational futures of the children; an increase in the children's acceptance of classroom assignments; increased intersubjectivity between students and teachers; and increased cultural congruence between school and community.

All of these—and other—factors may contribute to the character and scope of classroom events. However, what is of primary concern here is not the immediate causes of classroom activity (although these are in themselves quite important). Rather, the concern is to reflect on the deeper social meaning, the wider theoretical significance, of what happens in each social setting. In an attempt to assess the theoretical meaning of the differences among the schools, the work tasks and milieu in each will be discussed in light of the concepts used to define social class.

What potential relationships to the system of ownership of symbolic and physical capital, to authority and control, and to their own productive activity are being developed in children of each school? What economically relevant knowledge, skills, and predispositions are being transmitted in each classroom, and for what future relationship to the system of production are they appropriate? It is of course true that a student's future relationship to the process of production in society is determined by the combined effects of circumstances beyond elementary schooling. However, by examining elementary school activity in its social class context in the light of our theoretical perspective on social class, we can see certain potential relationships already developing. Moreover, in this structure of developing relationships lies theoretical—and social—significance.

The *working-class* children are developing a potential *conflict* relationship with capital. Their present school work is appropriate preparation for future wage labor that is mechanical and routine. Such work, insofar as it denies the human capacities for creativity and planning, is degrading; moreover, when performed in industry, such work is a source of profit to others. This situation produces industrial conflict over wages, working conditions, and control. However, the children in the working-class schools are not learning to be docile and obedient in the face of present or future degrading conditions or financial exploitation. They are developing abilities and skills of resistance. These methods are highly similar to the "slowdown," subtle sabotage, and other modes of indirect resistance carried out by adult workers in the shop, on the department store sales floor, and in some offices.[11] As these types of resistance develop in school, they are highly constrained and limited in their ultimate effectiveness. Just as the children's resistance prevents them from learning socially legitimated knowledge and skills in school and is therefore ultimately debilitating, so is this type of resistance ultimately debilitating in industry. Such resistance in industry does not succeed in producing, nor is it intended to produce, fundamental changes in the relationships of exploitation or control. Thus, the methods of resistance that the working-class children are developing in school are only temporarily, and *potentially*, liberating.

In the *middle-class school* the children are developing somewhat different potential relationships to capital, authority, and work. In this school the work tasks and relationships are appropriate for a future relation to capital that is *bureaucratic*. Their school work is appropriate for white-collar working-class and middle-class jobs in the supportive institutions of United States society. In these jobs one does the paperwork, the technical work, the sales and the social service in the private and state bureaucracies. Such work does not usually demand that one be creative, and one is not often rewarded for critical analysis of the system. One is rewarded, rather, for knowing the answers to the questions one is asked, for knowing where or how to find the answers, and for knowing which form, regulation, technique, or procedure is correct. While such work does not usually satisfy human needs for engagement and self-expression, one's salary can be exchanged for objects or activities that attempt to meet these needs.

In the *affluent professional school* the children are developing a potential relationship to capital that is instrumental and expressive and involves substantial negotiation. In their schooling these children are acquiring *symbolic capital*: They are being given the opportunity to develop skills of linguistic, artistic, and scientific expression and creative elaboration of ideas into concrete form. These skills are those needed to produce, for example, culture (e.g., artistic, intellectual, and scientific ideas and other "products"). Their schooling is developing in these children skills necessary to become society's successful artists, intellectuals, legal, scientific, and technical experts and other professionals. The developing relation of the children in this school to their work is creative and relatively autonomous. Although they do not have control over which ideas they develop or express, the creative act in itself affirms and utilizes the human potential for conceptualization and design that is in many cases valued as intrinsically satisfying.

Professional persons in the cultural institutions of society (in, say, academe, publishing, the nonprint media, the arts, and the legal and state bureaucracies) are in an expressive relationship to the system of ownership in society because the ideas and other products of their work are often an important means by which material relationships of society are given ideological (e.g., artistic, intellectual, legal, and scientific) expression. Through the system of laws, for example, the ownership relations of private property are elaborated and legitimated in legal form; through individualistic and meritocratic theories in psychology and sociology, these individualistic economic relations are provided scientific "rationality" and "sense." The relationship to physical capital of those in society who create what counts as the dominant culture or ideology also involves substantial negotiation. The producers of symbolic capital often do not control the socially available physical capital nor the cultural uses to which it is put. They must therefore negotiate for money for their own projects. However, skillful application of one's cultural capital may ultimately lead to social (e.g., state) power and to financial reward.

The *executive elite school* gives its children something that none of the other schools does: knowledge of and practice in manipulating the socially legitimated tools of analysis of systems. The children are given the opportunity to learn and to utilize the intellectually and socially prestigious grammatical, mathematical, and other vocabularies and rules by which elements are arranged. They are given the opportunity to use these skills in the analysis of society and in control situations. Such knowledge and skills are a most important kind of *symbolic capital*. They are necessary for control of a production system. The developing relationship of the children in this school to their work affirms and develops in them the human capacities for analysis and planning and helps to prepare them for work in society that would demand these skills. Their schooling is helping them to develop the abilities necessary for ownership and control of physical capital and the means of production in society.

The foregoing analysis of differences in school work in contrasting social class contexts suggests the following conclusion: The "hidden curriculum" of school work is tacit preparation for relating to the process of production in a particular way. Differing curricular, pedagogical, and pupil evaluation practices emphasize different cognitive and behavioral skills in each social setting and thus contribute to the development in the children of certain potential relationships to physical and symbolic capital, to authority, and to the process of work. School experience, in the sample of schools discussed here, differed qualitatively by social class. These differences may not only contribute to the development in the children in each social class of certain types of economically significant relationships and not others, but would thereby help to reproduce this system of relations in society. In the contribution to the reproduction of unequal social relations lies a theoretical meaning, and social consequence, of classroom practice.

The identification of different emphases in classrooms in a sample of contrasting social class contexts implies that further research should be conducted in a large number of schools to investigate the types of work tasks and interactions in each, to see if they differ in the ways discussed here, and to see if similar potential relationships are uncovered. Such research could have as a product the further elucidation of complex but not readily apparent connections between everyday activity in schools and classrooms and the unequal structure of economic relationships in which we work and live.

Acknowledgment

The research was funded by Rutgers University Research Council.

Notes

1. But see, in a related vein, Apple and King (1977) and Rist (1973).
2. The definition of social class delineated here is the author's own, but it relies heavily on her interpretation of the work of Eric Olin Wright (1978), Pierre Bourdieu (Bourdieu and Passeron, 1977), and Raymond Williams (1977).
3. For discussion of schools as agencies of social and economic legitimation see Althusser (1971); see also Anyon (1978, 1979).
4. While relationships of control in society will not be discussed here, it can be said that they roughly parallel the relationships of control in the workplace, which will be the focus of this discussion. That is, working-class and many middle-class persons have less control than members of the upper middle and capitalist classes do, not only over conditions and processes of their work, but over their nonwork lives as well. In addition, it is true that persons from the middle and capitalist classes, rather than workers, are most often those who fill the positions of state and other power in United States society.
5. Occupations may change their relation to the means of production over time, as the expenditure and ownership of capital change, as technology, skills, and the social relations of work change. For example, some jobs that were middle-class, managerial positions in 1900 and that necessitated conceptual laying-out and planning are now working-class and increasingly mechanical: for example, quality control in industry, clerical work, and computer programming (see Braverman, 1974).
6. The U.S. Bureau of the Census defines "poverty" for a nonfarm family of four as a yearly income of $6191 a year or less. U.S. Bureau of the Census, *Statistical Abstract of the United States: 1978* (Washington, D.C.: U.S. Government Printing Office, 1978, p. 465, table 754).
7. This figure is an estimate. According to the Bureau of the Census, only 2.6% of the families in the United States have money income of $50,000 or over. U.S. Bureau of the Census, *Current Population Reports*, series P-60, no. 118, "Money Income in 1977 of Families and Persons in the United States." (Washington, D.C.: U.S. Government Printing Office, 1979, p. 2, table A). For figures on income at these higher levels, see Smith and Franklin (1974).
8. For other similarities alleged to characterize United States classrooms and schools, but which will not be discussed here, see Dreeben (1968), Jackson (1968), and Sarason (1971).

9. Indeed, strikingly little teaching occurred in either of the working-class schools; this curtailed the amount that the children were taught. Incidentally, it increased the amount of time that had to be spent by the researcher to collect data on teaching style and interaction.

10. A dominant feeling, expressed directly and indirectly by teachers in this school, was boredom with their work. They did, however, in contrast to the working-class schools, almost always carry out lessons during class times.

11. See, for example, discussions in Levison (1974), Aronowitz (1978), and Benson (1978).

References

Althusser, L. "Ideology and Ideological State Apparatuses." In L. Althusser (ed.), *Lenin and Philosophy and Other Essays*. Ben Brewster, trans (New York: Monthly Review Press, 1971).

Anyon, J. "Elementary Social Studies Textbooks and Legitimating Knowledge." *Theory and Research in Social Education* (1978), 6:40–55.

Anyon, J. "Ideology and United States History Textbooks." *Harvard Educational Review* (1979), 49:361–386.

Apple, M. W. *Ideology and Curriculum* (Boston, MA: Routledge and Kegan Paul, 1979).

Apple, M. W., and King, N. "What Do Schools Teach?" *Curriculum Inquiry* (1977), 6:341–358.

Aronowitz, S. "Marx, Braverman, and the Logic of Capital." *The Insurgent Sociologist* (1978), 8:126–146.

Benson, S. "The Clerking Sisterhood: Rationalization and the Work Culture of Saleswomen in American Department Stores, 1890–1960." *Radical America* (1978), 12:41–55.

Bernstein, B. *Class, Codes and Control, vol. 3. Towards a Theory of Educational Transmission*. 2nd ed. (London: Routledge and Kegan Paul, 1977).

Bourdieu, P., and Passeron, J. *Reproduction in Education, Society, and Culture* (Beverly Hills, CA: Sage, 1977).

Bowles, S., and Gintis, H. *Schooling in Capitalist America: Educational Reform and the Contradictions of Economic Life* (New York: Basic Books, 1976).

Braverman, H. *Labor and Monopoly Capital: The Degradation of Work in the Twentieth Century* (New York: Monthly Review Press, 1974).

Dreeben, R. *On What Is Learned in School* (Reading, Mass.: Addison-Wesley, 1968).

Jackson, P. *Life in Classrooms* (NY: Holt, Rinehart and Winston, 1968).

Lampman, R. J. *The Share of Top Wealth-Holders in National Wealth, 1922–1956: A Study of the National Bureau of Economic Research* (Princeton, NJ: Princeton University Press, 1962).

Levison, A. *The Working-Class Majority* (New York: Penguin Books, 1974).

New York Stock Exchange. *Census* (New York: New York Stock Exchange, 1975).

Rist, R. C. *The Urban School: A Factory for Failure* (Cambridge, MA: MIT Press, 1973).

Sarason, S. *The Culture of School and the Problem of Change* (Boston, MA: Allyn and Bacon, 1971).

Smith, J. D., and Franklin, S. "The Concentration of Personal Wealth, 1922–1969." *American Economic Review* (1974), 64:162–167.

U.S. Bureau of the Census. *Current Population Reports*. Series P-60, no. 118. Money Income in 1977 of Families and Persons in the United States (Washington, D.C.: U.S. Government Printing Office, 1979).

U.S. Bureau of the Census. *Statistical Abstract of the United States: 1978* (Washington, D.C.: U.S. Government Printing Office, 1978).

Williams, R. *Marxism and Literature* (New York: Oxford University Press, 1977).

Wright, E. O. *Class, Crisis and the State* (London: New Left Books, 1978).

Index

Printed in the United States
211496BV00001B/4/P